D1291159

Number Twenty-one:

TEXAS A&M ENVIRONMENTAL HISTORY SERIES

Dan L. Flores, *General Editor*

BOUND
— IN —
TWINE

The History and Ecology
of the Henequen-Wheat Complex
for Mexico and the American
and Canadian Plains,
1880–1950

STERLING EVANS

TEXAS A&M UNIVERSITY PRESS
College Station

Library of Congress Cataloging-in-Publication Data

Evans, Sterling, 1959–
  Bound in twine : the history and ecology of the henequen-wheat
complex for Mexico and the American and Canadian Plains,
1880–1950 / Sterling Evans
    p. cm. — (Environmental history series ; no. 21)
  Includes bibliographical references and index.
  1. Twine industry—Mexico—Yucatán (State)—History. 2. Twine
industry—North America—History. 3. Yaqui Indians—History.
4. Great Plains—Economic conditions. I. Title.
  HD9999.C753M58 2007
  338.4'767771—dc22
                                                    2006039149

Some portions of this work have previously been published, in slightly different form. Parts of the introduction, chapter 1, and chapter 4 appeared previously as "Dependent Harvests: Grain Production on the American and Canadian Plains and the Double Dependency with Mexico, 1880–1950," *Agricultural History* 80 (winter 2006): 35–63, and are reprinted here with permission from the University of California Press. Parts of chapter 5 have appeared in three separate articles: "Prison-Made Binder Twine: North Dakota's Connection with Mexico in the Early Twentieth Century," *North Dakota History* 68 no. 1.: 20–36, © 2001, State Historical Society of North Dakota, Used by permission; "From Kanasín to Kansas: Mexican Sisal, Binder Twine, and the State Penitentiary Binder Twine Factory, 1890–1940" appeared in *Kansas History* 24 (winter 2001–2002): 276–99, Kansas State Historical Society; and "Entwined in Conflict: The South Dakota State Prison Twine Factory and the Controversy of 1919–1921," appeared in *South Dakota History* 35 (summer 2005): 95–124, South Dakota State Historical Society. These portions are used here with permission from those journals. Selections from poems "The Ri me of the Bucking Binder" and "A Last Farewell to the Bucking Binder" by Hugh Duddridge (from his self-published book *As Seen from My Seeder Step*) reprinted on pages 13 and 213 with permission from the family of Hugh Duddridge. The stanza from the poem "The Yaquis in Sonora in 1904" by Refugio Savala used as the epigraph of chapter 3 on page 67 is from *Autobiography of a Yaqui Poet* by Refugio Savala. © 1980 Arizona Board of Regents. Reprinted by permission of the University of Arizona Press.

ISBN 13: 978-1-58544-596-7 (cloth)
ISBN 13: 978-1-62349-047-8 (paper)
ISBN 13: 978-1-60344-448-4 (ebook)

To

my father, Cecil Evans,

and my uncle, Leroy Evans—

North Dakotans who remember 1936 all too well

as the year "we never touched a binder."

CONTENTS

List of Figures   ix

List of Tables   x

Preface   xi

Acknowledgments   xiii

Introduction: Dependent Harvests   xvii

1. On the History of Binders and Twine: Agricultural
   and Industrial Transformations in North America   1

2. Yucatán's Henequen Industry: Social and Environmental
   Transformations   32

3. Yaquis in Yucatán: Imported Slave Labor and the
   Sonora Connection   67

4. Twine Diplomacy: Yucatán, the United States, and
   Canada during the "Sisal Situation" of 1915   91

5. Prison-Made Twine: The Role of the Penitentiaries in the
   Henequen-Wheat Complex   121

6. Decline, Depression, and Drought: Economic and Environmental
   Change in the Great Plains and Yucatán, 1916–1939   161

7. Competition and Combines: The End of the
   Henequen-Wheat Story   197

   Conclusion: Bound in Twine   232

   Notes   241

   Bibliography   283

   Index   307

FIGURES

I.1. Map of the henequen-wheat complex   xxiv
1.1. Map of the North American wheat belt   2
1.2. McCormick reaper   3
1.3. John F. Appleby, inventor of the mechanical knotter   5
1.4. Farmer and four-horse team with binder   8
1.5. Harvesting with binders on bonanza farms in the
Red River Valley, Dakota Territory   9
1.6. Binder, header, and combine harvested areas of
North America, 1900–1950   15
1.7. McCormick Works twine mill, Chicago, 1900   16
1.8. Women workers at International Harvester twine
mill, Chicago, 1939   17
1.9. Ad for International Harvester twine   18
1.10. International Harvester pamphlet, 1937   19
1.11. International Harvester's "Prospy" tests binder twine   20
1.12. Foreign trade zone for U.S. sisal imports, Port of
New Orleans   23
2.1. The henequen zone, Yucatán Peninsula, Mexico   32
2.2. Henequen (*Agave fourcroydes*)   34
2.3. Plantation workers drying sisal fiber, Yucatán, ca. 1910   36
2.4. King Henequen (from cover of *El henequén*)   44
2.5. Rail lines servicing the henequen plantations, 1915–1918   49
2.6. Rasping shed and decorticator on abandoned
henequen plantation   55
2.7. Labor on a henequen plantation   55
2.8. Artist's rendering of Mayan worker harvesting henequen   64
2.9. Indian worker in the henequen industry   65
3.1. Map of Sonora showing Yaqui River and Valley, Mexico   68
3.2. Map of Yaqui diaspora   73
4.1. William Jennings Bryan inspecting a shock of wheat   99
5.1. Prison twine plants in North America   125
5.2. Interior of North Dakota State Penitentiary twine plant   132

5.3.   North Dakota State Penitentiary twine plant
       parade float entry   135
5.4.   Unloading bales of sisal from Yucatán, Kansas
       State Penitentiary twine plant   137
5.5.   Shipping binder twine from the Kansas State
       Penitentiary twine plant   150
6.1.   Growth of agriculture in the Prairie Provinces, ca. 1909   163
7.1.   Combine harvester, 1932   203
7.2.   Discarded binder along a fence line   206
7.3.   Cartoon in the campaign against imported binder twine   218
7.4.   International Harvester binder and baler twine ad campaign   224
7.5.   Drying henequen fiber in Yucatán, 1970s   227
7.6.   Worker baling henequen fiber, Yucatán, 1970s   228
7.7.   McCormick-Deering 123-SP combine, 1947   231
C.1.   World's largest ball of twine, Cawker City, Kansas   233
C.2.   World's largest single-handedly rolled ball of twine,
       Darwin, Minnesota   234
C.3.   The globalized fiber trade during the binder twine boom   236

TABLES

2.1.   Taxonomy and terminology for Yucatecan agaves   35
5.1.   Penitentiary twine mills in North America   124
6.1.   Henequen exporting arrangements, 1912–1930   175
7.1.   Total imports of binder twine into the United States
       by country of origin, 1925–1936   217

PREFACE

The redwoods on the foggy hills outside the window of the loft where I wrote this book represent a very different environment from that of the story within it. Here, I leave the Coastal Range and rocky coasts of northern California to address a part of history from the landscape of my origin and where I have returned—the flatter but every bit as beautiful North American Great Plains and how that region was linked from roughly 1880 to 1950 to Mexico's Yucatán Peninsula, an equally as flat and even more diverse place.

Those seventy years are when the Mexican state of Yucatán's henequen industry was linked to increased grain production, especially that of wheat, in the Great Plains. In those years, most American and Canadian farmers used an implement called a binder (or reaper/binder) to harvest grain crops. Binders used twine made primarily of the Yucatecan fiber crops henequen and sisal to bind the stalks into sheaves or bundles before being threshed. Binders were the harvesting machine of choice for hundreds of thousands of farmers across the grain-growing region of North America before most switched to combine harvesters that cut *and* threshed grain, thus eliminating the need to tie and shock bundles. The enormous demand for twine caused quite a growth spurt in the cordage industry, and several grain-growing states and Canada even subsidized their own twine manufacturing factories, situated within penitentiaries to make use of cheap convict labor, to offer a lower-priced twine to farmers. The interdependency created by these agricultural and manufacturing entities during this period form what I refer to as the henequen-wheat complex.

The three countries and these agricultural industries, then, were bound in twine. The dependency that emerged out of such a relationship had political, economic, labor, social, and environmental dimensions worthy of inquiry. Relating only part of this history would leave it incomplete; thus this study seeks to offer analysis on each of the angles to offer a more comprehensive and complete telling of the transnational henequen-wheat story.

This project began when I first started researching the topic for seminars in graduate school at the University of Kansas. Although I was working on a completely different topic for my Ph.D. dissertation, the "binder twine project" kept tugging at me, partly because it tied together so well my interest and doctoral field areas of study (modern Latin America, the American West, and environmental history). Later, as an American teaching Mexican history in western Canada at the University of Alberta and now at Brandon University in Manitoba, this book just seems to "fit" me in many ways. It is also partly a result of my own family background. I am originally from North Dakota, where my father was raised on a farm that relied on binders and binder twine during his youth. I fondly recall the stories of his days as a "bundle hauler" working on threshing crews, of his father and older brothers running the four-horse team binders, and even his stories of visiting the state penitentiary twine plant in Bismarck on school field trips. I remember the story of when the family purchased its first combine in 1941, his pointing out to me the old discarded binders rusting away in farmyard corners and showing me how they worked. And although my forebears never knew all the rather complicated, international, and multifaceted dimensions of binder twine production, the operation of the Evans farm near Turtle Lake, North Dakota, was also bound in twine.

ACKNOWLEDGMENTS

Because my work on this project lasted for several years, there are many people in Mexico, the United States, and Canada to whom I owe my sincerest gratitude. First, at the University of Kansas where I began this project when I was a graduate student in the 1990s, I thank my advisor Charles Stansifer for his pragmatic editorial comments on an early paper (which is now chapter 3) and for always taking a keen interest in this project then and since. Hailing from a rural background in western Kansas, Charley is the only scholar of the many mentioned here who has actually *operated* a binder! I am extremely grateful to Donald Worster, also at KU, whose strong and critical support of this project and others has been more encouraging to me than he will ever know. Graduate school at KU was made even better because of the cohort of students and faculty involved with Don's monthly Nature and Culture Colloquia at the Hall Center for the Humanities. Some of the most useful comments I received on any facet of this book came from when I presented "Bound in Twine" there. From that group I thank Kip Curtis, Jay Antle, Amanda Jones, Paul Sutter, Kevin Armitage, Mike Grant, Marc Becker, Don Wolf, John Egan, Mark Frederick, and Jim Leiker (who also accompanied me on my first trip to see the world's largest ball of twine in Cawker City, Kansas).

I also received important feedback from professors Anton Rosenthal (on an early version of chapter 3 that I wrote for his seminar on violence in Latin America) and the late John Clark and from my fellow Latin Americanist graduate students and friends Kathy Sloan, Kirk Shaffer, Lou Villalba, and Marc Becker. I owe a special thanks to my undergraduate research assistant Scot Vink, who made a road trip with me to Yucatán in the summer of 1996, helped me sort through references in the libraries and archives there, and shared travel "adventures" and fun times on the trip. Thanks to all who helped make KU the special place it really was during my grad school years.

Since then, I have used material from this book in classes that I have taught at the University of Alberta, Humboldt State University, and now at Brandon University, and I have benefited from students' enthusiasm for it. From Alberta, I thank Jaymie Heilman (now teaching at Dalhousie University) and Ryan Hoskins (whose co-written article I cite in the conclusion); from

Humboldt State I thank Clint McCowan, Chris White (now teaching at Marshall University), Geoff Kelley, Sam Sanford, and Fernando Calderón; and from Brandon, I thank Katie Pollock—all of whom went on to graduate programs. Research over the years has been made possible by grants from the Tinker Foundation, the Humboldt State University Foundation, and the HSU Emeritus Faculty Association. The time and space I needed to write the book came from a sabbatical leave granted by Humboldt State in the fall of 2004. I thank all of these organizations for their active support. Also, at HSU my historian colleague and friend Jason Knirck (now at Central Washington University) deserves my gratitude for his gentle but much-needed urging "to keep plugging away" on the book, as does my soil scientist and range management colleague Susan Marshall, for her constant interest in and encouragement on this topic.

There are too many archivists and collections personnel who assisted me in the twenty different national, state, provincial, and private archives or special collections where I conducted research to list here. However, I make special mention of Candy Flota García and Andrea Vergara Medina at the Archivo General del Estado de Yucatán in Mérida; Dr. Manuel Ramos Medina at CONDUMEX in Mexico City; Julia M. Brunni, Knowledge Center of Navistar International Transportation (formerly International Harvester Company) in Chicago; Lee C. Grady, archivist for the McCormick–International Harvester Collection, State Historical Society of Wisconsin; Carol Jennings at the South Dakota State Historical Society; and Cathy Langemo at the State Historical Society of North Dakota, for their exceptionally friendly and personalized assistance.

Projects such as this one are also fueled by the active interest and support given by friends and colleagues within the academy. For their unwavering enthusiasm and suggestions over the years, I want to thank (in Mexico) Luis Aboites, Michel Antochiw, Alejandro Tortolero, and Casey Walsh, and running into fellow Yucatecanists Terry Rugeley, Paul Eiss, and Ben Fallaw at various archives and special collections proved to be immeasurably valuable. I also wish to thank (in the United States) David Weber, Cynthia Radding, Evelyn Hu-deHart, David Yetman, Bill Beezley, Roderic Ai Camp, Adrian Bantjes, John Herd Thompson, Tom Isern, Mark Harvey, Hal Rothman, Neil Maher, Sam Truett, John Soluri, Lyn Bennett, Andy Graybill, Lise Sedrez, and, in a special way, the late John Wirth for his interest in the continentalist nature of this study. In Canada I thank Gerhard Ens, Ted Binnema, Stuart McCook, Bruce Shepard, Betsy Jameson, Gerald Friesen, Bill French, Jay Taylor, and the late Elinor Melville, who strongly encouraged me to continue studying topics in Latin American environmental history. In Cuba I am grateful to Reinaldo Funes. At Brandon University, I have been blessed with active interest and support for this project by my dean, Scott Grills, and by my colleagues in the departments of History, Rural Studies, and Geography: Jim Naylor (with whom I spent a memorable afternoon helping pitch wheat bundles at a binding-threshing demonstration at the Threshermen's Reunion in Austin, Manitoba, in July 2006), Morris Mott, Andy Pernal, Lynn MacKay, Tom Mitchell, George Hoffman, Ken Beezley, Ken Bessant, Doug Ramsey, Derek Eberts, and John Everett. For their extremely useful suggestions as panel commentators where some of this research has been presented at a variety of conferences, I am indebted to Angus Wright, Jeff Taylor, Carol Higham, Allen Wells, Kathy Sloan, and the late James Edgar Rea. And for their excellent editing skills and recommendations for journal articles of some of the previously published material herein, I warmly thank Janet Daly, Virgil Dean, Nancy Tystad Koupal, and Claire Strom. All deserve my thanks, but any errors of omission or of content or of translations from the many sources in Spanish are solely mine.

For publication of this book, I cannot thank the editor-in-chief of Texas A&M University Press enough for her instant enthusiasm for this work, her editorial assistant for getting it through the review process, their contracted copy editor Maureen Creamer Bemko for her extremely thorough attention to detail, and the Press itself for publishing works on environmental history and works that emphasize transnational, continental approaches. Benjamin Johnson (Southern Methodist University) and Geoff Cunfer (University of Saskatchewan) reviewed the manuscript, and their excellent recommendations went far to make it a much better product; I am deeply indebted to them. I also thank Wenonah Fraser, cartographer in the Brandon University Department of Geography, for so carefully and expertly creating the book's maps.

Finally, the book is a result of the warm support I constantly receive from my family. My mother and father have taken great interest in the project from the beginning, especially since it has this unique and intriguing family history angle. Yes, Dad, after all these years it's finally done! To you and Uncle Roy who worked so hard during those binder harvest years—good and bad—I dedicate the book. (Who would have believed there could be a history of binder twine?) I also thank my uncle, John Theios, who was a most gracious host to me on two archival trips to Madison, Wisconsin, and who has always taken great interest in this project. My wife Sheri was probably dismayed at such an undertaking, but nonetheless she supported me all the way through, including double-duty parenting while I was either on research trips or spending too many hours chained to the computer. I am unable to thank her adequately for all that support. And to our daughters, Alex! and Shelby Ann, I give huge hugs and thanks for being so understanding and patient throughout the creation of the book. But it represents part of their background history, too, which I hope they will pass along.

Introduction
Dependent Harvests

Mexico stands . . . as the world's largest producer of fiber suitable for binder twine. It is fortunate in having its immediate neighbor to the north, the world's greatest consumer of this fiber. On the other hand, the United States has been the largest producer of binder twine and is fortunate in having had a nearby source of fiber. For reasons of national interest it cannot afford to become dependent on a supply of fiber from the other side of the world.

—*Plymouth Cordage Co., memorandum to U.S. State Department, 1937*

BOUND in Twine is a continental tale. It is about the transnationalization, and indeed globalization, of the henequen-wheat complex upon which North American grain production depended for several decades. The importance of that agriculture, its growth and technological changes, speaks for itself, yet a broader understanding of the connections that made it possible has been absent from our discussions and literature on the topic. This book hopes to expose those dependencies and, in doing so, to suggest that scholars continue crossing national and disciplinary boundaries to uncover the broader and transnational aspects of history anywhere.

Farmers, historians, economists, and other scholars rarely think of Mexico when talking or writing about grain farming on the American and Canadian plains in the late nineteenth and early twentieth centuries. Yet grain harvests in those two nations were almost entirely dependent on two commodities from Mexico, specifically the Yucatán Peninsula: henequen (*Agave fourcroydes*) and sisal (*Agave sisalana*). These species of agave produce long, tough leaves from which fibers are extracted to make binder twine, rope, and other cordage products. Binder twine was used in binders—a harvesting implement that cut grain stalks and then tied them into bundles that could then be hand-gathered into shocks (or stooks, in Canada), with the grain heads oriented upward to avoid spoiling on the ground, before threshing. Between about 1880 and 1950, before the affordability and widespread use of combines that cut *and* threshed grain, hundreds of thousands of North American grain farmers came to rely on binders and the twine they needed.

A double dependency emerged in what I refer to as the henequen-wheat complex. The farming economy of the transnational Great Plains relied on Mexican fiber, and Yucatán's agricultural economy was almost entirely dependent on the binder twine market in the United States and Canada. These dependent harvests are part of a larger dependency theory that economists, sociologists, and historians advanced in the 1960s and 1970s to understand underdevelopment in Latin America (the so-called *dependista* school). The model applies to the henequen boom-bust industry quite well, as its incredible growth in the late nineteenth and early twentieth centuries that depended on U.S. and Canadian demand was followed by almost total collapse, from which Yucatán has yet to recover. Likewise, a series of economic, political, social, and environmental changes accompanied this phenomenon, thus meriting historical inquiry. The dependencies and changes are important to consider because they illustrate a North American tri-national economy that relied on the free exchange of commodities. They show clearly that one cannot study any of these national economies in isolation during this period; only with an understanding of the backgrounds of and interconnections between the three countries can the more complete history of North American grain production be told.

It should also be noted that a robust binder twine economy and culture arose across North America with the advent of the henequen-wheat complex, and citizens, from farmers to industrialists to politicians and national leaders (and the many folks in between), recognized the importance of this agricultural complex. I hope that readers will get a sense of that contemporary awareness from the many newspaper accounts, government hearings, and miscellaneous twine iconographies (as seen in advertisements, media attention, and other popular culture representations) that became a part of the story. In fact, twine was so important that a possible shortage of it nearly led to U.S. military action in 1915.

As such, the henequen-wheat complex fits neatly into the "social life of things" model that Arjun Appadurai and others have advanced in a book with that title (and with the apt subtitle, "Commodities in Cultural Perspective"). There, the scholars frame commodity trade patterns in a biography analyzing exchanges and arguing that things have, and have had over time, their own social lives and histories. Appadurai relates how commodities have been defined as "objects of economic value," but that "few will deny that a commodity is a thoroughly socialized thing." One of the book's contributors, Igor Kopytoff, expands on this idea by claiming that commoditization is a "process" with its own "cultural biography." He notes, "For the economist, commodities simply are. That is, certain things and rights to things are produced, exist, and can be seen to circulate through the economic system." But, "from a cultural perspective, the production of commodities must be not only produced materially as things, but also culturally marked as being a certain kind of thing."[1] Casey Walsh and others have taken this proposition to heart in an excellent volume on the social relations of Mexican commodities. Walsh and Elizabeth Ferry write in their introduction that commodity studies about Latin America have tended "to answer intellectual and political questions concerning rural class formation and political mobilization" or have examined "political and economic development in a region that has, since its conquest and colonization, been organized to produce primary materials . . . for a globalized market."[2] A number of engaging studies on various world commodities, from salt, sugar, spices, fish, rubber, coffee, tea, chocolate, potatoes, tomatoes, bananas, and even tequila, to mundane things such as motor scooters, Panama hats, and screwdrivers, also follow this analysis. And in another way, this history of the manufacture of twine follows the model of an expanding social historiography of industrialization and technology.[3] Thus, it is the objective of this study to offer a comprehensive and transnational history in the globalization frame of reference to which Walsh and Ferry referred and, in part, an environmental and social history of the seemingly common commodity of binder twine.

To unravel the many aspects of this history, *Bound in Twine* seeks to explore the different geographical and thematic angles. Chapter 1 deals with the history of binders and binder twine and the agricultural and industrial transformations they represented. It also deals with North American corporate interests, especially those of the International Harvester Company of Chicago, which discovered early on that it was profitable to import henequen and sisal fiber from relatively nearby Yucatán. The focus here is that of a dependency model, that is, how changes in the American and Canadian grain belt were linked to the flow of fiber from Yucatán. This sort of analysis has been absent in the agricultural historiography of the region.

In chapter 2 I discuss the henequen fiber industry's birth and growth in Yucatán, paying special attention to the social and environmental transformations that accompanied its development. Chapter 3 is a case study of the labor needs of the Yucatecan henequen industry. Due to a labor shortage in their state, henequen plantation owners came to rely on workers brought in from around the world, particularly the Caribbean region and other parts of Mexico. One such group that was brutally removed, and literally enslaved, to work in Yucatán was the Yaqui Indians from the state of Sonora in northwestern Mexico. The Yaquis' role in the henequen-wheat complex needs to be remembered and placed in its appropriate context. Thus, Yucatán and Sonora are linked, as I will work to show here, with the same theory of progress and development that characterized Mexico in the early years of the henequen-wheat complex—during the rule of Mexican president Porfirio Díaz (1876–1911) and his administration's campaign for economic modernization.

Further proof that there is a henequen-wheat dependency was the "Sisal Situation" of 1915. This crisis illustrates the intensity of the henequen-wheat dependency, and chapter 4 discusses the significant foreign relations aspect of the dependency. The Woodrow Wilson administration in the United States and the Robert Laird Borden government in Canada faced the possibility that the Mexican Revolution would disrupt fiber imports from Yucatán and seriously jeopardize North American farmers' ability to bind sheaves of grain produced during an unprecedented bumper crop. The U.S. State Department intervened with "gun-boat diplomacy" to ensure the supply of fiber. Once again, the result is a telling episode of dependency within the henequen-wheat complex. Thus, chapter 4 places the episode in its proper historical context and adds the Canadian dimension that is missing from previous studies on the topic.

Dependency is also reflected in the need for laborers to manufacture twine in the United States and Canada using the imported fiber. The finished product was not made in Mexico and then exported; it was more profitable for North American cordage companies to import the raw material and manufacture it into binder twine at their own factories. But to compete with International Harvester and other companies, various midwestern states and the government of Canada decided to manufacture twine by using inmate labor at penitentiaries. They could pay the convicts much lower wages, and the state could subsidize the construction and maintenance of twine-manufacturing plants. The labor issue discussed in chapter 5 has not received any attention heretofore in the agricultural or penological historiography of the United States or Canada. The prison labor angle shows very clearly not only the importance of twine to the era but also, and even more importantly, the degree to which governments would go to ensure its availability.

The henequen industry in Yucatán began to decline after World War I, however, and continued on a downward slide during the decreases in North American agricultural production caused by the Great Depression and drought conditions of the 1930s. But it was then that populist Mexican president Lázaro Cárdenas applied his agrarian reform policies to Yucatán. The interconnected changes wrought by all these events are the topic of chapter 6. Chapter 7 deals with the end of the story. It discusses the demise of the henequen industry as a result of competition from abroad and from synthetic fibers and from the fast-expanding adoption of the combined harvester (or "combine") that required no binding of grain crops on the Great Plains.

Bound in Twine thus seeks to expose these various aspects of North American transnational and agricultural history. The book was dependent on the sources available in a number of national, state, and provincial archives and private collections in Mexico, the United States, and Canada. Some parts of the book synthesize material from the extant literature, especially that of Yucatecan historiography, farm implement histories, and the ecological literature of the Yucatán Peninsula and the Great Plains. In this regard, the book will offer a synthesis of materials with new theoretical analysis based on continental-dependency and environmental history frameworks.

Various scholars have called attention to the need for this type of work, perhaps none more poignantly in regard to this study than renowned anthropologist Eric Wolf. In *Europe and the People without History*, Wolf wrote that "the world of humankind constitutes a . . . totality of interconnected processes"—"bundles of relationships" that "indicate contact and connections, linkages, and interrelationships." Wolf's "bundles" were not ones of wheat tied with twine, but the ones in this book are, and they represent the same kinds of transnational connections and interrelationships that he believed should be studied in order to develop an understanding of history's larger picture.[4] Applying this concept to transnational North American history has been central to works by Donald Meinig (volume 2 of *The Shaping of America*), John Wirth ("Advancing North American Community"), and Herman Konrad ("North American Continental Relationships")—a literature this book seeks to join.

Likewise, in a special issue of the *Journal of American History* in 1999, historian David Thelen provided a useful summary of the progress and direction in transnational history scholarship, suggesting that the discipline would "convey the open-endedness . . . to explore border crossings and to look critically at the nation-state itself."[5] That advice has been central to some of the more recent literature on North American borderlands history. For example, Samuel Truett and Elliott Young wrote in "Making Transnational History" (the introduction to their volume *Continental Crossroads*), "To understand . . . transformations, we must find ways to see beyond the nation even as we keep the nation in focus." The essays in their book, the ones in Bukowczyk et al. (*Permeable Border: The Great Lakes Basin as Transnational Region, 1650–1990*), and the ones in my own book, *The Borderlands of the American and Canadian Wests*, and the ones in Benjamin Johnson and Andrew Graybill's *Bridging National Borders in North America* have worked to do just that.[6]

On another level, Truett as well as Richard White and Ian Tyrrell have identified environmental history as being at the heart of a new transnational history, especially as it can relate to scale. Alfred Crosby has done much to advance this notion in his works about the transfer of commodities between nations and in expounding the theory of the "Columbian exchange."[7] Some scholars, such as Richard Grove (*Green Imperialism: Colonial Expansion, Tropical Island Edens, and the Origins of Environmentalism, 1600–1860*), J. R. McNeill (*The*

Mountains of the Mediterranean World: An Environmental History), and Thomas Dunlap (*Nature and the English Diaspora: Environment and History in the United States, Canada, and Australia, and New Zealand*) offer the big picture of environmental change across continents and oceans. Others, including Dan Flores ("Place: An Argument for Bioregional History"), Theodore Binnema (*Common and Contested Ground: A Human and Environmental History of the Northwestern Plains*), and Charles Chester (*Conservation across Borders: Biodiversity in an Interdependent World*), offer more bioregional, transboundary approaches to environmental history. All of these represent the kind of future environmental historiography that Donald Worster suggested would be "found in research that moves easily across national boundaries."[8]

These concepts can and should be applied to the rapidly developing field of Latin American environmental history. John Soluri, in his environmental and transnational history of the Honduran banana industry, advises that the field should "aim to write histories of commodity production that convey the heterogeneity and historical dynamisms of organisms and processes that tend to get lumped together as 'resources,' 'land,' or simply 'space.'" He adds that "by breathing life into these and other categories, we can avoid falling into the trap of environmental determinism while demonstrating the dynamic interplay between economies and ecologies, landscapes and livelihoods, and cultural and biological diversity." Those are valid and valuable points that this book attempts to consider.[9]

Bound in Twine thus speaks to a wide variety of scholars (and as one review suggested, puts them into conversation with one another), students, and the general public. It addresses themes pertinent to a variety of fields within history—agricultural, labor, business, economic, diplomatic, environmental—as well as themes of general U.S. history, especially of that period known as the rise of modern America (1870–1920), with its attention to technology and industrialization, or to regional studies of the Great Plains, the American/Canadian West, and North American borderlands (Mexican and Canadian). It also addresses themes important to the study of Mexican history, especially the *porfiriato* (1876–1911), revolutionary Mexico (1910–40), and post-confederation Canadian history (especially the history of the Prairie Provinces, agricultural history, and the history of U.S.-Canadian relations, and relations between Canada and Mexico). These themes should also be of interest to geographers, economists, farmers, and others interested in how such a seemingly innocuous commodity as binder twine could have such far-ranging implications. And as scholars study the tri-national effects of the North American Free Trade Agreement (NAFTA) or the Free Trade Area of the Americas (FTAA) in the post-1990 years, there could be useful comparisons made from this book's glimpse into a similar trade scenario that existed among the three North American nations from this earlier time period.

There are no previously published books devoted to the history of binder twine. There are no works on the interconnected, tri-national, agricultural relations between Mexico, the United States, and Canada during this time period. And there are no books that examine the henequen-wheat complex and its social, labor, and environmental implications. Where there is a more extensive literature is in Yucatecan historiography and the history of the henequen industry. For that I am indeed indebted to my colleagues in Mexico and the United States (especially Renán Irigoyen, Fernando Benítez, Gonzalo Cámara, and Eric Villanueva among others in Yucatán, and Roland Chardon, Gilbert Joseph, Allen Wells, Jeffery Brannon, Eric Baklanoff, Fred Carstensen, Diane Roazen, and Thomas Benjamin in the United States).[10] Their works, however, do not discuss relations with Canada, the prison labor dimension, environmental implications, nor the proto-NAFTA-style economic dependencies involved and perhaps do not cover adequately the Sonora connection. This book seeks to cast all of these dimensions and agricultural relations in their broader, North American historical context.[11] The henequen-wheat complex created a giant continental triangular set of relations, with points in the American and Canadian Plains where twine demand was highest, and in Mexico, both in Yucatán, where the majority of the fiber was grown for that market, and in Sonora, the origin of perhaps only a small percentage of fiber plantation laborers but whose agricultural trajectory changed radically when that labor force was removed to work in the henequen fields (see Figure I.1).

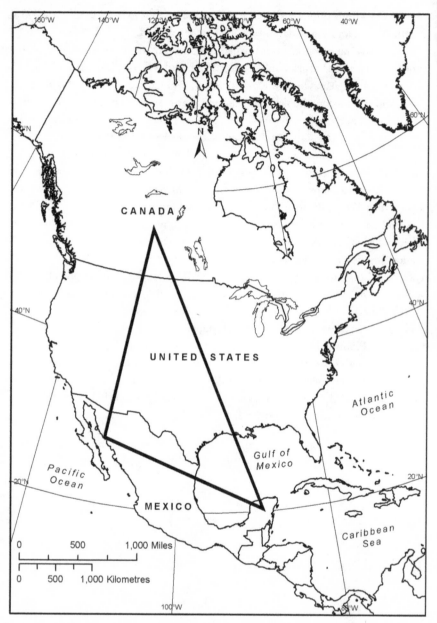

Figure I.1. Map of the henequen-wheat complex in North America. Courtesy Wenonah Fraser, Department of Geography, Brandon University.

BOUND IN TWINE

CHAPTER 1

On the History of Binders and Twine

Agricultural and Industrial Transformations in North America

> In 1830 a bushel of wheat had taken
> three hours to produce. By 1900 it took ten minutes.
>
> —*Howard Zinn*

THE history of the henequen-wheat complex begins with the transformation of the American and Canadian plains from a land of prairie grass where bison and later cattle grazed to a region of cereal grain production. As Donald Worster explains it, "The grassland was to be torn up to make a vast wheat factory: a landscape tailored to the industrial age."[1] In tune with this industrial revolution were farm implement companies that rallied to invent and mass-produce machinery that could not only bust sod and plow up the grassy rangelands but also increase and quicken the production of grain.[2]

The most important of those inventions was the mechanical reaper that Cyrus McCormick patented and demonstrated successfully in a wheat field near Steele's Tavern, Virginia, in 1831. Before the mechanical reaper, farmers had to harvest grain crops with the age-old scythe, improved only with the addition of the cradle that helped scoop the gavels of cut stalks into piles. The stalks would then be hand-gathered, tied into sheaves, and stacked in shocks to dry, after which it would be threshed to separate the grain from the chaff. McCormick's reaper was a horse-drawn machine with a moving cutter bar that cut the stalks with knives and a reel that laid them onto a platform where they could be hand-raked and later tied into sheaves (Figure 1.2). Although the reaper was seemingly a simple device, McCormick spent nearly a decade seeking funds to establish the McCormick Harvesting Machine Company,

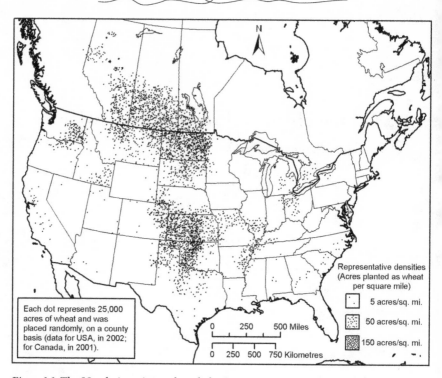

Representative densities
(Acres planted as wheat
per square mile)

☐ 5 acres/sq. mi.

▦ 50 acres/sq. mi.

▨ 150 acres/sq. mi.

Each dot represents 25,000
acres of wheat and was
placed randomly, on a county
basis (data for USA, in 2002;
for Canada, in 2001).

0   250   500 Miles

0   250 500   750 Kilometres

Figure 1.1. The North American wheat belt. Courtesy Wenonah Fraser, Department of Geography, Brandon University.

build a factory in Chicago, and market the reaper. Farmers quickly adopted the new machine. "The mechanical reaper was probably the most significant single invention introduced into farming between 1830 and 1860," according to historian Wayne Rasmussen, and "its advent marked the transition from the hand to the machine age of farming." The McCormick Company claimed in promotional literature that the reaper "marked the beginning of the successful race in which mechanical equipment on the farm has kept ahead of the world's demand for food."[3] McCormick biographer and industrial historian Herbert Casson takes this point further, arguing that without the reaper "the whole new structure of our civilization with all its dazzling luxuries and refinements would be withered by the blight of famine. The reaper has done more to chase the wolf from the door—to abolish poverty and drudgery and hand labor, than any other invention." He also went so far as to assert that the implement made possible "a nobler human race": "Every harvester that clicks its way through the yellow grain means more than bread. It means more comfort, more travel, more art and music, more books and education."[4] Regarding the reaper's impact on the United States, McCormick brochures stated that with farmers

The oldest Reaper alive! The father of them all. The original McCormick Reaper.

Invented by Cyrus H. McCormick, 1831.

Figure 1.2. The McCormick Reaper. Courtesy Wisconsin Historical Society (McCormick–International Harvester Collection, Whi-39559).

"growing a surplus of grain, transportation systems began to develop, new railroads were built over the fertile prairies of the middle west. Farmers went westward by the thousands, taking with them their precious reapers. Towns sprang up, and industry after industry was started. Thus, the invention of the reaper was the beginning of prosperity not only for the farmer, but for the nation."[5] Casson concurs: "This magical machinery of the wheat field solves the mystery of prosperity. . . . It makes clear how we, in the United States, have become the best-fed nation in the world."[6] Much of this philosophy was warmly repeated in 1931—the centennial of the reaper's invention. Farming and implement trade journals and newspapers around the United States honored McCormick with numerous accolades during the year. An article from the *Hutchinson (Kansas) News* is representative: "McCormick's Reaper put the cradle on its permanent peg in the museum. . . . It was to the Midwest what the cotton gin was to the South."[7]

Mechanical reapers represented a huge advantage to grain farmers in the 1850s and 1860s, but they still required a large amount of expensive manual labor. One worker, often the farmer's son, rode the horse, another raked the cut stalks off the platform, and others followed the machine gathering up the gavels of grain stalks, tying them with straw bands into sheaves (or bundles), and shocking them to await threshing. Some inventive changes occurred, like those introduced by the Marsh brothers from DeKalb, Illinois, who rebelled against stooping over to bind the bundles by hand. They invented the Marsh harvester, which added a riding platform so that a farmhand could ride along with the reaper and tie the sheaves as they were cut without ever having to bend over.[8] The devices were helpful and popular, but they were still labor intensive. Thus, implement manufacturers and inventors understood the need for a machine that could reap and bind the cut grain stalks into sheaves. John Heath of Warren, Ohio, is credited with having invented the first combined reaper/binder in 1850 using a complex mechanism and a spool of twine to bind grain bundles. It did not get much past the experimental stage, especially when just a few years later a number of inventors patented much simpler binders that used metal wire.[9] The most successful and popular model was one that Charles Withington invented and sold to the McCormick Company in 1872. McCormick started producing the Withington wire binder in 1877, and in the next few years it became popular with farmers as a labor saving implement. McCormick sold some fifty thousand of these fairly simple machines that would "seize a bundle, lock the wire about its middle, cut it loose, and toss it bound upon the stubble."[10]

However, while wire binders were comparatively simple to operate (needing a mere twist of the wire to secure the sheaves instead of a more complicated device to knot twine), they were not very efficient in tying bundles tightly, were hard on the hands of the harvest workers, and caused problems when livestock ingested wire that accidentally remained in the straw after threshing. This so-called "hardware disease" occasionally resulted in cattle mortality. Sometimes wire would interfere with the threshing machine's moving parts, and it often remained with the grain during separation, causing problems when the grain was milled into flour.[11] L. E. Sayre, a professor at the University of Kansas, noted in 1889, "Pieces of wire and nails would get into the machinery, and finally the feed . . . render[ing] [it] positively dangerous." What farmers needed, then, was to revisit the idea of a binder that could use a more flexible, digestible, and degradable product—a product like straw, cord, or twine that could tie bundles tightly. Sayre added, "Binding twine thus became an absolute necessity for cereal products."[12]

Two problems stood in the way of developing twine binders, however. The first was in creating a mechanical knotting device that would tie the bundles of wheat tightly without the need for manual labor. It was logical that some of the first patents for such a device were issued for straw binders, imitating but mechanizing the old-fashioned process of hand tying sheaves with straw bands. Inventions from 1858 to as late as 1905 focused on perfecting straw binders, especially since straw would be favored by farmers as a vastly less expensive alternative to wire, cord, or twine, and because it was digestible and degradable. The patented straw binders did not work very efficiently, and they were enormous, complicated contraptions that were not practical on farms.[13] Meanwhile, others were working to create a mechanical knotter for cord and twine. John F. Appleby (Figure 1.3) made the most successful one, leading Cyrus McCormick to proclaim him "one of the great names in the history of American invention."[14]

In 1857, when eighteen-year-old Appleby was working as a farmhand near Whitewater, Wisconsin, he declared that the reaper would be far more efficient if it could tie cut grain stalks into sheaves. As the story goes, he was inspired to invent a twine knotter by the sight of a girl playing with a Boston terrier pup and a jump rope. Apparently, when the girl accidentally dropped the rope on the dog's head, he shook himself and backed away, inadvertently leaving the rope in a knot on the ground. Appleby then carved from wood a sample knotter that supposedly could replicate the dog's twisting and turning motions, and he later fabricated the device in iron at a gunsmith shop. Merrill Denison writes that "upon such a seemingly trivial incident was based the 'beak' of the Appleby knotter, a mechanism which helped to people the Canadian and American wheat lands and dot them with thousands of grain elevators."[15]

Figure 1.3. John F. Appleby, inventor of the mechanical knotter that made twine binders possible. Courtesy Wisconsin Historical Society (McCormick–International Harvester Collection, Whi-24881).

Serving in the Union army during the Civil War put Appleby's inventiveness on hold. At war's end he picked up where he left off but learned that others had been tinkering with knotters. The most important of these inventors was Jacob Behel from Rockford, Illinois, who developed a "hawkbill" or "billhook" knotter in 1864. It had a movable jaw that could hook the twine, knot it tightly, and then cut it with a knife blade at the right length to bind a sheaf. The device, as one study explained, was what "turned the key that unlocked the problem of twine binding."[16]

When Appleby reentered the scene after the war, he worked to develop a whole new binder that incorporated Behel's billhook knotter, an improved packer, and other innovations. By 1877 he was running several successful cord binders mounted to Marsh harvesters and lacked only financial support to start manufacturing them in quantity. When he demonstrated his reaper/binder to implement maker William Deering, who had also been tinkering with binders, a deal ensued. An impressed Deering bought Appleby's patent, manufactured three thousand of the new reaper/binders under strict cover, and in 1879 "startled the country" by launching them on the market. C. H. Wendel has written that Deering's "Appleby twine binder . . . sold like wildfire and worked like a charm." Appleby later remarked, "To him [Deering] belongs the credit of forcing my binder on the market with sufficient energy to convince the farmer of its practicability."[17] Also impressed was implement maker Charles Marsh (of Marsh harvester fame), who by this time had given up a career in farm machinery to edit *Farm Implement News.* "No name is so well known among persons interested in harvesting machinery as that of John F. Appleby," he wrote in the trade paper in the 1890s, "and no machine ever swept over the world with such overwhelming rapidity—once it got started—as the twine binder."[18] Merrill Denison agreed, casting its impact into a greater world significance: "Next to the wheel, the cutter bar, and reel, the invention that did the most for agricultural mechanization was the automatic knotter. . . . It was this amazing device . . . which has exerted a more profound influence in the world's economy than any other of man's technological accomplishments, save possibly the locomotive."[19] It also triggered a veritable "battle of the binders," as Denison called it, between the various farm implement manufacturers. The competition became aggressive, and McCormick was right in the thick of it; his son Cyrus Jr. referred to it as "the harvester war."[20]

The Appleby binder, however, was never completely reliable in tying bundles tightly enough or in holding up under pressure, which often broke the cord knotters during harvest, as did simple friction. Meanwhile, the McCormick Company started to experiment with cord and twine binders a bit later, since its wire binders were still selling somewhat successfully. But by 1880, Cyrus McCormick Jr. saw that wire binders would soon go the way of the scythe, and he personally oversaw the development of different models of twine binders. Although some of the early twine binder models still had kinks, production of wire binders ceased in 1883.[21]

The second problem manufacturers had to overcome was finding the right kind of cord or twine that would work best in the binder's mechanical knotter and meet farmers' standards for tight bundles. Deering contracted with cordage manufacturer Edwin Fitler of Philadelphia to develop such a twine. Fitler used abacá fiber (also called manila hemp, made from fibers rasped from the bark of the banana relative *Musa textiles* from the Philippines) to create a strong but flexible twine. The new twine was made with hard twists (more turns per inch than any previous twine) that yielded seven hundred feet of twine per pound of pure manila fiber. Deering's experiments with the new twine were successful, and he sent it to be field tested in Texas, where winter wheat farmers reported that it gave "splendid" results. The Deering twine binder became "an immensely successful machine," as McCormick described it, and sold quickly in grain growing regions. McCormick knew that his company would have to catch up with Deering's, however. "With extraordinary rapidity," his son later wrote, he "adapted himself to the new circumstances," gained a license to manufacture the Appleby style binder, and by 1881 was "ready to do battle as before, valiantly, mightily, and victoriously."[22]

At the same time, McCormick was racing to develop a strong binder twine. His company was one of the first to experiment with sisal fiber from Yucatán, but it gave unsatisfactory results at first, straining the knotter and not moving through the mechanism smoothly. In time, however, the manufacturers discovered that an optimum blend of Philippine abacá and Yucatecan henequen or its similar relative sisal made very strong, rot-resistant, and insect-proof binder twine. A number of years later, the U.S. Department of Commerce confirmed that manila had greater tensile strength but that grasshoppers could later destroy it in the shock. Not so with the Yucatecan fibers because grasshoppers "do not consume sisal."[23] Also, because Yucatán was relatively close to the United States, henequen and sisal became the favorite fibers for cordage and implement companies' twines. It was also less expensive for farmers. Having addressed many of the problems of grain harvesting, the binder would "remain supreme for nearly forty years," as McCormick described it. As Canadian historian Grant MacEwan has written, "Of the factors which contributed most to the expansion of the western grain fields, none had more far-reaching influence than the mechanical knotter which permitted the use of twine."[24]

Farmers throughout the transnational Great Plains readily accepted twine binders, and they spread to the Midwest when manufacturers started making corn binders. One farmer-writer explained that a person with a team of horses (usually four horses but sometimes three) and a binder could do in a day what previously took six workers to do. Another wrote, "The binder reduced the man-hours required for harvesting by twenty-five percent."[25] McCormick advertised that the binder, which could harvest at a rate of about 2.5 to 3 miles per hour, helped to reduce harvest labor from what used to take hours down to ten minutes a bushel (Figure 1.4). The McCormick Company sold an average of 152,000 binders a year between 1897 and 1902, and after it merged with Deering and several other rivals in 1902 to form the International Harvester Company (IH), the firm sold 91,000 binders a year for the next decade. A U.S. Department of Labor report in 1939 indicated that IH sold more than half of all binders purchased in the United States. When the machines arrived by train in various places, townspeople and farmers often welcomed the deliveries with "implement parades." IH's *Harvester World* published pictures of such events in Springfield and Hastings, Minnesota, and Stigler and Centralia, Oklahoma. The caption of a picture in 1915 showing the arrival of 118 IH binders in Newkirk, Oklahoma, challenged, "If you know of a larger binder

Figure 1.4. Farmer and four-horse team binder harvesting wheat in Russell County, Kansas, 1912. Courtesy Kansas State Historical Society (Halbe Collection 224).

delivery, let us hear about it."[26] Depending on the size (six- or eight-foot cutter bars) and other options, most binders sold for around one hundred dollars in the early twentieth century—a third of what they initially cost—and thus were affordable for most farmers who could purchase them on credit and pay off the loan with that year's harvest. As early as 1911, farmers harvested nearly 90 million acres of small grain annually with binders.[27] By the 1920s many farmers were using tractors to pull the binders, although that practice added to the cost of labor (one worker to drive the tractor and one to operate the binder) and fuel. One report suggests that 1914 was the year when use of horse-drawn machinery peaked and when tractors started to become more affordable for farmers.[28]

Binders became useful for Great Plains farmers, the vast majority of whom had small-scale operations on 160 or 320 acres. However, they also played an important role in the development of large-scale farming throughout the region. Casson relates the story of a McCormick agent traveling in Texas who entered a bank in Amarillo to get acquainted with some of the local businessmen. A banker introduced him to a "big, roughly dressed" farmer who had just come in, mentioning to him that he might want to look at the salesman's catalogue. "Ten minutes later the big fellow looked up from the catalogue and

Figure 1.5. Harvesting with binders on bonanza farms in the Red River Valley, Dakota Territory, 1884. Courtesy Wisconsin Historical Society (Whi-36376).

asked, 'How much do you want for ten of these binders?' I nearly had a spell of heart failure, but I gasped the price. He said, 'All right; send 'em along.' " He also ordered a threshing machine, four tractor engines, and a half dozen plows. The banker then assured the salesman that he did not need to worry about the farmer's credit, confirming that he had more than $100,000 in the bank.[29]

On even grander scales were the so-called bonanza farms in the 1870s and 1880s in the Red River Valley of Minnesota and Dakota Territory—a short-lived phenomenon but important to the story (Figure 1.5). There, the remarkably flat and fertile terrain lent itself perfectly to huge, corporate-style wheat "factories." Regional folklore had it that a bonanza farmer claimed he had "seen a man on one of our big farms start out in the spring and plow a straight furrow until fall . . . [when] he turned around and harvested back."[30] The exaggeration may not have been too far off the mark. For example, Oliver Dalrymple's "farm" on the Dakota side of the Red River employed three hundred farmhands year round, grew wheat on thirty-two thousand acres by 1885, and was able to produce record-setting 23-bushel-an-acre harvests. Historian Kenneth Hammer writes that in 1880 with such harvests "there was concern that there would be not enough rail cars to carry the wheat to market. . . . [A]llowing 350 bushels to the car, [it] would require 32 cars a day for 45 days."[31]

There were others who invested in the Red River Valley, copying Dalrymple's methods to create what Hammer calls "a new style of frontier farming" and a "gigantic wheat production system" that emulated the "expanding industrial corporations of the eastern states." But without the technological changes in harvest machinery it could not have been possible. The binder "solved the problem," Hammer argues, showing how when the first binder arrived on the Dakota side of the Red River in 1878 it fascinated onlookers and became universally popular.[32] Sketches and pictures of the Dalrymple operation at harvest time show dozens of binders working in tandem to bring in the sheaves. Casson tells of when forty-seven European "commissioners," on a U.S. tour to visit the Chicago World's Fair, visited the immense Dalrymple farm and "saw a wheat field very nearly a hundred square miles in extent, with three hundred self-binders clicking out the music of the harvest. There were no serfs—no drudges—no barefooted women. And yet they were told that the labour-cost of reaping the wheat was less than a cent a bushel."[33]

The same could be shown of the giant wheat operations in eastern Montana and southern Alberta. Near the town of Hardin, Montana, Thomas Campbell had established the Campbell Farming Corporation in 1918, an operation that would become "the world's greatest wheat farm" with around 95,000 acres. Campbell was originally from the Red River Valley, and his views of corporate farming were informed by the successes of Dalrymple's giant operations and were only made possible by gasoline power. In fact, the world plowing record was set there circa 1920 when his workers used fourteen Aultman-Taylor gas-powered tractors to plow an entire section (640 acres) in one day. Harvest time required hundreds of workers and a panoply of machinery, including more than fifty tractors and seventy-two binders.[34] Up in Alberta similar but perhaps not quite as large operations were under way, especially near the town of Vulcan, where, as Paul Voisey has described it, "the flat, treeless terrain . . . encouraged mechanized wheat production on a mammoth scale." Mechanization there helped to provide wheat during the Great War in Europe and was relied on to harvest the record-setting bumper crops of 1915. For example, the Diamond Wheat Ranch "once used twenty-six binders in a single field," and at the Thompson Farm they "attacked 10,400 acres of wheat with fifty binders."[35]

The formation of International Harvester advanced the McCormick legacy, influence, and power in the farm implement world. That McCormick sought a merger with archrival William Deering illustrates his shrewdness. As Cyrus McCormick Jr. has written, "Deering was the rival McCormick had to fear—McCormick was the leader whose place Deering was trying to occupy."[36] Both companies had been commercially successful, although McCormick's history with the reaper established that company's strong agricultural legacy. McCormick had a better record in sales, but Deering had a better sense of investment for the future; he had controlling interests in iron ore deposits in the Mesabi Range of Minnesota, coal mines in Kentucky, a blast furnace in South Chicago, hardwood forests in Missouri, yellow pine forests in Mississippi, and plans to forge his own iron and steel, all of which Mc-Cormick jealously coveted. His son posited that if he "could provide his own iron, steel, and lumber, the basic raw materials of the agricultural implement industry, he might be able to reduce the cost of his machines."[37] McCormick and Deering had met three times prior to 1902 to discuss merging, but corporate details and the men's personalities and ambitions had prevented it. With Deering starting to age and McCormick backed by generous funding from J. P. Morgan, the chances for a merger improved. To bolster his efforts, McCormick acquired smaller implement companies: Plano Manufacturing, Milwaukee Harvester, and Wardner, Bushnell and Glessner. Milwaukee Harvester was "a ruling dynasty that had become extinct," as McCormick Jr. explained it, all of which helped the effort to buy out Deering. When the merger was complete, the all-powerful International Harvester Company had designs to be the world's largest farm machinery manufacturer. Two years later, IH acquired the Minneapolis Harvester Company (whose implements were known as "Minnies"), furthering the reach of the farm machinery giant. Headquartered in Chicago, IH's powerful implement empire helped make the Windy City the most important agricultural hub in the United States, or as historian William Cronon has called it, "nature's metropolis."[38]

But competition remained fierce. John Deere, Minnesota, Massey, and Case competed aggressively for the market and sold hundreds of thousands of binders across the grain growing Plains and Midwest. The Minnesota Company, located in the Stillwater State Prison and dependent on inmate labor, advertised in 1933 that its machine "embodies every feature that is necessary to meet the demand for a binder that can be depended upon." Most farmers in the far western Plains, eastern Washington, and California, however, preferred headers (which simply cut the grain heads and left the stalks standing) or, on bigger farms, the enormous early versions of the combined harvester-threshers (combines) for harvesting grain. In those drier regions, wheat crops were thinner and shorter and did not require binding.[39]

In Canada, as historian Tony Ward has written, there was "rapid adoption of the twine binder" as wheat production expanded across the Prairie Provinces. The first such machines started trickling into Manitoba in 1881 and into Alberta a year later. In western Canada "for a few hundred dollars," Denison explains, "the individual farmer was able to double [or] even triple his productivity and, to a very large extent, remove both the exhausting labor and psychological hazards of harvesting." Thus, as early as 1883—according to Denison, the most prosperous year ever for Canadian implement sales at the time of his study in 1949—some fifty-five hundred binders were in use in the Prairie Provinces, and most of those were made by the Massey and Harris companies. Their drop in price from the original Can$350 in the 1890s to Can$155 further popularized the implement. By 1915 even imported binders from the United States sold for around Can$105.[40]

The Canadian government, however, imposed tariffs on U.S.-made farm implements. They rose from 17.5 percent in the 1850s (primarily for early reapers used in Ontario prior to the wheat boom in the Prairie Provinces) to 25 percent in the 1870s (for wire binders) to 37.5 percent by the 1880s (for twine binders and other implements). The duty amounted to about $19 per binder, and in 1911 at the port in Winnipeg the government collected almost $4,000 in tariffs on imported binders.[41] Cyrus McCormick was clearly annoyed at such policies and petitioned the U.S. State Department to intercede on such matters, although the State Department did not respond to his request. He also sent twenty-five agents to Canada to help market his implements there, but the sales team had a tough time convincing farmers that the more expensive U.S. implements were better than the Canadian-made counterparts (primarily Massey-Harris). One agent wrote to company headquarters, "Canadians are clannish and strongly prejudicial." But although McCormick remained frustrated about this, he was unwilling to build manufacturing plants in Canada. Selling no more than a thousand binders in Canada in his lifetime, McCormick was greatly undersold by Massey-Harris, Deering, and other competitors. Even his son (who later ran IH) missed the mark when he thought the wheat boom would never last because one crop failure would ruin the region's entire economy.[42] Nonetheless, by the 1930s, in addition to its nearly one hundred U.S. agencies, IH established a string of "branch houses" across the Prairie Provinces to help sell all types of harvesters and other farm equipment. The Canadian branches were located in Winnipeg and Brandon, Manitoba; in Weyburn, Yorktown, Swift Current, Regina, Saskatoon, and North Battleford, Saskatchewan; and in Lethbridge, Calgary, and Edmonton, Alberta. Wheat-rich Saskatchewan was of particular interest to IH, which by 1914 maintained thirty-six agents, or "blockmen," and fifty-nine sales associates in the province.[43]

The strongest competition in Canada came from Toronto's Massey-Harris (M-H) corporation. M-H manufactured a line of binders for different conditions and farm sizes. In 1917 the company advertised the new Number 5 Binder as something farmers should buy for its "reliability, convenience, simplicity, [and] durability," adding that the "many thousands of farmers using M-H binders will tell you that on every one of these points, the M-H leads all others." In 1937 M-H argued that its harvesters were "the best binder made" and that they "cost less for repairs" and saved farmers money "by using less twine"—about "one and half inches on every sheaf." Two years later the company even advertised that its Number 16 Binder was best for "comfort and convenience," with a "new style roomy seat" and a high back for better support that "lessens fatigue."[44]

Whether purchasing Canadian- or U.S.-made binders, Prairie Province farmers bought many of the useful new implements, more slowly on smaller farms where reel-rake reapers still served their purpose well, especially for oats and barley, but at a much more rapid pace in other areas. The binder was at that time the most costly and complicated farm machine in existence, with thirty-eight hundred parts, making many farmers doubtful that it could withstand the pressure of repeated annual harvests and leery about the expense and headache of breakdowns.[45] But while "the early binders gave a great deal of trouble," Grant MacEwan acknowledges, "they were accepted at once and for nearly fifty years nobody considered an alternative." MacEwan also explains that the "most highly respected man in any rural community was the one who had demonstrated skill in repairing [the binders], especially the knotters."[46] Joyce Fieguth, from a German Mennonite family that immigrated to Rosthern, Saskatchewan, in the early twentieth century, reminisced, "I recall my little brother going to the field when Dad had had a particularly trying time with the old binder. He asked wisely and wistfully, 'Dad, ith thatan (Satan) under the binder?' . . . [D]ad could only say, 'Yo, Kleena (little one), I believe yes.' There had come a time when a weary farmer felt that indeed Satan was very intimately involved with the implement. Happiness was getting this clanging, jangling, banging piece of scrap metal around the field without a major break-down."[47]

Perhaps Saskatchewanian farmer-poet Hugh Duddridge captured this essence best in his poem "The Rime of the Bucking Binder":

> Some folks their pity waste on tramps
>   Or on the organ grinder;
>   My sympathy is with the man
>   Who rides the bucking binder.
>
> He rides, I said, but not for long,
>   He's mostly on the stubble,
>   A-poking around the pesky thing
>   And can't locate the trouble. . . .
>
> He's on again, but soon hops off
>   To tinker with the knotter
>   Great heavens! that arm is running loose,
>   It must have slipped the cotter.[48]

Occasional mechanical problems notwithstanding, most grain farmers were satisfied with their binders. Experience proved that many binders lasted ten years or longer, although in their early stages very few manufacturers dared to venture such a prediction. In 1910 *Harvester World* published a letter from Indiana farmer Peter Baily with a picture of his McCormick binder that he had "used for 24 years" and that was perhaps "one of the oldest machines in the state." A 1915 article in the *Nebraska Farmer* related the story of a "long-lived binder" owned by F. W. Chase of Pawnee County, Nebraska. He had used his McCormick binder for decades but claimed it had never missed tying more than three bundles an acre, that it still had its original canvas platform, and that he had spent only fourteen dollars on repair costs in all that time.[49]

The improved harvesting technology that binders represented (along with better plows, disk harrows, grain drills, seeders, threshing machines, and later combines) was what industry officials termed the "miracle of modern farm machinery." An IH booklet claimed the advanced implements were "saving the world from starvation" and "from fear of famine" with the surplus grain that the technology helped to produce: "America, with a surplus of foodstuffs, has been helping feed the world. Our ability to do this is the wonder and amazement of other countries who are not accustomed to the mass production methods." What did it all mean? According to Casson, "It means bread. It means hunger insurance for the whole human race. . . . It means the famine problem has been solved . . . for all civilized nations of the world." An ad campaign that IH prepared in the late 1940s showed a farmer pointing back in time to Thomas Malthus, who in 1798 forecast that mankind would not keep abreast of the world's food needs, saying "You were wrong, Dr. Malthus." It stated that the legacy of Cyrus McCormick and his mechanical reaper was the multitude of different farm machines—"the tools that help turn shortage into plenty."[50] Certainly, mechanization did not end world hunger, but the "tech solves" mentality seen in these kinds of ads and statements was prevalent at the time and represents how companies pushed sales.

Still, mechanization, coupled with a soaring world demand for grain, especially during World War I, did greatly accelerate the expansion of the wheat belt (Figure 1.6). Harvested acres of wheat in the United States jumped from nearly 36.7 million in 1890 to 69.2 million by 1938 (or, harvested bushels of wheat from 449 million to 920 million). The rate of increase in Canada was even more dramatic—from 42.2 million bushels in 1891 to more than 540 million by 1940. In 1940, 95 percent of the output came from the three Prairie Provinces, and the percentage of Canadian farms situated there climbed from 24.3 percent to 67.3 percent. Wheat acreage in the three provinces increased from almost nil to 27.7 million acres in the same time period.[51] The production of oats and barley increased in similar fashion. The boom is further reflected in the fact that Canada went from supplying 5 percent of the world's total exported wheat in 1911 to 40 percent by 1930. This dream of a "wheaten em-

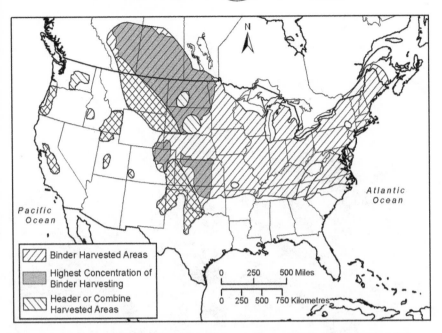

Figure 1.6. Binder-, header-, and combine-harvested areas of North America, 1900–1950 (adapted from map on p. 28 of Thomas Isern, *Bull Threshers and Bindlestiffs,* 1990). Courtesy Wenonah Fraser, Department of Geography, Brandon University.

pire," as John Bukowczyk has called it, was all made possible by a national rail strategy, government disposal of crown lands for homestead farmers, and a heightened world demand for cereal grains.[52]

Saskatchewan was especially well suited for the venture. The *Regina Leader* issued a report in 1892 called "Our Perfect Wheat" extolling the virtues of farming in Assiniboia and reporting how two North Dakota agronomists visiting the area were amazed with the wheat's lack of rust and its high gluten content. After Saskatchewan became a province in 1905, an agricultural extension bulletin claimed that the climate was ideal for producing "the world's best wheat" with a "high percentage of gluten of superior quality." Correspondingly, the number of farms went from 13,380 in 1900 to almost 56,000 in 1906, and their production increased from 4.3 million bushels of wheat to 50 million bushels in the same years—almost half the wheat production of prairie Canada, as Bill Waiser has documented in his book *Saskatchewan: A New History* (2005). It was all made possible by railroads, immigrant settlers (thousands of whom came from the United States), the development of new wheat varieties, and the use of farm equipment like sod-busting chilled-steel plows, disk harrows, and binders.[53]

Figure 1.7. McCormick Works twine mill, Chicago, 1900. Courtesy Wisconsin Historical Society (McCormick–International Collection, Whi-9752).

It is hardly surprising, then, that the binder-dependent grain expansion on the Great Plains "expanded the demand for fiber and twine geometrically," as one study calculated. An average of two to six pounds of twine was needed to harvest every acre of wheat, or seen another way, two pounds of twine were needed to cut a thousand pounds of grain, depending on conditions.[54] With such rapid adoption of binders the demand for twine was so immense by 1900 that it was estimated that more than half of all the hard fiber imported into the United States was being used for binder twine. For the next three decades, Americans consumed around two hundred thousand tons of binder twine a year and Canadians another thirty-five thousand tons annually.[55]

Cordage companies quickly retooled to manufacture greater amounts of twine, and IH launched itself into the cordage business by building four huge twine mills (in Chicago, New Orleans, Saint Paul, and Hamilton, Ontario) and by acquiring the immense Deering twine works, also in Chicago, for a total of 4,248 spindles and hundreds of spinners in each factory. It made the binders, so why not the twine? Its main Chicago twine mill was a huge structure standing five stories high and occupying nearly 500,000 square feet of floor space with a capacity to produce 30,000 tons of binder twine a year (Figure 1.7).[56] In fact, IH came to dominate the twine industry to such a large

Figure 1.8. Women workers at International Harvester twine mill, Chicago, 1939. Courtesy Wisconsin Historical Society (McCormick–International Harvester Collection, Whi-8897).

degree that by 1914 it was consuming nearly twice as much imported fiber— 584,000 tons—as the other significant twine manufacturers combined. Casson writes that at just one of IH's plants, "enough twine was twisted in a single day to make a girdle around the earth."[57] Its Saint Paul plant became somewhat known for its innovations and labor relations. According to an article in *Harvester World*, the mill was "a democratic community" with a "splendid spirit of co-operation." It was all made possible with the establishment of the Employees' Booster Club, a worker-run organization charged with the "promotion of cleanliness, health and safety through sanitation, ventilation and prevention of accidents."[58] In the Chicago plants, IH worked to create suitable working conditions and pay scales that would head off any attempt at unionizing. A company document in 1903 explained that it was IH's "firm opinion, in order to keep our employees out of unions, we must make them feel that they are receiving as much, or more, from us voluntarily as the unions could get by force." It employed a large number of women who made a dollar a day (ten cents an hour at ten-hour shifts) (Figure 1.8). Employee welfare was a big concern at IH's Deering twine mill, where women workers were outfitted in special caps, aprons, and shoes and given pie and coffee breaks in the factory's cafeteria.[59]

Figure 1.9. Ad for International Harvester twine. Courtesy Wisconsin Historical Society (McCormick–International Collection, Whi-9849).

At the twine works, "a bedlam of noise and fuzz," as Casson describes them, the pure fiber was put through eight different machines to comb and straighten it. Then, using giant spinners with bobbins, machines further reduced it to approximately seventy-five strands twisted 14.5 times per foot before being balled and packaged. Depending on the exact brand or fiber mixture, the balls averaged 500 to 650 feet of twine per pound and generally weighed eight pounds each. Finally, six to a bale, the balls were packaged and

Figure 1.10. International Harvester Company pamphlet, 1937 (file 92148, International Harvester Company records, IHCA/Navistar).

tied with 14 feet of lightweight rope for easily handling, and, as C. H. Wendel appropriately puts it, "Farmers could always find use for the extra rope."[60] IH published two different booklets entitled *The Story of Twine* (in 1931, the centennial of the McCormick reaper, and again in 1937 [Figure 1.10]). The company's promotional literature (Figure 1.9) asserted that in its "never-ceasing search for improvement," IH twine had "long been recognized as of unsurpassed quality" and that "better twine could not be made." The IH twine division also worked to improve the winding and balling processes and developed a patented reinforced cover that "did not collapse nor become tangled even after the twine in the ball [had] been used."[61]

International Harvester's biggest competitors were the established cordage manufacturers and rope works that wanted to get a share of the new gold mine in binder twine. The largest competitor, though still dwarfed by IH, was

Plymouth Cordage of Massachusetts, which had been manufacturing cordage
products since 1837. The company also had a Canadian twine mill in Welland,
Ontario. One business historian called Plymouth Cordage "the best managed
concern in the trade." Its specialties were ropes, twines, and cords, and thus
it was in better shape than some companies to compete quickly in the binder
twine race. "Plymouth Binder Twine is the stand-out for saving time during
busy harvest days," its advertisements proclaimed, and it ensured "full use
right up to end of the ball."[62] In 1909 and 1910 Plymouth went after IH in
an especially "bitter fight," with Plymouth telling farmers and other customers that "the line of battle has been formed." In a booklet entitled *What Every
Farmer Should Know about Binder Twine,* Plymouth advised farmers to go to their
hardware dealers "and have a good talk" and to "stand up for an open market."[63] Like the "battle of the binders" that was raging in the implement business, a battle of the twines now began in the cordage industry. IH enlisted
the help of "Prospy" (short for "prosperity")—the elfish cartoon character
bedecked in cornhusks and grain who "worked" for the company by selling
its variety of farming products (Figure 1.11). In 1910 he entered the twine-
selling business as a gimmick so that farmers and dealers would take note of
IH twine's durability.[64] Other large firms competing aggressively included the
Peoria Cordage Company of Illinois, the Hooven & Allison Company of Xe-

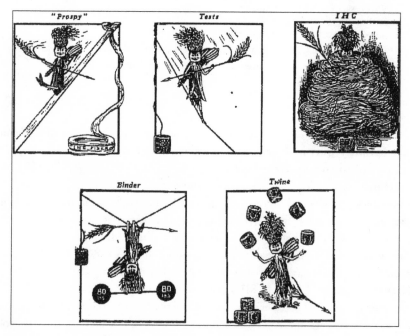

Figure 1.11. IH's "Prospy" tests binder twine (from *Harvester World* 1, March
1910).

nia, Ohio, the National Cordage Company and the Standard Rope and Twine Company, both of New York, and the Brantford Cordage Company of Brantford, Ontario, and Winnipeg, Manitoba, as well as smaller companies around the United States and Canada.[65]

Brantford advertised itself as "the world's largest exclusive binder twine manufacturers" and maker of "a twine of greater value and economy." But in 1918 a crisis of sorts developed when delivery of Brantford twine was stalled, threatening to ruin crops that could not get cut and bound in time. The fault was with the Canadian National Railway (CNR), not twine makers, when apparently ninety bales of binder twine balls were held up in Ottawa for three weeks in August around harvest time. One irate distributor from Forest Falls, Ontario, complained to the Railway Board of Commissioners that the CNR was out to "victimize their customers" and that the delay was "injuring business." "If the load does not arrive this week," he advised, "I cannot and won't accept it, for the harvest has begun . . . and my customers will have supplied themselves elsewhere." Brantford officials also wrote the Railway Board: "Twine is urgently required by consignee for the harvest which is now on." The CNR delivered the bales two days later.[66] Canadian farmers also had the choice of purchasing several brands made in Europe. Among the most competitive of those was England's Britannia binder twine and the Netherlands' Holland and Tip-Top brands. Britannia argued that Canadian farmers should buy British twine and thus help Britain buy more Canadian wheat. The Dutch brands, which were made from a different variety of sisal imported from the Netherlands' colony in Java, marketed their twines to Canadians with regional sounding names such as "Prairie Pride" and "Queen City."[67]

Unique to the cordage trade was that by 1891 the manufacturers had to compete against state-subsidized twine mills in penitentiaries. Officials at the Stillwater State Prison in Minnesota engineered the idea as a way to provide state farmers with lower priced binder twine and to keep inmates from being idle. Officials at the Ontario Central Prison in Toronto, the Kingston federal penitentiary in Kingston, Ontario, and state penitentiaries in North Dakota, South Dakota, Kansas, Wisconsin, Michigan, Indiana, Missouri, and Oklahoma followed suit in the early twentieth century, offering twines that were usually at least one cent a pound cheaper than the cordage company brands. Officials at Plymouth complained about the state-subsidized competition, estimating that the prisons had a production advantage of three-quarters of a cent per pound and that theirs was "the only industry in the country subject to prison competition."[68]

The variety in brands was matched by the variety of twines. Always the most expensive at more than ten cents per pound was Pure Manila twine, made from Philippine abacá. Then there were various manila-sisal mixtures (referred to as Superior Manila, Manila, and Standard Manila).

IH manufactured both a first-grade twine with International, Champion, and Deering tags, and a second-grade twine with the name of a company it had absorbed, Akron Twine and Cordage. The least expensive and most popular types were the Standard and White Sisal binder twines that were made of Yucatecan fibers, although for some reason the word "henequen" was never used commercially in the twine business the way it was in the fiber trade.[69] "Sisal" came to mean sisal *and* henequen, botanical nomenclature notwithstanding. An IH report in 1910 continued the confusion by wrongly stating that "the plant from which sisal fibre is produced is known in Yucatán as henequen." Either way, *Harvester World* noted its importance: "Ninety percent of all binder twine used in the United States or exported from the United States is made from sisal, and ninety percent of the sisal is grown in Yucatán." The *Washington Post* had reported on this dependency earlier, suggesting that "Yucatán produces nine-tenths of the world's sisal crop, and [it] composes nine-tenths of the binder twine used by American farmers in harvesting their grain crops."[70]

The huge increase in fiber use caused renewed interest in the scientific study of vegetable fibers and directed the U.S. government's attention to fiber economics. In 1911, the Department of Agriculture commissioned Lyster Dewey, a botanist in charge of fiber plant research at the USDA Bureau of Plant Industry, to conduct a study on the variety of marketable hard fibers, their natural histories, and their industrial utility for twine. His report, entitled "Fibers Used for Binder Twine," discussed the requirements needed for sturdy twine and provided short synopses and taxonomies of the various world fibers, such as abacá (manila), henequen, sisal, phormium (from New Zealand), mauritius (from the island of the same name), hemp, flax, and various Mexican agave fibers such as cabuya, istle ("Tampico hemp" or zapupe), and maguey. Dewey concluded by providing data on the recent surge in henequen, sisal, and manila imports into the United States for the binding of crops, showing that imports of henequen, "the sisal of the market," as he called it, had jumped from 39,000 tons in 1891 to more than 117,000 tons in 1911. "Should the market demand a similar increase during the next 20 years," he assured interested readers, "there is little danger of a lack of supply."[71] Parts of the report were also reprinted in the trade journal *El henequén* in 1916, illustrating its importance to Yucatecans. A dozen years later, F. I. Oakley published *Long Vegetable Fibres*, which updated some of the taxonomic, morphological, and life history data of hard fibers and dedicated some attention to their economic uses.[72]

To accommodate the growing flow of fiber from Mexico to the United States, the U.S. government established a free-trade zone at the Port of New Orleans to receive the fiber shipments from relatively nearby Yucatán (Figure 1.12). The free-trade designation opened the door to unlimited imports of raw fiber, but not manufactured twine or cordage products. The United States

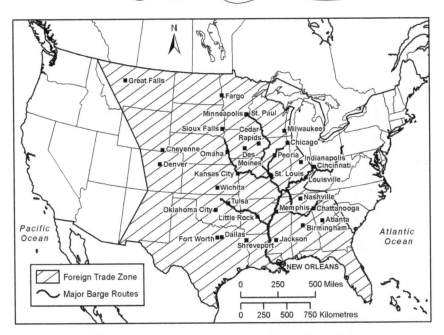

Figure 1.12. Foreign trade zone for U.S. sisal imports, Port of New Orleans (adapted from map "Foreign Trade Zone #2 Port of New Orleans" [pamphlet], International Harvester Co. records, documented series, file 441, box 394, Wisconsin Historical Society). Courtesy Wenonah Fraser, Department of Geography, Brandon University.

imposed a stiff tariff on any imported twine, effectively eliminating the threat of cheaper imports flooding the market.[73]

The government of Canada did the same. Canadian tariffs on farm implements extended to cordage and kept much of the twine out of the country at the end of the nineteenth century. But Canadian farmers clamored for an end to the three-cents-a-pound duty on imported twine. An anonymous pamphlet complained of the government's "combines" that controlled the manufacture and sale of twine and pointed to members of Parliament who were reaping unfair benefits from the government's involvement. The *Regina Leader* in wheat-rich Saskatchewan (then known as Assiniboia) was outspoken about the "absurd duty." "In the interest of the farmers of western Assiniboia, [we] raise our voices against the duty on twine," it editorialized in April 1892, suggesting that the duty amounted to "an annual tax" on farmers for a total of $144,000. The newspaper reprinted a long speech given in Parliament by Nicholas Flood Davin, the member from that region (and editor of the *Leader*), who argued that the government should reduce or eliminate the tariff so that twine prices could be reduced for his constituent farmers. The motion to eliminate the tariff failed, 107-to-63, a month later, and it failed again in 1893. The *Leader* also reported that most of the twine consumed in Canada was made there but that the 14 percent that came from the States was better, that a pound of Canadian twine was "much shorter" than a pound of U.S. twine. The author of a letter to the editor of a farmers' journal, however, argued that Canadian twine was "of good quality," supplied jobs to at least one thousand people, and prevented unfair competition from U.S. manufacturers.[74] Nonetheless, by the end of the century the strong populist organization Order of the Patrons of Industry lobbied hard for an end to the duties on U.S. twine. The Patrons sent petitions with more than twenty-five thousand signatures to Ottawa requesting that the tariffs be lifted. But the *Leader* reported that the Patrons were actually selling twine at "dearer" prices in Qu'Appelle, Saskatchewan, than those set "by the trade." The price of Canadian-made twine was more than halved, however, when it fell from eighteen cents a pound in the 1880s to seven cents by 1910.[75] The reduction was due in part to Canada's efforts to increase domestic production.

Twine was useful not for binders alone. It came to be one of those culturally ubiquitous and useful farm and household items that performed a million functions, perhaps like duct tape does today. Joyce Fieguth remembered this important cultural component when reminiscing about her childhood on a farm in a central Saskatchewan Mennonite community, which was undoubtedly similar to those of hundreds of thousands of people throughout the Great Plains: "Dad's overalls were more often than not, tied up with binder twine. Boots were another thing. Laces wore out before the sturdy split leather boots, so binder twine was the answer. . . . [I]t was suitable to tie up corral gates. It could be used to tie the rails of the fence to the posts or to trees that were already standing there. Harnesses were often repaired with twine."[76]

There was yet one other twist in the twine industry that deserves mention here. As demand for fibers suitable for binder twine accelerated, a race developed to control the importing of fibers to the United States. The competitors included some companies that were not cordage manufacturers but were involved in buying and trading fibers on the international market. The largest was Henry W. Peabody & Company of Boston. With its origins as a shipping firm, Peabody began trading in fibers in the 1860s, first manila from the Philippines. He had established a trading house in Yucatán for henequen by 1891.[77] The firm was the principal supplier of fiber for many of the smaller cordage companies and prison twine mills.

Around the turn of the century, the National Cordage Company of New York attempted to form a monopoly with Yucatecan fiber merchants. Quicker on the draw, McCormick entered into a contractual arrangement with Peabody to be McCormick's chief purchaser and importer of fibers. The agreement was a personal one between Cyrus McCormick and Henry Peabody in which McCormick lent Peabody an estimated $200,000, half the capital it needed to maintain Peabody's involvement in the sisal trade. In return, Mc-Cormick got the right to oversee Peabody's purchases in Yucatán. The deal not only pushed National out of the forefront of the hot henequen market but also paved the way for McCormick (and after 1902, IH) to maintain almost absolute control over imported Yucatecan fibers in what economists refer to as a monopsony (a monopoly on imports) or, according to another study, an oli-gopsony, since the IH trust included several different corporate entities. The deal had "fatal consequences" for National Cordage, as the trade journal *El agricultor* put it. From 1902 to 1915 IH controlled 90 percent of the Yucatecan fiber trade, and during 1910 alone it had a record setting 99.8 percent.[78]

Especially useful for this venture was an arrangement that IH made with prominent henequen growers in Yucatán that exemplified the monopsony structure. Now working with the principal producers (the *henequeneros*) and the principal importer (Peabody), IH created what critics called a "trust," which drove out the competition and controlled pricing. Historians Gilbert Joseph and Allen Wells argue that this scenario fits an "imperial collaborator model" and that IH's "invisible" or "informal empire" was its denouement as a "modern trans-national corporation" similar to the empire that United Fruit Company (UFC) maintained in the Caribbean Basin. Like UFC did with transportation in Central America, IH made serious, although eventually unsuccessful, at-tempts from 1903 to 1907 to take control of the Yucatecan railroads that were essential for getting fiber to the port for shipping. While IH controlled pro-duction and pricing, unlike UFC it never owned the plantations or any land in the henequen zone.[79]

With this trust structure firmly in place, IH became the largest fiber trader in the world. In 1902, for example, it garnered 90 percent of the binder twine market, although that figure would be reduced in later years.[80] IH claimed the trust helped prevent "frequent 'twine famines' and high prices" like those that occurred from 1881 to 1901. In 1881 demand was so high and a shortage so severe that binder twine sold for twenty cents a pound—nearly double the normal price. But with the merger of the several companies to form IH, the company had been able "to maintain a lower level of fibre prices . . . which has resulted in the lower price to the farmers of America."[81]

Twine helped the McCormick family become even wealthier, and IH be-came an even more powerful corporation, with its fiber trade helping to stimu-late a boom in Yucatán's economy. With that kind of wealth streaming into Yucatán, local historian Gonzalo Cámara Zavala proclaimed that McCormick had given "to humanity a very great benefit." Several Yucatecan and American investors were so appreciative that they proposed a new development in the

henequen zone to be named Ciudad McCormick (McCormick City), similar
perhaps to Henry Ford's rubber plantation in Brazil (Fordlândia), but Cyrus
McCormick Jr. rejected the offer.[82]

Not everyone was so fond of McCormick and the trust he had established.
Rival cordage companies screamed for anti-trust lawsuits, and the U.S. government investigated IH under the Sherman Anti-Trust Act. The legislature
of Minnesota, in an act of time-period populism for which the state was
known, even declared IH a monopoly in 1907.[83] It was at this time that grain-
dependent states and provinces in the Midwest and Great Plains established
penitentiary twine plants as an effort to bust the trust and provide cheaper
twine to farmers. But IH was able to hide behind dummy firms it controlled,
often without disclosing its holdings, or as a State Department special agent
charged with investigating IH's deals with Yucatán surmised, "Harvester was
again digging into its old bag of illicit tricks."[84] IH could not control the flow
of sisal from Yucatán to Canada, but its pricing policies affected what Canadian cordage firms would have to pay for sisal. Actually, in the henequen trade
records there is much evidence of direct sales of fiber to Brantford Cordage in
Ontario and to twine makers in Montreal and other places, but the prices they
paid were the ones dictated by IH/Peabody, plus shipping.[85]

Few Yucatecans were happy with the arrangement either. A plethora of
articles in area newspapers and trade journals denounced the monopoly. One
study counted fifty-five articles in Yucatecan publications in just a few years'
time complaining of IH's unhealthy role in the sisal industry.[86] El agricultor in
1908 pointed to "la International" as "the giant that dominates us" and that
makes "opulent earnings" from Yucatán's natural resources without many profits going back to the people. But the article preached a didactic message citing
"the magnificent lesson that this teaches" and how "we should learn from this
experience." The article finally invoked the law of natural selection, calling on
Yucatecans to be the "most capable" and the strongest in order to survive. Another article in the newspaper (reprinted from La revista de Mérida) called IH
"the tourniquet that squeezes Yucatán" and lamented the misappropriation of
the state's "only source of wealth"—henequen.[87]

Foreign reporters were not unaware of what was going on between a U.S.
corporation and an exploited Mexican state. Carlo de Fornaro, an Italian journalist researching Mexican politics and economics (whom Porfirio Díaz later
imprisoned for his writings) published an important exposé in 1915 entitled
"Yucatán and the International Harvester Company." It was a story, he said,
"of an American corporation [working] for the control of one of the richest
states in Mexico," how IH "absorbed" the vast majority of the fiber trade, and
how wealthy politicians and henequen growers colluded with IH to make it all
possible. However, as he reported, that very year the Mexican Revolution ar-

rived in the Yucatán Peninsula and forever ousted IH from its monopsonistic role in the henequen trade. "What Harvester Co. does not relish is the fact that the government of Yucatan after many years of oppression and exploitation has finally checked the American trust."[88] Indeed, 1915 marked the beginning of many changes, including the Yucatecans retaking control of their state and its henequen industry.

With the high demand for binder twine, dependence on foreign commodities to make it, and the disruption of events such as the Mexican Revolution, one might wonder why the cordage industry and farm implement manufacturers did not turn toward a fiber that could be grown in North America. For example, industrial hemp—true hemp (*Cannabis sativa*), sometimes called "Kentucky hemp"—had been a fiber staple for the production of paper and rope in the eighteenth and nineteenth centuries. For many years it was the number one cash crop in Kentucky and was grown extensively in Wisconsin and California and to a lesser degree in other states. A plant native to central Asia, where it had been used for cordage products for centuries (and continues to be), hemp did well in the temperate climes of the upper South and Midwest and did not deplete soil nutrients as fast as cotton or tobacco. Likewise, it did not yet in those years carry the misconceptions affiliated with THC (tetrahydrocannabinol), the psychoactive ingredient found in other, nonindustrial strains of *Cannabis* grown in the tropics or under special growing conditions that produce marijuana and hashish. The mythical connotation that all hemp is narcotic arose in the 1930s in great part through an active campaign engineered by William Randolph Hearst and Harry Anslinger. Hearst worried that hemp fiber could replace wood pulp, of which he had huge land holdings and investments for his newspaper, the *New York Journal*. Anslinger, essentially America's first "drug czar" (in the Franklin Roosevelt administration) combined his family connections to DuPont Chemical (which had recently produced a new chemical treatment process for converting wood pulp to paper) and his government position to outlaw the growing of hemp. The film *Reefer Madness* also did its part by exaggerating the dangers of marijuana and arousing popular opinion against it. In 1937 Congress passed, with a short and perhaps record-setting ninety-second debate, the Marijuana Tax Act, which made growing hemp cost prohibitive and required growers with paid permits to raise only plants that would not produce leaves, buds, or flowers—a horticulturally impossible task. The government granted a reprieve during World War II, when hemp was needed to make rope for ships. There was even a "Hemp for Victory" campaign and a film with the same title that the Department of Agriculture issued to promote the growing of industrial *Cannabis*.[89]

Cordage makers actually did experiment with fiber from the six- to ten-foot hemp plants in the 1880s and 1890s to see if its tensile and knotting qualities would make it suitable for binding. A Kansas study in 1889 showed that "hemp furnishes a fiber sufficiently tenacious for all the purposes of . . . binding-twine. It . . . does well in eastern Kansas, and in the early history of the state yielded handsome returns to the cultivator." The study warned, however, that hemp required "a rich soil and heavy manuring" and that it could be "an exhausting crop" on the farmland.[90] Extracting the pulp from Kentucky hemp also entailed a labor problem. Asian producers had developed water retting techniques to help extract the pulp, but farmers in the upper South were loath to adopt the measure because of the stench it produced in standing ponds and for the fear that livestock would ingest the polluted water. Therefore they relied on the old ways of "breaking" the hemp fibers—a difficult and time consuming task that required the use of wooden "hand brakes" that crushed the hemp stalks with repeated beatings. Then the fiber had to be cleaned. All in all, it was an expensive operation that farmers often could not afford for the low prices they would receive. Mechanical decorticators had been invented to help mechanize the process, but by then twine makers had discovered the better and cheaper fiber sources in Yucatán.[91] Likewise, hemp did not withstand other testing and fared poorly in experiments across the cordage industry, as manufacturers consistently found that henequen or sisal produced the stronger twine.

Wire grass, or American grass (*Carex stricta*), came next. In the 1890s, Minneapolis Harvester devised a twine made from wire grass, really a marsh sedge, that grew in profusion in the marshlands of Minnesota and Wisconsin and could be harvested with a reaper modified for swampy conditions. The company also developed a new Minnie binder adapted for wire grass twine, which was thicker and stiffer than most. A Wisconsin firm started the first grass twine business in 1896, although it soon incorporated into the American Grass Twine Company (AGT) of Saint Paul. AGT then bought out Minnie Harvester in 1900, making it one of the state's largest manufacturers for a brief period in the early twentieth century. While less expensive than imported fibers and despite ads suggesting that "wherever introduced, it leaps into immediate popularity," and embellished with farmers' statements that it tied a "nice, tight sheaf" and "makes stiffer bundles," grass twine enjoyed only meager acceptance because it was bulky and prone to insect damage. AGT sold its Minnie operation to IH in 1903 and concentrated its wire grass schemes on the more successful production of Crex brand carpets and wicker furniture. But, as Paul Nelson has written, not even IH "could make farmers buy the Minnie Harvesters," so it converted the Minnie facility to make more twine, not from wire grass, but from flax.[92]

IH launched the International Flax Twine Company in 1905, drawing on twenty years of experiments that William Deering had conducted on flax twine. So anxious was IH to have a locally grown fiber that it provided seeds and training to farmers growing flax. With an investment of some $1.5 million, the Saint Paul mill manufactured several thousand tons of flax twine a year from 1907 to 1912. And in Canada, a firm from Great Falls, Montana, established a short-lived flax mill in Saskatoon, Saskatchewan, for making binder twine and other products. [93]

Engineers at the Kingston Penitentiary in Ontario also spent considerable time and resources experimenting with flax. One enterprising individual, T. E. Mitchell, who had migrated from Scotland to Quebec and had experimented in his homeland with spinning jute into cordage products, had now taken up flax and sent the Canadian minister of agriculture, W. R. Motherwell, samples of his flax twine in 1907. Motherwell responded that at that time sisal and manila twine were relatively inexpensive and thus good enough for farmers' use. [94]

At the same time, the U.S. Department of Agriculture was studying various fiber crops and paying special attention to which ones could be grown in U.S. territory. Again, Lyster Dewey, from the Bureau of Plant Industry, conducted the research and wrote in his 1911 report that flax, hemp, and phormium were the only fibrous plants "at all suited for binder twine that may be successfully cultivated in the United States, exclusive of Porto Rico, Hawaii, and the Florida keys." The fiber from other plants, such as yucca and lechuguilla from the deserts of the Southwest were "too short and otherwise unfit for the purpose." So, could traditional agaves such as sisal be raised in those deserts? No, since "the winters are too cold for the successful growth of any agaves now cultivated for fiber production." However, sisal was being grown in the arid parts of Hawaii, and sisal, henequen, istle, and cabuya were being raised in Puerto Rico and in the Florida Keys on land "sufficiently high to escape being covered with salt water during the hurricanes." [95]

During and after the Mexican Revolution when the flow of sisal was threatened and actually halted for a while in what became known as the "Sisal Situation," cordage companies returned their attention to hemp and flax. In 1916 IH began a hemp farm on forty acres in the Red River Valley of North Dakota, expanded production to seven thousand acres by 1918, and contracted with firms in Grand Forks and Fargo to process the hemp fiber. By 1918 North Dakota was the fourth largest hemp producing state after Kentucky, Wisconsin, and California, which represented "a great future" for the state. [96] Similarly, Canadian farmers experimented with hemp in the Prairie Provinces. The Saskatchewan Department of Agriculture reported that in the vicinity of Rhein, Saskatchewan, hemp was being raised for a cordage firm in Portage la Prairie, Manitoba. "The farmers are finding hemp a valuable crop and are satisfied with the returns," a department memo stated, adding that there was "an incredible demand for its products and growing interest on the part of farmers, so that . . . the hemp industry in western Canada would appear to be well launched and to face a reasonably secure future."[97] Despite such boosterism, hemp did not enjoy a long success in the northern plains for the same reasons that farmers had discovered earlier.

In terms of flax, whose fibers are also used to make linen, farmers from North Dakota and Saskatchewan gladly sent samples to Saint Paul and Kingston for a number of years with renewed hopes of developing a local twine fiber market.[98] F. W. Van Allen of Rosetown, Saskatchewan, devoted a great deal of time to "treating the fibre taken from ordinary flax straw" and testing its utility in twine. He conducted experiments on flax cordage in 1917 in the basement of the Saskatchewan legislature building in Regina and exhibited the flax twine in the display cases in the building's entrance area, with the explanation, "Some thirty or thirty-five specimens of twine and cordage made from ordinary flax straw dug right out of a flax pile on the prairie as it was threshed in the usual way." His conclusions, like elsewhere, however, were that "the predisposition for mice, crickets, etc., to eat the twine in the field while the grain is in the stook" made flax an objectionable material.[99]

Later, IH began to experiment with other fiber crops to ensure a steady fiber flow for the robust binder twine market. It supported various fiber crop schemes around the United States and in the Philippines, Hawaii, Cuba, Puerto Rico, the Dominican Republic, Ecuador, and European colonies in Africa and Asia.[100] Some, but not all, panned out well, but there was always the distance factor and the resultant costs for shipping. Hope was perhaps brightest for sisal plantations near Matanzas, Cuba. There, in 1929 IH established the La Conchita Plantation, which produced 5 million pounds of fiber a year, and the Nuevitas Sisal Plantation (Compañía Hispano-Americana de Henequén, S.A.), which lasted into the 1930s. A company memo stated that Nuevitas was "a valuable source of supply from which to draw necessary raw material." This information was especially important because after the fall of Porfirio Díaz there was "Bolshevik control" of Yucatán, whose "henequen culture and sisal production came to ruin." Plymouth Cordage also invested in Cuban sisal land.[101]

Nonetheless, as late as 1923 the cordage industry and the U.S. Department of Commerce continued to worry about a Mexican "monopoly" and to conduct experiments, as one newspaper reported, for "the discovery of some fiber to take the place of sisal." The idea was first "to safeguard" U.S. industry "from price manipulations," the *Farm Implement News* noted, and second to investigate "the possibility of developing sources of supply of the raw material within the United States."[102] The idea was not new. During the chaos in Mexico during the late 1910s, corporate investors organized a company called the

United States Sisal Trust with the aim of starting sisal plantations in Florida. The company was to provide the fiber and market it with sales agents fanning out around the Great Plains to make "tie-ups" between "a guaranteed supply and a guaranteed market." One agent even visited with North Dakota's A. C. Townley, leader of the state's Nonpartisan League, which was always on the lookout to aid farmers, to try to sell the plan to his organization. While "not unfriendly to the idea," as one study put it, "he did not consider it sufficiently feasible to bother with." In the end, the U.S. Sisal Trust operations in Florida never took off.[103]

The Department of Commerce's study recognized that sisal *could* be raised in Florida, Puerto Rico, the Philippines (then still a U.S. "insular possession"), and even in California's Imperial Valley but that "serious impediments" needed to be considered, especially as it would take at least seven years to obtain the first cutting. It rejected the Philippines, perhaps prophetically, "because in the event of war this source would be cut off immediately." And in the continental United States, the schemes would not work as "the labor cost looms as the bogey."[104] The issue even came up in the 1936 presidential race when Republican nominee Alf Landon (from wheat-dependent Kansas) claimed that a new chemical procedure had been developed for decorticating sisal that would eliminate the hand labor—the reason it remained so inexpensive to import from Mexico. With the new processing, "we should be able to start producing henequen here soon."[105] But once again, that scheme did not materialize—sisal just was not to be grown in the United States.

Yucatecan sisal remained the fiber of choice. Hemp, wire grass, and flax all floundered; they could not produce a twine that could be tied tightly enough for farmers' satisfaction or withstand the pressure of the mechanical knotter, they were susceptible to being eaten by crickets, and they disintegrated in adverse weather. And sisal was still less expensive than importing other fibers from farther away. But that so many alternative fiber schemes developed, and that most took place in the wheat growing areas of the American and Canadian Plains, illustrates once again how the grain and cordage industries were so tightly bound in twine and that the linkages between regional economies were important. The history of Yucatán's henequen industry, how it developed so quickly, and how it transformed society and the environment is addressed in the next chapter.

CHAPTER 2

Yucatán's Henequen Industry

Social and Environmental Transformations

Yucatán es la tierra madre de esta fibra.
(Yucatán is the mother land of this fiber.)

—El agricultor, *November 1927*

THE invention of the power reaper/binder with its wondrous mechanical twine knotter created a "nearly limitless demand" for henequen and sisal fiber. By 1900 more than 85 percent of all binder twine in North America was made with Yucatecan fiber.[1] That reality set the Mexican state of Yucatán (situated on the northern third of the Yucatán Peninsula [Figure 2.1]) squarely in the henequen-wheat complex.

Yucatán became the center of the henequen empire because of geographic conditions that are optimal for agave plants but not much else of agricultural value. The fact is surprising in several ways. First, Yucatán is situated on a semiarid limestone karst that makes the land untillable. It thus appears, as one study found, to be "a hostile environment" with "inherent limitations." There is a lack of good soil and surface water, and the whole of the henequen zone "is . . . covered with a thin layer of soil and a dry, rugged scrub forest . . . with no mountains and few hills to deflect the unbearable heat." The forbidding land and its dense, scrubby vegetation confounded early European visitors and colonizers, with one writing that Yucatán was "the country with the least earth that I have ever seen, since all of it is one living rock," and another bemoaning its "deficiency in mineral endowments."[2] Friar Diego de Landa, a missionary to Yucatán in the mid-sixteenth century, wrote that "the land is very flat and clear of mountains, so that it is not seen from ships until they

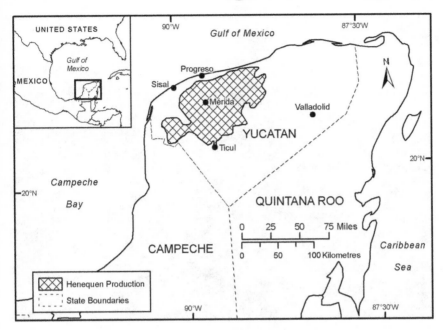

Figure 2.1. The henequen zone, Yucatán Peninsula, Mexico. Courtesy Wenonah Fraser, Department of Geography, Brandon University.

come very close. . . . This land is very hot and the sun burns fiercely. . . . Yucatán is a land of less soil than any I know . . . with very little earth, so that there are few places where one can dig down a fathom without meeting great banks of large rocks. . . . The country is excellent for lime . . . ; it is a marvel how much fertility exists in the soil on or between the stones."[3]

A Yucatecan mentioned to an American reporter in the 1930s, "I have always thought when God made Yucatán His original purpose was to use it for Hell. He neglected to give it any water or any soil."[4] Jutting out as it does between the Gulf of Mexico and the Caribbean Sea, Yucatán was isolated from the rest of New Spain during the colonial era and from Mexico after independence. The isolation resulted in a distinctly autonomous conditioning of the people there, "apart and different in both sentiment and jurisdiction," as one historian put it.[5]

In complete defiance of geographical determinism, the rocky soil and the hot, humid, but only seasonally rainy weather of the north central part of the state was an ideal environment for henequen and sisal—species native to the peninsula. Yucatán's average temperature of 77° F (25° C) helps to form the perfect agave growing conditions. The rocky soil and porous limestone and dolomite foundations—hundreds of feet thick—underlying the plantations

Figure 2.2. Henequen (*Agave fourcroydes*) growing near San Antonio Tehuitz, Yucatán. Photograph by the author.

allow water to percolate into the calcareous earth and form underground channels that drain into Yucatán's famous *cenotes* (large sinkhole wells). Soil scientists have long acknowledged that "soils containing a proper portion of calcareous earth are invariably rich in their natural state."[6] For Yucatán, the nutrients were derived from the remains of marine organisms, such as mollusks and corals, that were deposited on the ocean floor millennia ago.[7] Thus, that part of the state became the *zona henequenera* (henequen zone), an area of eighty-five hundred square miles (fifteen thousand square kilometers) that represents roughly one-third of the state (see Figure 2.1). The henequen zone is where growers produced 97 percent of the region's henequen fiber, with 97 percent of the land dedicated to fiber production. As Yucatecans have been fond of saying, "Es país que no se parece a otro" ("It is country like no other").[8] Even the name "Yucatán," as the legend goes, came from invading Spaniards, who heard Maya Indians say "*tectatán,*" meaning "I don't know," as a response to the invaders' queries of where they were.

The two fibrous plants that made Yucatán famous are in the agave family, that is, Agavaceae (but were formerly classified in the daffodil family, Amaryllidaceae): henequen (*Agave fourcroydes*) (Figure 2.2) and sisal (*Agave sisalana*), which are related to other Mexican agaves like the various yuccas

Table 2.1 Taxonomy and terminology for Yucatecan agaves

Botanical taxonomy	Mayan term	Spanish term	English term
Agave spp.	ki	los agaves	agaves
Agave fourcroydes	sak-ki (sacqui, sac-ci)	henequén blanco	henequen
Agave sisalana	yaxqui (yaax-ci, ya-ax-ki)	henequén verde	sisal
	che-elem-ki	agave de la costa	
	kitan-ki	henequén jabalí	
	bab-ki	henequén nadador	
	chukum-ki	henequén de fibra colorada	

Note: Blank spaces represent henequen and sisal varieties that have more specific names in Mayan and Spanish.

Source: Compiled from Benítez, Ki, 47–48; Irigoyen, ¿Fue el auge del henequén producto de la Guerra de Castas? 43; Chardon, Geographic Aspects of Plantation Agriculture in Yucatan, 14, 15; El sisal mexicano 1 (July 1927): 9. For further taxonomic history, see Orellana, "Agave, Agavaceae y familias afines en la Península de Yucatán," 82–87; Oakley, Long Vegetable Fibres, 138; Dewey, "Fibers Used for Binder Twine," 193–200; and Maiti, World Fiber Crops, 131–42.

(Yucca spp.) and the century plant (Agave americana, formerly Agave angustifolia or Agave tequilana), or in Spanish, maguey, from which the fermented drinks pulque and tequila are derived. While maguey is not native to Yucatán and does not thrive there, henequen and sisal are, and they survive in Yucatán's unique geography by storing water in their fleshy leaves. Although different species, they are similar plants. In the fiber industry, however, the generic word "sisal" (named after the small port town of Sisal on the west Yucatecan coast from which the fiber used to be shipped) came to refer to the fiber attained from both plants. The terminology in the henequen and Yucatecan literature gets confusing between Latin nomenclature, the common words used in English and Spanish, and the Mayan plant names used by the indigenous people of the peninsula (Table 2.1).

The Mayan names for the different plants indicated what they could produce. Yaax-ci (sisal) had longer leaves and was useful for cordage; sacqui (henequen) had a finer fiber and was used for hammocks. The literature is inconsistent as to the derivation of the Spanish word henequén. One source claims the word was adopted from the Mayan word nequen, which the Indians used for the cloth made from the fiber. Another argues that it was derived from the Incas in Peru, where Spaniards heard the Quechua word jeniquén that referred to fibers.[9] Related to the maguey, aloe, century plant, and other agave cacti, the succulents take seven years to mature but can last up to fifteen years with

-1826

Figure 2.3. Plantation workers drying sisal fiber, Yucatán, ca. 1910. Courtesy Wisconsin Historical Society (McCormick–International Harvester Collection, Whi-8081).

three cuttings of their spiny, spear-shaped leaves (called *pencas*) a year before a field needs to be replanted. Once planted there is little need for weeding, as the plants do not have much competition. Workers harvest the *pencas* with a machete and then transport them to a rasping shed where the fibrous pulp is macerated from the leaves with a decorticator. An acre of henequen yields fifteen hundred to two thousand pounds of fiber. The fiber is then strung out on wires in the open sun to dry (Figure 2.3) before being baled (usually in four-hundred-pound bales) and transported to port to be shipped out to cordage manufacturers. Every pound of dried fiber can produce up to five hundred feet of twine.[10]

All things considered, the plant was perfect for Yucatán, as the Italian journalist Carlo de Fornaro found when he visited the state in 1915: "Nature through centuries of selection made henequen the ideal plant impervious to inclemencies, droughts, to grasshoppers and other destructive pests. . . . The remarkable plant needs practically no cultivating, no irrigation. . . . The Yucatecans call it the noblest plant on the continent." So noble was it that local writer Manuel Escoffié called it the state's "crown of thorns . . . the crown that brought greatness to Yucatán." And the greatness and wealth that it brought was without favorable rivers, fertile agricultural lands, or valuable mines "with which the rest of Mexico was gifted."[11] The terminology is fitting since the word "agave" (the plants' genus), named by the Swedish taxonomist Carolus Linnaeus in 1753, is from the Greek word for "noble" or "magnificent." Yucatecan botanist Roger Orellana has written that the genus name "precisely" fits the agaves "for the durability of their leaves and the great resistance with which they survive adverse conditions and solar radiation."[12]

Because agave plants are native to Yucatán, they hold a place in the folklore of the Maya. The Indians tell the story of a henequen *penca* that cut the mythological sage Zamná, who wanted to add the plants to his herbarium. One of his servants then cut off the offending leaf and beat it continuously, which allowed the fibers to flow forth. (A different version has him tripping on a rock and his servants punishing the rock by whipping it with henequen leaves, thus revealing the fibers.) Zamná, who believed in omens and the greater significance of things in nature, then declared, "Life was born in the company of pain; [and] that through the wound was revealed a plant of great usefulness for the people." At that point, the ancient Maya rasped more fiber from the local plants and discovered many uses for it. Over time they made sandals, bags and baskets, thatch for roofs, traps and bows for hunting, and nets for fishing, needles from its spines, and many other household useful items. They also used henequen plants for decorative purposes. More unique uses included fashioning musical instruments from its components, fermenting its juices to make wine, and making a cloth wrap with which to bind prisoners of war.[13] Despite the legend, there is some debate among historians as to whether or not the pre-Columbian Maya used the fiber from the local agaves. However, Renán Irigoyen, in his definitive *Los mayas y el henequén*, argues that henequen was tightly interwoven into the lives of the Mayans, although the legend of Zamná could be a "recent invention." And as Roland Chardon concluded, the various age-old Mayan terms for the plants and their uses indicate that henequen was "a garden crop for family use . . . and also provided the necessary fiber for ropes and cordage in the Mayan economy."[14]

When the Spaniards invaded in the early sixteenth century they observed the Maya's use of henequen, but the Europeans adopted it for not much more than maritime rigging. Later in the century, however, written accounts show more interest in "*nequen*" (or as many called it, *cáñamo*, a generic hemp), and they describe how the Maya rasped the leaves and the many ways they used the fiber. For example, Hernández de Oviedo recorded that hammocks made from the strong fiber could be of great use for the armies in Spain, and Friar Diego de Landa mentioned in his *Relación de cosas de Yucatán* (1566) that there were "infinite things that could be made" from it. But while others alluded to the plant in similar ways, there was no colonial effort to cultivate the plant on a commercial scale for either local use or export.[15] Few Spanish colonizers actually settled in Yucatán. Those who did found the land unsuitable for agriculture, and as there were no mineral resources there for the Spaniards to exploit, they turned instead to raising cattle, for which the land was generally rather well suited. Finding success in exporting beef and hides to the more populous colony in Cuba, cattle ranchers increasingly began to cultivate plots of maize (*milpas*) to help feed a growing human and bovine population. However, when henequen became more economically important, the colonists' descendants, the Mexicans, began cultivating it on plantations. They learned how to do so from the Maya.[16]

By the end of the eighteenth century the Yucatecans had started to expand production of henequen, primarily for such useful things as rope, sacks, and hammocks. But after Mexico's independence from Spain in 1821, large-scale henequen cultivation started to take shape. The more autonomously oriented Yucatecans only reluctantly joined the Mexican nation and then only with stipulations that they have the rights to trade with whomever they chose and collect their own tariffs. With independence came the elimination of the restrictive Spanish tariff and mercantalist policies (requiring colonies to trade only with the mother country), which was useful when a young and growing United States was in need of naval cordage and becoming a steady customer for the emerging sisal industry in Yucatán. At that point the Mexicans who had inherited land began cultivating henequen on haciendas, or rather, they hired overseers and workers to do so while they seldom left the comforts of Mérida. And to work the henequen fields (called *henequenales*) the landowners needed greater numbers of field hands—peons or *campesinos*, many of whom were Mayan, who worked in a debt peonage arrangement with the landowner.[17] In fact, as the demand for fiber gradually increased, state officials in Yucatán recognized the economic opportunity that was unveiling itself and encouraged Yucatecans to plant more henequen. In 1828 the legislative body issued a decree requiring every citizen to raise at least ten henequen plants a year in their patios or yards, and they authorized municipalities around the state to begin converting community lands to *henequenales*. The mandate was successful enough that by 1830 local groups had organized the Compañía para el Cultivo y Beneficio del Henequén (the Henequen Growing and Development Company), whose objective was "to promote, increase, and perfect the planting, cultivation, and manufacturing of henequen and to facilitate in its sale." For such purposes, the company acquired the Chacsinkin Hacienda near Mérida and began what was probably Yucatán's first henequen plantation, with 20,880 plants.[18]

The industry grew. In the first few decades of the nineteenth century henequen was Yucatán's second greatest export commodity after logwood, which had a short-lived popularity in Europe for the dyes it rendered, and for the first time henequen exports surpassed those of beef and hides. Sugar, tobacco, and cotton rounded out other early export products, all of which depended on slavelike debt peonage labor, with sugar quickly replacing logwood as plantations expanded in coastal Yucatán. From 1830 (one year before Cyrus McCormick's invention of the reaper) to 1847, there was a steady increase in henequen exports, shipped from the small port of Sisal on Yucatán's southern coast.[19] By then many things had started to change, affecting all agricultural production on the peninsula. First, Yucatecans were alarmed at Mexico's return to conservative centralism with President Antonio López de Santa Anna's constitution of 1836 and his demands that Yucatán contribute 200,000 pesos of its own customs money to the federal government, in violation of the state's special conditions for joining Mexico. Thus, Yucatecans were in solidarity with Texans when the Lone Star republic seceded from Mexico, and they established warm political and trade relations with the independent Texans. They also toyed with the idea of announcing their own secession, passing resolutions for such in 1841 and forcing a Mexican naval squadron out of Yucatecan waters (with the aid of Texan gunboats). But soon realizing that their own independence was not economically viable, Yucatecans rejoined the Mexican nation on very favorable terms, although Santa Anna later reneged on most of the conditions.[20]

More significant was that the Maya had revolted en masse against the Creole (whites born in Mexico) planters and *ladino* (mixed blood) elites in what became known as the Caste War (1847–53). The uprising was in response to the confiscation of Maya lands, their impressment into hard labor on sugar plantations, the oppressive control of the Catholic Church, and a racist hierarchical social system that exacerbated the suffering of indigenous persons on the peninsula. Historian Terry Rugeley argues that the ongoing colonialist pattern of land confiscation, which was increasing due to expanding henequen production and Yucatán's entrance into agrarian capitalism, was one of the many causes of the conflict.[21] The prolonged violence resulted in a demographic collapse in which between 25 and 50 percent of Yucatán's population died due to war, disease, and starvation. The war also effectively put an end to the Yucatecan sugar industry and bankrupted the state treasury, causing local leaders and landowners to seek other avenues for commercial enterprises.[22] Those other avenues led right to what grew best in north central Yucatán—henequen. And, as one study put it, the spiny plant became "the center of Yucatán's economic life from 1860 to 1940."[23]

There was great hope that the plant would bring new opportunities for Yucatán. In 1869 the Mérida newspaper *La razón del pueblo* promised that henequen "will be known as the base of wealth and for public prosperity" and that economic growth seemed "to be destined by Providence." Production and exports seemed to validate this prophecy. In 1873 Yucatán exported 31,000 bales of henequen, but by the end of the decade the number had more than tripled, to 113,000 bales.[24] Thus began the henequen boom, a period from 1880 to 1915 that witnessed unbelievable growth in henequen exports due to the concurrent growth in the popularity of twine binders on the Great Plains in the United States and Canada. It took only four short years for the 1880 figure to more than double (261,000 bales in 1884), and by 1904 the figure had sextupled, with 606,000 bales shipped. More staggering, that figure was again nearly doubled in 1915—Yucatán's peak henequen year—when it shipped just under 1.2 million bales. Land conversion went from 87,000 hectares planted in henequen at the beginning of the twentieth century to a record of more than 212,000 hectares in 1916. The figure represented the fact that more than 70 percent of all the cultivated land in Yucatán was devoted to fiber production.[25] Yucatán's subsistence maize and cattle agriculture had been by this time truly transformed into a commercial monocrop economy.

In doing so, Yucatán entered the realm of other plantation societies throughout time. There has been some debate as to whether henequen was grown on haciendas or plantations, but the arguments are of semantics and translation. In Mexico, the Spanish term *hacienda* is used when referring to a large-scale operation such as those devoted to henequen. In English, if one accepts the working definition of plantation agriculture originally proposed by Leo Waibel as being that which is "characterized by the combination of agricultural and industrial functions in the processing of the export product on location," one can argue that Yucatecan henequen production fits this definition quite well. Scholars also argue that plantations have such commonalities as mutually exclusive cropping, an imported labor force, and a system of authority and force imposed on that labor regime for production of agricultural commodities to be sold in the world market—a scenario that also matches the Yucatecan henequen farming system.[26] Making Yucatán different, however, was that sisal and henequen were native to the peninsula, not introduced exotics like the products of sugar, coffee, and banana plantations. Geographer Roland Chardon explains that Yucatán was thus "unique among plantation areas . . . having a useful indigenous plant . . . and[,] using local initiative, management, technology, methods of production and, with minor exceptions, labor and capital, was able to supply a world-wide demand for its product on a large-scale basis." As others have pointed out, henequen was not a luxury product like sugar, coffee, or bananas; it was the raw material of an industrial product that became a necessity for harvesting grain. Rarely have plantation economies given rise to a significant manufacturing industry the way henequen underlay the binder twine industry.[27]

However, because henequen agriculture was superimposed on an earlier cattle-maize hacienda experience, there may be some hybridization of systems here. According to Eric Wolf and Sidney Mintz, haciendas tended to be family-owned units of property, whereas plantations elsewhere in the world were known for being agricultural estates often operated by corporations or associations of planters. In Yucatán, the henequen haciendas remained primarily family-run enterprises, but they were infused with large stocks of capital, often from abroad.[28] But the transformative experience here, as Chardon writes, was that henequen production became "a commercial plantation economy well integrated into a world trade pattern."[29]

There were other reasons for the rapid growth in the henequen industry besides the boom in binders. Henequen was far less expensive than Philippine abacá or Javanese jute to import into North America. In addition, Yucatecans believed it simply made better twine than other fibers. The trade journal *El henequenero* pointed out that henequen made the best twine in the world, proven to have the most uniform length and the best durability and to be the most able to withstand strain in machines. It was also resistant to moisture, rot, and insects. Yucatán was the "mother land of this fiber"; henequen was native to no other land.[30]

The Mexican government at both the state and federal levels helped spur growth in the henequen industry by enacting favorable legislation. For example, many planters wishing to expand their haciendas took advantage of an 1825 land colonization law that outlined how *henequeneros* could solicit title to public lands (*monte*) they had worked for four years. Also, in 1896 the government enacted the Yucatán General Treasury Law, which abolished all taxes on transporting henequen. More significantly, in the same year the federal government issued a decree that allowed individual private property titles to be granted to all who were working the public lands and *ejidos* (communal lands). But those lands had to be surveyed, an expense that was so inflated that a vast majority of the *campesinos* or Indians who were farming the lands had no choice but to sell out to wealthy landowning *henequeneros* who were waiting for such opportunities. By 1912, there were virtually no remaining *ejidos* left in the henequen zone. As Jaime Orosa Díaz has pointed out, everything about henequen was "undeniably in the best interests of the Yucatecans." Its production led to "economic progress" and was an "element of social transformation."[31]

It was a propitious time for Yucatán to have a growing agricultural industry. In the mid- to late nineteenth century international conflicts were impeding fiber imports to the United States. The Crimean War (1854–56) interrupted the flow of hemp, the main fiber for bagging and ropeworks, when Russia cut off shipments to western Europe. Later in the century, when twine was in greater demand, the abacá-rich Philippines became involved in a bloody war against U.S. occupation that caused fiber shortages and doubled the value of Yucatecan henequen. Combined, these international disturbances made henequen the "the principal source of public wealth for the state," as a Yucatecan official wrote in 1910.[32] As early as 1884, only a few years after twine binders appeared on the farm-implement scene, henequen had become the leading export crop of not only Yucatán but also Mexico as a whole. Thus, Yucatán just happened to be at the right place at the right time.[33]

The incredible growth of the henequen industry coincided almost exactly with the years of the dictatorship of Porfirio Díaz (1876–1911, a time period known in Mexico as the *porfiriato*). President Díaz waged a personal campaign to purge Mexico of any obstacles to his dreams of "order and progress" for Mexico. His closest advisors, known as *los científicos* (the scientists), had been schooled in the late-nineteenth-century concept of positivism propounded by European scholars Auguste Comte and Herbert Spencer. Many leaders in Latin America espoused positivism, a popular philosophical argument that supported liberal economic policy. Positivism underlay a doctrine of agricultural and industrial modernization, the belief that the state should direct the economy, and the idea that the government should promote engineering and technology in the national education system. It promoted the idea that private property was important in society, and this ideology thus favored foreign investment in mining and agricultural enterprises to stimulate economic growth. This scenario for economic development automatically excluded native peoples since many lived on the commonly held *ejidos*. Díaz did not hesitate to use military force against any real or perceived impediments to his goals for Mexico's economic modernization.

Díaz and the *científicos* used this positivist ideology to support increased exports of Mexican commodities for a Ricardian comparative trade advantage. Yucatán's henequen boom embodied all of these goals and reaped the best results for his administration's goals. "The smaller traditional plantations . . . were gradually consolidated into vast estates . . . run along scientific management principles geared toward the production of a single primary commodity for export," explains economist Eric Baklanoff.[34] A trade journal noted that sisal could be the agent to make Mexico a modernized country like the United States—that "example of a great agrarian nation . . . whose people are virtuous, patriotic, [and] in love with the land and the honesty of hard work." It suggested, "if Mexico could become [more] agricultural, its future could be assured forever, since as a young nation it has virgin and rich lands."[35] For his part, Díaz rewarded wealthy landowners in Yucatán with favors, including his administration's promotion of a labor regime that would keep henequen profits high. In typical dictatorial style, Díaz ruled harshly, eliminating political dissent and enforcing peace. As Allen Wells put it, "The sisal industry flourished . . . [transforming] Yucatán, traditionally one of Mexico's poorer states, into one of its richest." But true to positivist theory, the boom was dependent on foreign investment—financial resources that Baklanoff affirms "were obtained in great measure from New York banks and U.S. brokers at commercial rates of interest."[36]

Wealth came quickly—at least for the landowning families, investors, merchants, bankers, and fiber traders, known often as the *gente decente* (the decent people). It was reflected in Yucatán's capital, Mérida, which was Mexico's first city to be completely lit by electricity and was arguably the most modern urban center in the nation. Nelson Reed writes that the city's "streets were paved with macadam, . . . were traversed by horse-drawn streetcars, and numbered in the scientific way . . . in advance of Mexico City." One study called Mérida "the world's most active fiber market." Another claimed that Yucatán had become so rich in those years that it was never in need of financial assistance from the national government but instead was able to provide such assistance to other areas of the country.[37] The henequen boom caused the state and its capital to attract great numbers of people; the population of Yucatán grew by more than 100,000 in just thirty-three years (from nearly 284,000 in 1877 to 386,000 in 1900), and Mérida's growth rate was even higher.[38]

The demographic increases paralleled economic growth. Yucatán's Department of Agriculture and Commerce calculated in 1916 that the cost to raise henequen was $115 per acre and yielded a 53 percent profit on capital invested.[39] Some aristocratic landowners, however, received returns on their investments ranging from 50 to 600 percent, most of which came in the form of inherited wealth and land that they could reinvest in henequen expansion. The *gente decente* soon became entrenched in the habits of "hyperconsumption" characterized by European culture, clothing, music, and architecture that proliferated in the *nouveau riche* atmosphere surrounding those whom contemporary American journalist John Kenneth Turner called the "fifty henequen kings." They built colonnaded mansions on Mérida's fashionable Paseo de Montejo, sent their children to study in Europe, imported English cattle to start a pure Hereford stock, prided themselves in learning to speak French, and ordered Steinway pianos whether they knew how to play them or not. Wells has attributed such profligacy to the widespread belief in abundance theory—"the malady that afflicted many adventurous Yucatán investors . . . [and to] an almost religious belief that the henequen economy would survive the short-term bust cycles and enjoy lasting success." The *henequeneros* thus engaged in "conspicuous consumption" and "ostentatious living." Indeed, like King Cotton in the American South, King Henequen reigned in Yucatán (Figure 2.4). It was, as Gilbert Joseph argues, "order and progress, Yucatecan style." It was in fact Yucatán's *Época Dorada*—its "Gilded Age."[40]

Figure 2.4. King Henequen (from cover of *El henequén* 2 [May 31, 1917]).

Of course the aristocracy represented a very small fraction of the state's population. Yucatecan historian Eric Villanueva has pointed out that "the great majority of the population lived in poverty and in difficult conditions." By that time seven-eighths of the state's population was in some way or another devoted to the henequen industry and thus depended on the landed elites for their very survival.[41] Some benefited more than others. Baklanoff has explained that while henequen lifted "Mayan field hands far above the poverty found in other parts of Mexico," the local economy made only "modest progress toward manufacturing." Skilled and semiskilled employment did rise, however, with jobs created for the rasping machinery, railways, and telephone and telegraph systems and to accommodate the boom in construction. By 1900, Baklanoff writes, "The state had achieved a level of prosperity that was the envy of Mexico."[42]

There were a number of henequen families who came to predominate economically and politically. The Peón, Rendón, Montes, Ancona, Suárez, Regil, and Solís families and especially the Molina family established themselves in land, henequen, railways, the import/export trade, banking, business speculations, and politics to become known as the elite *Casta Divina* (Divine Caste), as Gov. Salvador Alvarado later labeled them.[43] Many were interconnected via marriages and business interests, forming an economic and political oligarchy that controlled Yucatán during the boom years. But one individual, Olegario Molina Solís, became *"el rey de los reyes henequeneros"* (the king of the henequen kings), *"capitán y amo"* (lord and master), or, as some called him, *"el civilizador de Yucatán"* (the civilizer of Yucatán).[44] He also was governor of Yucatán from 1902 to 1908, during which time he increased the number of schools in the state and paved Mérida's streets (giving the contract to a construction company he owned). So impressed was President Díaz with Molina's positivist emphases on economic growth and "scientific" modernization that he named him to the position of minister of development in the last years of the *porfiriato*. Molina faithfully believed that henequen was Yucatán's salvation and that trickle-down theory meant that wealth would spread around the state. His mantra for solving economic problems was "plant more henequen."[45] As governor, and with his powerful business O. Molina y Compañía, he was able to acquire hacienda after hacienda at below market values. He then required other growers to sell their fiber to him so that by 1913 he and his family clan owned 100,000 hectares (247,000 acres) of land—perhaps not as much as some of the immensely powerful oligarchs of northern Mexico but far more than anyone else in Yucatán. With that, he came to control 75 percent of the henequen trade.[46]

Of course the success of such a monopoly was in having a steady buyer. Molina and his son-in-law Avelino Montes, who ran the Molina family's export trading house, were astute enough to enter into a firm contractual relationship with International Harvester of Chicago and the multinational fiber trader Henry W. Peabody of Boston to clinch the export-import market. In October 1906, IH appointed Montes as its exclusive agent for purchasing sisal. Thus, by the beginning of the twentieth century IH controlled 72 percent of all henequen and sisal shipments from Yucatán and averaged 80 percent throughout the next fifteen years. The record year was 1910, when IH cornered a staggering 99.8 percent of the market—an economist's textbook case study of a monopsony. Wells and Joseph have called the relationship an "imperial collaborator model" that illustrated Yucatán's "stark conditions of economic dependence" and IH's "informal empire."[47]

There is more to the story, however. During what has become a much ballyhooed "secret meeting" between Cyrus McCormick of IH and Olegario Molina in Havana, Cuba, on October 27, 1902, there emerged an agreement outlining how Molina would use his powers to control the price of henequen and pay only those prices agreed upon by IH in return for Molina securing all the North American business. The agreement stated that "Molina and Co. are to use every effort within their power to depress the price of sisal fibre, and to pay only such prices from time to time as may be dictated by the International Harvester Company." The agreement was bad news for other henequen planters, as the pricing policy made them sell fiber at such low prices that they could hardly operate in the black.[48] An opposing viewpoint by some scholars, however, sees no "sinister, conspiratorial force," secret price manipulations, or an imperial collaborator model, especially given that IH's twine sales represented only a "wafer thin two percent" of the corporation's overall profits. The henequen empire belonged to Molina, they suggest, not to IH, which gained so little of its overall profit from its fiber dealings.[49] Instead, the thinking is that "less visible macroeconomic variables" caused normal price fluctuations, as Thomas Benjamin has argued. Various boom-bust cycles hit the henequen industry throughout the late nineteenth and early twentieth centuries, in part caused by growing competition from other fiber producing regions and geopolitical indicators such as the Spanish-American War. Benjamin concludes by stating that only once, in 1909, did IH interfere with the pricing of henequen and the purpose of that interference was to encourage the henequeneros to maintain a continuous supply of fiber for the market.[50] However, perhaps having the last word in the debate, historians Joseph and Wells counter that IH's profits were a difficult matter to gauge. For example, the fiber market that the company ended up controlling benefited their larger profit-producing implement business, especially the manufacture of reaper/binders that could not be operated without twine. And while the pricing policies perhaps benefited the aristocratic *henequeneros*, they perpetuated an artificially low world price for fiber that the landowners used as an argument to continue the slavelike labor conditions on their plantations.[51]

Taking advantage of the new demand for fiber also meant that Yucatán would be beholden to the whims of the international market and dependent primarily on a U.S. corporate trade relationship controlled by IH. However, the Yucatecans also knew that to some degree they had the upper hand in the dependency model. As the trade journal *El henequén* succinctly put it, "Without henequen, there will be no [grain] harvests."[52]

The destination records of Yucatán's millions of bales of fiber help tell the story of the henequen-wheat complex, with 1907 as a representative year. Yucatán exported a total of 611,845 bales of fiber that year, 90 percent (552,072 bales) of which was shipped to the United States. Canada, a distant second, imported 44,269 bales, or 7 percent of the total, and a variety of other countries (with Cuba and Great Britain leading, at 7,787 bales and 4,742 bales, respectively) followed with a combined total of only 3 percent of the total. Belgium, Germany, France, Italy, Austria/Hungary, Russia, Argentina, and Brazil each imported small quantities. Most of the bales heading to the United States were shipped to New York, Mobile, Chicago, Texas City, and New Orleans. Most of the sisal shipped to Canada arrived in Montreal, with secondary amounts going to Welland, Brantford, and Peterborough (all in Ontario), where there were large twine mills. As Fernando Benítez puts it, "Henequen binds the world's wheat."[53]

The transformations that stemmed from such a high demand for twine, along with all the conditions that set in motion the henequen-wheat complex, forever changed the environment of Yucatán. Botanist José Flores has described the original vegetation of the areas as a "low deciduous forest" of leguminous plants and cacti mixed with savannah and thorn-bush regions on its perimeters. Agaves such as henequen, aloe, and yucca were native to the peninsula and blended with other tropical angiosperms to create a varied landscape on the remarkably flat Yucatán terrain. The region was a "mosaic of vegetation . . . that provided a wealth and diversity of plant life."[54]

This landscape transformation was set in motion in stages. What first was a land of desert shrub and small subsistence farms was by the mid-nineteenth century becoming a patchwork of haciendas. But with the boom in henequen at the end of the century, haciendas and even the much-venerated cattle ranches were converted to plantations.

The shrubby desert landscape changed markedly as *terrenos baldíos* ("vacant" lands not used for agriculture) became *henequenales*. The change was fast; production climbed from 40,000 bales in 1875 to 600,000 bales in 1910. In 1901 growers converted 217,000 acres to henequen, but during the peak year of 1916, the number of acres converted to henequen had more than doubled to 524,000. By 1940 nearly 40 percent of the state was identified as the henequen zone.[55] Celebrating this transformation as a "victory of man against the desert," Benítez praises henequen as "the child of the desert" and the spiny leaves as "the green stars of the land." His description of the *henequenales*, while meant to be a panegyric of the industry, offers a poetic perspective on the landscape's ecological changes. He writes that the fields "are as beautiful as the vineyards in Italy or the olive groves in Spain. The plants, all straight and lined in their rows, . . . are ordered symmetrically on the sun-baked plain. [They] have an elegant severity, an economy of lines . . . a synthesis between the formal and the functional."[56] Such agriscape geometry prompted the poet Joaquín Lanz Trueba to pen in 1917 that the fields were like a "green carpet over the plain, symmetrically aligned in a rigorous order, in prolonged lanes of thousands and thousands of plants that seem to be offering their hands." Another study suggested that the fields appeared as "endless rectilinear rows of bluish-gray spines."[57]

This language of order, rigor, symmetry, and alignment in nature reflected the Porfirian ideal of order and progress and Mexico's quest for economic growth quite well. It described the much-coveted economic landscapes of a modernized Europe. It defied natural topography by lauding the landscape transformations that contributed to Díaz's call for modernization. Díaz and his *científicos* would no doubt applaud Benítez's statement that "every village in northern Yucatán is . . . a victory of man against the desert."[58] Thus, the descriptive language of the monocrop environment was matched only by the language that described the hoped-for wealth from henequen, its capital-generating potential, and its role as economic savior of the peninsula. For example, an editorial in *El henequén* praised the plant as "our rich agave—called 'green gold.' . . . It is the most noble of plants registered in the marvelous and fecund plant kingdom. That privileged treasure to its arid and . . . rocky grounds is . . . akin to a blessing from heaven."[59]

Now the plant was golden and a treasure, like the minerals from other parts of the republic. But while wealth came to a few in Yucatán, the agricultural and economic changes were only one part of the transformation story. As plantations grew, so did demand for crops and firewood to support hacienda managers and the workers and their families. With growth in mind, both the federal and state governments supported such changes and permitted the use of *terrenos baldíos* to be used to expand plantations. The state legislature passed a series of laws from 1888 to 1894 outlining such uses, all of which helped to spur henequen development and increase *latifundismo* (aristocratic landholding) at the expense of indigenous *ejidos*.[60] Petitions flowed into state authorities to request permission to clear *monte* for construction, firewood, and, most important, *milpas* (corn fields). In a letter to Governor Salvador Alvarado in 1916, for example, a farmer near the town of Kanasín complained of how agricultural productivity had fallen by 40 percent, necessitating "the search for more *monte* to be exploited for cultivation." He lamented how the increase in population had sent people scurrying to find more wood on vacant lands.[61]

As production expanded from the 1880s to the early 1920s, the Yucatecan landscape further changed with the development of a rail network throughout the peninsula. During the beginnings of the henequen industry, leaves arrived at the mills on the backs of mules and later on mule-drawn carts. But as the industry developed, the *henequeneros* needed a quicker and more efficient transport system, and rail lines were the answer. In the 1880s the state government starting authorizing concessions for movable Decauville narrow-gauge tram lines that used mule-drawn cars to bring henequen leaves from the field to

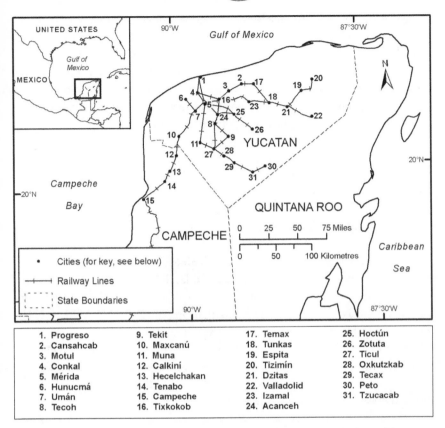

1. Progreso	9. Tekit	17. Temax	25. Hoctún
2. Cansahcab	10. Maxcanú	18. Tunkas	26. Zotuta
3. Motul	11. Muna	19. Espita	27. Ticul
4. Conkal	12. Calkiní	20. Tizimín	28. Oxkutzkab
5. Mérida	13. Hecelchakan	21. Dzitas	29. Tecax
6. Hunucmá	14. Tenabo	22. Valladolid	30. Peto
7. Umán	15. Campeche	23. Izamal	31. Tzucacab
8. Tecoh	16. Tixkokob	24. Acanceh	

Figure 2.5. Rail lines servicing the henequen plantations, 1915–1918 (adapted from
p. 31 of Francisco José Paoli, *Yucatán y los orígenes del nuevo estado mexicano,* 1984).
Courtesy Wenonah Fraser, Department of Geography, Brandon University.

the mills and to transport the dried fiber bales to port. It also started to build
regular, intermediate gauge tracks to connect various parts of the state with
the port at Progreso. The rail lines were so useful that the state expanded
the network to such a degree that by 1890 it had more than any other state
in Mexico. Some landowners built their own feeder lines, adding another
360 miles of rail to the system. By 1923, more than 4,000 miles of track connected various villages, henequen fields, and defibering plants throughout
Yucatán (Figure 2.5).[62] The accelerated transportation system enabled the
henequeneros to continue bringing more land into fiber production.

Meanwhile, technological advances resulted in more sophisticated and
mechanized rasping machines (or decorticators, called *desfibradoras* in Spanish) for separating the fiber from the leaves of the plants. The need for such
devices was great as the fiber had to be rasped out of the leaves within twenty-
four hours of harvest so it would not dry out. Thus, as Benítez has written,

creating the best rasping machine "became a peninsular obsession."[63] In the early nineteenth century, all retting of the leaves to render the fibrous pulp was done by hand—backbreaking, time consuming work that also wasted fiber. Early mechanical rasping inventions in the 1830s, such as rotating wheels with knives to separate the fiber, did not work well or were cumbersome. To stimulate ingenuity, in 1852 the state government established a prize for the best defibering invention. One entry in 1853 by the Yucatecan farmer/author Manuel Cecilio Villamor was a complex, animal-powered machine that could rasp three *pencas* a minute, but after continued use it destroyed the leaves and quickly tired the animals out. Inventors and engineers then raced to patent better and faster rasping devices, and the ones that worked the best over time depended on steam power (see Figure 2.6, p. 55).[64]

Steam required firewood to heat the boilers, quickening the depletion of *monte* wood cover. As growers converted more acreage to henequen, they needed more firewood to power the machinery. Certainly technology was leaving its mark on Yucatán's once-forested landscape. By 1917 forested land for firewood was so important for the industry that 240,000 hectares (593,000 acres) were classified as "vacant lands that provide firewood for the rasping of henequen fiber." As rasping intensified into the 1920s, Governor Felipe Carrillo Puerto decreed that *henequeneros* could cut wood to fuel their decorticators on the wooded vacant lands, and he even mandated that small farmers clearing land had to give the wood to planters if they needed it for rasping, instead of selling it for use as railroad ties.[65]

Those lands, however, were officially registered as part of the *zona henequenera*. In fact, a Yucatán land use report in 1917 showed the breakup of the state's forty thousand square kilometers (twenty-four thousand square miles): the henequen zone comprised a full 15 percent of the state's terrain (fifteen thousand square kilometers or nine thousand square miles that included henequen fields, *monte* for hacienda use, *milpas*, and small sugarcane fields); only 12.5 percent (five thousand square kilometers or three thousand square miles) of the state remained in *bosques* (forest). The remainder of the state's land was in coastal mangroves and the eastern and southern "transitional zones" that were "inappropriate for henequen production."[66]

The problems of deforestation in Yucatán were not unknown at the time, and some contemporary writers warned of its consequences. As early as 1878, for example, one concerned Yucatecan advised how "necessary it is to look a bit into the future" to see how "the lack of firewood" would affect people and industry if "the imprudent and disorderly destruction of *montes*" continued. He warned of the dangers of converting too many forests to *milpas* and of the alarming amounts of firewood and charcoal consumed annually in the henequen zone. Thus, it was beneficial to "avoid all imprudence in cutting the forests" and to "establish a system of replanting trees without waiting for what nature would do spontaneously." To do so would generate more oxygen—"so indispensable for health and life"—and would ensure a natural hydrological regime that would guarantee better harvests.[67] In 1882 an industrial chemist named Eugenio Frey conducted a study of Yucatán's forests that was later titled "The Utility of Forests." Frey bemoaned the "absurd and ridiculous theory" that forests stood in the way of progress. "On the contrary," he argued, "they are the strongest support and sustainer of it." He pointed out that he had seen unsuccessful farming in burned-over forest areas where the soil was left sterile and soon had to be abandoned. From the "history of so many denuded mountains" he gleaned important data regarding watershed hydrology and how forests served as "absorbents for the heat and exhalers for moisture."[68]

Some of this thinking informed political changes in the early twentieth century. As governor of Yucatán, Olegario Molina in 1903 took the first steps in "putting a finger in the dike" of the deforestation flood, as Víctor Suárez put it, to decrease "the immoderate cutting of forests" and to "regularize conservation . . . for the benefit of agriculture and public health." He created a local forests commission (*Junta Local de Bosques*) and appointed as its director Rodulfo Cantón, who "for twenty-five years had warned of the grave problems associated with deforestation." It is surprising that Molina, who was the largest landowner in Yucatán and had become truly wealthy from the henequen industry, would act so prudently on an environmental policy. If he were convinced that the future of agriculture lay with conserving hydrologic and forest resources, the financial value of conservation would be inescapable. However, according to Suárez, the forestry *junta's* proposals never had a chance to succeed; they were thwarted and "nullified by the incomprehension and lack of cooperation of the hacendados and farmers."[69]

Later, two articles published interestingly enough in *El henequén* in 1918 outlined the long-term disadvantages of forest destruction and called for conservation. The first, entitled "The Cutting of Forests," began by stating, "Everyday we are hearing more complaints among ourselves about the crude war that at times unnecessarily is being waged in our forests." The article lamented the "sad heritage [forest destruction leaves] to our descendants," the hydrology problems it causes, the important role forests play in providing oxygen for the air, and the environmental problems associated with eroded watersheds and valleys, circumventing successful agriculture in those areas. Rainfall was better absorbed in the undisturbed *monte*, the article continued, a characteristic especially useful in times of drought to sustain vegetation for soil cover and to avoid widespread desertification. It ended with a call to plant new trees.[70]

The second article, published some months later and entitled "Yucatecan Trees and Forests" by a proto-environmentalist writing under the pseudonym

Agrófilo (Agrophile), had similar warnings and advice. Agrófilo framed arguments chronologically, pointing back to the colonial years when the Spaniards
oversaw "the destruction of the Yucatecan forests" to acquire wood for various
purposes. Eventually such devastation led to policies in 1821 mandating that
every citizen in the various municipalities be required to plant five trees a year,
a requirement enforced by local authorities who were responsible for counting
the newly planted trees. They also imposed a moratorium on cutting trees that
were young or green. The idea was to infuse a "love for trees" in each community. Thus, "there was no need to lament the absence of Yucatecan trees
and forests." It indeed took the state government to "prevent the destruction of
forests in general . . . and their annihilation or total ruin." Agrófilo concluded
that all Yucatecans should "oppose the cutting of trees [and] the annihilation
of forests." The results would yield a "better climate and improved lands" and
a return to an "ancient and splendid Yucatecan garden."[71]

Other writers warned of the dangers inherent in monocrop agriculture.
In 1907, for example, a writer stated in El agricultor, "We repeat that it is good
to develop henequen, but quickly it appears that monoculture production, to
which we are now dedicating ourselves, is a very dangerous base for any country." The trade journal echoed these words in 1923 in an article entitled "Slavery to Monoculture." It told of the "undeniable truth that no-one doubts"—
being beholden to markets in North America—and the disadvantages involved
in not diversifying agriculture. It recommended more planting of corn, beans,
and sugarcane and more cattle grazing as a way of breaking the monocrop
culture.[72]

Those words, however, were rarely heeded in Yucatán's boom times or
in the henequen literature. It was not until 1977 that Víctor Suárez Molina's
book La evolución económica de Yucatán a través del siglo XIX, with its ecological
warnings about henequen production, appeared on the scene. In his section
entitled "Forests and Deforestation," Suárez addressed his concern that the
cultivation of corn had been one of the biggest culprits of forest destruction.
He showed how the rapid growth of milpa development in the late nineteenth
century (from 607,212 mecates of cornfields in 1883 to 1,269,000 mecates in
1893, with one mecate equaling four hundred square meters, or nearly a tenth
of an acre) caused problems associated with deforestation. For example, the
deforested lands were made worse when "torrential rains . . . hit the ground
without vegetated cover[,] eroding the land and causing it to lose even more
organic cover." All combined, forest clearing and the erosion that follows had
caused the ecological impoverishment of the henequen zone.[73]

Others have been equally critical regarding the environmental and economic impacts of milpas in the henequen zone. Moisés González notes that
milpa technology had been "primitive": burning down forests, planting the
seeds with a digging stick, and then moving to different land when the corn

patch was no longer productive. Friedrich Katz, however, discovered that by 1918 Yucatán corn production was considerably lower than previous years because plantation owners had been converting *milpas* to *henequenales*. Not only did this conversion accelerate the process of transformation and reduce the amount of land operated by *campesinos*, but it also meant that Yucatán had to import corn for subsistence needs. So great was the need in the 1920s that the federal government intervened to help bring in greater quantities from other parts of Mexico (primarily from Sonora) and from the United States.[74] Yucatán then experienced a cyclical dependency on the United States: first as a market for its henequen, and second as a source for foodstuffs to feed henequen workers. Worse, for the already impoverished majority of Yucatecans, importing such basics as corn sent prices sky high, higher than the national average.[75] Authorities in the state were aware of the problem. The trade journal *El sisal mexicano* in 1927 advocated the planting of more corn locally to feed the state's residents. Rebutting that article, however, the more conservative *El henequenero*, an organ of the wealthier *hacendados*, argued that there was not enough land available to convert to corn and repeated the line that there was little land in Yucatán good for raising any cereal crops: "If this were in Sonora, OK, but not here."[76]

The type of intensive plantation agriculture that henequen production represented was dependent not only on vast land transformations but also on a large labor force. Planting, cultivating (although henequen fields do not require a great deal of weeding), harvesting, rasping, drying, baling, and shipping the fiber crop required tens of thousands of year-round laborers (since henequen could be harvested three times a year with no regard to particular seasons), working in Yucatán's remarkably hot and steamy henequen zone. Benítez, who interviewed workers many years later to record their memories of the henequen experience, writes that the typical worker during harvest "would work covered in leaves, branches, and insects; was soaked in sweat, his hair matted with dust; and was almost transformed into a tree [himself]."[77] On average harvesting days workers would usually cut around one thousand *pencas*, but they often cut one and a half times or twice that amount. It was bloody work; workers wore heavy aprons to protect their legs and waists, but their hands would get badly cut and punctured from the sharp leaves. Benítez mentioned a worker's hands as "bloody yet in constant motion, almost independent of his body, contorted like an agonizing Christ." The journal *El agricultor* thus advised overseers to be alert to their laborers' bloody wounds that so easily could become infected.[78]

The laborers were usually Mayan indentured servants or actual slaves. Suárez explained the debt system to which most workers were bound: "They stayed in it as a consequence of the debts rooted to the farm. They could only abandon it by liquidating their debt or by having it bought out by another hacendado who would then take the peon to work on his own place to work off the [new] debt . . . [that] could only disappear with the death of the worker." He also explained that while the *henequeneros* did not invent such a system, they quickly took advantage of it. The system "existed in all of Mexico and in some places with characteristics that were even more inhuman."[79] In his important essay on violence and control on henequen plantations, Allen Wells fleshed out the "mechanisms of social control" that were used to maintain peace on the plantations and to optimize production. He cited how "apologists" for the labor system, including investors, *hacendados*, and even executives of International Harvester believed that the regime "stressed the symbiotic relationship between master (*amo*) and servant (*serviente*)" that spoke "to the conditions of labor scarcity." The elites believed in a colonial-era "paternalistic ethos"—that they were protecting the Indian workers from the dangers of the world outside the plantation. They even stated in the journal *El henequén* that Mayan Indians did not understand the concept of private property, laboring as they did on *ejidos*, and as such were "almost communists" who knew no better than to work on the plantations. *El agricultor* was even more racist in its assessments, calling Indians "indignant of civilization" and "apathetic by nature." But even with the labor shortages after the henequen boom, the growers treated the workers like slaves, kept them in debt peonage with company stores, and hired bounty hunters to capture them if they tried to escape. Landowners placed ads in Mexican newspapers offering rewards for the return of escaped servants.[80] The *henequeneros* seemed to follow to a T the old Yucatecan aphorism "*las cosas de Yucatán, dejarlas como están*" ("what is Yucatán's own, is best left alone").

Thus, the *henequeneros* took advantage of the large population of Mayan Indians native to the Yucatán Peninsula, displacing them from their villages to live and work on the henequen haciendas. Many of the Maya were captured rebels from neighboring Quintana Roo. A Yucatecan law established in 1855 prohibited the act of forcing Indians to work against their will, but with the Caste War over and with a fast-rising demand for fiber, the state legislature changed the law in 1863 to "declare in force the older laws that authorized forced labor" on the haciendas and in building the thousands of miles of Decauville tram lines throughout the state—the same transportation network that helped aid landowners in apprehending and returning any indentured workers who tried to escape (Figure 2.7).[81] The *henequeneros* classified the Mayan workers into *acasillados*, those who worked on the plantation and also resided there (often in substandard housing hardly fit for animals); "half-timers," who made up a large temporary, seasonal work force but were often worked longer hours and treated more harshly than full-time *acasillados*; and *luneros*, plantation residents who were allowed to farm *terrenos baldíos* with the stipulation that they give the landowner a certain amount of maize and that

Figure 2.6. Rasping shed and decorticator on an abandoned henequen plantation, San Antonio Tehuitz, Yucatán. Photograph by the author.

Figure 2.7. Labor on a henequen plantation: loading harvested *pencas* on rail cars, ca. 1910. Courtesy Wisconsin Historical Society (McCormick–International Harvester Collection, Whi-8092).

they help work the henequen fields, clean the streets, and perform other chores around the hacienda.[82] Mayan women on plantations followed traditional gendered divisions of labor. Some who were "salaried" were obliged to cook vast quantities of *pozole* (corn gruel) and corn tortillas—the standard *campesino* food regimen—for the many workers on the plantations.[83]

Although there was always a large population of Maya, they often did not meet the labor needs of the henequen plantations, especially in times of particularly high demand for fiber. The point is ironic in one way because before the henequen boom, the Creole Yucatecan elite were involved in *exporting* Mayan Indians to Cuba to be indentured (slave) workers on the sugar estates because a labor shortage was threatening harvests. The "infamous and painful" trade in Mayan Indians to Cuba lasted from 1847 to 1861.[84] But with the ever-rising demand for henequen, the landowners devised a variety of schemes to bring in Indians and hastily rounded-up workers from other parts of Mexico. In a program that became known as *el enganche* (the hook), labor-desperate *henequeneros*, in conjunction with the federal government, paid for teams of ruthless and greedy men (*enganchadores*) to round up thousands of laborers from central Mexico and Oaxaca (where in the late nineteenth century a labor surplus existed), prisoners of war, anti-Díaz political dissidents, criminals, vagrants, *campesinos* from the Bajío region, Yaqui Indians from Sonora, and, to a lesser degree, Huastec Indians from Veracruz. One study claimed this system "transformed [Yucatán] into a vast federal prison for Mexican criminals, recalcitrant deserters, and Yaqui prisoners of war" that was filled with "malarial labor camps."[85] Labor contractors hired by the *henequeneros* hoodwinked urban workers and literally expropriated rural *campesinos* to work in Yucatán. A contemporary account by a visitor to Mexico City described how *enganchado* workers were "practically shanghaied from the cities": "Often disease-ridden, almost inevitably soaked with pulque, captured and signed up for labor when they were intoxicated, these men were brought down practically in chain gangs by the contractors and delivered at so many hundred pesos per head. They were kept in barbed wire enclosures, often under ghastly sanitary conditions."[86] The deportation and enslavement of Yaqui Indians, identified by one scholar as "the most notorious use of coerced labor" in Yucatán, are so significant in the history of the henequen-wheat complex that they demand a full chapter (chapter 3), but some preliminary mention of this aspect of Yucatan's labor history is appropriate here.[87]

The *hacendados* also developed plans to bring in indentured servants from abroad. Plantation agents worked in Europe and Asia to lure workers to Yucatán with the same kinds of "contracts" they used in central Mexico. Called "foreign colonists," men came from Italy, Spain, the Canary Islands, Cuba (where workers were accustomed to working on sugar plantations), Korea (the origin of up to three thousand workers who came in two different waves), China, Japan, and even Java—all of which added to the protoglobalization of the henequen industry. Working as "contract laborers," these men basically lived in debt servitude and had little money to send home. The exact number of workers imported from overseas is not easy to deduce from port or hacienda records, but according to various studies the number was probably less than ten thousand from 1878 to 1910, when the schemes were carried out.[88] Altogether, between 1885 and 1910 the number of workers on henequen plantations tripled, although the combined number of all non-Yucatecan workers probably never exceeded 10 percent of the henequen work force and never really solved the labor shortage on the expanding plantations. Not fortuitously, however, it did aid in linguistically separating various groups to help prevent workers from organizing or rebelling.[89]

One problem with imported workers was that they were often not immune to tropical diseases. An outbreak of yellow fever in 1909 hit the Korean and Yaqui laborers hard. There was also a lack of adequate medical attention, and most arrived in Yucatán without having been immunized.[90] Those from southern Europe or eastern Asia earned too little to be able to send money home or to save enough to go off on their own. *Henequeneros* often judged the Chinese and Korean workers to be poor field hands and instead assigned them to domestic chores such as cleaning, cooking, and laundering. Few stayed on the plantations. Problems with learning Spanish, unfamiliarity with the agricultural techniques needed for henequen, and the feeling of being an outsider away from their own home and culture all led to the failure of the system.[91]

One contemporary report, however, came to some different conclusions. Esteban Flores, from revolutionary leader Francisco Madero's newly created Department of Labor and Social Security, toured Yucatán in 1914 to view the plantations. He mentioned seeing the small colonies of Spanish, Italian, and Korean workers in the henequen zone and observed that the *henequeneros* treated them well, provided homes and medical care, and "at times a small plot of land to cultivate" for their own gardens. Some of those *jornaleros* (day laborers), however, disliked Yucatán's extreme heat and never mixed well with local people due to the difference in language and cultures; consequently, some fled to "cooler climates" during the low work season. Others he met had been there ten or twenty years and seemed "content to have abandoned their homelands."[92]

But as Flores made clear, the "extraordinary scarcity of workers" was nearly at a crisis stage in 1914, threatening the henequen harvest. The growers "felt obliged to put the Indians to work, often settling them on their farms through inhuman means and maintaining them in . . . a state of dependence." For the local Maya, he indicated that many knew no better, that they did "not have aspirations," did not speak Spanish, eschewed "all notions of hygiene," and were "content to live without any other improvements not allowed by the overseer." He suggested that the only way to solve the labor problem was to send more laborers from other parts of Mexico.[93]

One of the places targeted was Tampico, in the state of Veracruz on Mexico's Gulf coast. There, *enganchador* Rafael Quintero, hired by the henequen hacienda owner Eduardo Bolio, rounded up groups of Huastec Indians to work in Yucatán. Bolio had contracted for fifty Huastec families, but Quintero returned in 1893 with ninety-two families, who were distributed among *henequeneros* needing laborers. According to Yucatecan archival documents, Quintero paid a local agent in Tampico twenty pesos per Huastec, but he was paid one hundred pesos for every worker delivered to Yucatán—netting him a substantial profit in the lucrative enterprise.[94]

Even more important, in the contemporary spirit of muckraking writers such as Upton Sinclair, Nelly Bly, and Ida Tarbell, journalist John Kenneth Turner alerted readers across the United States to the plight of the Yaquis. In 1908 Turner, a Californian who wrote for the *Record*, posed as an investor in order to research the treatment of plantation workers in Yucatán. He stayed on plantations, interviewed *henequeneros*, slave boat captains, and others involved with Yaqui removal and studied as much as he could about Porfirian policies of development. With his data, he published a series of articles on the henequen industry and on Yaqui deportation that first appeared under the title "Barbarous Mexico" in the *American Magazine* in 1909 and 1910. In London, a newspaper reprinted Turner's articles to much acclaim and popularity there. But to Turner's alarm, the *American Magazine* abruptly dropped the series when new editors took over—editors who presumably were opposed to publishing such a scathing attack. The change in circumstances forced Turner to publish some installments in the *Appeal to Reason*, the *International Socialist Review*, and the *Pacific Monthly*. He compiled the chapters and published them in book form with the same title in 1911.[95]

Turner's articles were popular; they caused a great sensation in the United States among such progressive leaders as Robert LaFollette and Mother Jones, and they caused a great deal of consternation among the ruling elite of Mexico. Officials there denied Turner's accusations about slavery and harsh conditions and banned the book, although it clearly made its way into the hands of many Mexicans. One who read it was Francisco Madero, leader of the early stages of the revolution and the first elected president after dictator Porfirio Díaz fled the country in 1911. Madero even told Turner in an interview two years later that *Barbarous Mexico* had contributed to the success of the revolution. Back in California, Turner stayed actively involved in the Mexican Revolution, especially with Ricardo Flores Magón and the Los Angeles junta of the Mexican Liberal Party.[96] The literature published then and now concerning henequen plantation conditions and Yaqui removal makes reference to Turner's important exposé.

Two other important works by travelers visiting Yucatán during this period corroborate Turner's accusations about the plight of the Yaquis and the appalling plantation conditions. The first was by British scholars Arnold Channing and Frederick J. Tabor Frost, who had gone to Yucatán to study the Mayan ruins but who spent considerable time in the henequen zone and saw firsthand the slavelike conditions. In their 1909 book *The American Egypt: A Record of Travel in Yucatan,* Channing and Frost were highly critical of the Yucatecan *henequeneros* and the policies of President Díaz, to which they devoted an entire chapter entitled "Slavery on the Haciendas." So appalled were these two men about what they observed that they wrote Díaz a letter outlining their concerns. The *American Magazine* published extracts from the chapter on slavery and their letter to Díaz, with the preface claiming that Channing and Frost's information added credence to Turner's essays, but curiously it did so only after the editors there had discontinued Turner's "Barbarous Mexico" series.[97]

Channing and Frost wrote that in Yucatán the daughters of enslaved Indians had "to submit to a systematic tyranny of lust which really is so base that it is difficult to write of in calm language." They went on to suggest that the Yucatecans had an "inconceivable cynicism . . . towards sexual excesses" that included "young sons of fourteen and upwards [who] are not restrained from, indeed they are often encouraged by fathers and even mothers in, indulging their boyish passions at the expense of the little Indian slave-girls."[98]

Near the same time, another Englishman and journalist, Henry Baerlein, published *Mexico, the Land of Unrest* (1913), in which he described the causes of the Mexican Revolution. He headed one chapter "The Slaves of Yucatán" but was far less critical of the labor system than were Channing and Frost or Turner. He briefly alluded to the plight of the Yaquis but primarily dealt with Mayan laborers, whom he also considered to be enslaved. He was contradictory in his account, however. At one point he mentions that "the masters are particularly kind to their dependents, for the reason that there is a scarcity of labour," but he later describes the brutality of whippings and includes a photograph of the lash wounds on the back of a Mayan worker.[99]

Adding to the laborers' misery were the unsanitary living and working conditions. The huts that the *henequeneros* supplied for the workers to "live" in were, as one study described them, "human beehives" with inadequate roofs and thirty to fifty people living under them.[100] The living arrangements bred diseases that were rampant on the plantations, with diarrhea being the leading cause of death among henequen workers. Many also suffered from pellagra, a vitamin B-12 deficiency that causes personality disorders and consequently led to many suicides. Workers received scant medical treatment, if any, for the illnesses. There were no schools for children of Indian workers.[101] Turner discussed what he called the *henequeneros'* "philosophy of beating." Different acts of torture were common, and one severe punishment referred to as "cleaning up" meant being whipped with wet ropes. They used beatings and whippings for punishments and warnings, and some used first-thing-in-the-morning lashings to start the workday.

Despite this preponderance of evidence, many Mexicans and Americans— then and now—have disputed whether there was ever slavery in Yucatán during the pre-revolution years. First, attempting to nip the issue in the bud as early as 1906 (a few years before Turner published his articles), Olegario Molina invited President Díaz to Yucatán to tour the area, to view the progress of the henequen industry, and, according to one study, to reject "as slanders the accusations of slavery in Yucatán." Channing and Frost alluded to how the henequen "millionaires" were "very sensitive on the question of slavery. . . . You have but to mention the word . . . and they begin a lot of cringing apologetics as to the comforts of the Indians' lives, the care taken of them, and the fatherly relations existing between the haciendado [*sic*] and his slaves."[102]

So at Molina's invitation, Díaz visited Mérida, making it his first trip to Yucatán in his many years as president. Referring to the controversial issue of slavery, the Channing and Frost account shows how the official state visit was a chance for the *henequeneros* to fasten the "bolts of the cupboard in which the family skeleton was hidden." The British visitors described the preparations: "Well, the President came. Never were there such junketings: . . . gargantuan feasts were served. Lucullus never entertained with more gorgeous banquets. . . . One luncheon party cost 50,000 dollars. . . . Triumphal arches of flowers and laurels, of henequen, and one built of oranges surmounted by the national flag, spanned the route." The preparations must have impressed the president. Channing and Frost reprinted Díaz's words at one of the big banquets: "'Some writers who do not know this country . . . have declared Yucatán to be disgraced with slavery. Their statements are the grossest calumny, as is proved by the very faces of the labourers, by their tranquil happiness.'" The Britons concluded that the whole feast was a "gigantic fraud, a colossally impertinent fake from the start." They then reasserted their insistence that a very brutal slave system existed in Yucatán and that the "millionaire monopolists" treated their Indian slaves "in a way an Englishman would blush to treat his dog."[103]

Using the evidence in *The American Egypt* and *Barbarous Mexico*, England's Anti-Slavery and Aborigines Protection Society brought the matter to the British Foreign Office in 1910. But an official there wrote back, explaining that Turner's allegations should be discredited due to the "sensational, highly coloured, and overdrawn" nature of his research. As for *The American Egypt*,

Channing and Frost "were but poorly equipped to formulate opinions" about Mexico, and the book "they wrote after a very brief visit to the country could have no weight or substance." The official also stated that the British consul in Mexico had condoned the deportation of the Yaquis as it was "was rendered imperative by their turbulence and resistance to authority." Mincing no words, the secretary of the society responded that the organization had "grave concerns" with Mexico's actions "to expropriate and exile the entire Yaqui nation to Yucatán" in a system involving "many thousands of human beings . . . in a bondage at once as cruel and hopeless as almost any form of slavery within knowledge of the society."[104]

Other reports and writings openly disagreed with the notion that slavery existed in Yucatán. When Turner's series started raising eyebrows, Mexican officials scurried to refute the reports, and newspapers favorable to Díaz published strong denials. Díaz even attempted to block circulation of the *American Magazine* in Mexico, causing the publishers to complain to the U.S. State Department and to U.S. Post Office officials. Even more vocal was the community of Americans living in Mexico City whose businesses and investments in Mexico had been stimulated by Porfirian policies. Leading that group was one E. S. Smith, who called for a writ of mandamus that would force the *American Magazine* to provide proof of the charges Turner was making against Díaz. Smith went so far as to appeal to President William Howard Taft to "prohibit use of United States mails to the American Magazine" due to how it threatened "libel against the whole Mexican people" as well as how it was "a disgrace and injury to American citizens in Mexico." Although Taft did not respond with any such sanction, Smith went on to publish an article entitled "The Truth about Mexico" in *Bankers Magazine,* which devoted an entire issue to why Mexico was still a good investment bet.[105] IH also joined in the chorus of denial. An article published in *Harvester World* stated, "Notwithstanding some of the magazine articles written on the subject, there is nothing in the nature of slavery in Yucatán. Every man is free and receives his pay as regularly as the workmen in the American factories."[106]

Debate on the topic has raged ever since. Two leading Yucatecan historians, Rodolfo Ruz Menéndez and Michel Antochiw, have argued stridently against the notion of Yaqui slavery. Ruz theorizes that in *Barbarous Mexico* Turner greatly "exaggerated and distorted on many occasions" the numbers and plight of the deported Yaquis. Stating that normal work hours on henequen plantations were from six to ten o'clock in the morning, during which workers harvested roughly two thousand *pencas*, Ruz argues that neither Yaquis nor anyone else could have worked as hard as Turner describes or for as many hours in the hot, humid conditions.[107] Ruz also points to a contract issued in 1900 by a local government; a government official informed the owners and operators of several haciendas in Yucatán and Campeche that they would need to enter into a contract to provide better conditions for the "rebel Indians from the Yaqui River" and their families who were still on their plantations. The contract stipulated that haciendas had to provide the Yaquis with paid wages, free living quarters, access to whatever firewood they would need from the hacienda's wooded lands, night schools in which "children of both sexes will receive elementary education," appropriate work clothes for laborers, and other provisions, all of which would be open to government inspections.[108] Ruz viewed the contract as proof that the Yaquis were not being mistreated. However, the contract's only clause indicating a penalty for infractions stated that fines (without specified amounts) would be charged for noncompliance, and there were no enforcement clauses at all. Because there is no proof that many similar contracts exited, one might wonder whether this contract was an anomaly.

Antochiw grants that the working conditions on the henequen haciendas were severe enough to be labeled "slavery," that "without doubt [it] was one of the most cruel social practices that took place in Mexico." He adds that the henequen labor system "came to substitute the older [form of] slavery" that used to exist in Mexico during the colonial period. But he claims the slavery accusations do not apply to Huastec or Yaqui Indians who worked in Yucatán. For example, he cites an article published in 1897 in *El eco del comercio* that rebutted accusations made by the "liberal Mexico City press," asserting that "Yucatán is not now nor has it ever been a slavery state" since Huastec Indian workers could redeem their debt and go free.[109] Specifically regarding the Yaquis, Antochiw has argued that scholars have put too much stock in Turner's writing. He claims that the journalist was purposely exaggerating the numbers of Yaquis deported and the harshness of plantation conditions for the sake of the popular muckraking genre of his day. He also points to what he called "an extraordinarily rare document"—the papers of a 1905 court case in which Antonio Cauché, a Mayan Indian, sued Audomaro Molina (brother of Olegario Molina) of the Xcumpich Hacienda for wrongful treatment of him and his wife on what he called "a true prison" of a plantation. Despite the graphic language Cauché used to describe hacienda conditions, the fact that he was able to sue proves for Antochiw that a state of slavery probably did not exist. Further, that Cauché lost his suit signaled that the allegations were nothing more than "defamatory libel."[110] The suit, however, dealt with Mayan rather than Yaqui Indians. Moreover, since it was filed against the might and power of the Molina family, the outcome was predictable.

Other works, on both Yucatecan and Sonoran fronts, dismiss the Yaqui enslavement by omitting any discussion of it. Esteban Flores never mentions the Yaquis in his contemporary study "La vida rural en 1914" nor does Keith Hartman in his oft-quoted thesis, "The Henequen Empire in Yucatán, 1870–

1910." Even more surprising are Eric Villanueva Mukul's omissions in *Así tomamos las tierras: henequen y haciendas en Yucatán durante el porfiriato* (1984), and those of José Velasco Toro in *Los yaquis: historia de una activa resistencia* (1988).

Perhaps the problem is with semantics and the problem of differing definitions of the word "slavery." Both contemporary and modern references to the labor regime in Yucatán have sometimes used the terms "peons," "laborers," "indentured servants," and so forth. After his visit to Yucatán, Baerlein noted the *henequeneros'* aversion to the term "slavery" and how they explained that it was essentially confused with how peons' debts were often bought by one *henequenero* from another, requiring the worker to move to a different plantation. That may have seemed like a slave system to an outsider, they said, but they ensured it was not the case.[111] Benítez explains that the henequen work regimen was a different "genus of slavery, one that pertained more to the past" in that the workers became "permanent debtors" who could never pay off their debt and interest by staying on the same hacienda, and thus they and their debt were transferred to another. Another traveler to the region in the early 1920s tried to follow up on the matter. Ernest Gruening, who in the 1960s was a U.S. senator from Alaska, wrote that the "Yucatecan hacendados denied little, although at the time with a new revolutionary governor, Felipe Carrillo Puerto, in the saddle, recollections of that nature were painful." He went on to relate how the *henequeneros* would always say that slavelike conditions were "on the other fellow's *hacienda*" and claim that they treated their "*peons* very much better than the rest." Gruening remembered that "the *hacendados* were unanimous on that point."[112]

With labor in a state of crisis on the plantations in Yucatán and with evidence that two-thirds of the enslaved Yaquis died in the horrid conditions under which they were forced to work, one wonders why the *henequeneros* would choose this type of brutal labor system. One study cites economic considerations to help answer the question. The *henequeneros* understood that boom times would be followed by lean years on the international fiber market, so maximum production when prices were high was of the utmost importance. When workers died, the growers figured that a great enough flow of newly imported Yaquis, at relatively low prices, would always be available to replace deceased slaves. Likewise, due to significant planter indebtedness, primarily to the North American trust and as a result of their own lavish consumerism, they at all times tried to keep production costs, including those for labor, to a minimum.[113]

Workers, then, were expendable, and the whippings and harsh conditions were to ensure maximum work and high, albeit short-term, yields. An oft-quoted Yucatecan proverb that suggests that "*los indios no oyen sino por las nalgas*" (the Indians hear only with their backsides) is a telling reminder of this condition. The painter/muralist Fernando Castro Pacheco graphically

Figure 2.8. Artist's rendering of Mayan worker harvesting henequen (from *El henequén* 1 [April 30, 1916]).

portrayed these gruesome work conditions in his artwork, as Jeffery Brannon and Eric Baklanoff have written, "showing the peons being crucified on the spiny henequen plant." Yucatecans themselves were fond of claiming that they were "impaled on the fibrous spines of the hardy cactus."[114] Many works of art and popular culture around Yucatán and in the literature reflect this image (Figures 2.8 and 2.9). One of Castro's beautiful murals, painted on the wall of the courtyard of the *palacio de gobierno* (capital building) in Mérida, shows an Indian laborer bearing the weight of an enormous bale of henequen on his back—bearing the years of weight, the legacy of torture, and the process of

Figure 2.9. Artist's rendering of henequen worker carrying a large bundle of *pencas* (cut henequen leaves) (from cover of *El henequen* 3 [November 15, 1918]).

exploitation and dependency. Revolutionary leader and governor Salvador Alvarado recognized the burden when he stated that henequen was the "link in the chain" from the colonial slavery of the past to the servitude of Indians in his day, or as Benítez explains in his important book *Kí: el drama de un pueblo y de una planta,* "That which for other peoples is such a love for farming, here is a hatred, hatred and desperation."[115]

One can conclude that labor conditions on the henequen haciendas were as horrible as those of other plantation-slave societies. The overwhelming majority of people who made up the work force were Mayan Indians from Yucatán, but the *henequeneros* also benefited from the importation of peasants and Indians rounded up in other parts of Mexico. The Yaqui experience in Yucatán is especially relevant since the Mexican government wanted to rid Sonora of that population so as to begin a Yucatán-like, export-oriented agricultural system there. A discussion of the background, connections, and implications of that experience—an integral part of the henequen-wheat story—follows in the next chapter.

CHAPTER 3

Yaquis in Yucatán

Imported Slave Labor and the Sonora Connection

Those who were caught were cast in jail,
"Las embarcaciones ya se van"
Was then made a song and tale,
Yaquis taken to Yucatán.

—*Refugio Savala, from "The Yaquis in Sonora in 1904"*

AFTER Refugio Savala was born in a Sonoran village in 1904, Mexican soldiers took his mother from her tortilla stand and held her in jail to await deportation to the henequen fields of faraway Yucatán. Amazingly, unlike most of the other thousands of detained Yaquis, she talked herself free and hurriedly moved her family to safety in southern Arizona—a refuge (and hence the naming of her son) from the *política deportadora,* or deportation policy, of Porfirio Díaz.

The story of Yaqui deportation from Sonora (in northwestern Mexico) to the Yucatán Peninsula is based on a complex set of factors. Decades of war between the Mexican military and the Yaqui nation, Mexico's push for agricultural modernization, international business interests in commodity monoculture, and deep-seated ethnic hatred all merged to write a violent chapter in the history of early twentieth-century Mexico. Equally important, as we have seen, Yucatán's *henequeneros* were in dire need of laborers, as the North American demand for fiber continued to expand exponentially. These factors and their noteworthy results, including what happened to the Yaquis' land in Sonora when they were deported, add the Yaqui and Sonoran dimensions to the henequen-wheat complex and are a vital part of the story that needs to be understood in its broader context.

Two opposite sides of Mexico's vast periphery represented places that

President Díaz and his *científicos* were particularly interested in developing economically. One, as we have seen, was in the southeast, on the henequen-rich Yucatán Peninsula where only a few decades earlier a significant organization of rebel Maya known as the *cruzob* had been fighting for autonomy. The other was in the northwest, in the state of Sonora, where Apache, Mayo, and Yaqui Indians had been, according to Díaz and his advisors, blocking the path of economic modernization and progress. By the late nineteenth century, Díaz oversaw a "pacification" campaign to drive *indios bárbaros* (hostile tribes) from their homelands so that their lands could be open to modernization schemes, often funded by foreign investments. But, as one study has appropriately suggested, "the term pacification became a euphemism for genocide."[1]

The Yaqui side of the pacification campaign in the northwest merits a brief review here as that native group's destiny became tied directly to the economic development of Yucatán. The Yaqui homeland was in southern Sonora at the mouth of the Yaqui River, which drained much of the state's eastern mountainous area and created a delta of some of the most fertile land in Mexico despite the harsh scrubland terrain (Figure 3.1). The Yaquis, related linguistically to Aztecan groups in south central Mexico, developed their own culture,

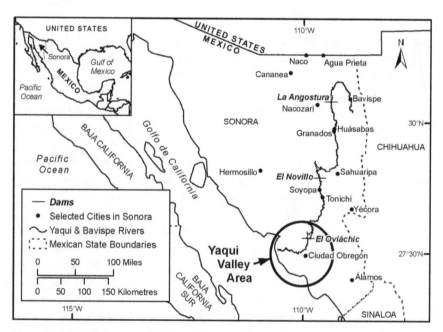

Figure 3.1. Map of the state of Sonora, Mexico, showing the Yaqui River, its three major dams, and the Yaqui Valley. Courtesy Wenonah Fraser, Department of Geography, Brandon University.

religion, tribal organization, and language.[2] They thrived for centuries in this arid valley by developing a practical system of flood-plain irrigation using the Yaqui River's seasonally cyclic runoff, learning to defend their resources and livelihood from invading forces that over the years included other native groups, Spaniards during the colonial era, and eventually the Mexican army.[3]

The first trouble with an independent Mexico came in 1825 when the Yaquis, under the leadership of Juan Banderas, had to confront a force of Mexican soldiers who came to collect taxes that the Yaquis refused to pay. Forging an alliance with other northern Mexican indigenous groups, they drove the Mexican soldiers away. Midcentury, however, the Mexicans redoubled their efforts and invaded Yaqui lands, destroying property and capturing and killing many Indians. Mexican soldiers burned 450 Yaquis to death inside a church in the village of Bácum in 1862 and killed 200 Yaquis at the Battle of Buatechive in 1885. Many more died when a smallpox epidemic ravaged the valley. At that point most survivors fled to find work elsewhere in Sonora, and others established active resistance centers in the Sierra Bacatete just east of their lands. Meanwhile, the government "settled" 4,000 remaining Yaquis into eight villages along the Yaqui River—the only semiautonomous Yaqui villages that exist today in the entire region.[4]

Thus, the Yaquis became known for their tenacious resistance and resilience. Many times when state and federal forces thought they had overwhelmed the Yaquis and were about to declare the campaign against them to be at an end, the Indians would come back even stronger. In a report for the Sonoran legislature in 1888, Vice Governor Ramón Corral (who was very much in the forefront of the military battle against the Yaquis and who would later become a three-term governor of Sonora and eventually vice president under Díaz) explained that while his forces thought the campaign was finished at the end of 1887, "the Yaquis, even more warlike and tenacious, continued sustaining the war in small groups in the Sierra Bacatete. . . . [T]he Yaquis persisted."[5] Renowned Mexican poet Amado Nervo in his tender short story "La yaqui hermosa" ("The Beautiful Yaqui Woman"), referred to this Yaqui characteristic as a "wild, almost epic, tenacity."[6] Yaquis honored the resources of the valley that gave them the strength to resist.

It was the same Yaqui Valley that powers in Mexico during the *porfiriato* came to covet. Three successive governors in the late nineteenth and early twentieth century—Luis Torres, Ramón Corral, and Rafael Izábal, known as "the triumvirate" in Sonoran history—were staunch supporters of Díaz and aggressively believed in modernization and economic growth. Torres worked to bring the railroad to Sonora in 1880, thus opening up the state to mining and export agriculture. He confiscated hundreds of thousands of acres where Sonoran indigenous groups had been living and created a colonization system for Mexican and foreign investors. These acts were in tune with Díaz's *política colonizadora* (colonization policy), especially for areas of sparsely populated *terrenos baldíos* and areas identified as likely to be productive for agriculture.[7] A government-sponsored "scientific commission" (Comisión Científica de Sonora) identified such lands in the 1890s and early 1900s and joined in the chorus calling for local indigenous groups to be removed in order to advance modern agriculture in Mexico.[8] Torres himself expropriated some 400,000 acres of the Yaqui Valley for his family's ranching and farming enterprises.[9] His brother Lorenzo—a brigadier general and interim chief of the First Military Zone in Sonora—in 1901 issued a decree "in the name of civilization" to the soldiers under his command congratulating them for their perseverance in "striking a terrible blow to the barbarism" of the Yaquis. He thanked them for their "efforts in returning to the . . . peaceful dominion of the Republic the great and rich Yaqui" region whose wealth would advance the country's "peace and progress."[10] With few choices available, many Yaquis had to work in the copper mines in northern Sonora or on the haciendas of the wealthy Mexican landholders.

In the spirit of their past resistance efforts, the Yaquis revolted in 1885. Their leader Tetabiate formed a rebel unit of Indians that engaged in skirmishes and guerrilla warfare against the landowners and the Sonoran troops who backed them. In the 1890s, federal troops intervened. Tetabiate and the government reached a peace agreement in 1897 that provided for "repentant" Yaqui rebels to become "colonists"—in their own valley—and for federal troops to leave. Díaz hoped that by "seeing every Yaqui behind a plow," the valley would peacefully prosper and modernize. But the *federales* did not leave, and the fighting that broke out in early 1900 led to the Battle of Mazocoba, which resulted in four hundred Yaquis dead, eight hundred to a thousand taken prisoner (many of whom were women and children), and nine hundred forced to flee to the Bacatete Mountains.[11] Fighting intensified from 1902 through 1907 despite the Mexican army's numerical superiority and modern weapons (Mauser rifles). The outnumbered Yaquis resorted to guerrilla activities and fighting with bows, arrows, and rocks.

Sonora's secretary of state, Alberto Cubillas, worked to keep Vice President Corral informed about the Yaqui pacification campaign. In May of 1908, Cubillas explained to Corral that state troops would assist federal troops in ensuring that the Yaquis hand over all "their arms and munitions" in an "absolute and unconditional surrender." As that month progressed, so did the campaign against the Yaquis, with Cubillas informing Corral, "I think that there remains no other choice but the complete deportation of the tribe." Corral continued to loom large in the government's policy making and maintained such great influence with Díaz that at one point the president had anointed Corral

to be his successor, although the revolution altered that plan. At a huge ban-
quet in 1910 to honor this announcement, Díaz offered a toast to Corral's "zeal
for the welfare of the country . . . and enthusiasm for progress," and he invited
the guests to "drink to the progress of Mexico, under a sky of prosperity and
prestige."[12]

By then some of the American investors were assisting the Mexican government in supplying weapons to Sonoran troops "clandestinely from across
the border" in Arizona. However, Arizona territorial governor Joseph Kibbey
issued orders against the sale of arms to Yaqui Indians.[13] The wars continued until 1911 and became, as Ramón Ruiz describes them, "the curse of the
porfiriato"—costing the federal government more than 50 million pesos and
hundreds of lives since 1885, not to mention the Yaquis' loss of life, land, and
way of living.[14]

What started as an effort to "colonize" Yaquis and remove them from the
valuable land of the Yaqui Valley ended up being an unabashedly racist campaign of extermination.[15] Policies shifted from state strategies against Tetabiate
and his rebels to intimidation and violent harassment of any Yaqui, with the
goal of annihilating the entire tribe. In 1902, when the turn-of-the-century
census data revealed that roughly 15 percent of the population of Sonora was
Yaqui, Izábal, the newly elected governor, ordered that all Yaqui Indians age
sixteen and over be required to wear identification passports. Those caught
without such registration were subject to arrest and deportation. By 1905 this
law was used to detain any Yaqui whom officials even slightly suspected of
rebel involvement, and Izábal ordered that the persons be arrested "with all
their families, so that not a single Yaqui remains, neither big nor small." One
year later officials used the law to arrest persons merely for being Yaqui; as the
governor explained, "Frankly, I don't see any other solution for these *indios*."
He had the implicit support of a wide array of Sonoran merchants, bankers,
cattle ranchers, and business leaders.[16] Yet Izábal also could practice political
spin on the matter. He wrote to a group of nine Yaqui captains in 1904, saying
that "in the war I have treated the Yaquis with humanity, but I have also had
to punish you severely."[17]

Izábal's reign of terror for racial cleansing manifested itself in other ways.
The governor enlisted the services of Colonel Emilio Kosterlitzky, commander
of the federal rural police (*los rurales*) in Izábal's area of northern Mexico, and
assigned him the task of capturing Yaquis fleeing to Arizona. For those who
attempted the flight to the border, the trips were, as many Yaquis told anthropologist Edward Spicer, "desperate journeys." Kosterlitzky's men caught parents carrying babies and children through the desert at night, separated them
from their families, and often tortured and imprisoned them to await hanging
or deportation. Hundreds not as fortunate as Refugio Savala's family, which

made it to Arizona, had to watch as the Mexican troops took their children, who were then adopted by waiting couples or used as house servants in Sonora's capital, Hermosillo. Many children became homeless. Raquel Padilla Ramos explains that the breaking up of families was a method of breaking up the tribe, as the family was the "base and moral sustenance of the tribe during the war." Izábal also created a complex surveillance system and intimidated many Yaquis into spying on others, including their own family members. The informers became known as *torocoyoris*, a Yaqui term meaning "like a Mexican."[18]

Kosterlitzky's efforts included meeting with U.S. officials along the border to solicit their support. On the U.S. side, however, the policy was to accept the escaping Indians as political refugees, especially since Arizona mining and railroad companies were taking advantage of the low-cost labor that the Yaquis provided. That situation changed in 1906 and 1907 when an economic depression caused layoffs in the mining and railroad industries. The U.S. Department of Commerce then agreed to stop Yaqui migration into the United States. U.S. officials enlisted the help of Arizona Rangers to hunt down Yaquis and deport them across the border.[19] The Sonorans were indeed content with such cooperation. Louis Hostetler, the U.S. consul in Hermosillo, notified his superiors in the State Department that Governor Izábal had told him that he was "very highly pleased at the action of our government in taking steps to stop the entrance of the Yaqui Indians into Arizona . . . as that carried out will certainly end the Yaqui trouble in a short time."[20]

Important to the U.S. side of this story is that American officials were aware of the climate of terror into which they were returning the Yaquis. Hostetler had kept the State Department abreast of the Mexican campaigns against the Yaquis and how they were being deported to the henequen plantations. He wrote in early 1906 that Sonorans "desire to rid the country of the entire lot [of Yaquis]," and he later explained that "all Yaquis caught are summarily dealt with. Those found and not suspected of being on the warpath are shipped with their families to Yucatán, as the officials have determined to get rid of the whole tribe."[21] United States authorities were also aware of John Kenneth Turner's series "Barbarous Mexico" and its critical portrayal of Mexico's brutality toward Yaquis. But despite these accounts, the "political refugee" status for fleeing Yaquis was not reextended to them, nor did other aid come to them from at home or abroad.

This history is in itself is perhaps not so different from many other conflicts between indigenous groups and an advancing national state in the western hemisphere. There are three things, however, that make the Yaqui case unique: the duration of Yaqui resistance through the colonial and national periods, the relative lateness of the continuing conflict (early twentieth century, compared to mid- and late nineteenth century for the "pacification" of most

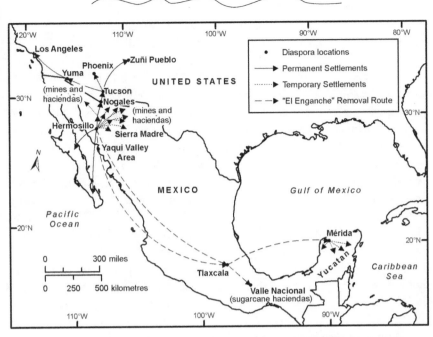

Figure 3.2. The Yaqui Indian diaspora (adapted from p. 159 of Edward Spicer, *The Yaquis: A Cultural History,* 1980). Courtesy Wenonah Fraser, Department of Geography, Brandon University.

other North American Indian groups), and the deportation and enslavement of the Yaquis to faraway plantations in Yucatán. Calling it the "Yaqui diaspora," Spicer claims that the Yaquis "became the most widely scattered native people of North America" (Figure 3.2). He notes that "not even the Cherokees, whose deportation in 1835 from Georgia to Oklahoma had initiated a scattering over the United States, were so widely dispersed."[22] (Interestingly, in 1898 and 1905 two groups of Cherokees from Oklahoma formed colonies in the Yaqui Valley. Originally, there was to be a colony of twenty thousand Cherokees, but by 1898 the colony comprised thirty Indians from Oklahoma.[23]) Those Yaquis who successfully fled to Arizona established the Pascua community in Tucson, which remains today the largest Yaqui enclave in the United States. Others moved to Yuma, Arizona, and Los Angeles, California. Yaquis often refer to the diaspora as the *ruta de exilio* ("the exile road").

It is important to consider that at the core of Yaqui exile was a strong element of racism that influenced policy making. Tetabiate's biographer, Palemón Zavala Castro, noted that evidence for racist thought underlying the removal policy was rooted in "the battle of the books": three influential works from the early twentieth century that advanced the theory of Yaqui inferiority and of the need for extermination and/or deportation.[24] The first was Fortunato

Hernández's *Las razas indígenas de Sonora y las guerras del Yaqui* (1902), which openly called for extermination or deportation and which Zavala Castro believed to be the origin of the philosophy of genocide. The Díaz administration commissioned the second work, written by Colonel Francisco Troncoso. His book, *Las guerras con las tribus yaqui y mayo del estado de Sonora* (1905) continued the explicitly racist themes. The Yaquis, he stated, "abhor civilized people," had an "inclination for theft, murder, destruction, vagrancy, [and] drunkenness," and that "if an energetic remedy is not employed, over time they will lose whatever good qualities they do have."[25] Troncoso's words, however, would ring oddly unfamiliar to many in Sonora. As one scholar has written, the Yaqui River valley was an "area of the country with the least criminality, and its Indian inhabitants . . . the least delinquent." Further, many *hacendados*, ranchers, and mine managers depended on Yaqui labor, and they regretted losing that resource when the people were deported.[26] Some of those *hacendados*, however, were not always in the good graces of Sonora's ruling triumvirate, nor did they always agree with Díaz's policies. At one point a group of these influential Sonorans corresponded directly with President Díaz to request a slowing of the deportations. Thus, some scholars have argued that an additional possible reason for deportation was to punish those various anti-Díaz *hacendados*.[27]

The final work influencing government policy was Federico García y Alva's *México y sus progresos: album-directorio de Sonora* (1905–1907), which propounded similar anti-Yaqui dogma. Calling the Yaquis "a continual obstacle" and "a hindrance for the wealth and progress of the state," the book suggested that the solution was "in uprooting them . . . sending them to another region of our territory, the farthest away possible, to where their natural savagery can be molded to the necessities of the new soil. . . . This solution is hard, but is efficient, necessary, and required."[28] Díaz heeded this advice; after 1907 the policy was "total deportation."[29] Yucatán was indeed the place "farthest away possible" yet still on Mexican soil, and the "new soil" for the Yaquis was planted in henequen.

The robust racism and desire for Yaqui lands could make one think that annihilation would have rid southern Sonora of the Yaquis, if that were the precise end desired. Genocide was possible, given the military superiority of the Mexican army, so why not just continue the war of extermination? The answer revolves around the need for labor. Spicer concluded that the decision was part of the government's hope for the Yaquis to "be educated properly" and for their "hostility [to] be bred out of them."[30] And perhaps that could be more easily accomplished with the Yaquis serving as slave laborers instead of time in prison, especially since, as Refugio Savala has noted, deportation was considered a logical next step because of the overcrowded jails in Sonora.

Due to the high number of Yaqui prisoners taken by the Mexicans in the wars, there was simply no space left in the jails around the state or in the penitentiary in Hermosillo. The seemingly obvious answer was to ship them out.[31]

Daniel Cosío Villegas traces the original idea of deportation back to a Sinaloan planter named Joaquín Redo who, due to his desire for cheap labor, started calling for the roundup of Yaquis. His view of Yaquis as the answer to his own labor needs began to pop up elsewhere in Mexico, including Yucatán.[32] None of these plans was based solely on a particular region; there was very much a top-down element coming from members of Díaz's administration, including Vice President Ramón Corral (from Sonora) and Minister of Development Olegario Molina (from Yucatán). Díaz himself "sanctioned and applauded this draconian measure," using his War Department to bring the Yaquis to Yucatán. In so doing, the government would come across as a benevolent protector of the Indians, giving them a second chance to become "civilized" and to work for the good of the country instead of being annihilated. With a removal policy Mexico could proceed with the modernization dreamed of by the *científicos* and leaders of the Yucatecan and Sonoran peripheries, which, as Evelyn Hu-deHart puts it, "was killing two birds with one stone."[33]

There is considerable debate on when deportation started and ended. Some scholars point to 1900 as the year when the deportations began, or at least when henequen hacienda contracts start showing evidence of Yaquis arriving in Yucatán. Others argue it started as early as the 1880s and 1890s, or, as John Kenneth Turner noted, in 1905, when the deportations "began to assume noticeable proportions" after having been "carried out on a small scale at first." Others suggest it was not until as late as 1908, when Díaz issued a decree ordering that "every Yaqui[,] . . . men, women, and children . . . be gathered up by the War Department and deported to Yucatán."[34]

Sonoran officials happily complied. Sonora's secretary of state, Alberto Cubillas, wrote to federal officials in Mexico City, assuring them that the Sonoran government would be "apprehending all those who live peacefully in the ranches and haciendas to deport them." And General Lorenzo Torres stressed to Cubillas that "we must take out of Sonora all the Yaquis, all without exception . . . and proceed with the deportation . . . we will take out rebels and *pacíficos* [nonrebels]."[35] Nonetheless, the deportation started gradually, perhaps to avoid further upsetting Sonoran *hacendados* and mine managers who themselves were dependent on Yaqui labor. Raquel Padilla Ramos suggests that those Sonorans believed that "an immediate deportation would have adversely affected the whole economy of Sonora."[36]

A leading scholar of Yaqui history has called the *política deportadora* "one of the most notorious acts of the Díaz regime." The removal process was brutal. Government forces and *enganchadores* rounded up thousands of Yaquis (and according to Turner, some Pima, Opata, and other Indians from Sonora whom *enganchadores* had "tagged as Yaquis" due to their similar appearance).[37] The officials packed them into boxcars bound for Sonora's port of Guaymas, shipped them by boat down the coast to Tepic (in the state of Nayarit) or Salina Cruz (in Oaxaca), and then again by cattle car and long, arduous marches across Mexico to the Gulf port of Veracruz. One account in the Yucatán press in 1900 reported that 250 Yaqui women, primarily widows from the Yaqui wars, and children had to walk in a "forced march" from Salina Cruz all the way across the Tehuantepec isthmus to Yucatán.[38] Those who went via Veracruz had to board another boat to Yucatán's port of Progreso and then go by local rail or on foot inland to the henequen haciendas. From Sonora the whole exile road was a wretched, month-long journey of nearly three thousand miles, or as one historian called it, "an incomprehensibly horrible voyage."[39] Officials separated children from their parents en route and set up holding camps along the way. Padilla Ramos argues that Yaqui women were likely the first to be deported since their absence would destabilize the family unit. The *henequeneros* had also quickly learned that Yaqui women were "just as strong as men" and that the widows could do twice as much weeding as men in the same amount of time.[40]

There were many different people who profited or benefited from the deportation business: soldiers, business owners, *hacendados*, politicians, *enganchadores*.[41] Turner learned from Colonel Francisco Cruz, "chief deporter of Yaquis," that Cruz earned $10 for each Yaqui delivered to officials. At the time of the interview he had already made $157,000 and was jubilant at his orders to deliver fifteen hundred more Indians as quickly as he could. "Ah yes," he proclaimed, "I ought to have [a] comfortable little fortune for myself before this thing is over." He explained how the Yaqui slaves fetched $65 a piece in Yucatán. "Who gets the money?" he asked rhetorically. "Well $10 goes to me for my services. The rest is turned over to the Secretary of War." But that was "only a drop in the bucket." He told Turner, "Every foot of land, every building, every cow, every burro, everything left behind by the Yaquis when they are carried away by the soldiers, is appropriated for the private use of authorities of the state of Sonora." And Ramón Corral himself reportedly made three pesos per Yaqui sold (with a peso in those days roughly equivalent to a U.S. dollar).[42] Assuredly, there were many others at all points along the exile route who profited from selling supplies, food, and services to the soldiers overseeing the Yaqui deportation.

Mexican forces deported the majority of Yaquis to Yucatán, but they also sent some to Oaxaca to work on sugarcane plantations. They sent others to Quintana Roo (then a territory east of Yucatán), others to Campeche (the state south of Yucatán), and some they incarcerated in Hermosillo. They hanged others on the spot, as Hu-deHart puts it, "in an aura of selective terror."[43]

Scholars have had great difficulty in discerning the exact number of Yaquis who were deported and enslaved on henequen plantations; it is a number that will never be known with any precision. Despite the fact that the *política deportadora* came from Mexico City, there are no federal accounts of it, and those people involved with the trade itself kept very few records. Upon learning this, Turner suggested that the business was done quietly, a fact that has helped fuel the antislavery theory among Yucatecanists.[44] So what methodologies can be used to try to trace Yaqui removal numerically?

In Sonora, reports from 1903 to 1907 to the state congress in Hermosillo confirm that the *enganche* included categories such as Yaqui men, women, women with babies, and children and whether they were to be deported (approximately 2,000) or imprisoned.[45] For Yucatán, Turner's *Barbarous Mexico* includes important data from his conversations with Francisco Cruz, who said he had transported roughly 15,700 Yaquis to the Yucatán Peninsula between 1905 and mid-1908. For the first half of 1908 alone, he figured, there would have been 500 Yaquis—the "capacity" of the government boats leaving Guaymas, Sonora—per month. Later Turner figured that a total of 8,000 Yaquis had been deported to Yucatán in one year. Similarly, the London-based Anti-Slavery and Aborigines Protection Society investigated the Yucatán labor scene and concluded from sources that the number of slaves was between 6,000 and 12,000.[46] One could argue that these figures mesh with what Spicer determined by drawing on his many years of anthropological studies. He has written that the Yaquis' population of about 20,000 at the turn of the twentieth century dropped to 5,000 by 1908, although part of the loss could be attributed to those fleeing to Arizona. In another work he put the number of deported Yaquis at between 5,000 and 6,000.[47]

The disparity has caused scholars to check other sources. Cosío Villegas consulted the 1910 census, which listed only 2,757 "Sonorans" living in Yucatán.[48] That figure, however, would not show how many Yaquis had been deported in the ten years preceding or how many had died or escaped. It also highlights the terminology problem. Records avoided the term "Yaqui," using instead "Rebel Indians from the Yaqui River," "*Sonorenses*" (Sonorans), "*rebeldes*" (rebels), "*extranjeros*," (foreigners), and "prisoners of war" when referring to deported laborers. But as Padilla Ramos found, port records *did* use the word "Yaqui" (along with "prisoners of war"), especially as health officials conducted quick surveys of passengers when they disembarked at Progreso, listing ailments or diseases. Those records identified hundreds of Yaquis as having influenza, chicken pox, yellow fever, and smallpox, diseases that would have made their already difficult passage unimaginably worse, but the records also indicated clear patterns of how many Yaquis arrived at Yucatán's main port and when. Likewise, she did a thorough check of Mérida's newspaper, *La revista de Mérida*, which announced such things as "1,000 Yaquis being guarded by the 10th Battalion in Yucatán" and "500 Yaquis arrive" on various days. It often reported to which haciendas the Yaquis were being assigned. One hundred Yaqui arrivals, for example, were headed to Olegario Molina's plantation in March 1908; other large groups were sent to Manuel Peón's hacienda. From those sources Padilla Ramos computed that a total of 6,432 Yaquis were deported, noting in bold that "the number is in no way definitive." Similarly, Allen Wells discovered that the Mexico City newspaper *El imparcial* reported in July 1911 that 4,000 Yaquis remained on plantations that year—figures that corroborate Spicer's numbers.[49]

Unfortunately, none of these sources indicates the exact number of Yaquis deported. They do show that large numbers—in the thousands (Gilbert Joseph accepts Turner's "almost 16,000 deported Yaquis")—survived the *enganche* and the brutal *ruta de exilio* to work in Yucatán.[50] Those individuals were a part of the henequen-wheat complex and, with their forced labor, production costs for twine were kept low, to the benefit of farmers in the United States and Canada.

The numbers look much more gruesome when attached to names on lists. There in the Sonoran archives are pages and pages listing the names of those killed, captured, detained, and incarcerated, lists of Indians waiting to be deported, lists of Yaqui prisoners, and lists of Mexican couples who "received Yaqui children on order of the Secretary of State." One list had the names of seventy-nine children ready to be deported; another had the names of mothers and children, ages one to ten, and indicated how many babies were still at their mothers' breasts. In 1905 alone, the lists contained the names of 1,925 Yaquis in these various categories, eerily written in pencil, as one can imagine the clerk doing while the terrified detainees waited in lines and holding areas.[51]

Individuals get lost in number crunching, so the personal accounts of those who endured the reign of terror and removal are particularly valuable. There are only a few such accounts available, and their messages are often absent in the historical and economic literature of the henequen industry. Luckily, anthropologist Jane Holden Kelley worked to record the memories of several elderly Yaqui women in the 1970s, and a cultural support organization for Sonoran indigenous groups recorded similar testimonies of Yaquis in their eighties and nineties who remembered the campaign against their people. Their accounts, the memoirs of the Yaqui Indian Rosalio Moisés, the first-hand experiences and interviews of John Kenneth Turner, who traveled part of the way with deportees, and several foreign travelers' accounts from the time are all useful for gaining an understanding of the violence and tragedy of the extermination policy and deportation.

When Turner wrote that Yaquis in Sonora "were merely hunted" by the Department of War, Dominga Tava, a Yaqui woman born in 1901, could relate. She recalled when President Díaz ordered five thousand troops to quell the Yaqui rebels (among them her own family), when the military chased them around the Sierra Bacatete where they were hiding, and where she contracted smallpox. In her seventies, she had not forgotten the hunger, illnesses, cold, and other hardships of a mobile life as a child hiding in the mountains. She knew what it was like to be hunted.[52]

Josefa Morena was a young mother during deportation, and her memories are heart wrenching. The train car she rode in was more like a cell, with all the Yaquis "stuffed in like goats" with no place to lie down or to relieve bodily functions. The boat from Guaymas to Tepic was even worse, and she and her baby became ill. The baby died of hunger and thirst at Tepic, and when she begged to be able to bury him, the guards forced her at bayonet point to go back to the post, which she did, weeping the whole way. She then rode in a cattle car from the coast to Guadalajara, and on to Veracruz. After the slave boat to Progreso, she was "bought" and ordered to do kitchen work for the field workers on the Manuel Peón plantation. She was beaten and whipped several times, once while pregnant. She lost a total of seven babies during the exile years.[53]

Rosalio Moisés recalls that when he was a youngster in Sonora his family decided to flee to Arizona after the army hunted and deported many of their friends and relatives, among them his grandfather, whom officials interrogated and tied up. They sent him in a boxcar to Guaymas to be shipped to Yucatán. "That was the last time we saw my grandfather," Moisés lamented. "He was gone forever. . . . He was the last shoemaker in all the Yaqui tribe." And because the family had depended on his income, those members who escaped deportation "did not live well. . . . We were always hungry." He recalled the terror in his community: "[Children] . . . were given away like puppies. Girls over twelve were given to . . . soldiers. Babies were killed by knocking their heads against trees. . . . Governor Izábal was called *el segundo dios* [the second god] . . . [because] the Yaqui men were sorted into three lines. Men in one line were to be killed; men in the second line . . . deported; men in the third line were released to work another week."[54]

Ramón Velázquez, from the Yaqui village Pótam, was thirteen years old when he fought with his family in the Sierra Bacatete after officials confiscated their land in the valley. He recalled that many persons in his village "were taken away as slaves to work in other states or were tricked by the government and relocated to Yucatán to work the maguey [henequen]." Another woman, Dominga Ramírez, remembered when soldiers barged into her family's home and gave them only minutes to gather a few belongings before being deported. She herself was "bought" at age four or five to be raised as a servant on a Yucatecan hacienda.[55] Alberto Martínez Valdéz was six years old in 1910 when soldiers abducted his family, took them on the journey to Yucatán (on which "they made the elderly walk long distances at bayonet point," causing his grandmother to die en route), and then handed them over to *hacendados* in Mérida who bought them for fifteen pesos a head.[56]

Conditions on the plantations were often as bad as those on the deportation trains and ships. After visiting some haciendas and witnessing the Yaquis' conditions, Turner described the "pitiful misery" of their lives—"half starved," served only one meal a day of beans and corn tortillas, sometimes with rotting fish; with scarce and foul water—locked up at nights, thrown in deep holes, frequently beaten and whipped, forced to work from 4:00 A.M. to sunset (even if sick), and killed at will by their masters. Sexual abuse of Yaqui women was commonplace. Hacienda foremen required pregnant women to work and often tore babies away from their mothers. They often forced Yaqui women to "marry" Mayan or Chinese laborers. "We do that," a planter explained, "to make the Chinamen better satisfied and less inclined to run away. And besides, we know that every new babe . . . will . . . be worth anywhere from 500 to 1,000 pesos cash!"[57]

The death rate for Yaquis in Yucatán was extremely high, with two-thirds dying within their first year there.[58] A major reason for the high mortality rate was the extreme humidity, which was in direct contrast to the dryness of Sonora. Centuries earlier white planters had argued that Africans could tolerate heat and hard work better than Europeans, and some voices began to echo that idea, suggesting that the Yaquis had some kind of racial adaptability to the humid conditions. In fact the opposite was true; Yucatán's climate was one that constantly afflicted the Yaquis with tropical diseases. A newspaper article summarized the situation well, saying that Yaquis had been taken "from their fertile soil and benign climate to the death-breeding climate of Yucatán." The experience was one of exile and slavery, or as Turner called it, "Siberia . . . [but] hell aflame."[59]

Like slaves in any society, some Yaquis attempted to escape. There is no way to know how many attempted or succeeded, and their flight rarely meant freedom. Officials caught and punished or killed many who tried to run. Some reportedly chose to escape to the tropical forests of Tabasco. Distance, the unfamiliar region, and a lack of resources made it nearly impossible for most escapees to make it back to Sonora. Some who did were recaptured and redeported to Yucatán or, according to Rosalio Moisés, "taken to Mexico City and turned loose."[60] Actually, there were few opportunities for Yaquis back home since their land had been parceled out to investors. Sadly, the same was true after the Mexican Revolution, when the revolutionary forces finally "freed" the Yaquis. Josefa Morena remembered that in Sonora there "was no work available" and that upon her own return, she felt "totally uprooted" and did not feel like she "fit in" within her own Yaqui community.[61]

Students of comparative slavery would wonder about the incidence of slave revolts in Yucatán, especially given such a strong history of Yaqui resistance. Yaquis were involved in a significant uprising on a sugarcane plantation at Catmís, Yucatán, in 1911, but unlike the slave rebellion history of colonial Brazil and the Caribbean, and to a lesser degree of the American South, there is no evidence of massive Yaqui slave revolts on the henequen plantations.[62] Among the Yaquis in Yucatán the slave experience was relatively short, fifteen or so years, compared to the other slave histories in the Americas. Also, because the Yaquis were so severely mistreated, nearly starved, and constantly afflicted with illnesses, the mortality rate was severe (as high as 60 to 65 percent, according to Turner), and as a result the energy level was low among survivors, making it virtually impossible for an organized rebel front to develop.[63] Also, the *henequeneros* maintained tight control over their workers, meting out a variety of harsh punishments such as whippings and separating Yaqui family members from each other. They also created ethnically mixed work groups of Yaquis, Chinese, Koreans, Mayas, and Mexican peasants so as to thwart Yaqui-initiated rebellion plans with multiple language barriers, since many Yaquis spoke only their indigenous language. The *henequeneros* were well aware of the Yaquis' notorious uprisings in Sonora and knew that keeping them separated would prevent their mobilization in Yucatán.[64]

Some Yaquis who had escaped or were released enrolled in the Mexican revolutionary armed forces under General Álvaro Obregón of Sonora, whom they saw as a home-state liberator. Obregón had made a significant offer to the Yaquis, promising he would reimburse them and restore their lost lands if they would fight in his army.[65] A report written early in 1915 showed that thirty Yaquis had escaped plantations to join the First Battalion (later a part of Obregón's forces). Likewise, several hundred Yaquis fought for the Yucatán state militia in which, according to Governor Eleuterio Ávila, "they received good treatment." Wells and Joseph found that by 1915 nearly half of Yucatán's 800-man Cepeda Peraza Battalion, "the most reliable Yucatecan force," were Yaqui Indians and that 900 Yaquis were recruited into the Pino Suárez Battalion to fight the Huertista army.[66] In addition, 500 "captured Yaquis" fought with the revolutionaries in Quintana Roo, although the idea of rearming Yaquis was a matter that some considered the "joke of the war." Later that year many Yaquis had already broken away from supporting Obregón. The *Mexican Herald* reported that of an original "powerful column" of 7,000 Yaqui soldiers, only 140 remained with the Sonoran general's forces. "They were fighting for the agrarian problem" and the right to return to their homelands—issues that Obregón did not prioritize after all.[67]

The deportations ebbed and flowed with larger macroeconomic market forces. Most authorities on the topic point to 1908 as the peak year for deportations, after which, due to falling demand for henequen fiber, they abruptly came to a halt for a while.[68] The Mexican Revolution ended the deportations completely in 1910, and Francisco Madero promised the Yaquis a boat to return them to Sonora. However, as one study has pointed out, approximately 4,000 Yaquis were still in their "miserable situation" in 1911 awaiting passage out of Yucatán.[69] Thus, many Yaquis continued working in the henequen fields. Records show that as late as 1913, for example, officials found a total of 112 Yaquis ("twenty-eight men, eighteen youth, and sixty-six women and children") still living and working on *henequenero* Anilio Pérez Machado's "Finca Copó."[70] Slavery itself officially came to an end in 1914 when the Constitutionalist forces under Salvador Alvarado marched on Yucatán, ousted the Yucatecan leaders who were proponents of the forced labor, and decreed an end to indentured servanthood on the peninsula. Using assertive language against the "barbarity" of such slavery, the Constitutionalists decreed the *liberación de los servientes endeudados* on September 11, 1914.[71] Despite the decree, some *henequeneros* were reluctant to give up their Yaqui workers. In 1914 the owner of the Hacienda San Francisco would not release the 35 Yaquis he had in his employ when a local official arrived to pick them up.[72]

Thus, slavelike conditions persisted for many Yaquis in Yucatán until they were able to return to Sonora—a gradual process that according to some accounts lasted until 1930. In her study on the topic, Padilla Ramos suggests that the Yaquis' return had to make it seem like they had been "pacified, so as not to anger the Yucatecan *hacendados* who had paid money for them." And some, though not many, Yaquis felt compelled to stay in Yucatán, especially if they had married Mayan or Cuban spouses. Another study argues that many of the Yaquis in the Yucatán state militia who fought during the revolution had become "completely assimilated" and also chose to remain on the peninsula after the war.[73] Descendants of these Yaquis remain in the Mérida area today.

The Yaquis clearly viewed the revolution as a liberating movement. An Arizona newspaper reported in the summer of 1911 that a "formal delegation" of eleven Yaqui "chiefs" had passed through Arizona en route to a meeting with Francisco Madero to discuss the return of the deported Yaquis and a return of their lands in the "fertile acres along the Yaqui River."[74] Madero never instituted any land reform policies for the Yaquis, but he did help arrange for their transfer out of Yucatán. Many of the returning Indians ended up back in the eight *rancherías* along the Yaqui River (the semiautonomous areas established earlier), where appropriately enough one *ejido* near Ciudad Obregón, Sonora, is even named "El Henequén." A Yucatecan official testified in 1916 before a U.S. Senate committee investigating the fiber industry that "the Revolution had brought freedom" to the henequen workers.[75] And for those Yaquis who did stay in Yucatán, conditions were probably better on the plantations due to the more enlightened policies of the new state government that the revolution ushered in.

Unfortunately, the revolution's role in ending Yaqui slavery did not curb the harsh anti-Yaqui racism that existed across Mexico or the apathy about their plight in the United States. The *Mexican Herald*, for example, reported in 1915 that when Yaqui troops in the Mexican army charged with finding a fugitive entered an American club in Mexico City, club employees barred the doors and did not allow the Yaqui troops to enter or any Americans to leave, presumably for their own safety. The matter subsided only when the fugitive, who was in the bar, escaped.[76]

Far worse, a headline in Mexico City's *Excélsior* on January 1918 announced that "Ten Thousand Yaquis Will Be Sent to Yucatán." The front-page article, with tellingly racist language, explained that one thousand families would be "deported" due to the "resistance of their race," that they belonged to certain groups that continued rebelling against the government. The arrangement was based on a post-revolution labor shortage in Yucatán and was part of a plan created by a newly formed state henequen regulating commission to bring nineteen thousand workers into Yucatán. The *henequeneros* signed a contract with Salvador Alvarado (despite his liberating of the Yaquis in Yucatán four years earlier) that would be "based on Porfirio Díaz's [system when] the Yaquis thrived [in Yucatán] and worked well with the Mayans whom they had befriended." The article also rekindled the old stereotype that argued that "because they are acclimated to the heat of Sonora they will soon be acclimated in Yucatán."[77]

Evidence shows that the government enlisted "only" fifteen hundred Yaquis, and many of those were transferred to agricultural jobs not in Yucatán but elsewhere in southern Mexico. Likewise, Alvarado ensured that the transfer would be nothing similar to the earlier *enganche* and that the Yaquis would be treated as immigrant workers rather than as slaves. Five days later, however, *Excélsior* reported that Sonoran governor Plutarco Elías Calles (who would serve as president of Mexico in the 1920s) had announced his initiation of an "active campaign against the Indians" and that "the Yaquis [would] be rigorously punished."[78] Calles enlisted the *federales* to hunt down Yaquis as late as 1926, again forcing many to flee to Arizona. But the Yaquis were not welcome in the United States. The U.S. Army captured escaping Yaquis near

Nogales, Arizona, and Secretary of State Robert Lansing gave permission for
Mexican troops in Ciudad Juárez to travel quickly to Naco, Sonora, through
U.S. territory in search of the Yaquis. And up to ten years later, the United
States continued deporting many of the Indians to Sonora.[79]

Equally racist were the sentiments of Martín Luis Guzmán, the editor of
El imparcial (despite the newspaper's name). Writing in his memoirs of the revolution, which became the vastly popular book *The Eagle and the Serpent* (1928),
Guzmán reminisced about a rail journey he had taken through Sonora during
the revolution. He wrote disparagingly of not only the Yaqui Indians he observed aboard the train but also their land: "It was a Mexican Far West, newer
than that of the United States and with less promise of industry, less machinery, less energy; and with greater aboriginal influence which was revealed in
the use of mud as a building material, but as barbarous on the other, more so
perhaps, its brutality unrestrained by a tradition of civilization, and ignorant
of all amenities invented by human culture. The civilizing influence of the Je-
suit fathers had had no time to flourish in those regions, currents of savage life
still floated in the tragic, miserable atmosphere, in which every feeble better
impulse was crushed out by the uncontrolled passions of men who respond
to none but the zoological stimuli."[80] Guzmán's thoughts were ever present in
the minds of positivists in Porfirian Mexico: to modernize and civilize northwestern Mexico meant ridding the southern, most fertile part of the state of
the "hostile" Yaquis. The removal would also provide a hoped-for edge against
the labor crisis in Yucatán. But what were the long-term results for Sonora? A
consideration of those results provides a clearer picture of how Sonora became
connected to the henequen-wheat complex.

The persecution, deportation, and enslaving of the Yaquis had predictable
long-term effects on the tribe. In addition to the terrorism and violence they
endured on a personal basis, for the Yaquis as a whole, as Spicer found, "the
social and psychological effects had deep consequences" and "the anguish of
the period was never forgotten." Dominga Ramírez explained that growing up
in Yucatán she was ignorant of Yaqui religion and never saw public displays
of Yaqui rituals; for many years the exiled Yaquis could not celebrate the traditional *fiestas* that are so important to their cultural identity. And the Yaqui
Indians whom Hu-deHart came to know all referred to the deportation years
as "the most terrible phase of their history"—a time of severed relationships
and broken families which was "devastating in a society where the family is a
strong cultural institution." Worse than the military campaigns, deportation
"broke down the spirit of the Yaquis," which certainly was the intent of the
política deportadora.[81] Meanwhile, the government confiscated Yaqui lands and
sold them to investors from other parts of Mexico, the United States, and a
few from Canada. Approximately 100 million acres of land in Sonora became

the property of such landholders as William Randolph Hearst, copper mining baron William C. Greene, the Phelps-Dodge Company, the *Los Angeles Times*, the Cargill Corporation, and others. Sonora quickly came to have the second highest rate of U.S. capital investment in Mexico (after Veracruz, with its oil resources). A common thought in Mexico in those days was that "it's New York capital that pushes Don Porfirio, and it's Don Porfirio that pushes Mexico."[82] To facilitate the process, the government allowed foreign investors to build a railroad from Arizona to the Yaqui Valley. Officials then transformed the map of the valley by creating a grid system of 100-hectare square parcels to be sold to the investors and colonizers; the Yaqui Valley became the only place in Latin America to replicate the U.S. style township and section system that is based on the 1785 Northwest Ordinance. Now the valley was one of symmetrical square parcels, irrespective of topography, climate, or water resources. One investor taking advantage of this newly designed system was the Mexican Land and Colonization Company, which acquired vast amounts of the area's *terrenos baldíos*. Another was the Richardson Construction Company of Los Angeles, which owned 100,000 acres of the valley—much of it a gift from Díaz's minister of development, Olegario Molina, who was also the largest handholder in Yucatán and who profited greatly from the Yaqui labor pool sent from Sonora. As Henry Baerlein put it in 1913, the Yaquis in Yucatán could only "dream about their distant valleys that, alas! were all too fertile."[83]

With the Yaquis out of the way, Díaz undertook all these efforts as part of his plan to make the Yaqui Valley the country's flagship region for modern agriculture and transform Sonora into the breadbasket of Mexico. With advances in irrigation technology, Díaz's plan seemed feasible. In 1885 Francisco Troncoso praised the Yaqui Valley, saying that it could produce "great yields of all types of grains, plants and fruits . . . from wheat to sugar cane, from corn to cotton" and that the lands were "immeasurable for the raising of all types of livestock." "There exists there," he concluded, "a great unexploited source of rich and varied productions that only needs the pacification of the tribes and the labor and intelligence of civilized man, to give abundant fruits and to change the face of the State."[84]

The Richardson Construction Company (or as it was known in Sonora, Compañía Constructora Richardson, or CCR) took the lead in developing the land for these ideals. It introduced an irrigation system of diversion wiers, canals, and lateral and feeder lines, and it began to lobby the federal government for the construction of the Yaqui River's first upriver dam—La Angostura, completed in 1937. (By the 1950s there were three high dams and reservoirs on the Yaqui [see Figure 3.1].) Thus, the water could be controlled for even flows to the colonizing settlers who had purchased parcels of land from CCR.[85] Sonora then became known as the "Mesopotamia of Mexico," "the Empire State of the West Mexican Coast," and the "Agricultural Cornucopia" of the country. With 7 percent of the nation's total agricultural lands (788,000 hectares), 60 percent of which had irrigation systems in place, it soon became the most agriculturally productive state in Mexico.[86] Of that agricultural land, 50 percent is in the valley of the Yaqui River—the "Nile of Sonora" and the "Granary of the Republic."[87]

Fittingly enough for the "Granary of the Republic," Sonora's number one crop was wheat. Government reports reveal that Sonoran wheat harvests steadily climbed in this era (from 19.6 million kilos in 1905 to 30 million kilos in 1925, with a "considerably better" harvest projected for 1926–27). A popular variety of the cereal developed in the region even bears the name "Sonora wheat." Sonorans—defiantly proud to be in the land of flour, not corn, tortillas—and now with access to steady flows of water for wheat fields, also became dependent on mechanized agriculture for grain harvests. One government report suggested that wheat was the easiest and least expensive crop to produce, partly due to its "great economy of wage workers . . . due to harvesting machines."[88]

Many of those harvesting implements were American in origin. As early as 1888, a report from the U.S. consulate in Guaymas, Sonora, related how for that year "the wheat crop [in Sonora] was an abundant one, . . . [and that] agricultural implements and machinery of American manufacture are coming into general use."[89] Another report from 1890 showed that American agricultural settlers in Sonora and Sinaloa were bringing their American farm machinery with them. The report alluded to a group of two hundred colonists from Kansas who were of "communistic ideals"; they had settled in Topolobampo (south of the Yaqui Valley and just inside the state of Sinaloa) and had come "well supplied with . . . agricultural implements."[90] Many of those implements included binders to harvest the region's excellent wheat crops. Federico García y Alva even included pictures of farmers harvesting wheat with binders in his 1905 book on progress and modernization in Sonora.[91] With the climate, the lush, irrigated fields, the ready availability of implements, the proximity of points from which to import them, and the fact that many agricultural colonists from North America were accustomed to using such implements, it is not surprising that many wheat farmers in Sonora harvested with binders.[92]

Cyrus McCormick had recognized this growth in Mexico and of course agreed with Mexican development-minded economists and government leaders that agriculture there should be more modern and mechanized. As early as 1870 he sent equipment to be tested in Mexican fields. So great did the demand for farm implements grow that soon after the merger in 1902, IH started exporting machinery to Mexico via the creation of the International Harvester Export Company. According to an article in *Harvester World* in 1911, however, the company recognized that modernizing agriculture in Mexico would "be a long slow process" because "of the great surplus of cheap peon labor that has to be supported principally from the farms of the country." The article explained that it was "only natural that this class should dislike to see the harvesting machines taking the place of the hand sickle, for at harvest time they are supposed to get somewhat better wages than during the remainder of the year." Still, in the 1890s and early 1900 Mexican landowners bought many binders and headers for their wheat harvests. IH operated in Mexico until 1911 when the revolution cut the relationship off, but afterward, in 1919, IH made a "direct sale to the Mexican government," sending six rail cars of machinery "for the rehabilitation of agriculture in Mexico," as one company communiqué on the topic explained. In 1947 IH opened its own implement manufacturing plant in Saltillo, Coahuila, for more direct marketing in Mexico.[93]

Most of the binder twine used by Mexican farmers came from homegrown fiber in Yucatán, and in the 1920s through 1940s their twine was manufactured by Yucatecan cordage companies. In fact, those companies became alarmed when farmers in northern Mexico started harvesting with combines, dramatically reducing their demand for sisal twine. Thus, the henequen-wheat complex's triangle is complete: labor from Sonora, which aided in the production of fiber in Yucatán; exports of henequen from Yucatán that were manufactured into binder twine in the United States and Canada and eventually made it back to Sonora in the form of binders and twine made of Yucatecan fiber; and exports of Sonoran produce to the United States and Canada. In describing the role of the *porfiriato* in this scenario, Evelyn Hu-deHart suggested that "it was surely no coincidence that the Díaz government effected this happy marriage between Sonora and Yucatán."[94] Actually, it was more of a ménage à trois comprising Sonora, Yucatan, and the U.S./Canadian unit. It was a clear case of protoglobalization based on a North American dependency model that predated NAFTA by a hundred years.

The problem with this triangular or global view is larger than just economic rationalizations for modernized agriculture and export commodities. The Yaqui part of the henequen-wheat complex (including deportation, enslavement, and complete transformation of their lands) was never mentioned or even alluded to in any binder twine promotional literature. In fact, denial ran deep. In his sympathetic history of International Harvester, *Romance of the Reaper*, Herbert Casson even wrote that "the harvester is the best barometer of civilization. It cannot go where slavery and barbarism exist."[95] Yet the slavery part of the story needs to be told; it needs to be understood in a broader globalized context, not just as a gruesome byproduct of Mexican modernization efforts during the *porfiriato*, notwithstanding how contradictory the Mexican policy was in showcasing modernized agroindustry while at the same time relying on the most colonial of labor systems.[96] That International Harvester and other cordage manufacturers, implement dealers, farmers, and eventually consumers of grain products throughout North America benefited from the reduced price of binder twine fiber afforded by indentured Mayan, Chinese, and other imported workers and by Yaqui slave labor is not only an important component of this story but is also symbolic of oppressive labor regimes, past and present, wherever corporate exploitation occurs.

Others have argued, however, that the henequen industry was hardly dependent on the imported Yaquis—that "only" eight thousand to sixteen thousand Indians were deported from Sonora and that all imported workers represented only about 10 percent of the work force during the henequen boom.[97] Numerically, no doubt that is correct. But some plantations had one hundred or more Yaquis workers and depended on their labor. More important is not what Yaquis represented for henequen, but what henequen represented for Yaquis—how they too were bound in twine. That fact has been overlooked and has resurfaced only recently through the voices in Raquel Padilla Ramos's *Yucatán, el fin del sueño yaqui* and Montserrat Fontes's novel about the Yaqui deportation, *Dreams of the Centaur*.

Turner's articles (and eventually his book *Barbarous Mexico*) worked to bring attention to the matter, and his writings did cause some people in the United States to rethink their once bright opinion of Porfirio Díaz and his methods of modernizing Mexico by bringing order and progress. In his introduction to a 1966 edition of Turner's book, Sinclair Snow compared the impact of *Barbarous Mexico* with *Uncle Tom's Cabin*, by Harriet Beecher Stowe: "Both books caused untold numbers of complacent Americans to take a new look at their immediate neighbors and to revise their opinions of their leaders and their social and economic institutions."[98] But did Turner's book actually do that? Where was that revision of opinion directed? Snow never mentions binder twine, dependent farmers, International Harvester, the cordage industry in general, or cheap bread for that matter—all of which required the use of indentured servants and slave labor in Yucatán. Turner's writings did not generate the great manifestations, sympathy strikes, boycotts, petitions, or mass protests against Yaqui slavery that developed in response to other contemporaneous muckraking issues and progressive causes such as child labor, the meatpacking industry, and workers' rights in North America. Perhaps that meant it was not publicized enough, that readership was limited to a progressive elite or socialist audience who read such literature. But news of Indian mistreatment in Mexico was widespread in newspapers and magazines across the United States.[99] Are there effective protests or consumer habit changes today in response to sweat-shop labor conditions in Third World countries that produce less expensive products for North American consumers?

Turner's work in the long run did not cause much change; very few Americans, and Canadians for that matter, in the first decade of the twentieth century worried or cared about the plight of native peoples in their own countries, let alone in any other. In fact, at about the same time period that Turner was releasing his accusatory articles on Yaqui slavery, another American reporter who had traveled in Mexico, Marc Reynolds, published an equally scathing article in *Harper's Weekly* in 1908 entitled "The Scourge of the Yaquis." With the telling subtitle, "Why American Lives and Capital Are Menaced by a Handful of Savages," Reynolds described Sonora as being completely ravaged by these "Simon-pure Indians, with no mixed blood." "Not only is the situation serious for the Mexican people," he concluded, "but it is very serious for American capital invested in Sonora." He illustrated the article with a variety of pictures of hanged Yaquis swinging by their necks from trees, with such captions as "the kind of Yaqui preferred by the terrorized citizens of Sonora."[100] Reynolds's readership in *Harper's Weekly* was probably greater than that of Turner's in the *American Magazine,* or especially in the *Appeal to Reason.*

Thus, farmers loading their binder's twine-can and shoppers buying bread and other grain products assuredly did not think about, or know about, the labor conditions that helped make it possible for them to purchase those items at relatively low prices. Nor did they think of their role in the entire complex. Turner never asked them to; his aim was for Americans to revise their understanding of a barbarous Mexico. And as important as his work was to expose the evils of the *porfiriato* and perhaps the U.S. government's relations with it, it effected no consumer or policy shifts, the way the writings of Nelly Bly brought change to mental health care in the United States. In fact, he offered no suggestions at all for what readers should have done after having become more enlightened.

Government officials in the United States, however, were already aware of the plight of the Yaquis. As we have seen, a paper trail outlining the tragedy of Yaqui genocide and removal began at the U.S. consulate in Hermosillo. It predated Turner's exposé, but like the journalist's work it did not cause any changes with regard to U.S. foreign policy. Naturally, there was no basis for it to accomplish such changes, given the U.S. government's similarly disastrous federal Indian policy, removal mandates, and wars against American Indians throughout the nineteenth century and assimilationist policies in the twentieth.

What the inaction means, not surprisingly, is that the highest priority of U.S. and Canadian twine manufacturers, farmers, and consumers was the lowest possible prices. That interpretation is supported by the fact that outrage *did* occur across several sectors of the manufacturing and agricultural industries during the "Sisal Situation" of 1915 and again after the Mexican Revolution when a Yucatán state regulating commission raised fiber prices significantly on the international market, as we shall see in the next chapter. The price increases reflected greater henequen labor costs and were designed to provide a greater and more evenly distributed income, as well as benefits such as education, for Yucatecans—economic policies missing in pre-revolution Yucatán. With the price increase, there *was* considerable outrage, and it found its way to the State Department. With that outrage came demands that the United States take action, with some business leaders and farmers even calling for a U.S. military occupation of Yucatán to reduce the price of sisal.[101]

That the racism and violence inherent in Yaqui deportation, and the North American apathy toward it, continued after the Mexican Revolution that deposed Díaz suggests that the lures of economic modernization remained stronger than the goals of justice and land reform, which to this day have not materialized for the Yaqui people. None of this inertia is surprising, of course, but it needs to be kept in mind if one is to understand this period of Mexican history, the major role played by corporate interests in the United States and Canada, the power of the heavy market demand for twine, and the interconnected dependencies that arose in an unregulated, free-trade, international economy.

CHAPTER 4

Twine Diplomacy

Yucatán, the United States, and Canada during the "Sisal Situation" of 1915

The situation is so serious as to menace the
entire grain-growing sections.

—*Secretary of State William Jennings Bryan, 1915*

T HE year 1915 proved to be a landmark one for the henequen-wheat complex. It was the year that the Mexican Revolution hit Yucatán—a fact that
the Woodrow Wilson administration in the United States and the Robert
Laird Borden government in Canada had to confront when the revolution
threatened the supply of sisal fiber for binding that year's harvests of wheat.
But it was to be no regular harvest throughout the Great Plains and Prairie
Provinces; it was a bumper crop year, the best since records had been kept and
until the 1950s. Thus, the results of this set of circumstances deserve a separate chapter, showing as they do the degree to which the United States and
Canada had become dependent on henequen.

Mexico's revolution had begun five years earlier in 1910, when Francisco
Madero of Coahuila, in northern Mexico, rallied troops to oppose the rigged
reelection of Porfirio Díaz, who had ruled Mexico since 1876. Madero's principal interest for Mexico was political reform—in the form of ousting Díaz
and formulating a new constitution based on a more democratic change of
president every six years. Other revolutionaries elsewhere in Mexico called
for more significant changes. Emiliano Zapata of Morelos and his followers fought for land reform—for the right to farm their own communal fields
without intervention by private or foreign investors. Political and economic
independence, especially from the United States, was a rallying cry of Pancho

Villa in Chihuahua, as were economic growth and political reform the political banner of Álvaro Obregón in Sonora. Madero and his troops were triumphant in the early stages of the revolution. Díaz fled to Paris, and Madero became provisional president while the regional factions continued fighting for their various causes. When forces loyal to Díaz, led by Victoriano Huerta, assassinated Madero, a counterrevolution and civil war ensued across Mexico. Venustiano Carranza, close friend of Madero and also a leader from Coahuila, then became *primer jefe* (first chief) of the revolution and led the Constitutionalist forces. Carranza and the Constitutionalists were victorious over Huerta by June 1914, and then Huerta also fled the country.

Carranza recognized the value of Yucatán's henequen industry; it would help fund his revolutionary ideals. He recognized that by 1915 nearly 90 percent of the binder twine used in the United States, about 200 million pounds annually, was made from Yucatecan fiber—a trade that had made Yucatán arguably Mexico's wealthiest state.[1] The state and its rich henequen fields had been spared of revolutionary warfare due to the control the powerful *henequeneros* wielded over potentially rebellious workers. Thus, as one scholar put it, "While the rest of the Republic made war, Yucatán made money."[2]

After the fall of Huerta, whom many wealthy *henequeneros* had supported, Carranza appointed Major Eleuterio Ávila as military governor of Yucatán to oversee the revolution's goals there. Ávila, a Yucatecan, issued a proclamation outlawing slave labor on the plantations, but the *hacendados* and agents of International Harvester made sure the ruling was never really enforced. The henequen oligarchs learned that they could manipulate Ávila, and they returned to their pre-revolution power structure.[3] Soon many of the *henequeneros* were backing another leader in Yucatán, the former Huertista colonel Abel Ortiz Argumedo, whom Ávila had appointed commander of Mérida and who now assumed leadership of the rebel, or antirevolutionary, forces in Yucatán.

To counter such a move, and to ensure that the Constitutionalists received the henequen taxes, Carranza replaced Ávila with the non-Yucatecan Toribio de los Santos as state governor. De los Santos reinstituted the proclamation against forced labor and promised to carry the goals of the revolution to Yucatán. He also made himself the head of the Henequen Market Regulating Commission (Comisión Reguladora del Mercado del Henequén, or CRMH). Early in his term, however, the rebel *henequeneros* aligned with Ortiz Argumedo, who had formed a military force against de los Santos and had started negotiating fiber sales to the United States, even seeking a sort of U.S. protectorate. In February 1915 Carranza had advised de los Santos that "sufficient forces" were on their way "to combat the rebels" and that "reinforcements" were ready to leave for Mérida.[4] IH, via its contacts with the fiber trading firm of Avelino Montes, kept in close touch with these events as they were unfolding in Yucatán. The company attempted to purchase as much henequen as possible, and move to safety the funds with which to buy the henequen, before the revolution interrupted any of its contracts to supply fiber to its clients and to its own twine mills.[5]

Carranza assigned General Salvador Alvarado to the Yucatán Peninsula to lead the forces known as the Army of the Southeast, which would break the stronghold of the *hacendados* under Ortiz Argumedo. "That's why I've sent you to Yucatán," Carranza wrote Alvarado, "not only to command the Army of the Southeast, but also to receive the government of the state. . . . I cannot accept from the Yucatecan rebels anything but for them to submit unconditionally to this *primera jefatura.*"[6] Alvarado, who was originally from Sinaloa but had grown up in the Yaqui Valley of Sonora, envisioned truly revolutionary economic change, including the breakup of the henequen plantations and a redistribution of benefits for Yucatecans as a result of increased fiber prices demanded by the new socialist, government-run henequen industry.[7]

Many people in Yucatán were glad to see Alvarado's troops march into their state in early 1915, and they communicated their avid support of Carranza's Constitutionalists. A group from Mérida wrote Carranza, inviting him to Yucatán to bring to the state his ideals, which represented "the ideals of the people here." Another supporter assured Carranza that the "Yucatecan heart and soul beats for the Revolution . . . to give freedom to the people." And people in Progreso and Mérida who supported land re-division, divorce laws, and the idea of freedom greeted Carranza's decrees on those matters "in huge crowds and [with] ovations."[8]

But an even larger faction of *henequeneros* and their forces was growing under Ortiz Argumedo. They had ousted Governor de los Santos and other Carrancistas by mid-February. The *New York Times* reported that some growers had asked for U.S. aid "in saving their crop, so much needed for the wheat harvest here. . . . The people of Yucatán did not wish to take part in the revolution."[9] Carranza knew he had to get control of those rebels and the 1.5 million pesos cash that was in the CRMH that they controlled to help fund his Constitutionalists forces.[10]

Thus, Carranza's plan was for Alvarado's troops to advance steadily from the south in Campeche and work toward Mérida to secure the henequen industry and eventually all of Yucatán. Alvarado worried about having enough reinforcement troops ready to meet him, since the "enemy forces are veterans and really know the land." But Carranza promised that he would send fifteen hundred men with artillery by boat to Progreso "to incorporate themselves" into his unit.[11]

Progreso, Yucatán's port, then became the focal point of Carranza and Alvarado's strategy. It would be through that port that Ortiz Argumedo's rebels in Yucatán would receive arms and supplies from U.S. arms makers, a point not lost on the Constitutionalists. By February 13 Alvarado had notified Carranza that the steamship *Honduras* was set to leave Galveston, Texas, with supplies for the rebels in Yucatán. "We must work to avoid the ship's arrival with whatever means are possible," he urged in a message to Carranza. He later wrote that the coasts should be secured to ensure that the *Honduras* and other ships not be allowed through: "Let me make known to you just how indispensable it is that a gunboat be sent to the Yucatecan coast."[12]

Carranza agreed. He responded on February 14, saying that Alvarado should "be ready for battle." The next day he ordered the gunboat *Tamaulipas* to sail from Veracruz to Progreso "to make effective the closing of the port." He mentioned how the ship had "precise orders to avoid any conflict with foreigners, limiting itself to notifying them that the port was closed and to avoid any communication with the 'traitors' [rebels]) and any boats" that came to supply them. He hoped the *Honduras* could be detained in Havana.[13] Meanwhile, Carranza received word two days later that another ship had left Galveston bearing arms and money for the Yucatecan rebels. Alvarado sent word back that he had found out that "the true cause of the Yucatecan movement was resistance of key privileged [landowners] to stop the Revolution from planting its reforms [in Yucatán]."[14]

By early March, Carranza had ordered the gunboats *Zaragoza*, *Melchor Ocampo*, and *Bravo* to Progreso as part of a naval blockade of the port. Using encoded messages, both Carranza and Alvarado kept in close touch with the commander of the *Zaragoza* to enforce the blockade.[15] From Carranza and Alvarado's viewpoint, sealing the coast by ordering a naval blockade of Progreso was the logical way to prevent Ortiz Argumedo and the Yucatecan rebels from getting arms and other supplies that could be used against the revolutionaries. And it apparently was working by mid-March when Carranza learned that the U.S. ship *Honduras* headed to Yucatán was docked at Key West, Florida, and that the *Phanfilder* had slowed its path from New York to Yucatán. "It's indispensable that the vigilance over the port be effective," he reminded Alvarado in mid-March, "as all of the supplies headed for us could be diverted to the rebels."[16] And indeed there were many messages sent from the Pearce Forwarding Company of Galveston and from Andrés García of El Paso saying how their orders for rifles, cartridges, ammunition, saddles, uniforms, and other military supplies for Carranza's army were all being held up so that Ortiz Argumedo's forces would not be able to commandeer them.

The blockade was also good for CRMH. Because Ortiz Argumedo and his militia had jeopardized the supply of fiber, the blockade successfully stopped any illegal deals between the rebel *henequeneros* and IH or other entities in the United States. Eduardo Robleda, a fiber dealer out of Havana, Cuba, who

had worked for Avelino Montes, testified later that the blockade had effectively thwarted the deals that Ortiz Argumedo had tried to make during his
takeover of the Yucatecan government. "Consequently, I was not worried by
[his] threats," Robleda said, and the fiber supplies were saved for the CRMH,
which distributed the henequen income more equitably.[17]

But the blockade also meant that commodities on contract and ready to
be exported from Progreso would be tied up. The first complaint came from
the Royal Bank of Belgium, surprisingly enough, which was financing a shipment of chicle from Quintana Roo (east of Yucatán) for the American Chicle
Company chewing gum manufacturer. The chicle shipment was held up in the
port of Progreso, and the Belgians demanded "release" of the "illegally taken"
chicle.[18] Carranza resolved the issue for the Belgian and American chewing
gum interests later that month.

A financially more important commodity that Carranza's blockade halted
was fiber. Industry officials claimed that 200,000 bales of already contracted
henequen and sisal fiber, 119,000 of which belonged to International Harvester, were detained during the blockade.[19] Cordage manufacturers, implement dealers, and farmers viewed the stoppage as an imminent disaster at
a time when farmers in the United States and Canada had significantly increased their planting of grain. The problem lay in the fact that fiber supplies
had been depleted with the excellent 1914 harvest, and the demand for twine
was soaring to meet increased grain production for World War I. With increased planting of grain and excellent weather conditions, North American
farmers expected a record-setting year for wheat. Kansas newspapers had
been reporting such conditions around the time of the blockade. Headlines in
the *Topeka Daily Capital* in February announced "1915 Wheat Crop Is Good"
and "Wheat Crop Prospects Better Than in 1914." The articles discussed how
the winter wheat was in "first-class shape," how the crop was "tip-top," and
how there had already been "plenty of moisture," thus giving the "promise of
another bumper year." Conditions for wheat, especially in the central part of
the state, the newspaper predicted, "were never better." Newspaper reports out
of Manitoba were similar. One announced that increased wheat production
for the war effort in 1915 would yield harvests exceeding those of the previous
five years by 35 million quintals (with one quintal equaling 100 kilograms, or
about 220 pounds).[20] Thus, when the *New York Times* reported that Carranza's
blockade of Progreso threatened a shortage of binder twine for that "summer's
bumper cereal crops," it was illustrating no small matter.[21]

The *Times*, issuing front-page coverage of the blockade and the reactions to
it, referred to the incident as the sisal situation, as did other media, the cordage
industry, and the U.S. State Department. Carranza's reasons for the blockade, however, were somewhat misrepresented by the State Department, never

made clear in the North American press, and never fully explained by historians in the years since. Shortly after the blockade began, for example, a Kansas newspaper reported that the State Department had declared that the embargo was due "to differences between Carranza factions at the port"—an impossibility since the Carrancistas in Yucatán were not divided among themselves. Later, the *New York Times* in a front-page story announced that the port had been "closed to all commerce" by Carranza, thus interrupting "the exportation of henequen from Yucatán to the United States . . . to punish the Yucatecans who . . . [had] expulsed the Constitutionalists from the peninsula."[22] Nowhere in the State Department records, or in the media at the time, was there any explanation as to how Carranza and Alvarado had managed to stop U.S. arms from reaching anti-revolution Yucatecan rebels or how it had prevented illegal henequen deals between Ortiz Argumedo and cordage companies. Likewise, most historians who have studied U.S. foreign policy in Mexico during this time period do not mention the blockade or U.S. reaction to it. Two who did were Gilbert Joseph and Arthur Link. Joseph provided considerable coverage of the "Sisal Situation" in *Revolution from Without,* his authoritative work on Yucatán during the Mexican Revolution, but did not go into any detail about the reasons for the blockade. Link incorrectly assessed the reason by writing that "Carranza closed the port . . . to prevent the export of a large quantity of sisal hemp that American manufacturers of binder twine for reapers desperately needed, in order, it seemed, merely to spite the United States."[23]

Journalists during this period did work to inform interested parties about the sisal situation and also encouraged them to seek redress. Newspapers in the American and Canadian plains and farm and implement trade journals kept readers alert to the issue and how it could potentially affect them. In March the *Topeka Daily Capital* told Kansas readers that the State Department had made the embargo of sisal fiber known to American manufacturers and that the blockade had already caused "an immediate suspension" of work at Peoria Cordage in Illinois. In North Dakota, the *Grand Forks Weekly Times-Herald* ran both news articles and editorials about the blockaded fiber. It kept readers updated on how negotiations were progressing but also called on the government to take additional action. One editorial suggested, "The time may come when it is necessary for this country to take forcible steps to bring some order out of Mexico."[24]

Interestingly, as far as henequen operations were concerned, there was less disorder than might have been expected. A fiber-exporting agent who was connected with Avelino Montes and H. W. Peabody reported later that he was in Mérida when the blockade was first imposed but that "everything was peaceful and order was being kept." He and other agents continued working to keep fiber orders moving but had to deal more closely with the CRMH. What made things tricky for IH and other fiber importers was dealing with governments as they changed quickly during the revolution. One IH representative reminisced some years later that issuing peso notes for fiber purchases was no easy matter "at a time when it was extremely difficult to ascertain what government in power was a de facto or de jure government."[25] Yet, for others in the business the revolution represented an opportunity to save money. A fiber dealer who worked to supply the Kansas State Penitentiary twine plant suggested that henequen prices in early 1915 were lower due to "the unsettled conditions in Mexico," where in "times of greatest unrest . . . Mexican money is always cheapest." "We pay for all sisal in the money of the republic," he explained, "and when they are in greatest turmoil, Uncle Sam's dollar will purchase more Mexican dobies [pesos]. They need ready cash and will sell for less."[26]

Still, the blockading of Progreso caused immediate reaction in the cordage industry and among implement manufacturers, penitentiary twine factory officials, and farmers throughout the Great Plains. The first official complaint came from the Plymouth Cordage Company and was directed to Venustiano Carranza via the Mexican embassy in Washington, D.C. On March 6 Mexican ambassador Juan Amador wired Carranza that Plymouth Cordage had contacted his office, explaining that it desired only to send a boat to fetch the sisal fiber that was ready to be exported and "guaranteed with satisfaction to this government" that it would not abuse any other travel or export restrictions (referring to shipments of arms). Carranza, however, remained unmoved. The next day he responded to Amador tersely, stating that it was "not possible to permit importations nor exportations . . . from that state." To a fiber representative in New York he had written that the blockade was indeed "constitutional" and that "soon the question for that state would be resolved."[27]

The messages were hardly enough to allay the fears of industry and farm representatives. Now, fearing trouble for their business abroad, they contacted the U.S. State Department, headed by William Jennings Bryan during the first Woodrow Wilson administration (1913–1917). Bryan's and Wilson's reactions to the sisal situation are historically significant, and thus some background on their working relationship and how they formulated U.S. foreign policy toward Mexico is instructive.

William Jennings Bryan was a player on the American political and cultural stage from 1890, when he was a thirty-year-old Democratic congressman from Nebraska, until his death in 1925. Known for his championing of specific causes, such as the free coinage of silver against the gold standard (made famous by his "Cross of Gold" speech at the 1896 Democratic National Convention), corporate trust busting, women's suffrage, world peace, Protestant fundamentalism, opposition to the teaching of evolution, Prohibition (he served only grape juice at State Department functions and dinners), tighter government regulation of corporations, and terminating government subsidies for private industry, he was also well known as a remarkable orator, delivering speeches frequently at Chautauqua gatherings, churches, and political events. His work on so many fronts earned him such nicknames as the "Boy Orator of the Platte," "Great Commoner," "Peerless Leader," "Champion of Democracy," "Defender of the Faith," "Prince of Peace," and even the "Fundamentalist Pope." With such rhetorical ability and name recognition, Bryan became the Democratic Party nominee for president three times (at age thirty-six in 1896, again in 1900 [both times against William McKinley], and in 1908 against William Howard Taft).[28] In 1912, however, he turned down offers to run again, and, instead, at the Democratic convention he supported Woodrow Wilson over Champ Clark of Missouri for the nomination. Bryan's support clinched the nomination for Wilson on the forty-sixth ballot. Bryan then wholeheartedly supported Wilson's campaign, often speaking on his behalf. When he was elected, Wilson knew for political reasons that he had to reward Bryan with a sort of consolation prize, and he offered him the State Department. Bryan eagerly accepted, but he soon discovered, as Edward Kaplan has written, that "the president would be his own secretary of state." Wilson biographer Arthur Link explained this tendency as the president's "extreme individualism in conducting foreign affairs," describing how his philosophy was that "the President should lead and the Congress should follow." His "egotism[,] . . . his conviction that he was an instrument of divine purpose[,] . . . his sense of destiny[,] . . . his awareness of his own intellectual superiority[,] . . . and, above all else, his urge to dominate" allowed him to take "wide latitude" in conducting foreign policy. With Mexico, Wilson often "bypassed the State Department by using his own private agents, ignored his secretaries of state by conducting important negotiations behind their backs, and acted like a divine monarch in the general conduct of affairs."[29] He allowed Bryan to have more say on issues in Nicaragua, Haiti, and the Dominican Republic, but, while often soliciting Bryan's advice, he preferred to handle Mexico more personally.[30]

Thus, Secretary of State Bryan, hailing from grain-rich Nebraska (Figure 4.1), and President Wilson received letters and telegrams urging the United States to take action against the naval blockade of Progreso that was stopping the flow of the fiber needed to make binder twine. It is interesting to note here that for many years Bryan had been known as a "crusader against trusts" but soon would be developing policies that would benefit International Harvester. Earlier in his career, Bryan had lambasted IH for exploiting workers, being a monopoly, and unfairly benefiting from government subsidies. Cyrus McCormick so despised Bryan and these forms of "Bryanism" that he deserted the Democratic Party in 1896 and declared that if Bryan were president, the McCormick Harvesting Company (not yet merged into IH at

Figure 4.1. William Jennings Bryan on his farm in Nebraska, inspecting a shock of wheat. Courtesy Nebraska State Historical Society (RG3198-PH-52).

that time) would have to close down. The situation became even stickier when Wilson was elected president in 1912. McCormick and Wilson were personal friends; McCormick had even contributed $12,500 to Wilson's campaign. He offered more funds, but upon Bryan's advice Wilson rejected the offer. However, Wilson did accept corporate campaign donations from IH that amounted to $53,500. Two members of the IH board of directors, brothers Thomas and David Jones, were also Wilson's close friends and served as Princeton University trustees. Thus, while Wilson criticized other trusts and monopolies in his campaign speeches, he never mentioned IH.[31] As president, his policies toward Mexico benefited the corporation in many ways.

Furthermore, Bryan, as a U.S. congressman (1890–1894), had opposed subsidies of twine, a brave move for a representative from a grain-producing state.[32] As secretary of state, however, he was forced to contend with a strong cordage lobby during the sisal situation. Representatives of U.S. cordage companies traveled to Washington to urge the Wilson administration "to take steps against the actions of Mexican authorities who . . . placed an embargo on the shipment of sisal hemp," especially since the fiber at the port was already under contract to be shipped. An official of the Michigan State Penitentiary (which ran a twine mill) accompanied the delegation, who, according to a Plymouth Cordage representative, got "more attention from Secretary Bryan than anybody" because Bryan favored the state-run twine plants over corporate ones such as IH. Gov. Arthur Capper of Kansas, a Republican who had made the state's agriculture one of his chief concerns, especially with regard to the war effort, cabled Bryan, saying, "I am informed that blockade of Port of Progreso Yucatán makes it impossible for the State of Kansas to secure sisal for its prison plant. I earnestly hope that every endeavor will be made to raise the blockade so that we can secure this necessary supply of sisal for Kansas grain producers."[33]

The lobbying pressure forced the Wilson administration to deal with the sisal situation. First, Secretary Bryan issued pleas to Carranza in Veracruz, the provisional "capital" of Mexico where Carranza had set up his *primera jefatura,* to open Progreso on behalf of the cordage and farming interests. Bryan's agent or special envoy in Veracruz was John R. Silliman, who received the State Department messages and passed them along to Carranza. The State Department also worked to respond to the interested parties and keep them alerted to any progress in Progreso. For example, Bryan responded to Governor Capper's letter, saying that "Dept has made earnest requests of Caranza [*sic*] to re-open port progresso [*sic*] and permit exportation of sisal hemp, but requests have met definite refusal and caranza [*sic*] states that he will not permit such exportation at present and that the port will remain closed as a means of subjugating district."[34]

It was that kind of "futile parleying," as Arthur Link described it, that frustrated President Wilson.[35] He was clearly ill equipped to deal with Mexico's revolution and civil war, as some of his earlier policy blunders had already testified to. When Victoriano Huerta took control of the government in 1914, Wilson felt compelled not only to avoid recognizing his government but also to intervene by assisting with his ouster. In doing so he relied not on informed Latin Americanists at the State Department nor on the American chargé d'affaires in Mexico City but rather on his own special agents. He commissioned a journalist and the former governor of Minnesota, whom Arthur Link described as having "neither experience in diplomacy nor any knowledge about Mexico," to try to negotiate a solution to Huerta's illegal takeover.[36] In an attempt to force Huerta out of power, in April 1914 Wilson ordered the U.S. Marines to occupy Tampico and Veracruz. These cities were Mexico's important ports on the Gulf of Mexico and situated in the oil-producing district, in which there were significant U.S. commercial interests. But the landing of the marines in Tampico led to an ugly incident over the American flag, intensifying already hostile anti-American feelings in Mexico. Worse, when Wilson ordered U.S. forces to seize Veracruz, four thousand marines landed at the port but were met with stiff opposition by Mexican forces. During the ensuing fight, nineteen Americans died and seventy-one were wounded, facts that shocked President Wilson, who had ignorantly expected no opposition. Even the Carrancistas, whom Wilson was supporting against the Huertistas, were opposed to an American military presence in Mexico. Finding himself on the verge of what could have been a prolonged war, Wilson accepted an Argentine-Brazilian-Chilean proposal for mediation and backed off. By July, Carranza's forces had gotten the upper hand over the Huertistas, Huerta had fled Mexico into exile, and Carranza had become the "first chief," although Wilson did not officially recognize his government.

Critics began to call Wilson's policies toward Mexico "watchful waiting," complete with the "Wilson Tango" that involved "one step forward, two steps backward, side-step, hesitate." The "tango" was particularly apparent in the way Wilson would deal with the binder twine interests during Huerta's interval as president of Mexico. International Harvester, for example, continued purchasing large quantities of fiber during those months, even though many of the profits were going to support Huerta and his illegal government. Alarmed, Secretary of State Bryan wrote the president, asking, "Do you know anything we can do?" Wilson replied, "I'm concerned . . . but do not see anything we could do in [these] circumstances."[37]

In early 1915, Wilson had to confront new problems with Mexico. With Mexico in the throes of its civil war there came word that the lives and properties of the twenty-five hundred Americans and twenty-three thousand other foreigners (many of whom were European) living in Mexico City were being threatened by crossfire from the incoming forces of Venustiano Carranza and Álvaro Obregón versus those of Emiliano Zapata and Francisco "Pancho" Villa. Wilson demanded a guarantee for their safety, and not being satisfied with any of the responses, on March 6 he issued a stiff ultimatum via John Silliman, saying that the U.S. government would hold them personally responsible for any harm or suffering inflicted upon the American colony there. The message did not specify what kind of action the U.S. government would take, but the implication was that an expeditionary force would be sent to Mexico City to rescue the foreigners and that worse retaliatory measures could follow. Along with sending the memo, Wilson ordered the U.S. Navy to dispatch an additional battleship and a cruiser to Veracruz, where the navy already had a force stationed just offshore. Refusing to go through Secretary Bryan, Carranza replied directly to Wilson, denying that foreigners were ever endangered in Mexico City but promising them all possible protection. The issue more or less defused itself when shortly thereafter both Obregón's and Carranza's forces left Mexico City, having accomplished their goal of taking the capital for the Constitutionalist cause.[38]

Thus was the diplomatic backdrop and the mood at the time of the sisal situation. Annoyed with all aspects of the matter and frustrated at Carranza's unwillingness to honor Yucatán's contractual obligations for henequen shipments, Wilson discussed the matter with his Cabinet on March 12. Secretary of Agriculture David Houston advised the president that 200 million pounds of twine were used annually in the United States to bind grain crops and nine-tenths of that twine was made from Yucatecan fiber exported from Progreso.[39] Wilson then wrote Secretary Bryan about his decision to send Carranza a second ultimatum: "I think we are justified in all the circumstances in saying to Carranza that we cannot recognize his right to blockade the port to the exclusion of our commerce; that we are just to beg him to recall his orders to that effect; and that we shall feel constrained, in case he feels he cannot do so, to instruct our naval officers to prevent any interference with our commerce to and from the port. . . . [W]e are doing this in the interest of peace and amity between the two countries and with no wish or intention to interfere with her internal affairs, from which we shall carefully keep our hands off. I hope that your thinking has led you to a similar conclusion."[40] It had. Bryan responded the next day, telling Wilson, "I feel as reluctant as you do . . . but I believe it as real a kindness to Carranza as it was to Huerta. . . . While Carranza may take offense to it, chances are he will not, and we can assure Villa and Zapata of our purposes, and in case we came in conflict with Carranza we are in a position to restrain the employment of force within the smallest possible limit, just as we did in Veracruz. At Progreso there would be no reason for landing a force or taking charge of the port."[41] Bryan then relayed Wilson's note to Silliman for the latter to deliver to Carranza. Wilson notified Secretary of the Navy Josephus Daniels of the decision, and Daniels ordered the armed cruiser *Des Moines*, stationed off of Veracruz, to move to Progreso to back up the ultimatum.[42]

In some ways, Wilson and Bryan's decision was predictable based on their previous approaches to and actions in Mexico. But in other ways, they are surprising based on their earlier writings and avowed philosophies. Wilson had emphatically been opposed to the "dollar diplomacy" of his predecessors, Theodore Roosevelt and William Howard Taft, and had emphasized that opposition throughout his campaign for president. He had made known his ideology toward Latin America early in his tenure as president. At a cabinet meeting in March 1913, he proclaimed, "The United States has nothing to seek in Central and South America except the lasting interests of the peoples of the two continents, the security of governments intended for the people and for no special interest group or interest, and the development of personal and trade relationships . . . [that] shall redound to the profit and advantage of both and interfere with the rights and liberties of either."[43]

Later that autumn, Wilson addressed the Southern Commercial Congress in Mobile, Alabama, and further outlined his philosophy toward Latin America. He told the delegates that he hoped the United States would draw closer to Latin America with "common understanding," not through "interest" which "does not tie nations together." He explained that he would free Latin America from unfair investment and subordination from foreign capitalists, and he criticized past gunboat policies to collect debts with high interests, as Taft had ordered in the Dominican Republic.[44]

Bryan had been even more overtly opposed to dollar diplomacy. His biographers have shown clearly how the Great Commoner stood against American interventionism, especially for the sake of U.S. business, with one explaining that when Bryan became secretary of state, "it appeared that 'dollar diplomacy' would finally be eradicated." Earlier, Bryan editorialized against it in his periodical *The Commoner* and stated in a speech in 1910, "Gunboats should not be used to protect American investment." And in his first year as secretary of state, he made clear to Wilson that the United States should respect the rights of Latin American republics "to attend to their own business, free from external coercion. . . . We must be relieved of suspicion of our motives."[45]

Another biographer, Kendrick Clements, provides clues on how Bryan's philosophy could possibly have meshed with his decisions, or support of Wilson's decisions, on the sisal situation. Clements explained that "the central goal, as Bryan saw it, was to increase American political and economic influence without imperialism . . . [that] would reduce any risk of foreign intervention." But instead of continuing with the old ways of Taft, Bryan had hoped to achieve the objectives of American policy abroad "by winning the hearts and minds of the people." For those reasons Bryan had opposed the Platt Amendment regarding U.S. interests in Cuba, the Panama Canal Treaty (engineered by President McKinley), and the Roosevelt Corollary to the Monroe Doctrine (which explicitly stated that the United States had the right to intervene in the affairs of other Western Hemisphere nations). Thus, Clements defines Bryan as a "missionary isolationist" and a "cultural imperialist" who "was so sure that democracy and Christianity offered the routes to earthly perfection and eternal salvation that he could not imagine that other peoples would not embrace them eagerly if only they could be given the good news." His foreign policy therefore "embodied a curious paradox—a resistance to imperialism and intervention coupled with an eagerness to guide, instruct, preach, and otherwise meddle in the internal affairs of other nations."[46] Surprisingly, there is no record of a response from the *primer jefe* to either Wilson or Bryan on this matter; he had been in close touch with them on other issues. Nonetheless, Carranza ordered the port to be reopened on March 13, nearly one month after he imposed the blockade. Some accounts suggest that he lifted the blockade *before* he had received Wilson's ultimatum from Silliman.[47] In fact, on March 18 the media quoted Carranza's agent in Washington, Juan Amador, as saying that Carranza reopened the port on his own without any threat from the United States and "without any pressures of any kind." "The Mexicans are not seeking any international complications," Amador explained, since at the time they were "engaged in a great civil strife for the purpose of changing the social conditions of their country."[48] Carranza realized by this time that the Constitutionalist forces were winning the battles in Yucatán, thereby precluding the need to maintain the blockade to prevent Ortiz Argumedo's forces from acquiring supplies. Further proof of the argument is that on the same day he reopened the port Carranza sent word to his general in Quintana Roo that Salvador Alvarado's troops had "completely defeated" the rebel Yucatecans and that they had taken prisoners, even from among "members of the Mérida's aristocratic families."[49] Some of the Argumedistas fled to Cuba; Ortiz Argumedo himself sailed for New York with a good deal of the Yucatecan treasury. But Carranza's timely decision, either immediately before receiving Wilson's note in anticipation of U.S. resolve or indeed if it were made after, was assuredly based on the fact that he knew the last thing the Constitutionalists needed was a naval attack by the United States.

The North American media, however, unanimously perceived the blockade's removal as a win for Wilson and the cordage and grain interests. The *New York Times* reported in a front-page article that Wilson had "informed" Carranza "in emphatic terms" that unless the Mexican gunboat *Zaragoza* was recalled from Progreso that "the United States would . . . issue instructions to the commander of the armed cruiser *Des Moines* . . . to prevent any interference with American ships." Some foreigners in Yucatán, including Americans, in fear of what would happen when Carranza's troops arrived, sought sanctuary on the *Des Moines*. On March 17, the newspaper continued to alleviate concerns by reporting, "The Yucatán situation was further relieved" when the Mexican gunboat *Zaragoza*, of "Carranza's diminutive navy," sailed out to sea away from Progreso.[50]

Responses to the reopening of the port of Progreso were predictably joyous in the American and Canadian plains. In South Dakota, the *Sioux Falls Argus Leader*, the state's largest newspaper, ran a front-page article announcing the "relief of the situation" and how "a crisis" had been averted by "urgent representations of the United States." It related how cables "pour[ed] into the White House and State Department," stressing that "unless sisal were obtained through Progreso, the harvest of this year's crops would be embarrassed." The report concluded that the people of Yucatán, who obtained much of their food and supplies from outside sources, "were as anxious that the embargo be raised as the United States." The next day, the newspaper quoted Wilson as saying, "American representations and notes had been effective." A Kansas newspaper reported that U.S. warships had "received orders to protect commerce from unauthorized interference." The front-page story told how the *Des Moines* had been sent to prevent interference with commerce at Progreso and how the Wilson administration used the argument that "the right of a *de facto* government to close a port in its possession is not recognized" to pressure Carranza into ordering his gunboat *Zaragoza* away, thus clearing the way for "two ships laden with hemp" to leave Progreso. The next day the newspaper ran the headline "Raising Blockade Will Help Kansas," and the accompanying article mentioned how the news was "welcomed by farmers" since existing fiber supplies would have lasted only about another month, which could have closed the penitentiary twine plant. At that point, closing the twine plant "would have meant a great loss to the wheat growers of Kansas." The article concluded that it was due to the "insistent telegrams" from Kansas's members of Congress, Gov. Arthur Capper, members of the Board of Corrections, the warden of the penitentiary, and the many retail dealers and farmers' organizations that were all "influential in persuading the [Mexican] government to re-open the port." On the same day, another Kansas newspaper reported that Carranza's blockade was canceled and that the Mexican leader would "enforce all factions to respect freedom of trade." It went on to report, incorrectly, that Yucatán then sought to secede from Mexico to become a protectorate of the United States.[51] The article did not mention that only a minority renegade faction under Ortiz Argumedo had briefly talked of such a U.S. alliance.

Other coverage was more succinct. The *Kansas City Star* ran a more militarist-toned front-page article headlined "Carranza Needs a Threat." It suggested, "The United States had prepared to back up its demands with the cruiser *Des Moines*." In North Dakota, the *Fargo Forum* headlined that Carranza was "compelled" by the United States to lift the blockade, saying, "This government served notice on Carranza that the Port of Progresso [*sic*], through which practically all the Sisal used in making harvesting twine for this country is obtained, must be kept open." The *Daily Tribune* of Bismarck echoed this sentiment the next day with the front-page headline "Freedom of Commercial Communications Must Be Preserved Says Note." Relating to farmers' worries, the article showed how Wilson's action was aimed at "assuring the supply of sisal hemp needed for the American harvest." And finally, the *Grand Forks Weekly Times-Herald*'s headline story "Wilson Means Business in Mexican Muss" praised the president for being so determined that all factions in Mexico "be compelled to respect the lives and property of foreigners."[52]

Some Canadian newspapers (e.g., the *Toronto Globe*) followed the story too, but perhaps not as closely as their American counterparts. None of the major wheat belt newspapers in the Prairie Provinces carried many stories about the potential crisis, although the *Calgary Daily Herald* did mention that "the United States was determined to raise the blockade" and if necessary was prepared to use force to do so.[53] Instead, coincidentally enough, on the very day of Wilson's ultimatum to Carranza, the prairie newspapers covered the story of a new twine manufacturing plant planned for Calgary. The *Manitoba Free Press* reported that the Western Canada Cordage Company Ltd. would employ 375 workers, produce twenty-seven tons of binder twine a day, and cater to markets in Alberta and Saskatchewan. The plant was being built because of the more than four million dollars' worth of twine that was imported into western Canada from the United States in 1914—an amount that could be better spent at home. But just as important, to avoid the potential problems in the flow of sisal from revolutionary Mexico all of the raw material (manila) to be used in this new plant would come from the Philippines, New Zealand, the Hawaiian Islands, and the west coast of Mexico, which produced other kinds of fibers, albeit in far smaller quantities than the amounts of henequen grown in Yucatán. Also on the same day, the *Saskatoon Phoenix* reported that Saskatoon would be home to a new flax mill that a company out of Great Falls, Montana, was building. But as discussed earlier, flax ultimately failed to produce a good binder twine.

Perhaps some of the best analysis of the sisal situation was in the *Nebraska Farmer*. A March 24 article with the simple but poignant title "Entwined" spelled out the importance of henequen to American agriculture and the strong dependency on it that had resulted: had the blockade continued, American farmers "would have been strictly 'up against it.'" "It was urgent that the fiber keep coming in order that the factories might make it into twine in time for use this year. . . . This is another instance showing how closely the world is knit together commercially; even the efficient harvest of our crops may sometimes be dependent upon diplomacy."[54]

The sisal situation was far from over, however. Despite a reopened port, by mid-March there were rumors both false and illogical (since it was well known how badly Carranza needed the income from a robust harvest) about revolutionaries destroying the henequen fields or of the *hacendados* themselves destroying the fields to prevent the Carrancistas from capitalizing on them. The rumors fueled industry representatives' worries about the larger situation in Yucatán. Peabody officials in Boston sent a stern message to their field rep in Mérida, advising him that their customers were "absolutely relying upon us to keep their mills running and either we must continue to get sisal out of Yucatán in good-sized quantities, or these mills will have to shut down and the Western farmers will see their crops rot in the fields." With that in mind,

IH and Peabody encouraged their fiber buyers to protest directly to the State Department, and a huge quantity of messages arrived on Secretary Bryan's desk on March 19 and 20.[55] Peoria Cordage Company wired Bryan with the misinformed message that Carranza's army in Yucatán represented "a serious menace to the supply of sisal fibre and hence of binder twine" and indicating its hope that "all possible pressure will be brought to bear to keep that army of Yucatán [away] as the arrival will mean destruction of fibre and consequently shortages of twine supply." Similarly, the Hooven & Allison Company of Xenia, Ohio, telegrammed Bryan, urging that Carranza "be prevented from obtaining possession of sisal. [It is] feared [he] may burn it. In that event it will be absolutely impossible to supply [the] binder twine requirements of the American farmer." A representative of the John Rausehenberger Company of Milwaukee wrote that his company was informed that "sisal and sisal plantations" were "being destroyed" and urged the State Department "to take action to stop such destruction."[56]

Officials from state penitentiaries sent messages repeating the rumors. Warden J. D. Botkin of Kansas urged "action to stop destruction of sisal as failure to get it will cause enormous loss to our farmers." Warden E. J. Fogarty of Indiana wrote that he was "reliably informed" that "none of the commodity, so vitally important to the American farmer and American industrial institutions, is able to reach . . . the port." And Warden C. S. Reed of the Minnesota prison system indicated that Yucatecan sisal was of the "utmost importance" to Minnesota, "one of the largest wheat-producing states," since there had recently been a drought in the Philippines that reduced the amount of manila his prison could get for making binder twine. Whitlock Cordage of New York went one step further, requesting that the State Department intervene to "have the state of Yucatán declared neutral territory [during the Mexican Revolution] thus ensuring harvesting crops." A couple of days later Whitlock wrote Bryan, asking, "Cannot Washington do something to improve the desperate conditions of farmers and manufacturers, even to intervention?" Bryan responded that the State Department was continuing in "its efforts to relieve [the] sisal condition." Also advocating Yucatecan neutrality was Columbian Rope Company of Auburn, New York. It wired a dramatic message suggesting that because Carranza's army was destroying the plantations, "inflicting on the farmers . . . a loss impossible to compute," that the sisal industry needed U.S. protection to "safeguard the interests of manufacturers, the farmers of the country, and humanity at large."[57]

According to the messages sent to the State Department, the various cordage companies and twine manufacturers were getting their misinformation from newspapers and implement trade journals. A representative from the Hatfield and Palmer Company of Indiana cited as "common knowledge" the imminent destruction of the henequen fields by Carranza's forces and how that would be such a "serious situation for our farmers." Other companies made similar petitions to the State Department. Wall Rope Works of New York told Bryan that "to enable grain crops to be harvested the United States should take immediate action." A telegram from the New Bedford Cordage Company of New York was even more urgent: "We hope this government will take action so that the twine and cordage industry will not be crippled."[58]

Bryan worked to answer such concerns. He wired IH, Peoria Cordage Company, and twelve other henequen interests in the United States that this new aspect of the sisal situation was "receiving the Department's attention" and that "day-to-day instructions" were being sent to Yucatán. As proof, on March 20 Bryan cabled the U.S. consul in Progreso to explain the situation: "We are using our influence with Carranza for the protection of the industrial interests of Yucatán and we have a right to expect the people of Yucatán to consider the interests that Americans and other foreigners have in the sisal, both growing and baled." Second Assistant Secretary of State Alvey A. Adee responded to the Hatfield and Palmer Company that Carranza was no further danger to the flow of fiber to U.S. twine manufacturers.[59] The same day Bryan telegrammed special envoy Silliman, saying that he had been receiving all these reports of Carrancistas burning henequen fields in Yucatán, fields that would take six (actually, seven) years to restore before henequen leaves could be harvested for fiber. "It is impossible to believe Carranza would authorize or tolerate such action on the part of his followers," he wrote, adding that he should get the message to Carranza's followers not to take part in any henequen destruction. Silliman responded a few days later with the news that Carranza had been "sick in bed three days with lumbago" but that his representatives told him that there had been absolutely no threat to burn sisal plantations. Carranza had, however, been alerted to the rumors of such destruction. He was informed by Salvador Alvarado and his ambassador to Washington, Eliseo Arredondo, of stories in the press about henequen being threatened, but he maintained there was no basis to the rumors.[60]

Alvarado's message, however, provides clues to some possible origins of the rumors. He wrote Carranza to say that the Associated Press stories on the matter denied that the rumors were merely "false accusations by reactionaries"; they were more likely due to the "new direction of the railroads" that he and his troops had taken over. That new direction included detaining the railroad cars of Avelino Montes as part of Alvarado's overall plan to break the Montes-IH monopoly.[61] There was also news that the Carrancistas had destroyed the railroad station in Mérida. Thus, the cordage industry was becoming concerned about the railways, since they were the primary means of getting henequen to the port at Progeso. For example, a telegram from the Edwin Fitler Company of Philadelphia had mentioned how Carranza would not allow railroads in

Yucatán to bring the fiber to port. The message ended by asking Secretary Bryan, "Can you do anything to facilitate matters?"[62] Bryan announced soon thereafter that he had met with President Wilson on the matter and that he would work to his "fullest extent" to keep Yucatecan railways running and the bales of fiber moving from the various haciendas to the port. On the same day, March 18, word came that Wilson, bending to pressure about this perceived new threat to railroads, had ordered the U.S. Navy to commission another gunboat off the coast of Yucatán for a few days as a backup to the *Des Moines* for "protecting foreign interests." The U.S. Navy sent the collier *Brutus*. The measure was to create a "moral effect . . . on the authorities of Yucatán . . . until they have given definite assurances . . . that they will provide adequate railroad facilities for all American dealers without discrimination by favoring the *Comisión Reguladora* or anyone else."[63] Wilson's message, intoned with his typical moral superiority, seemed to have the desired effect. After consulting with Alvarado, Carranza complied with Wilson's request and made available the railroad cars to transport henequen for IH, Peabody, and other cordage companies.[64]

While the State Department continued to notify twine manufacturers of these developments, it turned its attention to the next order of business: the safe transfer of sisal at Progreso to the waiting customers. The *Washington Post* reported that the "chief obstacles in the way of moving [the] supply" of fiber was a scarcity of labor and shipping facilities at Progreso. IH officials had written Bryan that they viewed "with great concern" how these issues were jeopardizing their contract with Avelino Montes for securing their bales of fiber. Bryan had already authorized agents on board the *Des Moines* to use "large sums of money" if necessary to protect IH's contract. Also, he had already notified Silliman to "please urge General Carranza [of the] vital importance of this contract." But the henequen was secure; IH responded on March 25, one day after Silliman's reassurance, that it had received word from Yucatán that its contract would be honored and that its bales of fiber would soon be shipped to the United States.[65]

Equally important, the Wilson administration authorized using U.S. warships to deliver the money for the sisal in Yucatán and to return with the valuable fiber since commercial ships had not been allowed to dock there during the blockade. Representing sisal purchasers, Edward Heidrich of Peoria met with Secretary of the Navy Daniels to petition the government to use a warship to transport gold bullion to pay for the henequen shipment due to the difficulties that were occurring in Yucatán.[66] Daniels agreed, and on March 24 the collier *Jupiter* carried $625,000 in gold from vaults in Galveston, Texas, for advance payment to the henequen growers; the ship then delivered twenty thousand bales of fiber to New Orleans. Daniels's agreement to this

arrangement, representing a unique government subsidy of commercial enterprise, was widely reported in the press. The *New York Herald*, always a strong
proponent of business interests, referred to this example of government
assistance to private industry as a "novel proceedure" [*sic*] and wondered about
the wisdom of delivering the gold to Carranza's agents in Yucatán instead of
to the planters to whom the fiber belonged, many of whom were opposed to
Carranza and had fled the state. Other merchant steamers started to make the
voyages for fiber soon thereafter.[67]

The importance of the renewed shipments was not lost on interested parties in the Great Plains. A telling editorial in the *Bismarck Daily Tribune* perhaps best exemplified the sentiment: "That the United States has taken a hand
to protect the supply of sisal is good news to North Dakota farmers. A tenth
of the wheat grown in the United States is raised within the borders of this
state, so no state . . . is any more interested in the sisal market. The decision of
the federal government to send a warship with sufficient gold to facilitate the
movement of 20,000 bales of sisal is probably unique, but conditions in Mexico
call for unique action. . . . The interests of the American farmers are intimately
bound up in the presence of the sisal market."[68]

Daniels also ordered the battleship *Georgia* to move to Progreso as a way
of showing force and protecting the transport of henequen. The *New York Sun*
claimed that "unless the United States shows its teeth[,] sisal fibre so urgently
needed for the manufacture of twine to bind this year's crops in this country
and Canada will not move northward as promised by the Mexican authorities." The article reminded readers that "Canadian farmers [were] just as vitally concerned" about not being able to bind their harvests.[69]

Canada had issued no official statement regarding Carranza's blockade or
the U.S. reaction to it. Prime Minister Robert Laird Borden had his attention
focused more on the war in Europe, where by 1915 Canada had fifty thousand soldiers aiding British forces. However, with these renewed threats and
rumors the Borden government began to monitor the situation very closely,
but via the British ambassador to the United States; it did not send a special emissary to the United States or to Mexico, and it did not rely on the
Canadian Ministry of External Affairs. This move was nothing unusual, as
London maintained control over Canadian foreign policy until 1931. During
these events, the British ambassador to Washington, Sir Cecil Spring Rice,
met daily with Secretary Bryan and kept in close touch with Prime Minister
Borden and the governor general of Canada about what he called the "deplor-
able situation in Mexico." But the British and Canadians were quick to defer
to the United States. Spring Rice posited to Governor General Sir Edward
Grey on March 24, "The only Power who can do anything to remedy [the situ-
ation] is the United States Government . . . and it must not be forgotten that

they have a large force within striking distance."[70] Spring Rice then wrote to Bryan, saying he was glad that the United States had taken "serious steps . . . to secure the export . . . of Sisal Grass [*sic*] for twine. . . . Canada is deeply interested in the export for the use of Canadian farmers, and many British houses . . . have invested large sums. . . . I am confident therefore that your government in the common interest of the agricultural population of this continent will be ready to co-operate . . . in the preservation of this most important industry. . . . [D]estruction will entail a shortage . . . from which every farmer in this continent will suffer. . . . I have no doubt that the protection afforded by your government will be extended to every one with absolute impartiality and with a single view to securing low prices for the American farmer."[71]

Despite all of these measures, the rumors persisted. "Sisal Supply in Danger" screamed the front-page headlines of a Bismarck newspaper. The article cited reports that revolutionaries were "burning stores of sisal and threatening growers and shippers with heavy taxation and penalties." The *Toronto Globe* headline claimed "Canada's Hemp Supply Endangered at Yucatán" but assured readers that Ambassador Spring Rice was conferring with U.S. officials on the matter in the interests of Canadian farmers. The article stressed that "steps [would] be taken to prevent any interference with the shipment of the much-needed product" and that the United States "gave notice" that gunboats "would be used if necessary."[72] In that regard, Spring Rice continued to keep Canadian officials abreast of developments. He wrote the governor general that the growers in Yucatán were "in some anxiety as to the possibility of making exports by the port of Progreso, as trade of the port has recently been interfered with by an armed vessel employed by the Carrancista authorities. I understand however the United States Government are alive to the importance of keeping open this source of supply of twine." And in a report attached to his letter, Spring Rice outlined the implications of a fiber shortage, especially given that the fiber trade from other places combined (East Africa, New Zealand, the Philippines) amounted to 30,000 tons annually, compared to the 160,000 annual tons from Yucatán. Further, East Africa's supply (primarily from German-controlled Tanganyika, now Tanzania) was unavailable due to the war in Europe. The fiber was needed quickly "because any delay . . . could easily occasion a world-wide disaster," he wrote. "It would be impossible to harvest the crops by hand," especially since the farmers had planted an "enormous acreage of grains" due to the war in Europe and were taking advantage of "the high prices so that more twine will be needed this year than in the past."[73]

More messages arrived on Bryan's desk about how "insurrectionists" had burned fields and warehoused bales of sisal. Implement companies, such as McCluskey Brothers of Billings, Oklahoma, and Gulbro Implement of

Pekin, North Dakota, sent typical messages regarding the rumors. Politicians got into the act as representatives of their states' farm, implement, and penitentiary twine factory concerns. Bryan heard from North Dakota's Sen. Asle Gronna, Rep. Patrick Norton, and Secretary of State Thomas Hall and from U.S. senators William Thompson and Joseph Bristow of Kansas. He also heard from Ambassador Spring Rice on behalf of Canadian wheat growers and from Secretary of Commerce William Redfield, who had been getting requests from Peoria Cordage for "daily updates" on the sisal situation. A new concern was that fields of istle, whose fibers were used to make cheap rope and brushes, were being threatened near Monterrey and San Luis Potosí in northern Mexico. Bryan responded to most of the messages with the stock line that his department was "making vigorous efforts to relieve the sisal hemp situation." Under Secretary Robert Lansing responded to Redfield that the State Department was getting daily updates from the *Des Moines* off the coast of Progreso. The department kept in close touch with more than thirty different cordage manufacturers, relaying cable messages it received from the *Des Moines* showing that by March 27 there had been no problems with cargo ships getting to port or with loading bales of fiber.[74]

Bryan also alerted Spring Rice so that he could give Canadian officials the same news. Spring Rice did so, passing on the reports that regular shipping had resumed and that there should be no further worries about the exportation of sisal to Canada. A few days later, he relayed the message that despite the rumors, no "wanton destruction" in the sisal fields was occurring, no crops had been destroyed, and fiber was being loaded onto ships without incident.[75] As for official policy toward the revolution and Carranza's leadership, Canada, a dominion within the British Commonwealth, would follow Great Britain's direction. Spring Rice outlined what that would be in early April. Sounding about as ambivalent as Wilson and his "watchful waiting" approach, he spelled out for Canadian officials that "we should have no candidate and no policy, except solely the policy of friendliness to that Power which is able to keep order so long as it keeps order and in the places where order is kept." He also made clear that the United Kingdom had worked to demonstrate to all factions in Mexico that it had "absolutely no political ambitions nor any desire for exclusive commercial advantage" in Mexico and that the Mexicans "nourish[ed] no suspicion" about that. Remaining consistent with earlier foreign policy, the British and Canadians would continue to defer to the Americans on any decision to threaten military force again in the event of an interruption of sisal exports. Spring Rice referred to this policy as Wilson's plan for "partial intervention," of which he seemed critical: "I have spoken with the President on this subject and it is with the President that the decision rests. He is not apt to take advice and it is probable that when he arrives at a decision it will be without previous consultation and without the foreknowledge of the general public."[76]

The scenario, so replete with misinformation and innuendo, must have been extremely frustrating for Carranza and other Mexican officials. The Carrancista ambassador to Washington, Eliseo Arredondo, had made clear that his compatriots knew that depriving North Americans of henequen risked a substantial loss of revenue to both Yucatecan and Mexican national treasuries and thus was to be avoided. Carranza had even thought of bombarding the port during the height of the struggles against Ortiz Argumedo, but his better judgment stopped that plan when he realized that such action would have destroyed so many bales of henequen ready to be shipped.[77] Arredondo emphasized that after Alvarado's army was successful in defeating the Yucatecan rebels, Carranza was willing "to have the whole [henequen] crop go to the United States and to afford all the necessary facilities, so that the exportation may take place without any impediment from our part." And as one authority has pointed out, "No evidence can readily be found in either Mexican or Yucatecan archives suggesting even the rumor of a threat on the part of Alvarado or the *hacendados* to burn the henequen fields."[78]

As for Bryan and U.S. State Department officials, there assuredly was some level of frustration involved, especially since all of the information they were getting from both Mexicans and Americans in the region contradicted the rumors. Yet he was not above being influenced by the talk of burned sisal, and he did expend energy trying to avert that kind of disaster. In mid-March he resorted to a new tactic: he responded to an offer from a third country, Cuba, to pressure Carranza not to have any of his supporters destroy henequen fields. He wired the U.S. legation in Havana to take up Cuban president Mario Menocal's offer "to help in whatever way he could," especially in light of the "necessity" of binder twine, the increase in demand for grain due to the war in Europe, the drought in the Philippines that was decreasing manila hemp shipments for cordage production, how there was simply no other commodity available to make binder twine, and how, if the Yucatecans had to replant henequen due to destroyed fields, it would take no fewer than six (or seven) years for the new plants to mature. "Please say to President Menocal that interference with the harvest and shipment of sisal from Progreso is threatening a great loss to the farmers of the grain-growing sections of the United States and other countries," Bryan pleaded, "and ask him whether he is in a position to urge upon Carranza such action as may be necessary to give relief at once."[79]

The response from Havana reiterated Carranza's denials of involvement in any sisal destruction or obstruction of shipments.[80] By the end of March, Carranza had declared "that everything in the state of Yucatán" was "pacified." He had sent word to the commander of his gunboat *Zaragoza* directing him to "take whatever means are necessary" to ensure passage of the cargo ships hauling fiber. And by April 5 he had given assurances that henequen was being shipped without any interruption. Bryan at that point wired Senator Gronna of North Dakota, saying, "I have the honor to inform you that sisal hemp is now being shipped from the State of Yucatán and that no further interference with shipping at that place is expected." He had sent a similar message to Secretary Redfield over in Commerce, reiterating that the "sisal situation had been so cleared up" that it was "unnecessary to bring further pressure to bear."[81] Especially grateful to hear such news was Cyrus McCormick Jr. In fact, he and other officials from IH called Bryan on April 8 "to thank the Department for the services rendered in the matter of securing sisal," as Bryan reported to President Wilson, adding, "He [McCormick] said that the manufacturers of binding twine all very much appreciated the help rendered." Wilson was pleased to hear that his friend McCormick had contacted Bryan about this matter. "Thank you for telling me this," Wilson replied, adding, "I am glad they are alive to what we have done. It was right and courteous of them to thank us."[82]

Despite all assurances, the crisis appeared to worsen in some sectors of the cordage industry. Bryan was undoubtedly displeased to receive an article from a Syracuse, New York, newspaper issued on April 3: "Twine Shop Shuts Down Owing to Lack of Sisal." The article, which was entered into State Department documents, related how "several hundred people were thrown out of work." Later that month the general manager of IH wrote to Bryan about such shortages. Following up on McCormick's call to Bryan, this manager wrote that his company was being unfairly accused of hoarding its stocks of newly arrived sisal and not honoring contracts to supply fiber to other companies. He pointed out that IH had actually distributed to various manufacturers 16,780 bales of fiber received from Avelino Montes.[83] With fiber shipments thus making their way from field to factory, it is noteworthy that for the *third* time President Wilson ordered a gunboat to Yucatán on April 20. Apparently, another scare about sisal crop destruction had surfaced, so Wilson had the navy move the *Olympia* to the area as a warning for the Mexicans to maintain order.[84] The gunboat's services, like those of the *Des Moines* and the *Brutus*, however, did not end up being needed.

By summer everything seemed to have settled down. Newspapers in July quoted Carranza as having announced that "commerce in Yucatán is entirely free" and that "whatever sisal may be needed by cordage manufacturers . . . can be obtained." The *New York Herald* reported that Carranza had once again denied ever holding up any fiber shipments and that Yucatán growers were able to fill any orders that the twine mills needed.[85] By late spring, the State

Department had heard from the U.S. Navy (which was still monitoring the trade between Yucatán and the United States) that there had been a significant rise in the exportation of fiber: 22,000 bales were exported in February, before the blockade, 55,000 in March, after the blockade had been lifted, and 97,000 in April. Of those 174,000 bales, 122,000, or 70 percent, were contracted for the Avelino Montes–IH supply chain.[86]

All of this news was vitally important because, as the weather forecasters had predicted, that season's harvests were indeed record setting. The spring rainfall levels had been perfect, and farmers later that year had the best crops of their lives. American farmers harvested more than 1 billion bushels of wheat—the only time production hit the billion-bushel mark between 1866, when the Department of Agriculture starting keeping records, and the 1950s. North Dakota farmers led the way, harvesting nearly 160 million bushels of wheat—50 million bushels more than their nearest competitors in Kansas.[87] Yields in Canada were similar. What Vernon Fowke referred to as "the fabulously bountiful crops of 1915" and John Herd Thompson called the "spectacular crop in 1915" was Canada's nearly 400-million-bushel harvest, most of which came from the three Prairie Provinces. That total was nearly double Canada's previous production high.[88]

It was one of those quirks of coincidence that 1915, the year the Mexican Revolution hit Yucatán and Carranza imposed the blockade that prompted fears of a twine shortage was also the year that American and Canadian farmers enjoyed their best bumper crops to date. Through it all, twine manufacturers raced to keep up with demand during harvest time. In fact, farmers in Saskatchewan were more than alarmed that August when a "serious holdup" of rail cars of twine on the Thunderhead Branch of the Canadian Northern Railway (CNR) at Dauphin, Manitoba, en route to Pelly, Saskatchewan, threatened to ruin "thousands of acres of over-ripe wheat." As one Mossbank, Saskatchewan, dealer telegrammed William Motherwell, the province's secretary of agriculture, "No twine. Crop shelling. Kindly advise what is best to do. Is there no hope of immediate relief?" Motherwell promised "to do everything possible" and then contacted CNR and IH, which assured farmers that a carload of twine had just left Chicago bound for Pelly.[89]

Nonetheless, cordage firms and farmers continued to be highly displeased with the fiber suppliers in Yucatán. IH wanted to assure them that their demand for twine to harvest that summer's bumper crop would be met, and the company petitioned for an American warship to make regular patrols off of Progreso to ensure uninterrupted shipment of fiber. The company argued that "without the moral influence of an American naval vessel, the situation of American interests is unsafe." This time, however, Navy Secretary Daniels refused the request, arguing that U.S. ships were needed elsewhere; he sent

no gunboats in the summer of 1915.[90] Later that year when the revolutionary government of Salvador Alvarado revamped the Comisión Reguladora del
Mercado de Henequén and significantly raised the price of sisal on the world
market, IH and the entire cordage industry once again petitioned the U.S.
government for intervention. This time their request was for legal and economic sanctions, not military force.

The sisal situation occurred during what some historians have identified as
a turning point in the history of world events and in how the United States
responded to international concerns. The Wilson years (1913–1921), as Arthur Link has explained, were "a time of far-reaching attempts to confront
and resolve the dilemma posed by the existence of private economic autocracy
in a political and social democracy. Abroad it was a time of revolutionary upheaval in countries near and far, of cataclysmic world war, and of portentous
shifts in the balance of power that threatened to crumble the foundations of
the international community."[91] Wilson had to confront this scenario early in
his first term as president, and as was the case with Mexico, he had to address the issues while having only limited understanding of, and experience
in, the region. The sisal crisis also came toward the end of William Jennings
Bryan's brief but action-packed two-year term as secretary of state. Disagree-
ing strongly with Wilson's plans to build up an army to send into combat in
Europe and because of his staunch opposition to war in general, Bryan ten-
dered his resignation from the Cabinet on June 9, 1915. One of his final acts
as secretary was regarding Mexican matters. Three days before his resignation he had advised Americans living in Mexico to leave the country. Wilson, glad to be rid of Bryan, eventually replaced him with Under Secretary of
State Robert Lansing.
    Bryan returned to his many other causes and to his desk at *The Commoner*
in Lincoln, Nebraska. A couple of years later when the United States was
starting to increase its involvement in World War I and when the harvests
were not as good as they were in 1915, Bryan advocated decreased wheat consumption at home to save grain for the war effort in Europe. In a speech in
Houston, Bryan referred to the limited world wheat crop of 1916 and called
on Americans to continue sacrificing by consuming fewer wheat products at
home, calling it "the lightest burden imposed by the war."[92] In May 1915 he
had suggested to the president that the United States organize a relief program for the people of Mexico, similar to what had been done for Belgium:
"It would certainly make a favorable impression upon the people there and it
might soften the antagonists." Although Wilson replied in a one-sentence letter, "I agree with you that this is the right way to handle the matter," the project was never carried out.[93] Bryan lived but a few years longer, dying in 1925

immediately following his intense involvement as a prosecuting attorney in the Scopes "Monkey Trial" in Dayton, Tennessee.

For his entire life, as Edward Kaplan has written, "Bryan never realized the inconsistency of his Latin American policy. . . . [He] never understood that when he used military force, he was doing the same thing his predecessors did."[94] Apparently he had forgotten the battle between U.S. Marines and Mexican forces that resulted in the deaths of nineteen Americans, the wounding of seventy-one more, and countless Mexican casualties. Perhaps he had also forgotten that he had recommended to the president that two additional battleships be sent "into the neighborhood" around Veracruz.[95] Likewise, during the height of the sisal situation and only a few days after Wilson and Bryan had conferred about sending a gunboat to Progreso, they conferred again about a blockade in Europe against Germany. Bryan told the president, "My own idea is that we cannot afford to make merchandise a cause for the use of force."[96] Then in September 1915, only months after agreeing to send gunboats to Progreso for the sake of the cordage industry, Bryan once again wrote in *The Commoner* about the evils of "interests behind interventionism": "Intervening on the behalf of business is not in the name of humanity, or the welfare of this country, but for the benefits of those who have interests there."[97]

Indeed, Bryan had other opposing thoughts and actions. One biographer claims that Bryan went from being a "crusader for social and economic reform to a champion of anachronistic rural evangelism, cheap moralistic panaceas, and Florida real estate" and of being "for social and economic betterment, even while he closed his eyes to the evils of the Ku Klux Klan."[98] And apparently he never perceived the contradictions in how he went from opposing government subsidies for the twine industry to later being so actively involved in supporting a far greater expenditure of public funds to send warships to protect the fiber supply. And what happened to his crusade against trusts during the sisal situation? Kendrick Clements explains: "The aim of 'busting' a trust was in conflict with the goal of helping the American farmer, and the farmer seemingly could not be helped without resorting to the coercion of Mexico."[99]

As for Wilson, he was certainly guilty of his own contradictions. He was on record supporting the Spanish-American War and proclaiming occupation of the Philippines to be good both for extending U.S. markets abroad and for teaching order and self-government, even if it meant using force. Later, he switched to a belief in "moral diplomacy," if more in words than in actions.[100] In the summer of 1915, he issued a statement on U.S. policy toward the Mexican Revolution. Alarmed at how the revolution had devolved into a civil war between various factions, the president stated, "In these circumstances the people and government of the United States cannot stand indifferently by and do nothing to serve their neighbor. They want nothing for themselves in

Mexico."[101] This statement of policy was blatantly the opposite of what had been in force just been two months previous, during the sisal situation. Concluding, he once again demonstrated his ignorance for the gravity of Mexico's complex crisis and advocated a bland, unrealistic solution: "This government will be very constrained to decide what means should be employed by the United States in order to help Mexico save herself and serve her people."[102]

The next year, 1916, brought an even more compelling reason for Wilson to confront issues in Mexico and his own dilemma over the use of moral diplomacy versus armed threats and invasions: Pancho Villa's raid on Columbus, New Mexico. Once again, Wilson chose the former. On March 9, exactly a year after the sisal situation began, Villa led a group of five hundred men across the border from Palomas, Chihuahua, to avenge the United States for helping Carrancista forces defeat his army at Agua Prieta, Sonora, and Ciudad Juárez, Chihuahua, and also for what he believed, mistakenly, was an agreement that President Wilson had made with Carranza to make Mexico into some kind of U.S. protectorate.[103] The Villistas killed seventeen Americans and shot up the town. A garrison of the 13th U.S. Cavalry stationed in Columbus quickly mobilized and retaliated, killing one hundred Mexicans in the process and sending the rest back across the border into Mexico.

Villa's act of aggression was too great a match for Wilson's moral diplomacy. By March 15 (coincidentally the anniversary of Carranza's lifting of the blockade) the president had commissioned Gen. John "Black Jack" Pershing (assisted by a young lieutenant named George Patton) to lead an expeditionary force into Mexico to capture Villa. With seven thousand men, including the 10th Cavalry's African American "Buffalo Soldiers," and eight thousand horses, Pershing led the Punitive Expedition into northern Mexico. In addition to manpower and horsepower, the expedition had bulky tanks, trucks, motorcycle-mounted machine guns, and even an aero squadron of biplanes, the first time any of those were used by the U.S. military. For seven months the U.S. force tried to bring Villa to justice. Despite the considerable technology, much of it questionable for an expeditionary force in the deserts and canyons of Chihuahua, the mission failed. Pershing and his soldiers never did find Villa after spending more than half a year and $130 million in his pursuit.[104]

A pertinent side note to the story is that William Jennings Bryan, out of public office for over a year at that point, went on record as strongly opposed to the Punitive Expedition. Returning to his more peace-oriented side, the former secretary of state demanded Pershing's withdrawal from Mexico when it appeared that U.S. actions were coming perilously close to war.[105]

Sandwiched between Wilson's ignominies of the marine invasion of Veracruz in 1914 and the Pershing Expedition in Chihuahua in 1916 was his response to the sisal situation in Yucatán. Fortunately, unlike the other two

shows of force, there was no loss of life for the binder twine cause. It was certainly less dramatic, less costly (although assuredly expensive enough), less
publicized, and hence is less known than the other American misadventures
in Mexico. The press accounts of the situation were there, and often on the
front pages, but dwarfed by other world events in spring 1915, primarily those
in Europe. The Greeks and Armenians fleeing the Turks at the Battle of the
Dardanelles, the Germans' zeppelin raids over Paris and their increased use
of submarines, and the Italians' preparation for entering the war all had much
larger headlines. There was also considerable coverage of the many national
events of the time, but squeezed between stories of women's suffrage assem-
blies, Billy Sunday revivals, and presentations by Helen Keller, there was
news from Mexico. Newspapers covered the long-lasting Battle of Celaya and
Pancho Villa's exploits in the Mexican civil war. Newspaper coverage of the
henequen crisis clearly shows that the U.S. government's efforts to protect the
free trade of a commercial commodity for the benefit of North American business and agricultural interests was important to the American and Canadian
public. Published sentiment ran strictly in favor of the use of force to persuade
Carranza to lift the blockade, to guarantee the safety of the henequen fields,
and to ensure the safe transport of fiber to and from the port of Progreso.
Yet the Wilson administration presented no alternatives and exhibited very
little patience with or understanding of what was happening in Mexico. Had
he just waited, perhaps even just a few more days, the blockade most likely
would have been lifted; it may already have been in the process of being recalled. Had officials more carefully investigated the rumors of henequen and
railroad destruction they would have found no cause for such alarm. On both
accounts, Carranza needed to secure the henequen sales just as badly as U.S.
and Canadian agriculture needed the fiber. Instead, Wilson relied on gunboat
diplomacy, a tactic from past administrations that both he and Bryan were on
record opposing.

However, it is interesting to note that America's response to the sisal situation may have been the last U.S. episode of gunboat diplomacy, at least in the
style of Theodore Roosevelt, William Howard Taft, and as we can say now,
Woodrow Wilson.[106] The tactic can be identified as part of an American "no
duty to retreat" philosophy, which was carved out of the violence of America's
frontier past and which during the late nineteenth and early twentieth centuries came to characterize U.S. foreign policy.[107] Despite Carranza's denials,
the tactic worked against Mexico and for U.S. commercial interests in 1915
but was not used per se by future administrations. Other forms of invasions,
CIA interventions, orchestrated coups, and military actions represented newer
forms of dollar diplomacy to support American economic interests abroad but
replaced gunboats in U.S. policy in Latin America (and elsewhere), especially

during the cold war. It is of interest to note that in the midst of the sisal situation, on March 29, 1915, President Wilson spoke at a luncheon on board the Argentine battleship *Moreno* docked at Annapolis, Maryland. The media proclaimed, "Wilson Predicts That the Americas Will Be Bound by Close Ties." The president was quoted as having said, "We are rapidly approaching the day when the Americas will draw together as never before and it will be a union not of political ties, but an understanding of mutual helpfulness."[108] He was not necessarily addressing the commercial ties between North America's grain belt and the Yucatán Peninsula, but his thoughts on "mutual helpfulness" ring familiar in the history of binder twine. Two parts of the Americas, the transboundary Great Plains and Mexico, were bound by close ties from the 1880s through the 1940s when demand for sisal fiber and the demand for wheat and other grains generated mutual dependence. So interdependent were these regions that the sisal situation commanded the rapt attention of many sectors of the U.S. government—Department of State, Department of Commerce, Department of the Navy, Department of Agriculture, and the office of the presidency, as well as Canadian and British officials. So interdependent were they that the U.S. government sanctioned use of the U.S. Navy to transport funds for fiber payment and even to ship fiber for private industrial interests. So interdependent were they that the United States more than once was ready to use military action to safeguard the flow of fiber in 1915. And so interdependent were they that the press, from New York to Bismarck and from Saskatoon to Wichita, provided front-page coverage of the events surrounding a threatened supply of binder twine. Britain's Ambassador Sir Cecil Spring Rice had captured the essence of that interdependence when, while lobbying for the Canadians, he told Secretary of State Bryan, not once, but twice in the same letter, that the sisal concerns were in the common interest of the people of this *continent*—both in the United States and Canada.

The same is true for Mexico. Despite his lofty words, Wilson's idea of intercontinental "mutual helpfulness" was absent from U.S. foreign policy during the Mexican Revolution. There was no show of solidarity against monopolies and corporate control of the Yucatecan haciendas. There was no support of the Yucatecan people who clamored for land reform and for increased henequen profits to go toward education and social services, drastically needed in their state after the tight control of the henequen oligarchs. There was no call for a "New Freedom" for those Yucatecans. No, the sisal situation reflects just how far the United States was prepared to go to "prevent any interference with our commerce"—ultimatums and the old standby of gunboat diplomacy—all for the seemingly simple commodity of binder twine.

CHAPTER 5

Prison-Made Twine

The Role of the Penitentiaries in the Henequen-Wheat Complex

We have saved the farmers of this state $200,000 during the operation of the twine plant as a difference between the State price of twine and the Trust price. It has acted as a leveler of prices and there is no telling how much the farmers would have to pay for twine if it were not for the State's Twine Plant.

—*Ole Swenson, warden of the South Dakota State Penitentiary, 1913*

ONE of the least known aspects of the history of the henequen-wheat complex is the role played by North American penitentiaries in the manufacture of binder twine. The literature on henequen, the fiber industry in general, and U.S. and Canadian agricultural history has either ignored this aspect entirely or alluded to it only in passing. Yet the prison twine industry is an integral part of the larger story of cordage manufacturing and represents in a clear way what governments would do to provide a much-needed commodity for farming: subsidize twine manufacture by using convict labor. This aspect of the larger henequen-wheat story has a variety of dimensions worthy of study. Like any industry, prison twine manufacturing has a context (prison labor history in general), a history of its specific origin (why and how prisons were chosen to manufacture twine), and different agricultural, economic, and political events that affected it over the years. All enter the story here.

The idea of using prisoners as workers is quite old. Ancient civilizations from China to Egypt to Peru used convicted criminals and prisoners of war as slave labor for galley crews, construction projects, and agricultural work. The practice continued throughout the world, but by the eleventh century prisons in Europe placed emphasis on convicts working to pay off the expense of their incarceration. By the sixteenth century, "workhouses" for vagrants appeared in England (e.g., Bridewell), and these facilities emphasized work as a reformative program rather than just reimbursement of expenses. The concept of reform was the genesis of prisons as distinguished from jails ("gaols"), with the prison representing a "correctional alternative" to the jail's purpose of punishment. It was in prisons in eighteenth-century France that the idea of prison "industry" was born.[1]

The practice continued in the nineteenth and early twentieth centuries, when it became controversial; philosophers, sociologists, psychologists, penologists, and prison reform activists endlessly debated the merits and pitfalls of prison labor, especially the concept of rehabilitation versus economic return. In his influential book, *Discipline and Punish: The Birth of the Prison*, Michel Foucault, ever concerned with the analysis of power relations, focused on the way prisons used labor to shape and discipline the inmates.[2] The history of labor in the prison twine mills that developed later may not touch on all of this debate, but the theory behind them does.

Prison labor as a legislated penal institution began in North America in 1794 at the Walnut Street Jail in Philadelphia—the first penitentiary in the United States. In Canada, inmate labor began in 1835 at the old Kingston Penitentiary in Ontario when prison authorities assigned six prisoners to stone cutting work. The governments of both countries viewed convicted criminals as a cheap source of labor that reduced the costs of their upkeep and helped to pay for other prison programs. Among the first prison-made products were shoes, boots, and clothing, some of which were for inmate use and some for sale to the public. As early as 1828, the U.S. federal prisons of Auburn and Sing Sing in New York state were paying for themselves "due in large part to convict labor."[3]

The practice continued into the nineteenth and twentieth centuries, most infamously perhaps in the American South, where chain gangs dressed in stripes broke rocks and served on road crews.[4] At the end of the Civil War, prisons throughout the South were so overcrowded that state authorities devised a contract lease system that provided penal labor to private industry in a contractual, low-wage arrangement. Railroads, coal mines, road construction firms, and cotton plantations were quick to take advantage of the cheap labor (often consisting of former slaves arrested on trumped-up charges), especially as the South was attempting to rebuild after the devastating war. But the arrangement meant that many other workers, especially union members, lost their jobs to inmates, causing predictable tension. Unions spoke out strongly against the system. By the mid-nineteenth century penitentiary administrators in the northern United States and in Canada sought to expand inmate work and looked to private industry for its expertise on production. The benefits would be twofold: private industries would use the cheap labor to make products for sale on the open market for considerable profit, and prisons would increase their income to cover operating expenses.[5]

While entrepreneurs and prisons benefited financially, the convicts often received severe punishments for not meeting production quotas and endured harsh and often unsanitary conditions. In addition, the competition with non-convict workers led to greater unemployment outside prison walls. Labor unions led mass efforts against the practice, resulting in New York's abolition of it in 1887. Things boiled over in Tennessee in 1891–1892 during the Coal Creek Rebellion, when officials of a coal mine barred union miners from working and instead leased convicts from a nearby prison at far lower wages. The union miners fought back, stormed and burned the prison, and liberated four hundred inmates. With that, the mine company halted its use of convicts and rehired the union miners.[6] The incident signaled the end of the contract lease system nationwide as states around the country passed laws against it. The practice had effectively ended in Canada by 1886.[7]

The trade union movement in the United States and Canada continued to be a powerful voice against prison labor in general, not just the contract lease system. With convict labor estimated to be worth only one-third the value of free labor, unions in both countries decried how it represented a threat to "jobs, markets, and profits" and began to lobby for legislation to restrict the practice.[8] They were first successful in Canada, where by the 1890s the federal penitentiary in Kingston, Ontario, had geared its tailoring operation for government use only, making clothing only for prisoners, guards, the North West Mounted Police, First Nations through an Indian Department program, and messenger boys at the House of Commons, and making mail bags for the Canadian postal service (with a mailbag repair service—one of the only such ones in the world). Prime Minister John Macdonald's tariff policies instigated the changes to stimulate Canadian industrialization, since industry and labor in Canada despised competition from convict labor as much as they did from other countries.[9] In the United States debate continued to rage on penal labor during the so-called Progressive Era when humanitarian organizations worked to end or restrict it, arguing that it was demoralizing to inmates who needed religious and moral training instead. By then, prisons were developing industrial and educational programs to reduce prisoner idleness and to reform prisoners by teaching them skills, although many consumers complained of poor quality products resulting from prisoners' lack of incentive to do good work.[10]

During the depression of the 1930s the issue again became contentious in the United States when jobs were even scarcer, prompting unions to fight for increased legislation to protect workers against prison labor. President Franklin Roosevelt's support of the initiatives resulted in a host of New Deal policies and laws on the matter: the Hawes-Cooper Act of 1929, the Ashurst-Sumners Act of 1935, and the Sumners-Ashurst Act of 1940, which criminalized as federal offenses the transport and sale of prison-made products across

Table 5.1 Penitentiary twine mills in North America

Penitentiary	Location	Years in operation	Number of spinners	Annual output	Usual number of inmates employed
Stillwater State Prison	Stillwater, Minn.	1891–1957	525	18–24 million pounds	225
Ontario Central Prison	Toronto, Ont.	1892–1915	n.d.	< 1 million pounds	n.d.
Kingston Penitentiary	Kingston, Ont.	1894–?	n.a	< 1 million pounds	30–40
North Dakota State Penitentiary	Bismarck, N.Dak.	1899–1964	120	3 million pounds	60–80
Kansas State Penitentiary	Lansing, Kans.	1899–1947	120	3 million pounds	60–80
Indiana State Prison–North	Michigan City, Ind.	1906–1924	100	3 million pounds	66
Michigan State Prison	Jackson, Mich.	1907–?	200	6–12 million pounds	60–80
Missouri State Penitentiary	Jefferson City, Mo.	190?–?	n.d.	200,000 pounds	n.d.
South Dakota State Penitentiary	Sioux Falls, S.Dak.	1909–1950	100	3 million pounds	60–80
Wisconsin State Prison	Waupun, Wisc.	1910–1954	140	4.5 million pounds	60–80
Oklahoma State Penitentiary	McAlester, Okla.	1916–?	n.d.	< 1 million pounds	n.d.

Note: n.d. indicates that no data were available.

state lines.[11] The legislation effectively limited prison industries to small-scale manufactured items, such as license plates and road signs, for state use. The government relaxed the laws with the outbreak of World War II, when Roosevelt signed an executive order in 1942 that permitted prisoners to manufacture materials; the need to manufacture goods for the war effort took prece-

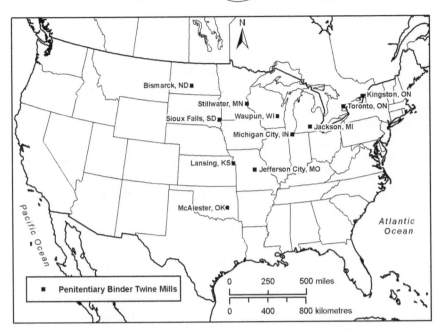

Figure 5.1. Prison twine plant locations in North America. Courtesy Wenonah Fraser, Department of Geography, Brandon University.

dence over industry and union protectionism. Canada did the same, but at war's end in 1945 both countries discontinued the practice.[12]

By the late nineteenth and early twentieth centuries penitentiaries were producing many different products in their shops and factories: clothing (especially prison wear for their own inmates), mattresses, cement blocks, sheet metal, furniture, brooms and brushes, shoes and boots, hosiery, cooperage, carpeting, woolen and cotton goods, laundry products, kitchen utensils, children's toys and sleds, and even, ironically enough, at Canada's Kingston Penitentiary, locks and keys. Many prisons had their own gardens, farms, livestock, poultry businesses, coal mines, rock quarries, sawmills, flour mills, print shops, tailor shops, leather shops, bookbinding shops, cabinetmaking shops, blacksmith shops, brick factories, and iron works. The Kingston and Minnesota penitentiaries were unique in having competitive and successful farm machinery factories that made a wide assortment of implements. And eleven prisons (nine in the United States and two in Canada) established their own binder twine plants (see Table 5.1 and Figure 5.1).

The germ of the idea to create prison binder twine plants evolved as a direct response to the monopoly that the McCormick Harvesting Company of Chicago came to have in the fiber trade and twine business by the late nineteenth century. As discussed in chapter 1, McCormick's control of sisal acquisition and binder twine production gave it the chance to control the price of twine. The McCormick "trust" caused policy makers in agricultural states and Canada to think that prisons could add binder twine manufacturing to their industries to help their farmers while creating useful work for inmates. It was authorities in Minnesota who pioneered the idea in the 1880s and who established the world's first penitentiary binder twine plant in 1890.

The twine plant at the Stillwater State Prison was begun with relatively low start-up costs of thirty-five thousand dollars. The prison purchased its first twine-making machinery from a Belfast, Northern Ireland, firm and from a Cincinnati cordage company that had gone bankrupt. When the prison's new twine plant began operating in 1891 it employed sixty convicts (and seventy-six by 1893) who were able to produce an average of six thousand pounds of twine per day, but with a machinery and fiber stock capacity of ten thousand pounds a day. The plant at first used industrial hemp (i.e., true hemp, *Cannabis sativa*) from Kentucky, but by 1907 it had switched to Yucatecan sisal for standard twine and Philippine abacá or manila for a more expensive binder twine, most of which was brokered through the firm of Henry W. Peabody & Company of Boston.[13] By buying from Peabody, penitentiary administrators learned they could avoid going through McCormick or, after its merger with other implement companies in 1906, International Harvester. The sisal was of good quality, and the marketing department advertised it accordingly, noting in their catalogues that it was the "policy of the management to buy only the best grades of sisal and manila fibres."[14]

The twine plant generated profits almost immediately. The plant's first ten years of business (1891–1900) netted more than $26,000 a year. The annual profit figure had climbed into the six-digit range by 1904, with a record of more than $436,000 in 1919. From 1899 to 1943 the plant earned more than $9.5 million for the prison. By 1917 profits were so great that the state's legislative manual went so far as to call the Stillwater Prison "the greatest revenue producing public institution in the world." Apparently thrilled with the profits and the running of the mill, in 1915 prison officials ordered several henequen *pencas* (the long, sharp sisal leaves) from the Yucatecan fiber trading firm of Avelino Montes in order to display them in the prison offices.[15]

With such good binder twine, state officials thought, why not make the binders too? By 1907, the Stillwater State Prison had a full-scale implement manufacturing business making binders, rakes, disks, and many other implements using the simple but appropriate name, "Minnesota Farm Machinery." Minnesota's prison-made binders developed an excellent reputation, especially with their ability to avoid making loose bundles—a characteristic farmers greatly appreciated so they would not have to get off the harvester and retie a

bundle. Many grateful farmers and implement dealers wrote letters of praise
that were often used as testimonials in the Minnesota catalogues. To be sure,
many of the customers used prison-made twine on their prison-made binders.
In 1915 administrators agreed that the twine should be labeled accordingly
("prison twine" or "Minnesota Prison Twine") to avoid any confusion with
commercial brands.[16] To keep up with all the industry news and marketing
plans, administrators began to have monthly "twine conferences" and "farm
machinery conferences." The meetings kept prison officials alert to changes
in the cordage business, fiber prices on the international market, sales strategies, and other corporate-style business concerns. News of Minnesota's success in making twine in its prison factory reached Yucatán and was welcomed
there as yet another good market for henequen. The trade journal *El henequén*
in 1916 reprinted Warden Reed's biennial prison industries report that showed
increases in twine production and profits.[17]

Louis Robinson, who evaluated the various Minnesota prison industries in
the 1920s, wrote that the Stillwater binder twine plant started out of "fear of
the 'cordage trust' of the 1890s and early 1900s, . . . for the express purpose of
preventing a monopoly in binder twine, and insuring [*sic*] the wheat growers a
supply of twine at low prices." Critical of its origins, he argued that the plant
"was made possible by the dominance of agricultural interests in the state. It
is the old story of tariff over again—one set of producers opposed to another."
From a business point of view, however, he praised the Stillwater State Prison
as "the shining example of what a state-account industry can do financially.
By means of its binder twine and farm machinery plants, it has supported
itself since 1917." He added that through its industries the prison ran with a
net surplus.[18] According to Minnesota's governor at the time, Theodore Christianson, the twine plant was the best venture at the prison. Speaking at a national governors' conference in 1930, Christianson related how binder twine
could be mass produced with little effort to help run the penitentiary without
a deficit. So great was "Minnesota's success with binder twine," as Robinson
correctly noted, that it "influenced half a dozen mid western states to install
twine plants."[19]

The first place to follow in Stillwater's footsteps, however, was not in a
state; it was in a province. In Canada, administrators at Ontario's Central
Prison in Toronto had experimented with some seventy-five different prison
industries by 1910. Inmates there had made everything from piano stools to
commode seats, and the prison established a corn-broom factory, blacksmith
shop, toy shop, greenhouse, and bakery.[20] By the early 1890s, it had installed
a binder twine plant for the benefit of farmers in Ontario. In 1894 a regional
newspaper stated that "at a time when the combines [IH trust] had succeeded
in virtually crushing out competition in the manufacture of binding twine

with the result of increasing the price to the farmer in a burdensome degree, the Ontario government came to the rescue." The article reported that prison officials were looking for a new industry for the inmates, since the prison's brickmaking factory had closed down. Thus, "the thought suggested itself that the binder twine situation gave opportunity for an experiment in economics," showing that the commodity could be made and sold to farmers "at a fair price." The story provided the complete details of the materials and equipment used to make binder twine and the details of the process itself. At that time, the Central Prison was making twine from a mixture of sisal and manila hemp, but most of it was the superior quality twine made from the manila.[21]

The Central Prison was a logical choice for the twine factory. In contrast to the Kingston Penitentiary's industries, the Central Prison was the first to use sophisticated machinery and advanced mechanical procedures. While it was in operation it was also financially successful, generating much-needed revenue to run the prison. Compared to other prison industries, the twine factory generated the best cash flow for the institution. However, its reputation for cruelty and financial mismanagement prompted provincial officials to close the prison in 1915—in the boom years of the binder in North American agriculture, meaning that the prison's twine plant ultimately had little impact on Canadian farming.[22]

More important to Canadians was the establishment of a twine mill at the Kingston Penitentiary, a federal correctional institution in Ontario, which opened for production in 1894. Labor at Kingston, the first federal penitentiary established after Canada gained dominion status in 1867, had for many years centered around the vast limestone deposits in the area—the reason the site was chosen for the prison in the first place. Limestone was always the prison's most important focus of production, with inmates cutting stone in the quarries and constructing buildings and walls with the sturdy rock. As the saying went, Kingston was "built of limestone and rules."[23] Working with stone was notoriously difficult, however, and by the end of the century officials were looking for alternative uses for inmate labor, such as shoemaking, tailoring, and making doors in a factory, and farming. The goal was to make the institution self-supporting while assisting in the reform of the convicts by instilling a strong work ethic.[24] In the early1890s, prison officials established a binder twine plant.

The idea emerged one year after Minnesota opened its twine plant at the Stillwater State Prison. By 1892, James Moylan, Canada's federal inspector of prisons, had received estimates for spinners and start-up costs from machinery manufacturers in New Jersey and Ohio. But his primary source of information was the warden's office of the Minnesota prison. Stillwater wardens were quick to offer advice and services, despite the fact that Canada's efforts could cut into the market for Minnesota twine across the border. Information from Stillwater was about twine making capacities, inmate employment numbers, machinery prices, fiber choices, sisal brokers, and sales strategies.[25] Inspector Moylan commissioned Kingston prison warden Michael Lavell to inspect the binder twine plant at the Central Prison in Toronto in 1893. Lavell reported that Central's twine mill "works admirably and turns out excellent twine." But as one historian has argued, the Kingston Penitentiary was always somewhat technologically behind the "expensively outfitted" facility in Toronto, that it "often turned to the Central Prison for technical support." Thus, "in emulation of the Central Prison," Kingston developed a twine industry, although the smaller prison's "technical superiority was biting proof" of Kingston's "own inferiority."[26]

Nevertheless, the Kingston twine factory was completed on March 31, 1894, and its opening seemed to excite people from across Canada and into the United States. The contractor who built it (from Saint John, New Brunswick) notified Warden Lavell: "The binder twine plant being installed by me in the Kingston Penitentiary is now complete and ready for operation. I would like you to come down to the room this morning and see it running. I feel you will be pleased with its working." Eager individuals from Regina, Saskatchewan; Peterborough, Ontario; and Winnipeg, Manitoba, wrote to officials in Ottawa asking to be considered for the role of Kingston binder twine representative for their respective cities. The Dominion Bag Company of Montreal, Quebec (with its logo of a cat being let out of a bag), along with another company from Toronto, sought and received the bagging contracts for the finished balls of twine. The bags were made of cotton and jute from India. The J. C. Wilson Company (also of Montreal) won the contract for making the tags for the twine bags. A company representative argued persuasively for the business, saying that the tags would be helpful "in order that the farmer may know from what end of the ball he is to draw the twine, and also enable him to see at a glance the quality of twine that is being supplied." Various hemp brokers from New York and cordage machinery makers from Montreal and New York requested bids and received contracts. The Canadian Pacific Railroad pursued contracts for shipping the manufactured twine to farmers throughout the country. Trade journals and newspapers in the prairies carried announcements of the prison-made twine. Articles appeared in *The Commercial* (Winnipeg), the *Saturday Night Review* (Portage la Prairie, Manitoba), and *Hardware and Metal* (Toronto). The first load of the Kingston Penitentiary twine headed to the Prairie Provinces arrived in Winnipeg on July 30, 1894—in time for that year's spring wheat harvest.[27]

Despite the accolades, the Kingston plant failed to expand employment significantly, never employing more than forty inmates at any one time, and it was troubled by a series of events that resulted in scandal. One study noted that the "the venture was difficult to discipline, made little profit, was not re-habilitative, [and] produced many accidents due to the dangerous equipment." Complaints came in about faulty twine and how the prison was unfairly cutting into the open market for cordage. The result was that the Ministry of Justice conducted a special inquiry in 1899, only a few years after the plant was installed.[28] While the prison administration recognized the problems, it opposed calls for shutting down the plant. As one warden wrote, although "the twine factory is not an easy place to discipline . . . [it] is a blessing compared to idleness, and I hope that no move will be made to abolish it in this prison until it is decided to substitute something better."[29]

By the end of the 1890s, other penitentiaries had established twine factories. North Dakota and Kansas had prison twine mills up and running by the turn of the century, and Indiana, Michigan, Missouri, South Dakota, and Wisconsin had theirs operating a decade later (see Table 5.1). In Indiana, starting a prison twine plant was the brainchild of Gov. J. Frank Hanly, who believed in corporate trust busting and inmate reform and in 1916 was the Prohibition Party's nominee for president of the United States. He persuaded the Indiana legislature that a prison twine plant would not only employ sixty-six inmates and generate revenue for the state but also be competitive against IH and its high prices for twine. Soon thereafter, Michigan's governor Fred Warner, noting the successful results of the plants in Minnesota, North Dakota, and Indiana, sought and received his state legislature's approval to create a twine plant at the Michigan State Prison.[30] Oklahoma, which became a state only in 1907 and did not have a prison until 1908 (sending its prisoners before that time to the Kansas State Penitentiary), established the last of the state prison twine plants in 1916. In terms of size and production, Minnesota's twine mill was always far in advance of the others. As shown in Table 5.1, Stillwater had four times the production capacity and output than the other state prisons, and it employed more than twice as many convicts as others. Michigan and Wisconsin were always second and third, respectively.[31]

That several of these prison twine mills (the two in Ontario and the ones in Michigan, Indiana, Wisconsin, and Indiana) were east of the core wheat belt reflects the changing nature of North American agricultural geography in the late nineteenth and early twentieth centuries. While many farmers in those places had traditionally grown some wheat, by this time most had switched to corn or hay (for dairies). Farmers in Minnesota had grown vast amounts of wheat as late as 1900 but raised very little after 1920.[32] Assuredly, then, much of the binder twine made in these midwestern penitentiaries was for corn binders, as that implement grew in popularity with farmers who raised corn. In some ways it is curious that other wheat producing states, such as Illinois,

Iowa, Nebraska, Texas, Colorado, Montana, Washington, and California, never created prison twine making facilities (although wheat growers in western states usually harvested with headers and early combines that required no binding, and the Washington State Prison in Walla Walla did have a fiber sack factory for a number of years). Authorities in Iowa and Nebraska had discussed the idea for their respective state penitentiaries in Fort Madison and Lincoln, but apparently the plans never came to fruition.[33] More surprising is that Manitoba, Saskatchewan, and Alberta—Canada's top wheat producing provinces—never had their own prison twine factories, presumably due to their smaller populations (with most Anglo settlers not arriving in the prairie region until the early 1900s), later provincial designation for Saskatchewan and Alberta (1905), small territorial prisons without space for a twine mill, and a lack of capital for start-up. But some people in the region did suggest establishing a prison twine plant at the Stony Mountain federal penitentiary in Manitoba. In response to the Canadian government's high tariffs on imported U.S. twine and the high prices of commercial twine, the *Regina Leader* in 1892 editorialized, "We hope the government will . . . commence manufacturing of binder twine by the prisoners at Stony Mountain, and if possible at Regina." While recognizing that Regina's jail was hardly big enough to support a twine mill, the farm supporting newspaper "hoped in Manitoba the Penitentiary there will [be] manufacturing twine soon" and somewhat naively suggested that "very little machinery is required; we can grow the hemp, and the government could send a man up to teach the prisoners."[34] But the idea never took hold; Stony Mountain never established a twine mill. There were also no binder twine factories at any U.S. federal penitentiaries, including that of Leavenworth in wheat growing Kansas (perhaps due to its proximity to the Kansas State Penitentiary in Lansing—literally minutes away—but mainly because there was no federal initiative to establish one there). In neither country were any twine factories located in women's prisons.

As with Kingston, several of the states with prison twine plants benefited from friendly start-up advice from Minnesota. North Dakota officials had contacted Henry Wolfer, warden of the Stillwater State Prison, to inquire about financial allocations and output capacities for the size of their state and its agricultural enterprise. Echoing his advice to Kingston officials, Wolfer recommended a facility that could produce ten thousand pounds of sisal twine a day and estimated an investment of $25,000 for machinery. North Dakota would also need about $200,000 to build, stock, and insure the plant. Wolfer even recommended that his own assistant twine plant manager in Minnesota be hired as superintendent of the Bismarck plant. Needing such an experienced person, North Dakota hired him at once. The state legislature then approved the overall plan and floated a bond to cover the expenses. The state

Figure 5.2. Interior of North Dakota State Penitentiary twine mill, Bismarck, North Dakota. Notice the piles of raw sisal and spinning machinery. Courtesy State Historical Society of North Dakota (E0329).

hired architects, brought in experienced twine mill operators, purchased the equipment, and secured quality Yucatecan fiber via a hemp broker in New York. On March 24, 1900, everything was in place and the entire operation was tested in the presence of the Prison Board and other dignitaries and guests. "It worked smoothly from the start," wrote one observer, "and to the entire satisfaction of [the plant superintendent]" (Figure 5.2).[35]

It was Oklahoma, however, that probably did more homework than any other state on how to start a prison twine plant. Coming late to the game (1916), Oklahoma governor Robert Williams personally contacted officials in seven states with prison twine plants, asking about such matters as start-up costs, revolving funds, output capacities, numbers of inmates that could be employed in a plant at the state prison in McAlester, and how many spinners to obtain. Authorities in all seven states responded in the spirit of cordial helpfulness and without any rancor at all regarding how Oklahoma's prison twine factory might compete with theirs (although at that time only Wisconsin, Minnesota, and Michigan were selling twine out of state). The wardens of Indiana and Kansas not only gave a great deal of useful advice but also invited Governor Williams and his warden to visit their facilities to see in person how a twine mill could operate in a prison setting. The Indiana warden's response was very realistic and cautious, suggesting that his twine plant "has been fairly successful, but the sailing has not been smooth. Opposition by the large manufacturers and prejudice against prison made twine have been constant handicaps." The Kansas response noted that "binder twine is chiefly made of Sisal Fiber . . . [which] is produced in Yucatán and can be purchased at any time." The superintendent there emphasized that quality was of primary concern in the competitive binder twine market. On that note he had a unique suggestion that certainly no other prison could claim. He advised officials at McAlester to seek out the "number of good operators in your Oklahoma State Prison who learned the trade while they were confined in the Kansas State Prison" (before Oklahoma's statehood and establishment of its prison) for their experience at running the spinning and baller machinery.[36]

Reasons for establishing prison twine plants varied. Most were designed to bring in hard cash to sustain a revolving fund for the running of the penitentiaries and thus avoid drawing on scarce state funds. Only a couple of years after Kansas opened its prison twine plant, Gov. Willis Bailey announced to the legislature that he was pleased with its "reasonable degree of success" and called on the plant to be maintained and continued so that its profits could be accumulated "to protect the revolving fund from loss." South Dakota officials described their revolving fund as a tax that had been voted in by the people of the state to be used as "working capital" and how "nothing [could] be paid out of [it] except by a Legislative act." Oklahoma used most of its penitentiary twine plant profits for the building of additional cells and projects at its smaller prisons around the state.[37]

A primary reason for establishing the plants was the idea of reducing prisoner idleness. A past president of the American Correctional Association expressed this thinking well: "Ours is a society built on the work ethic and enforced idleness deprives offenders of self-respect and a sense of purpose. The danger of having large numbers of inmates with no constructive outlet for their energies can be overcome by a balanced program that employs as many persons as possible in productive labor."[38] Such was the case in North Dakota when during its first year of producing prison twine (1900) with eighty prisoners employed, the warden viewed the new factory as a place that would provide "employment for those inmates who were under these conditions obliged to be supported in idleness." According to a later prison brochure, without the twine plant the "unfortunate men" at the penitentiary would have to be "locked up in their cells most of the time and would not have the opportunity to earn money for themselves." The same could be said of all the prison twine factories. In fact, a visitor to the Kansas State Penitentiary in 1923 cleverly remarked in a letter to Gov. Jonathan Davis that "the place where the binding twine was [made] resembled a hive of busy bees. There was not one single idle workman to *bee* seen from the time we entered the building til we left it."[39]

An even bigger reason for establishing the state twine plants was so that the state's farmers could cut their costs. In Minnesota prison officials calculated that by 1907 their less expensive twine had saved the state's farmers an estimated $750,000 since the prison began its cordage operations. The warden of the South Dakota prison figured that in the four years between 1909 and 1913 his twine plant had saved the farmers in his state a total of $200,000 "as a difference between the State price of twine and the Trust price." He also noted in a letter to Gov. Robert Williams of Oklahoma that his prison twine plant had served as a "leveler of prices," that there "was no telling how much farmers would have to pay for twine if it were not for the State's Twine Plant." Kansas officials felt likewise, with the warden writing to Williams that his twine plant could "manufacture twine at 1¢ per pound profit and still undersell the Trust price 1¢ per pound."[40]

In North Dakota, the prison warden recognized these advantages as early as 1902 and noted that besides creating work for otherwise idle convicts, the cordage plant demonstrated "that the consumers of twine in the state . . . have reaped no small benefit by being enabled to buy their twine at materially lower prices than they could have done if the twine plant had not been installed." The pamphlet mentioned earlier also pointed out that the inmates' work at the factory made available to the farmers of the state a "high quality Binder Twine at cost plus only a small profit." Thus, the prison factory was serving as a "price regulator in the binding twine market"; since its opening in 1900 it had already saved customers hundreds of thousands of dollars. The warden explained in a 1922 report that "a savings of a cent a pound to the farmers who buy this twine means more than $250,000." In reality, he continued, the prison had "operated to reduce the general level of prices more than three cents, thus making an annual savings to farmers of between $700,000 and $800,000." The report concluded by saying that the twine plant was one of the "most valuable assets" and "the most important manufacturing industry" in the state.[41]

To prove all this to the public, enthusiastic officials promoted the North Dakota twine plant in a variety of unique ways. Stamped on packages of twine, invoices, and even the prison's biennial report of 1901–1902 was the announcement, "You Are Urgently Invited to Visit the Twine Plant at Your Earliest Convenience." Visitors to the Bismarck facility included school groups who toured the state penitentiary and got to watch the twine being made (as the author's father did in the late 1930s). Many farmers made the trip to Bismarck to purchase their binder twine directly from the prison (which the author's relatives also did). And for further public relations, the state prison issued educational pamphlets in 1911 and 1925. In the first one, entitled "North

Figure 5.3. North Dakota prison twine parade float entry. Courtesy State Historical Society of North Dakota (0395-4).

Dakota Twine and Cordage Company: A State Institution and Enterprise," the warden wrote, "It is of vital importance to you, as a taxpayer, that this industry should be operated and maintained on a paying basis. The product is guaranteed in every respect; it is second to none. . . . You will find that the prices are right, and terms liberal. . . . [Y]ou are cordially invited to come out and inspect the plant." The brochure contained pictures of not only "how twine is made" but also of the sisal industry in Yucatán and manila from the Philippines (although the North Dakota plant over time used very little of this more expensive fiber), and it mentioned other fibers such as New Zealand hemp and African sisal. The public relations schemes seemed to work. By June 1902 the plant's entire supply was sold out. In the first two years of operation, the state had sold more than 2 million pounds of binder twine.[42] The North Dakota Penitentiary also showcased its twine on floats in local parades (Figure 5.3) and even displayed it at a booth at the Great Exposition in San Francisco in 1915.

Kansans boasted similarly about their twine facility. It was built and run "in the interest of the Kansas farmers," a warden explained in 1914. According to a state Board of Corrections member, state law prohibited running the plant for profit, stressing that the mission was "to give the farmers of Kansas twine at cost of production," allowing the state to sell twine at always around a cent per pound cheaper than other brands. An additional financial benefit was that the plant became so successful that its profits paid the wages for all Kansas prison inmates working in other industries and farms.[43] Farmers in South Dakota accrued even additional savings on their prison-made twine from the penitentiary in Sioux Falls. There, a warden had expressed in 1912 that the state twine plant had been established "with the idea that the farmer might reap the benefit of the industry by being able to secure their twine at reasonable prices." And indeed they did, he was happy to note, buying their prison twine at two to five cents a pound less than twine sold by the "trust." Even at those prices, the prison generated considerable revenue—more than seventy-two thousand dollars since it had opened three years earlier in 1909—which allowed the twine factory to run in the black.[44]

Interestingly, henequen trade journals in Yucatán published many of these kinds of reports that kept growers informed about what was happening in their North American market. The journal *El agricultor* noted in 1907 that prison twine plants were providing benefits to state governments, inmates, and farmers and that they gave "a certain blow to the big corporations." Later that year it reported on the specific prices for manufactured binder twine coming out of places like Bismarck, Jefferson City, Michigan City, and Lansing—towns that most Yucatecans, even the wealthy ruling henequen families, would not have known or cared much about prior to their sending shipments of sisal there. And the journal *El henequén* even reprinted the Minnesota prison warden's annual binder twine plant report on an entire page of a late 1916 edition.[45]

Part of the reason that twine prices could stay so low, especially in the early years of the prison plants, was the wardens' close involvement in acquiring sisal. The most pertinent example of this hands-on management was when the wardens of Minnesota, North Dakota, and Kansas traveled to Yucatán in December 1901. They designed the trip to purchase their raw materials on location, "where practically all the sisal fiber produced in the world is grown," as North Dakota's warden N. F. Boucher later wrote, "for use in our respective plants." Boucher made no mention in his report of how he and his colleagues found the balmy, tropical climate of Yucatán, especially compared to December in North Dakota and Minnesota, but he did relate how he acquired five hundred bales of henequen at "3/8 of a cent [per pound] under the market price in New York" and that arrangements had been made for "future purposes . . . at a saving to the state of 1/4 to 3/8 of a cent per pound." The wardens also confirmed shipping arrangements for their purchases—by boat to New Orleans, then up the Mississippi River, then by freight trains to Stillwater, Bismarck, or Lansing (Figure 5.4).[46] State records do not indicate that the wardens, or their successors, made other trips to Yucatán. They

Figure 5.4. Unloading bales of sisal from Yucatán at the Kansas State Penitentiary twine plant, Lansing, Kansas, 1936. Courtesy Kansas State Historical Society (FK2.7*21).

probably did not, as arrangements for future sales had been made on this trip, and, by the next decade, henequen sales were often via the Peabody Company that handled sales for many state prisons, especially as the prisons needed to compete with IH, and later were restricted by the policies and prices that the Yucatecan henequen regulating commission (CRMH) had set.

Like all industries, the penitentiary twine business across North America had its fair share of problems. Most of the low points in the industry's history, however, were due to situations outside of prison officials' control. For example, the issue of convict versus free labor continued to plague the penitentiaries. Plant managers had to deal with constant fluctuations in demand (due to inconsistent harvests and variable weather conditions), in fiber prices (controlled earlier by IH and Peabody and later by the CRMH), in policies made law by legislatures, and so forth. Some had to deal with poor management and financial problems, especially during the depression. Others had inmate troubles that resulted in riots, strikes, and damaged twine. Three of the factories sustained serious fires that temporarily halted operations.

Local examples of concern about penal labor competing with private business surfaced at the penitentiaries around the turn of the century, although their twine factories were not much affected by the earlier contract lease system. In Kansas, trade union and mining interests worked to end the system, starting with the Kansas Federation of Labor, which began lobbying against it as early as 1873. The state legislature passed a law outlawing the contract lease system in 1899—the year that the prison opened its twine factory.[47] Michigan and Indiana passed similar laws in 1900 and 1904, respectively, again with little impact on their twine mills. In Minnesota, people's concerns about convict labor at the twine plant in Stillwater competing against private industry came to light in 1915 when letters to the editor of the *Minneapolis Morning Tribune* decried the use of prison labor. One writer argued that inmate labor decreased incentive for other companies to move to the state, especially if the prison expanded its use of prisoners at such low wages.[48] It was not an illogical argument. According to a contemporary study, most prison-made goods did not compete that significantly with commercially manufactured products, but not so with binder twine. In that line, the prisons, especially in some states, such as Minnesota, represented a real threat to the commercial twine market. The cordage industry responded with bitter protests, insisting that twine making was a poor task for prisons to adopt because saving money on labor was only a minor part of the overall manufacturing expense and that there were too many seasonal and financial risks involved for it to be profitable.[49]

Other elements beyond prison authorities' control that affected twine production included a worker's strike, which took place at the Kingston Penitentiary in Ontario in January 1899 when forty inmates working in the twine shop staged a sit-down strike. They were actually protesting the overcrowded cells and other harsh conditions at the prison, but the strike spread from the "binder twine gang" to the "stone pile gang" and then the next day to the "masonry gang" and the "blacksmith gang."[50] The strike only temporarily halted operations; the plant was up and running again soon after the strikers were punished. Later that year, inmates at the Stillwater State Prison in Minnesota staged what became a violent insurrection in the binder twine plant. The source of the unrest was animosity toward a particular guard rather than issues about the plant itself, but the uprising stalled plant operations. The inmates planned the action in secret using notes on the bobbins to tell inmates to stop working on their machines, and one prisoner hurled a piece of iron off of a spinner at the guard, with a full-fledged fight among workers and guards ensuing. The riot became bloody, prompting the warden to inquire, mistakenly, if the inmates had used the sisal fiber lying around in the shop to wipe the blood from their hands. After the warden placed the fighting workers in solitary confinement, the twine plant was back in operation the next day.[51]

The first fire to affect a prison twine plant was in Ontario's Central Prison in 1909, and it caused the factory to shut down for seven months. Authorities never did determine whether it was caused by accident or arson, but later that year they reopened it. The prison itself remained open only until 1915 and thus its twine plant had less of an impact on the overall binder twine needs of Canadian farmers than did the Kingston Penitentiary.[52] Another major twine plant fire occurred at the Indiana State Prison–North in 1924. That fire took more than a day to extinguish because the oil-treated sisal could smolder for a long time. The blaze destroyed the prison's twine plant, at a loss of $175,000, which shut the factory down.[53]

A fire that destroyed the Kansas State Penitentiary twine plant in Lansing in 1913, however, had implications worthy of more in-depth study here. For Kansas, usually the top wheat producing state in the United States, in the year 1913, when farmers started to expand grain-growing operations significantly across the state, having a fully operating twine facility that offered reduced prices for binder twine had already become a necessity. There was no discussion of whether the prison twine plant would be rebuilt or not; it reopened for manufacturing early the next year.

The fire occurred on April 12, and front-page coverage of the disaster in area newspapers was sensational and varying, especially as to how the fire began and the role of the inmates in either starting it or helping to extinguish it. The fire destroyed all of the walls in the plant within forty-five minutes and, according to the *Topeka Daily Capital*, it spread to the twine storeroom, where the "oil-soaked twine balls caught like [gun] powder." The room soon became a "cauldron of flame," with water having no effect. As for inmate involvement, Gov. George Hodges, who immediately traveled to Lansing to inspect the burning factory, said, "Those who hazarded their lives in saving others or the property of the state would receive great consideration when they came before the board for parole." The *Kansas City Star* excitedly reported that Warden Julian Codding and his son were "on guard with drawn revolvers during the excitement . . . ready to fight to the death should any of the imprisoned men try to escape."[54] None did. Firefighters extinguished the blaze that afternoon before it could reach the cell house where the majority of the inmates lived. Likewise, as the *Topeka Daily Capital* related, about 2.5 million pounds of binder twine (the actual amount was 1,384,870 pounds, as officials reported later) "went up in smoke," causing a loss of about $700,000. Included were all the accounts and records because the twine mill's business office was destroyed along with the factory. The *Topeka Daily Capital* added that Governor Hodges, "standing in the lurid glare of the flames," spoke with the warden about rebuilding and said that "certain action" would be taken at once.[55]

Two days after the fire Warden Codding provided a detailed report of the damages to Governor Hodges and pointed out that only one-third of that year's twine orders could be filled. However, that estimate was unfortunately optimistic. By spring of 1914, only one-twentieth of the orders were filled due to the lack of twine created by the fire, and the many canceled orders forced farmers to purchase the higher-priced brands. Codding had tried to warn farmers and solicit their support during this time. In a letter to customers he described "the disastrous fire" as an "act of Providence" that "no-one regrets . . . more than the Board [of Corrections] and myself." He requested that they send cash or money orders for the next year's twine orders, explaining that the prison needed the money "to get the plant going again."[56] He then contacted machinery brokers to order spinners, ballers, and other supplies to outfit the factory.

Prison officials, however, found that to be easier said than done. By May they were experiencing difficulties finding the machinery and the available sisal, and rumors flew that IH was somehow making equipment hard to come by and raising its price of twine to take advantage of the market in Kansas where customers could not buy the prison-made product. A member of the Board of Corrections wrote a letter to the *Kansas City Star* asserting that IH "jumped the price of twine two cents [a pound] since the burning of the Kansas prison twine plant."[57] The response from IH headquarters was indignant and defensive, as shown in a letter from IH president R. C. Haskins: "The price of binder twine has gone up all over the world. . . . [B]ad trade conditions in Yucatán have sent up the cost of raw material. . . . Every mill at home and abroad, and every prison twine mill in America has been compelled to increase twine prices this year. Our prices . . . were not increased since your fire." And regarding the equipment, he argued, "Your letter darkly hints that someone has taken options of all available twine machinery to embarrass the state of Kansas." In addition, the IH twine mill manager indicated that a variety of manufacturers had new spinners and twine-making equipment for sale and that cordage companies back East had used available machinery.[58]

Warden Codding at least had the backing of Governor Hodges throughout these trying times. He sent another letter to him soon after the fire, thanking him for his "self-sacrifice" and the "manly spirit you showed toward this institution and toward us during our recent calamity" and this "very dark period of my life." Hodges responded with his full support: "I was glad I could be with you. . . . I have the same interest in your institution that all good Kansans should have." He also indicated that while "hampered by want of money," he hoped the state could "rebuild a bigger and better" twine facility and that he had called a special meeting to take up the matter of funding. And then in a postscript befitting any politician, he added, "I am glad to know you will save one carload of twine for the farmers of Johnson County."[59] Hodges was a Democrat from Olathe, Kansas (in Johnson County), who had won his 1912 gubernatorial race on Woodrow Wilson's long coattails and due to a factional split in the Republican Party. The twine load for his home county, however, did not have enough political benefits for Hodges to overcome the traditional GOP advantage, and Republican candidate Arthur Capper won the governor's seat in 1914.[60] Hodges's letter of support did not sufficiently ameliorate Warden Codding's predicament. The fire in the twine plant, the funding and equipment acquisition problems, and news from the twine plant clerk that there were many uncollected (and probably, uncollectible) accounts from farmers around the state all caused him to resign in June 1913.[61]

The new warden Hodges appointed was Jeremiah Botkin, who took an active role in rebuilding the plant. By the end of the year it was completed, with 120 spinners (20 more than the old plant), fire-proof walls, and a sprinkler system. It was, according to one prison official, "an exact duplicate of the International mills."[62] Warden Botkin noted to the governor that it was "running full blast . . . like the works of a first-class watch." The first twine rolled out on January 2, 1914, in a factory now made to produce an estimated 3 million pounds of twine per year. Later that month, Botkin sent Hodges some samples from the plant along with another letter that explained the twine making process and illustrated very clearly the ties between grain producing Kansas and Mexico : "I am sending you today . . . a ball of twine, together with a nice bunch of sisal, which you may desire to place in your office. The sisal came from Yucatán . . . and was made from the fiber of the cactus [*sic*] leaf. . . . We are all proud of our twine mill."[63]

It is unknown whether Hodges displayed the sisal fiber and the ball of twine in his office—he may have been the only top state official to have those items sent for official gubernatorial display. But equally important, Botkin's gift symbolized the fact that the prison mill was back up and running by 1914. That was the year in which Kansas farmers experienced their most abundant wheat crop to date (172,750,000 bushels, not surpassed until 1928 with its 173,185,000 bushels). It was also the year that wheat production in Kansas surpassed that of corn—"the deposed king," as one account put it, representing "a sharp increase in wheat rather than a decrease in corn."[64] As was discussed in chapter 1, much of the demand that fueled the increase in production was due to World War I and America's effort to help keep its European allies' armies fed. For the 1914 bumper crop, that meant that Kansans used 20 million pounds of binder twine, 15 percent of which came from the penitentiary twine factory. Unfilled orders for 5 million pounds more prompted a frustrated Warden Botkin to write that such a figure showed "how impossible it is for us to supply demand." Even double shifts, producing 16 thousand pounds a day, could not fill the orders.[65] Later that year, based on a great harvest, Botkin lobbied for an expansion of the twine plant, even though it had only been a year since the rebuilding. He suggested that because the mill was producing "hardly a drop in the bucket compared with demands," the state construct two other twine plants that could produce 9 million pounds annually plus an extra storage warehouse to replace the one that burned. With such additions the dealers and farmers could "control the price of binder twine."[66]

It was a sound proposal, especially considering that more Kansas farmers were eager to buy the twine and the state would be able to make good on a solid financial investment. But his hopes were dashed with the gubernatorial election of 1915 in which Republican Arthur Capper, who, although making agriculture one of his chief concerns, especially with the war effort, cut state spending and did not support the expansion of the twine mill.[67] This turn of events was surprising in some ways; the factory was not only operating solidly in the black but also turning a good profit for the state. The Board of Corrections reported in 1915 that the twine plant was "one of the most profitable manufacturing concerns" in Kansas. And in 1916 the plant did even better, selling $204,000 worth of twine—almost doubling the previous year's total. A new warden reported to Capper that the prospects for the next year were just as good since the plant had nearly 1.5 million pounds of raw sisal in storage and a great deal of finished twine ready to distribute.[68] Capper, however, showed his support for the state's farmers and for the prison factory in other ways. He actively supported the state's efforts to keep the price of the prison-made twine 1 to 1.5 cents per pound cheaper than "the trust twine," and he endorsed a plan to give farmers a discount for cash payments for their orders. Representing the sentiments of many farm families across the state, one farmer wrote the governor, "You can hardly believe how much your efforts have been, and will be, appreciated. Keep on."[69] The prison did exactly that, especially with the growing popularity of its twine during the postwar years when wheat, now going to help the people of wartorn Europe, still fetched wartime prices. Kansas farmers continued expanding their wheat acreage, creating an even larger demand for prison twine, which the factory simply could not meet. Some farmers started to drive to Lansing in the northeast corner of the state to buy it on site.[70]

In some ways the above troubles pale in comparison to the problems that the South Dakota State Prison twine factory in Sioux Falls had to confront in 1919 and 1920: sabotaged twine. Various inmates employed in the plant had cut large amounts of twine into small segments as they were being balled. Their actions caused a great deal of grief among farmers and farm supply deal-

ers and stimulated a special legislative investigation in early 1921 into the operations of the twine factory itself. As one member of the Board of Charities
and Corrections, which oversaw the prison for the state, put it, "We got into a
bad snarl."[71]

It is difficult to discern exactly how and when the snarl was discovered.
South Dakota officials would investigate those questions, but first they had to
deal with a large quantity of ruined twine and angry farmers. The Farmers'
Grain Dealers Association received the brunt of the complaints and became
the organization representing farmers and elevator operators demanding compensation. Its general secretary solicited complaints and received a flurry of
letters from affected parties all over South Dakota, which were then entered as
evidence in the investigation. Not unlike the time when fiber was embargoed
at the port of Progreso, Yucatán, in 1915, the controversy became known in
the state as the "Twine Situation." One farmer's letter perhaps best explained
the problem: "The twine is a bad mess, much of the twine is cut. . . . [A] farmer
found balls of twine stuffed with rags. Personally I have had a bad time with
this prison twine, I am thru with it. . . . [W]hile cutting grain we find a loose
bundle, get off and examine [the twine] can, and find a lot of cut twine. . . .
This we pull out as far as we can find it and throw it away, lace and needle
and start again, and perhaps . . . lace needle several times on account of cut
twine. [It] entails a considerable loss in *twine,* in *time lost,* and *loose bundles cause*
a *loss* of *time* in *shocking* and *loss* of *time in loading, waste of time in pitching* grain
at [the] separator."[72] Later, during a hearing on the matter, the same farmer
complained about the "cut and chopped" twine and how during harvest when
"that goes on continually . . . a person's patience is worn out."[73] An outraged
co-op operator, left with five thousand pounds of prison twine he could never
sell, wrote in complaining of the "considerable trouble" his customers had had
"on account of a good deal of [the twine] being cut right in the balls, purposely
by some of the workers in the plant." Another elevator operator left with a
large quantity of ruined twine wrote of similar problems with it and that "the
farmers would not trust it now." Indeed, the "Twine Situation" was a big matter of discussion at the state Farmers' Grain Dealers Association convention in
January 1919.[74]

A number of complaints compared the prison twine with that of other
brands when discussing why they had to drop their orders with the state penitentiary. One angry farmer wrote that he had purchased two hundred pounds
of twine, but because "in the center of about ten balls the twine was cut in
lengths about one foot long," he threw out his entire lot and the next year
bought IH twine. "It cost more," he explained, "but I don't like to have trouble
in the harvest." In the same vein, a dealer who had exclusively sold prison
twine for years canceled his order for 1920 and wrote, "The small difference

in price between the prison twine and the Deering or other twine makes the price no object to a farmer who is in a hurry to get his crop out."[75]

Representing the dealers and farmers, the Farmers' Grain Dealers Association took these concerns directly to the governor of South Dakota, Peter Norbeck, along with demands for reimbursements to farmers who had purchased the sabotaged twine, and for the governor to call a special session of the state legislature to make the appropriations. The legislature took up the matter the following summer and created a special committee to investigate the prison operations.[76] Prison officials testified before the committee that they had caught inmates using shoemaker's knives to cut the twine as it went around the baller so that the balled twine did not have the appearance of being irregular. Unfortunately, the discovery came too late, after much of the bad twine had been shipped. They also spoke of how "considerable" amounts of the twine had been returned to them for re-balling, which cost three-quarters of a cent per pound to do, a process conducted with the advice of a New York cordage company. The prison warden testified that personnel problems were at the root of the problem: "To my mind, it isn't possible for this institution to make a twine as perfect . . . as can be made by the Plymouth people who have the same men year after year. We have a man here and he serves a year or two years and . . . and then we have to instruct a new man. We have to teach them how to operate the machine, how to run the thread, teach them to ball the ball."[77] The twine plant superintendent, who had worked at Plymouth Cordage for eleven years before taking the position at the prison, agreed and added that there were too many transfers of inmates in and out of the factory—they would transfer to the prison farm, kitchen, garden, or be paroled just as they learned the factory work. Yet he argued that the South Dakota twine was usually of good quality: "To be honest, I would say it would be a trifle inferior, but not much. I have had Plymouth twine that is not as good as ours, and I have had better."[78]

Discovering who was involved and why was a more difficult matter. Prison officials identified four convicts they believed were the culprits; some were caught in the act, and the officials maintained that the suspects had probably conspired with others. But what were their reasons for cutting the twine? Several theories emerged from the committee's proceedings. Some committee members were convinced that the episode was part of a larger conspiracy to get back at the state, a move organized by inmates who were members of the radical labor union Industrial Workers of the World (IWW, whose members were known as the "Wobblies"). One board member testified that all of South Dakota was suffering "from I.W.W. sabotage. . . . They burned elevators and corn cribs, damaged crops, and they supplied the very worst type of man we have had in the prison, and they did all the damage." The theory was backed up by the fact that one of the principal twine cutting convicts was an IWW member and by hearsay that Wobbly literature was wrapped in some balls of damaged twine.[79] Although officials admitted such a conspiracy was possible, they did not think that was the main reason. The guards never heard talk of any plots, none of the IWW literature was presented as evidence, and, as historian Herbert Schell has written, Wobblies during the era of World War I were often scapegoats—they "were suspect whenever acts of violence . . . occurred" in the state.[80]

As testimony continued, the committee learned that a more probable reason for the twine sabotaging was as a way for the inmates to get even with the former warden who had promised them privileges, including early parole, but who did not come through on his word. As the committee pursued this line, however, it became aware of other work-related and prison-related grievances that, as the convicts testified, led to acts of revenge. Complaints like poor medical service, insufficient food, the unpleasant task of working with wet and rotting sisal fiber, "inhumane" treatment and brutal punishments by a former deputy warden, and poor pay (eight cents an hour for nine-and-a-half-hour shifts) were common. The plant superintendent tended to agree: "The men were pushed from those unsanitary cells to that dusty, noisy, greasy twine plant and back again, and it bred dissatisfaction."[81] Thus, the majority of the testimony led the legislative committee to conclude that the most probable reason for sabotaged twine was inmates' revenge against a despised prison administration, not political protest.

Perhaps more important to state officials was ensuring that such misdeeds be prevented in the future and that the plant remain open. They heard from the state examiner, who said that the factory was a "valuable asset to the state" by keeping "a leverage on the outside trust in charging exorbitant prices." He quoted a farmer who had pleaded, "Don't let them destroy the twine plant. The only time it caused any trouble was . . . [when] we had the cut twine." Another farmer volunteered, "I wish this plant would keep right on making twine. I think that if it hadn't been for this twine plant, twine would have been a good deal higher for us." He also mentioned that the prison twine was not much different from other brands and that he and his neighbors wanted the plant to remain open, especially since the other companies' twine "went up so terrible high"—five to ten cents a pound more than the prison's.[82]

The press in South Dakota echoed those sentiments. "State Twine Plant Not to Be Abandoned" announced the front-page headlines of the *Sioux Falls Argus-Leader* at the end of the hearings. Despite "trouble with disgruntled workers" and how "poor quality and cut twine the last two seasons ha[d] so destroyed public confidence," the factory would remain open, the damaged twine would be discarded, and the prison would sell its remaining stock.[83] The preventive measures must have worked, as there were no more problems of sabotaged twine or records of further disturbances at the prison's twine plant. It remained in operation until 1950.

In North Dakota, the penitentiary twine plant in Bismarck did not undergo dramatic events such as riots, fires, or sabotaged twine; its operations ran fairly smoothly from when it opened in 1899 until the 1920s. Then, however, a problem developed that affected the plant's financial stability and demanded considerable time and attention from twine plant officials. The issue that arose was a significant problem in the collection of notes on binder twine delivered to customers. Minnesota suffered from the same problem for twine sales, especially in 1925.[84] In the 1920s, wheat prices dropped dramatically after demand for grains had significantly subsided with the end of the war in Europe. Farmers throughout the Great Plains felt the slump acutely, especially since they had to pay higher prices for twine; many simply could not pay their bills for it. North Dakota prison records include several large boxes of notices from plant business manager Thurman Wright to farmers and dealers around the state, a majority of them directed to the northwestern part of the state, about their unpaid bills. His standard form letter on the matter read that "we are not writing letters to you about this note because we like to write you, but because we want you to pay the note and interest. If we cannot cause you to pay it by writing letters to you, we shall be compelled to refer it to our attorney for action."[85]

Interestingly, the letters farmers wrote in response to Wright's notice create a kind of microcosm of the social and agricultural history of the region at this time; the letters dealt with crop yields, weather problems, personal health conditions, and general economic issues that farmers faced in those days and that affected the state's twine plant. Representative of many was the response in October 1923 from a farmer in Donnybrook, North Dakota, who owed $40.65. In his letter he explained, "We have not thrashed [*sic*] at present and when I do get some plowing done before it freezes up as we can haul grain when it is froze but cannot plow if we are going to farm . . . we got to watch our time." That same autumn a farmer from Kenmare, North Dakota, who owed $33.69 responded to Wright's notice by saying, "I have paid up my twine bill both this year and last, [but] I have had an accident and have not been able to be about much lately. We were badly hailed and crops [were] very poor. It is almost impossible to meet any obligation of any kind this year." Wright understood these kinds of farming conditions and often tempered his letters accordingly. To a dealer in Tolley, North Dakota, who owed the twine plant $289.00, for example, he wrote, "We understand that threshing was exceptionally late in your vicinity, due to weather conditions and the large volume of crops, . . . but we need to make settlement."[86] Such correspondence also illus-

trates the extent of the involvement of the prison twine plant with area implement and hardware dealers, and the extent to which those dealers came to rely
on the prison industry to meet their binder twine needs. There were hundreds
of such stores around North Dakota, most of which were small, family-owned
enterprises struggling to survive just like their farmer customers in the early
twentieth century. They relied on and benefited from their prison twine sales.

Survival for farmers, dealers, and the twine plant itself became even
tougher in the 1930s. The factory's business office sent more overdue payment
notices to the farmers and dealers during that droughty decade, and the managers of the plant had to learn to be creative in making ends meet to keep the
plant running with less cash available from customers. One avenue they re-
searched was to acquire the least costly fiber on the market. In the fall of 1929
North Dakota officials began watching the Yucatán henequen market very
closely, mainly via the Peabody firm of Boston. "We remind you that we are
the only House that still has a branch in Yucatán," a Peabody representative
wrote to the penitentiary in Bismarck, adding that "our neighbors have folded
their tents like the Arabs and silently stolen away." Peabody kept a close eye
on the situation with Yucatecan growers and their distributor, the CRMH,
and dutifully made "confidential deals" for the North Dakota prison to acquire
"brushed" or "special marked" sisal, to buy when prices started to drop, to
monitor what IH was doing with prices, and so forth. The firm also alerted
Bismarck when competing sisal growers in Haiti and Africa offered better
prices for fiber.[87] Tough times and stiff competition meant making the prison's
purchasing dollar go as far as possible.

The situation also called for penitentiaries to compete more intensely with
other manufacturers, including other state prisons. Going against giants like
IH was no easy task; as early as 1904 McCormick Harvesting Company had
decided to compete with the lower-priced prison twines around the country by making a "cheaper" generic product called "Plain-tagged Twine" that
came without the McCormick, and later IH, logo. But unlike the prison-made
twines, IH's Plain-tagged brand was made by blending flax and other fibers
with sisal to create a lower quality product.[88] Understandably, the cordage
industry was alarmed that prisons would undersell commercial manufacturers
and, as some prisons would do, guarantee their prices to be always lower than
that of commercial twine. The industry also considered it unfair that public
taxes were used to support farming, which they argued in reality brought little financial return to state residents because the lower binder twine prices
were offset by higher taxes to pay for all the expenses involved with manufacturing subsidized twine.[89] Thus, IH, Plymouth Cordage, and other companies kept close tabs on what their state-funded competitors were producing,
where they sold twine, and what kinds of profits they were making. In a con-

fidential memo to IH in 1933, Plymouth listed each penitentiary's production outputs between 1925 and 1931 (predictably, the highest was in Minnesota with 24 million pounds a year, and Michigan second with 10 million pounds), and for some (like South Dakota's plant) how many pounds of twine were on hand to be sold. The report also highlighted how Wisconsin twine was sold in eleven different midwestern states. Plymouth included the entire Minnesota State Prison Industries business statement for 1929 and seemed pleased to announce that "competition from private industries in twine has reduced the profits of this activity."[90]

In Canada, especially during World War I, shortages of twine caused many Canadian farmers to demand U.S. twine, via legal or black market routes. Often the Michigan and Wisconsin state prisons sold twine across the international border, and more commonly it was smuggled into Canada for willing farmers wanting to pay less than the prices of commercial Canadian twine. Manufacturers such as Brantford Cordage of Ontario tried to stem the tide by arguing that U.S. prison-made twine was of inferior quality ("irregular and unreliable") due to the "class of labour" in the penitentiaries ("free labour factories"). They even asserted that the twine bore labels "intended to mislead the public" of its origin, which would lead to "grave injustices to [the] farmers" of Canada, and they lobbied strongly for increased border inspections of twine to keep out the Michigan and Wisconsin prison twines. Also, the United Farmers of Manitoba passed a resolution in 1928 requesting that the government continue its inspections to keep defective twine off the market. It sent a copy of the resolution to the Canadian minister of agriculture, W. R. Motherwell. And as late as 1937 IH was still advising farmers to avoid the less expensive off-brands like those made in state prisons. In the brochure "The Story of Twine," IH warned farmers that when "you have a chance to buy at lower prices . . . you have no assurance that this saving will not be more than offset by short weight, short length, or lost time due to breaks in the binder."[91] Unfortunately for South Dakota in 1919 and 1920, that scenario was altogether too real, albeit rare.

For a while it also became a real scenario in Kansas. In 1918 and again in 1930 complaints poured into the prison about "inferior twine." "Why can't the prison turn out as good [a] twine as the private manufacturers?" an attorney representing Fredonia, Kansas, farmers inquired directly to Gov. Clyde Reed. He claimed that the prison twine was "of inferior quality . . . [with] heavy places and light places" causing the binder's knotter to bind up and break. He also cited how some farmers complained that the twine went only three-fifths as far as trade brands and that it was not being treated to prevent damage from crickets. He related how one farmer was so angry that he dumped his stock into a granary and went to town to buy another brand. Another was so frustrated at the twine for being "as thick as one's finger [in places], while in other places it only consisted of three or four strands of sisal," that he threw it all into the river. "It's a matter of serious concern to farmers of Kansas," the attorney wrote, and should "be investigated and remedied."[92]

But state officials fought back. A Board of Corrections member investigated the situation and found that the Fredonia farmers were "entirely mistaken." He reported to the governor that many farmers praised the twine's quality and that it equaled any other sold in the state. He wondered if the complaints might have stemmed from other manufacturers: "Sometimes the competitors, particularly . . . International Harvester Co. and the John Deere Co., grossly misrepresent Penitentiary twine." The prison warden also wrote the complaining attorney, making a solid case for the prison. He argued that the prison sold twine at cost, which had "saved many thousands of dollars to the farmers" as a "bar to the exorbitant prices by combinations," how a "long list" of merchants handled it without complaint, how farmers often were "disgusted with other twine" and bought "ours because their neighbors recommend it," and how the occasional "faults" had been "grossly exaggerated" since the prison twine "remained in big demand . . . year after year." He challenged the lawyer to make his own comparisons by checking balls from other companies.[93]

Officials from state prisons also started having much closer contact and aggressive competition with each other in the 1920s and 1930s. The problem stemmed from the fact that some states had policies forbidding the sale of prison-made twine across state lines and some did not. The legislatures in North Dakota, South Dakota, and Kansas mandated a no-out-of-state-sales policy to ensure that sufficient binder twine was available for their own farmers, and the policy was strictly enforced. In Kansas, for example, the penitentiary's warden explained to an inquiring firm that the prison had "refused to sell a pound outside the state and [had] required all dealers to promise to sell their [prison-made] twine only to Kansas consumers."[94] The South Dakota warden in 1913 further clarified the issue when writing to Governor Williams of Oklahoma: "We have no trouble in selling our twine and could in fact sell considerably more. . . . The manufacture of twine by means of convict[s] at a state prison is not out of harmony with the 'state-use' plan in the management of prisons. . . . The agricultural interests are so interwoven with the prosperity of the entire state that the manufacture of twine . . . is part of the recognized 'state-use' plan."[95]

The policy soon became unpopular, however, especially when the CRMH raised its fiber prices dramatically in 1915. After that, inquiries for cheaper Kansas-made twine came from Oklahoma, Missouri, and Texas and from as far away as Idaho. Typical was the letter from a farmer in Oklahoma who

Figure 5.5. Shipping binder twine from the Kansas State Penitentiary twine plant, ca. 1900. Courtesy Kansas State Historical Society (FK2.7PE1900c*2).

appealed directly to Kansas governor Arthur Capper in April 1917: "I seen a piece in your paper [*Capper's Weekly*] where you was selling binder twine at 13 cents a pound. . . . We are in need of 300 pounds and would be glad to hear from you." Another Oklahoman complained to Capper that in his town they were paying twenty cents a pound for twine compared to Kansas's price, which was seven cents lower. Perhaps the Oklahomans could not get enough of their own state's prison-made twine, as their facility in McAlester was never one of the major prison twine producers. The letter from Idaho was from a dealer who explained that due to a "shortage of twine in southern Idaho" farmers would need the Kansas twine. Each inquiry, however, received a short note back, indicating, "The State Prison cannot sell twine outside the state of Kansas."[96]

Some farmers in neighboring Missouri plotted a way to get the twine anyway. Apparently Missouri's state penitentiary twine plant in Jefferson City was too small an operation to keep up with the demand in its own state (indeed, records show that in 1914 it was the state that was buying the least amount of sisal fiber, a mere 2,000 tons compared to Minnesota's 43,400 tons or South Dakota's 11,300 tons).[97] So it would not be too difficult for Missourians living near the state line to travel into Kansas and buy large quantities of less expensive twine. Governor Capper plainly did not like this out-of-state "scheme to buy Kansas twine," as he put it in a letter to the Kansas prison warden, arguing that "certainly we don't want to sell twine to Missouri farmers when a great many Kansas farmers are complaining that they cannot get our twine." The warden responded by saying that the subject was a "delicate one," but that his business manager had "the matter in hand."[98]

Keeping up with demand seemed to be a constant problem for the prisons in Kansas and North Dakota—the two biggest wheat producing states. A Kansas warden in 1914 wrote how frustrated both he and farmers were when his prison had unfilled orders for 5 million pounds of binder twine. The figures showed "how impossible it is for us to supply the demand," even when the plant went to double shifts that produced sixteen thousand pounds a day.[99] At times, politics even played a role in who would get the twine. For example, Kansas governor George Hodges wrote the warden in May 1914 that one group of supporters in need of twine consisted of "very strong Democrats and good business men" and "friends of this administration." Thus, he continued, "if there is any way that you could edge in and give these gentlemen 10,000 pounds, please do so." And when another carload of twine ordered for Anderson County had not yet arrived, farmers there went right to the governor's office with the complaint, and his staff then contacted the prison. The response indicated that orders were "being filled as fast as possible" and that the prison was "doing everything that human endeavor can do to supply twine."[100]

The supply/demand issue only got worse in Kansas when Arthur Capper was elected governor in 1915, the year the Board of Corrections reduced the price of twine by one cent per pound (a 15 percent cut). A board member announced that the prison twine would be "the cheapest ever, and of the best quality . . . [and] will run between one and two cents [per pound] cheaper than that from outside" and that it would yield a savings of approximately $30,000 to the state's farmers. It was all made possible with the prison's purchase of five hundred bales of Yucatecan sisal at $4.29 a bale, "the cheapest in the history of the plant." But with those prices, the twine became even more popular. Thus, when orders could not be filled, some farmers once again wrote directly to the governor. His office responded that the plant was running at "full capacity until harvest time . . . [but that] most of the output is spoken for."[101]

Similarly, in North Dakota the demand for state twine became especially strong in the early 1920s. After a drought in 1921, farmers had good crops, creating "an extraordinary heavy demand for our twine," according to the plant manager then. In fact, by the close of the 1922 harvest the factory experienced an "inability to fill all orders as received" and advised customers to "secure twine elsewhere." Prison officials then increased the capacity of the twine plant for the next season so that it could produce 4 million pounds, which would still equal only 13 percent of the state's twine consumption in 1922. The plant manager was optimistic: "With abundant labor and our proximity to the almost inexhaustible lignite [coal] veins of the state providing an inexpensive fuel, we should . . . meet the competition of other plants."[102]

Tension also arose in both wheat states about distribution and sale of the prison-made twine, especially when there were supply and demand problems. Prisons had traditionally sold twine directly to farmers, but some retailers (hardware and feed stores, implement dealers, grain elevators) were able to acquire the twine and sell it for slightly higher prices. The issue first surfaced in North Dakota soon after its prison started to produce twine. In 1901 the penitentiary sold 78 percent of its output directly to farmers or farmers' organizations and the rest to dealers, but in 1902 farmers represented only 57 percent of sales and dealers 43 percent. The trend seemed to present a problem for some Fargo area farmers, who complained that they could not get prison twine and that dealers were being preferred over the farmers. The complaints must have worked; in 1903 and 1904 only 20 percent of the prison's output was sold to dealers.[103]

In Kansas similar scuttlebutt arose in 1914 when Grange members and other farmers heard that the prison was selling scarce twine to "jobbers" (wholesalers who sold to retailers). One angry Grange member complained to Governor Hodges about it. "Since this twine factory was started to benefit farmers," he wondered, "why was this twine sold so early in the season to Jobbers?" Hodges relayed the complaint to the warden, J. D. Botkin, who countered with press releases to local newspapers and circulars sent to Democratic publications and precinct members around the state to suggest to farmers and their organizations that the accusation was untrue.[104] Those efforts did not make the problem go away; in fact, the issue of twine sales to jobbers only got worse around the time Arthur Capper replaced Hodges in 1915. The new Republican governor discovered that Botkin was trying to withhold twine shipments to farmers' organizations or to sell it to them at higher prices. One organization representative wrote Capper that his group's members felt "sore about it" and that they thought the plant "was built for their benefit" but that it seemed like the jobbers "had bought up this twine in order to shut the farm organization out." Since Kansas farmers "pay 3/5 of all taxes" in the state, he argued, "they should have first chance on the out put of the plant." Capper intervened on their behalf, ordering the Board of Corrections to ensure that jobbers did not get the scarce twine—acts that made him even more popular with farmers throughout the state. A Grange member from south central Kansas wrote to applaud his efforts: "This grange commends the actions that you took and is with you almost to a man, Democrats and all."[105]

But there was also a growing competition from some prisons that had vigorous campaigns to sell twine outside their states. This caused the twine producing states to agree to a half-cent per pound surcharge on any out-of-state twine sold, a policy that would encourage customers to buy their own state's product but at the same time make it more profitable for those states with a capacity to produce more than they could use. Three such states were Minnesota, Wisconsin, and Michigan. Minnesota's intense twine sales campaign was part of its much larger farm implement production and sales business in general. Actually, in the early years of the twentieth century, the binders needed to be marketed more heavily than the Minnesota twine, which as one report stated, "did not need any pushing"—farmers and dealers were eager to get the less expensive, state-made product.[106] Thus, Stillwater prison officials actively advertised their products and employed sixteen full-time sales representatives who had their own "territories," most of which were in Minnesota but some of which included other states in the region. Some of the sales agents complained that their territories were too large, comparing them with those of the IH sales associates whose sales areas never included more than fifty towns. In great crop years such as 1915, Minnesota could not keep up with the demand from North Dakota and South Dakota and had to cancel orders. It was also one of the largest suppliers for farmers and dealers in Nebraska (which never had a prison twine facility), selling three hundred tons of twine in the state in 1922 and projecting sales of more than three times that amount for 1923. According to the sales reps, Nebraska dealers sold the less expensive Minnesota prison twine at the same prices as they sold the commercial twine.[107] As the largest prison twine facility in North America, and feeling the sharp competition from IH, it had to keep orders flowing in to keep the spinners and ballers running and the inmates employed. At one point there was a discussion on how to keep the men occupied while they were waiting for sisal bales to arrive and during other shop lulls. Officials developed a "stored sisal" plan to keep fiber available for such times, and the warden even suggested that the inmates use excess fiber to make mattresses for the prison.[108]

Wisconsin was even more aggressive. As a state whose geography was more suited to dairies than wheat farms, it is somewhat surprising that the state prison in Waupun became such a big twine marketer, especially since it was never a big producer of the product. In 1914 it purchased only 8,650 tons of sisal fiber from Yucatán, making it one of the smallest prison twine factories in the nation.[109] Ten years later it was purchasing even less: only 1,906 tons of Yucatecan sisal and 305 tons of manila hemp. Yet records show that in that year, 1924, it marketed and sold binder twine in twenty different states, garnering a profit of $62,353 for Wisconsin. The state's farmers and dealers were its primary customers, of course, but what is interesting here is that it sold twine in four other states that had their own thriving prison mills (Michigan, Minnesota, North Dakota, and Kansas), but not in the other two (South Dakota and Missouri). Surprisingly, Minnesota was its third biggest buyer. The rest went to grain producing states such as Illinois (its second largest customer), Indiana (whose prison mill was closed by this time), Iowa, Nebraska, Colorado, Montana, and Washington, and lesser amounts to states back East and in the South.[110]

South Dakota was probably not a Wisconsin twine customer in 1924, due to a bad experience it had had with it a few years earlier. In 1918, a particularly good year for wheat in South Dakota, the prison plant in Sioux Falls could not keep up with demand and was forced to buy one hundred tons of twine from the Wisconsin state prison. South Dakota prison officials traveled to Waupun "to inspect their twine," and as the warden later wrote, "while we do not believe their twine was as good as that manufactured by the South Dakota Penitentiary, still we were satisfied at that time that it would meet all the requirements."[111] But a farmers' elevator representative wrote that the "Wisconsin Brand" twine was bad: "the crickets cut the twine so badly that considerable loss has been sustained in twine and waste of grain." He then asked the state for an "adjustment for damage"—fifty-nine hundred pounds of twine—to eighteen farmers in his area. The warden responded that it would have been "impossible" for the prison to fill such an order. He further explained that "all twine was damaged by crickets last year—ours, Wisconsin's, Plymouth's, McCormick's [IH], Deering . . . in fact, all twines which were used in South Dakota . . . were more or less damaged" and that "one twine was not damaged any more than another." He concluded by stating that his Sioux Falls plant would no longer contract for any more out-of-state product, but "as there seemed to be a shortage of twine in this state, we did all within our power to supply that shortage."[112] In Minnesota, twine makers kept grasshopper damage in mind and worked to create better proofing against insects. The sales agents in Nebraska boasted that the Minnesota twine was a better against crickets than most other twines and was even better than the "Cricket-Proof Brand."[113]

The competition between penitentiaries and private manufacturers began to frustrate prison and state finance officials in Kansas. There, not only was it difficult to keep up with aggressive competitors but the state's demand for binder twine started dropping significantly in the mid-1920s as many Kansas farmers had been switching to combines (with no need for twine) to harvest their crops. To keep the twine mill running, especially given the amount of

investment the state had put into it after the fire only a decade and a half earlier, and to keep up with other producers, they knew something would have to
change. So, by the late 1920s they persuaded the legislature to allow the prison
to start marketing its twine out of state. As a result, in 1929 the prison sold
a whopping one-third or more of its twine production (724 tons) to a dealer
in Iowa.[114] The next year, to continue researching what they could be doing
better, Kansas governor Clyde Reed commissioned the state budget director,
E. L. Barrier, to travel to Stillwater to see how Minnesota could still be producing so heavily and competing on the market so aggressively, and how Kansas might be able to emulate some of those activities. Barrier's post-trip report
argued that after seeing Minnesota's operation, he knew that the Kansas system was "absolutely out-of-date." He then recommended that Kansas adopt
a direct sales and marketing campaign instead of just relying on implement
dealers and hardware stores. Governor Reed sent the proposal to the State
Board of Administration, which killed it, believing it "would antagonize the
dealers throughout the state."[115]

Then, as if things were not already bad enough for the prison twine factories, a price war broke out in April 1932 when IH and Plymouth Cordage
reduced their prices by three-fourths of a cent. That caused Minnesota to drop
its prices to six cents a pound for twine, a fact noted in a letter from industries
superintendent M. C. McMillan to the manager of North Dakota's factory.
G. D. Wagar, secretary of the Bismarck plant, responded two days later to
both Minnesota and South Dakota officials, inquiring if they were going to
continue lowering their prices. McMillan replied that "on account of the two
Dakota plants we are sorry to make prices as low as we were forced to, but
Wisconsin always seems to wish to make exceptionally low prices." He also
advised looking into Javanese sisal, which at that point was selling for less
than Yucatecan henequen.[116]

Warden J. T. Jameson of South Dakota's penitentiary replied soon after,
saying that "we, no doubt, will reduce our price 75 cents a hundred so as to
be in line with Stillwater, Minnesota. This price is ruinous, but it cannot be
helped." Jameson and other prison officials had started lobbying for an end to
South Dakota's no-out-of-state-sales policy as early as 1921, when they were
squarely back in business after the earlier twine cutting episodes.[117] By the
1930s their wish had come true; the restriction was lifted to help with cash
flow, and they were selling twine to customers in southern North Dakota and
elsewhere. With that in mind, Wagar wrote Jameson in Sioux Falls asking
how the "rule of 1/2 cent higher [price] outside South Dakota" would be enforced. "What is to stop dealers and other customers in North Dakota going
to your dealers in South Dakota close to the border and buying twine at your
prices?" asked Wagar. He requested Jameson's help in seeing that such prac-

tices were not allowed since the state prison's plant did "not solicit business in South Dakota [and had] no dealers there." Jameson's terse response illustrates the competitive nature of the business and the times: "We are not going to deviate from our announced price. . . . We are not caring whether we sell outside the State or not. . . . We deemed it necessary to make the price equal to Minnesota, because they are serious competitors of ours in this territory."[118]

Wagar was also concerned about Minnesota's encroachment in North Dakota in the early 1930s. Stillwater prison officials, still complaining about Wisconsin's twine prices and how IH and Plymouth were "fixing" prices, were at least considerate enough to have advised Bismarck in 1932 that they had sold more than a million pounds of twine to North Dakotans—60 to 80 percent of which was distributed via a company in Minot, North Dakota. Thus, Wagar wrote to Minnesota's McMillan, stating, "We believe it would help our sales if I could assure our dealers in that territory that your dealers on the Minnesota side would not push sales in North Dakota." More civil than his counterpart in Sioux Falls, McMillan replied that his factory was already oversold and that he hoped North Dakota would have a good crop and have "no trouble disposing of your entire output. . . . It is our aim to work with your state as far as possible at all times."[119]

But the competition only got worse. Michigan entered the fray in 1934 when North Dakota twine officials learned that farmers in Erie, North Dakota, were buying Michigan prison twine for only slightly more than the price at which it was being sold in Michigan. J. D. Battcher, who replaced Wagar as secretary of the twine factory in Bismarck, asked the Michigan warden how that could have been possible, considering the high freight costs involved in moving twine all the way from Michigan. The response came back that Michigan had been selling year-old twine—none from their current production.[120] Worse, relations between the two rival Dakotas did not improve when the warden in Bismarck received a notice in 1935 from the South Dakota attorney general about a "claim versus you and your state of $1,005.35 for twine purchased from our state." The letter concluded by blandly asking, "Will you kindly take the necessary steps to clean up this balance?" The North Dakota prison warden responded that no one at his institution knew anything about such a purchase and that they had no records verifying it.[121] The amount was never paid.

Interestingly, much of this interstate competitiveness did not go unobserved by the henequen interests in Yucatán. Trade journals there kept a close eye on all facets of binder twine manufacturing and sales in North America, including the penitentiaries' role in production and how they competed with private industry. In March 1935 one such journal even ran a story entitled

"The Competition of the Prisons in the United States," listing which states by then did not have laws regarding the sale of prison-made items in the free market. But it was also during this time period that some states, including Michigan, were going to the "state-use system," which mandated that goods made by convicts would be for state institutional use only, thus excluding them from the general market.[122] But 1935, the year that the Hawes-Cooper Act prohibiting interstate commerce of prison-made goods went into effect, would be the last year that private industry would have to be concerned about the problem and the last that prisons would have to worry about competition from other prisons.

Thus, in the dusty, low-harvest mid-1930s, the efforts of the state prisons to maintain what market they could, to stay competitive against the private manufacturers and other prisons, and to continue to generate savings for their states' farmers helped to preserve their factories through the rough times. Aggressive marketing, however, could not make up for the dwindling crops, which adversely affected the twine plants. In Minnesota in 1933, for example, Gov. Floyd Olson signed a decree imposing price reductions on the price of twine to help farmers in his state and to move the prison's twine stocks. The decree was even reported in Yucatán, where nervous henequen growers closely followed the bad crops and resultant economic conditions in the *grandes llanuras* (Great Plains).[123] In South Dakota, the prison warden announced in 1936 that "owing to the severe drouth" he was forced to curtail production dramatically. "This leaves most of our men who have been employed in the twine plant idle, which increases our problem," he wrote, also mentioning that he had been studying "possible ways of keeping the men busy." Compounding the problem were cricket and grasshopper infestations that ravaged South Dakota farms in the 1930s. The prison by that time was adding oil to its twine balls, like the commercial producers did, but it hardly slowed the problem. In 1938 a particularly bad grasshopper infestation damaged many crops, and the factory increased the oil treatment by 15 percent. But by 1939 the bad harvest had resulted in a net loss of more than seventy-eight thousand dollars for the South Dakota twine factory.[124]

Although the bad harvests in the Great Plains during the 1930s reduced prison-twine production, there were other factors that contributed to its demise. For those prisons that sold twine out of state, the Hawes-Cooper Act further reduced their market. By then, prison industries in general were in decline. According to one study, at the beginning of the twentieth century roughly 85 percent of all prison inmates were employed in prison industries, but by 1940 the number had dropped to 44 percent.[125] After legislation limited the manufacture of commercial goods in prisons, inmates had fewer industrial opportunities. States came to rely on them to make such state-specific products as license plates and road signs, although most prisons retained their carpentry and furniture making shops and other smaller ventures.

However, the primary reason for the decline and eventual disappearance of the prison twine plants coincides with the end of the binders, binder twine, and the henequen boom in general: the gradual development and affordability of combine harvesters that cut and threshed grain crops without the need to tie bundles. The combine so reduced the need for twine that penitentiaries gradually reduced operations from 1940 onward (even earlier in Kansas, where farmers adopted the combine sooner), and most were closed by the mid-1950s. For example, the Wisconsin State Prison twine plant slid from a profit of more than sixty-two thousand dollars in 1924 to a paltry thirteen thousand dollars in 1940. By then, the plant was down to a total of two sales representatives who primarily negotiated deals for the sale of twine to other state and county institutions. In South Dakota, the penitentiary warden reported in 1950 that his prison twine plant was "a mere shadow of its former self. . . . The situation has become acute and new industries to employ prison personnel are now most important." With that in mind, a few of the prison plants converted some of their operations to the production of baler twine for haying. Wisconsin did so first in 1948, followed by South Dakota in 1949, and North Dakota in the early 1950s with its NODAK Baler Twine. The South Dakota warden wrote that baler twine would not "nearly be able to account for the volume lost in the binder twine business . . . [but could] be of some assistance."[126] But baler twine manufacturing, while perhaps assisting the prisons with replacing some lost binder twine jobs, did little to help Yucatán's henequen industry. Originally baler twine was made of sisal (by then much of it coming from Cuba, East Africa, and Java), but cordage manufacturers began to switch to synthetic polyethylene for baler twine in the mid-1950s and 1960s. Thus, one by one, the major penitentiary twine mills in the Great Plains ceased operations: Kansas in 1947, South Dakota in 1950, Wisconsin in 1954, and Minnesota in 1957. North Dakota, the state where farmers continued using binders the longest, straggled on with a very limited production until 1964.

The penitentiary binder twine experience yields several important conclusions. Most importantly, it suggests how dependent on a foreign commodity the grain growing regions were and how globalized the agricultural industry and economy were at the end of the nineteenth century and during the first half of the twentieth. It shows very clearly that sisal fiber, 90 percent of which came from Yucatán, was of such importance to the governments of several states and Canada that they agreed to subsidize its importation and production into binder twine for the benefit of their farmers. But what was the nature of this subsidized benefit? Could the prison twine plants be classified as a socialist experiment in an otherwise free-market agricultural economy? As early as 1904, Walter Thomas Mills addressed that question using the example of the twine mill in the Kansas penitentiary. In his book on socialist and collectivist principles, *The Struggle for Existence*, Mills posited that the twine mill was "an instance of public ownership . . . together with cheap labor. . . . So [that as] long as the government is administered by a political party controlled by capitalists, any industries administered by the government cannot in any way be said to be either examples of Socialism or steps toward socialism."[127] It is difficult to know how many Kansans or others in the Great Plains may have read Mills's book (some would perhaps have been relieved to know their government was not turning toward a socialist economy), but the passage speaks to important points. For example, prison officials in Kansas and elsewhere soon learned that savings could be won by dealing directly with henequen producers in Yucatán or through competitive fiber brokers instead of going through McCormick (or later IH). Such direct negotiation resulted in greater savings for customers. That governments intervened for commodity production in a free-market climate represents without any doubt a policy far from capitalist thought or traditions. However, the federal government never nationalized the industry or put it under the control of any one state government. No level of government in the United States ever came to control the flow of the raw materials for twine or the modes of production for its manufacture, and no government outlawed or even discouraged competition from the private sector. Instead, the government organizations subsidized, without tax money, a small part of the overall industry. The cheap convict labor and heavy demand kept the prison factories in the black.

Still, anomalies emerged in this economic scenario. In reality, only Minnesota's penitentiary ever supplied more than 20 percent of its state's binder twine needs, with most providing between 12 to 15 percent of total state twine sales. The figure is surprisingly low for the amount of effort poured into twine production: prison wardens becoming fiber-grade experts and sisal purchasers, with some even traveling to Yucatán to make the right connections; governors and legislatures intervening on behalf of their prisons' twine factories, arguing at length about the benefits to farmers, but often, surprisingly, halting efforts to expand production capacity that would have provided even more low-cost twine and employed even more "idle" convicts. Add to that the large-scale alarm that prison twine factory incidents (fires, riots, sabotaging) generated relative to the small scale of the prisons' twine sales, and one can see that government officials and the general public obsessed to some degree on the importance of their twine facilities. However, at the national level the prisons gave private cordage firms reasons to worry. All prison production combined averaged 25 percent of the total amount of twine manufactured in the United

States between 1914 and 1935, with that figure being as high as 32 percent in 1935.[128]

Finally, the idea of cheap penitentiary labor is pertinent not only to the discussion here but also to the ongoing controversy surrounding it. The Kansas penitentiary paid inmates working in the twine plant 3.75 cents per day for ten-hour days (changed to eight-hour days in 1915) plus room and board, such as it was.[129] The pay was similar to that of other penitentiaries in the region and far below the wages of factory workers in the outside world. Depending on one's point of view, that is either acceptable or not—prisoners were incarcerated to prevent them from re-committing crimes and for corrective reform, with the possible side benefits of learning a trade. More to the point, the governments involved in creating prison twine mills saw an opportunity to reduce inmate idleness while supplying an important commodity to farmers at below market prices, a point understandably criticized by corporate cordage manufacturers but widely applauded by participant farmers. While the prison twine making industry was probably not as harsh as other prison labor had historically been (excepting some comparatively minor complaints about the mills' conditions), the theory of worker exploitation for poor pay for the benefit of another industry irritated progressive reformers and has been hotly debated ever since. In fact, in the 1990s and later the controversy significantly intensified. Organizations such as the Prison Activist Research Center and books like *The Celling of America,* especially part IV, "Workin' for the Man: Prison Labor in the U.S.A.," call attention to the continuing problems of inmate exploitation in the "prison industrial complex."[130]

Fittingly enough, the last remnant of a prison twine factory that remained standing into the twenty-first century was where it all started, the place that was always the largest producer of prison-made twine: the Stillwater State Prison in Minnesota. In 2002, however, it burned to the ground in an arsonist's fire. The land was destined to be developed for condominiums, so prison officials and historic preservationists pulled bricks from the rubble and put them up for sale at the Warden's House Store and Prison Museum Gift Shop in Stillwater.[131] Their legacy, unknown to most brick purchasers, to be sure, reflects part of a complex tale in North America's agricultural past.

CHAPTER 6

Decline, Depression, and Drought

Economic and Environmental Change in the Great Plains and Yucatán, 1916–1939

The application of the Agrarian Law in the sisal zone of Yucatán . . . is now an
imperative economic necessity—an undeniable act of social justice.

—*Lázaro Cárdenas, president of Mexico (1934–1940)*

THE years from 1916 through the 1930s featured dramatic economic and
environmental changes in North America, and together they had a significant impact on the henequen-wheat complex. First, with a heightened
demand for grains during World War I, the demand for Yucatecan fibers
greatly increased—demands that both wheat farmers and henequen planters
welcomed. However, the political changes resulting from the Mexican Revolution's success in Yucatán ushered in economic changes for the state's henequen
industry and aroused contempt in North America's cordage and agricultural
industries. Once again the U.S. government proceeded to intervene, this time
with Senate hearings, Federal Trade Commission rulings, Commerce Department investigations, Department of Justice lawsuits, statements by the
Departments of State and Agriculture, and attempted litigation against the
Yucatecans by the U.S. cordage industry. It was then that the henequen industry started experiencing a serious decline. In the 1920s, the postwar economic
slump led to business declines for grain farmers and twine makers and further
declines for henequen growers. The postwar decline was made far worse for
all by the Great Depression and drought of the 1930s.

"Wheat will win the war" was an oft-heard rallying cry in North America
during World War I. In that crisis, the Turks had blocked wheat exports from
Russia, causing a huge demand in Europe for North American grain, which

caused prices to soar. Historian Gerald Friesen noted that wheat prices were
so high in Canada during the war that "prairie farmers pressed all available
land into cultivation and went into debt to expand their farms even more."[1]
In Saskatchewan and Alberta the number of acres "improved" for field crops
jumped from 844,000 in 1901 to 26.3 million just twenty years later. In Manitoba the amount of acreage under cultivation more than doubled (from 2.7 million to 5.8 million).[2] The Canadian government, via the Ministry of Agriculture, launched a vigorous campaign to lure farmers west, calling the Prairie
Provinces "the Last Best West" (Figure 6.1). American farmers of the Great
Plains were equally as aggressive, especially when prices shot up from around
a steady dollar a bushel in the decade before the war to more than two dollars
a bushel by its end, a price guaranteed by the Food Control Act of 1917. Between 1914 and 1917, wheat prices rose by more than 50 percent. The increase,
as historian Donald Worster describes it, put farmers "into a happy dither"
and enabled them to further mechanize their operations to plant and harvest
more wheat. Encouraged by the Wilson administration's various wartime
campaigns, often cloaked in patriotism, farmers in Nebraska, Colorado, Kansas, Oklahoma, and Texas by 1919 had increased wheat acreage by 13.5 million acres—11 million of which came from plowing up native grasslands that
had never been tilled.[3] A similar transformation took place in the northern
plains at the same time. Wheat harvests in Minnesota, North Dakota, South
Dakota, Montana, and Wyoming jumped from 100.5 million bushels in 1890
to 276.5 million in 1918.[4]

For the entire American and Canadian plains region, grain crops replaced
native grasslands and forever changed the prairie landscape. "The fact is,"
Worster continues, "the bloody conflict in Europe had a profound impact" on
the Great Plains and "hastened trends already under way." A Kansas newspaper headlined that "Our Food All Goes to the Allies" and related how the
state's farmers were exporting more grain to Europe, including Germany.[5]
The British declared in 1915 that they would consider grain and food headed
for Germany contraband; it was as detrimental as sending the Germans weapons or ammunition. And farm machinery manufacturers were happy to com-
ply with the wartime calls to increase the production of grain, out of a sense
of patriotism and to acknowledge that there would be fewer harvest hands,
thus hastening the need to mass produce more machinery and thus reduce the
need for labor. An International Harvester (IH) report in 1916 stated, "Our
country's entrance into the European War has placed additional responsibilities upon the agricultural implement industry to supply the farmer with labor-
saving devices for planting and harvesting the crops."[6]

Wheat for the war meant twine for the wheat. Farmers used on average
six pounds of twine for every acre of wheat, depending on conditions. In

Figure 6.1. A promotional poster issued by the Ministry of Agriculture celebrates the growth of agriculture in the Prairie Provinces, 1909. Notice the field of stooked wheat, bundles tied by a binder and stacked together to dry before threshing. Courtesy Library and Archives of Canada / Bibliothèque et Archives Canada (C083564).

Kansas alone, farmers used 10,000 tons of binder twine in 1914, and more
would be needed for the expanded crops of 1915. Nationally, the United States
would need more than 200,000 tons a year, and Canada, an additional 30,000
tons or more.[7] Henequen producers in Yucatán and twine manufacturers in
the United States and Canada rose to the wartime challenge. Production
in Yucatán climbed from around 550,000 bales in 1910 to 1.5 million bales
by 1915.[8] In the United States the cordage industry increased production of
binder twine to meet the demand, with 90 percent of the fiber supplies coming from Yucatán. In Canada's seven cordage plants, the production of twine
came to account for nearly 90 percent of all cordage products manufactured,
although slightly under half the amount was made of Yucatecan sisal or henequen, the remainder coming from Philippine manila and other fibers. Overall,
the amount of Canadian-produced twine more than doubled in one year alone,
from 16.3 million pounds in 1919 to 34.7 million pounds in 1920.[9] With that
in mind, the U.S. government placed the fiber trade under the jurisdiction of
the powerful wartime U.S. Food Administration (1917–1919). It was with this
agency that the cordage industry and the henequen growers would have to
learn to work quite closely for the duration of the war.

President Wilson established the Food Administration as a means for
regulating and distributing foodstuffs and commodities for the war effort.
Directed by his appointee, the Stanford engineer and humanitarian Herbert
Hoover (known as the "Food Czar" in this position), the agency addressed the
rising price of twine during these years. The worry was that additional costs
for farmers could threaten the harvests, which were desperately needed in the
war's final phase. Thus, the agency created the Division of Chemicals, Sisal,
and Jute to manage the importation and distribution of those commodities. To
lead the division, interestingly enough, Hoover appointed H. L. Daniels—the
former chief of International Harvester's fiber department.[10] Daniels immediately summoned his colleagues in the twine business to a conference in Washington to meet with Hoover and discuss sisal and twine prices and ways to increase output for the war effort. The cordage companies' representatives were
happy to oblige but complained later that the federal agency had no definite
plan of action and that time and effort were being wasted in mere discussions.
Nevertheless, at Hoover's urging, they agreed to sell their twine at no more
than the cost of the fiber plus the manufacturing expenses and "a reasonable
profit" that the agency would determine. They also agreed to a policy mandating that the cordage firms buy sisal only from the Food Administration, which
would import it from Yucatán and other sources. It would now be the Food
Administration that dickered with the Yucatecans over prices and supply.[11]

Soon, however, the Food Administration joined the cordage industry in
their worry about recent events in Yucatán that could impede the flow of the

much-needed sisal. They were especially worried about increased prices after the revolution. Salvador Alvarado, military commander and governor of Yucatán, had formed an agrarian reform commission and started the process of reapportioning land, the effects of which alarmed North Americans.[12] However, Alvarado never instituted anywhere near a complete land reform policy for Yucatán; that agenda would have to wait until the presidency of Lázaro Cárdenas in the late 1930s. Alvarado's post-revolution land redistribution ideology was based more on rural workers becoming small landowners in *non*-henequen lands—such as corn plots (*milpas*), livestock pastures, and "vacant" public lands (*monte*). Because he viewed the henequen industry as essential to Yucatán's continued modernization and as a source of revenue for the national cause, he feared that breaking up vast plantations could potentially threaten their economic stability, which could be ruinous for the overall welfare of all classes in the state.[13] In fact, with the exception of Olegario Molina, who had fled, most of the large land-holding *henequeneros* or "Casta Divina" learned to work with the new governor and benefited economically and politically from their new alliance with him. Most even became avid members of the political party, the Socialist Party of the Southeast (known by its Spanish acronym PSS), that Alvarado established in Yucatán. Despite the name, the party never represented a Marxist, class-conscious entity. Instead, it became, as historian Ben Fallaw has described it, "centered around concepts of individual rights (*libertades*), secularism, and state intervention in the economy," owing as much to "classical liberalism and anarchosyndicalism as to historical materialism."[14] Thus, the Casta Divina remained an integral part of the ruling political organization that would be in power through the next two decades. As wealthy *hacendado* Hernando Ancona exclaimed, "The Revolution has given me more than it has taken."[15]

Alvarado was more "revolutionary" in abolishing the *henequeneros'* use of corporal punishment, debt peonage, and slave labor, and in his reactivation of the Comisión Reguladora del Mercado de Henequén (CRMH), or as the fiber industry, press, and governments simply called it, the Reguladora, in November 1915. The revived CRMH became the next big worry for cordage interests and the U.S. government, especially during World War I. The *henequeneros* had established the CRMH in 1912 as way to increase the valorization of fiber in the world market by imposing a tax on production and by warehousing vast quantities of baled sisal until market prices rose. However, although it was a quasi-government entity, CRMH remained in the hands of its wealthy *henequenero* members and was controlled by the Avelino Montes–IH monopoly, thus achieving few of its propounded benefits. It collapsed completely when rebel and anti-revolution leader Abel Ortiz Argumedo fled Yucatán with the Reguladora's remaining 5 million pesos ahead of Alvarado's successful entry into the region. Montes fled to Havana at the same time.[16]

Alvarado's plan in 1915 was to put more teeth into the Reguladora, making it into a more stringently government-run organization, especially in mandating higher prices, with profits to be shared with the Yucatecan people instead of going to the old Montes-IH alliance. The new arrangement mandated that all henequen growers sell their fiber to the CRMH, with two-thirds of the sales going back to them (indicating that the *henequeneros* would continue to benefit under Alvarado and the PSS), and the remaining one-third going to the government for social services. The plan would be accomplished with CRMH's creation of a permanent Wall Street office in New York staffed by director Victor Rendón, a physician and *hacendado* from one of the old Casta Divina families. For start-up loans of more than 10 million dollars for five years and financial management and operating funds in the United States, the Reguladora created a "trust" consisting of four banks that became known as the Pan-American Commission. The new commission comprised the Royal Bank of Canada, the Canadian Bank of Commerce, the Equitable Trust Company of New York, and the Interstate Trust and Banking Company of New Orleans to assist with CRMH's financial needs. The Reguladora then set out to establish its own prices for Yucatecan fiber, regardless of the capitalist ideal of allowing the market to determine prices; its policy became known as the *política alcista* (policy of high pricing). During the next three years, CRMH raised sisal prices by nearly 400 percent for North American buyers, from 13.2 cents per kilogram in 1915 to more than 50.6 cents in 1918—doubling Yucatán's export earnings during Alvarado's three-year term. The state government also raised railroad rates by 300 percent and warehouse expenses by 200 percent. The extra money then went to finance an increased bureaucracy in Mérida, to raise field hands' and decorticating plant workers' wages, and to fund hundreds of new schools and libraries.[17]

North Americans were outraged at such quick price hikes on raw fiber and argued that one monopoly had replaced another. The parties involved were predictably similar to those who screamed the loudest during the blockade of Progreso and the rumors of burned henequen fields: cordage companies, farmers, implement dealers, penitentiary officials, and congressional representatives from wheat states. Officials in Canada were equally alarmed.

As early as March 31, 1915, the *Cordage Trade Journal* bemoaned "increased taxes of hemp by the Mexican government" and complained, once again, directly to the State Department. Some manufacturers and government leaders blamed IH and its long-standing monopoly with Avelino Montes for the changes, but the company was quick to deny the charges and to blame CRMH. An article in IH's trade journal *Harvester World* in December tried to dispel the idea that the company was making exorbitant profits on its twine sales, showing that earnings on twine averaged less than one cent per pound. It argued that the drastic price increases over the past year were due to how CRMH's "syndicate with several American bankers" was maintaining "a price not justified by the market conditions." It also suggested that the supposedly "philanthropist" side of the agreement was not working to alleviate poverty in Yucatán since most of the money from henequen sales went to the growers, who were "wealthy owners of large plantations—many of them millionaires."[18]

The mainstream press echoed these concerns. In December 1915 the *New York Times* ran a lengthy article on the topic, proclaiming in headlines that "Yucatán Monopoly Hoists Hemp Prices" with the objective "to oust" IH. It quoted Victor Rendón, who bemoaned how IH "formerly controlled the entire hemp industry of Yucatán" and was "in effect a monopoly which injured the growers and laborers of Yucatán by depressing the price of their product and by loaning money at exorbitant interest rates." However, as the story related, the new prices were seriously hurting the American farmer, and the CRMH was becoming monopolistic by not only driving IH out of Yucatán, but also by driving smaller cordage firms and independent fiber brokers out of the business.[19]

To the *Times*'s credit, the majority of its article contained Yucatecans' responses to the charges. "I admit that we can to a large extent control the market," the article quoted Rendón as having stated (although he would later argue that the *Times* misquoted him). But "the reason for the formation of the commission," he explained, "was to secure to the [henequen] farmer a fair price. . . . not less than 10 percent profit on his invested capital." He argued that this new arrangement would be far superior to the years when the Yucatecan growers were "at the mercy" of IH and Plymouth Cordage and when they "were poor and had to borrow money [from IH and Plymouth] . . . at 10 percent interest." Then, "the contracts of the loan required the farmers to sell their crops to the agents of these companies at from 1/4 to 1/2 cent less than the prevailing market prices." Concerning the accusations that higher prices were enriching CRMH, Rendón answered that "whatever profit accrued to the commission would be divided among the growers quarterly." Finally, he played down the extra expense for the American farmer by calculating that an increase of one cent per pound "would cost the grower of grain upon 100 acres of land the insignificant sum of from $2 to $3." Thus, the big fiber customers "will be coming to me offering me higher prices than we are asking," he asserted, "in order to assure their supply of the fiber on account of the difficulty in obtaining it from other sources."[20]

Most industrialists and farmers did not buy Rendón's explanation. Countering, a hardware dealer from Starkweather, North Dakota, complained about the dime-a-pound increase to his U.S. senator, Porter McCumber: "Before the Spanish-American War I sold sisal twine for 6 cents a pound and made a fair profit. . . . Then American bankers formed a trust in Yucatán. . . . They have controlled the price ever since. . . . And we are absolutely at their mercy."[21] Representing farmers in its area, an editorial in a Concordia, Kansas, newspaper decried CRMH's policies and even suggested that it was now IH that was being victimized by "this unholy combination of American capital with the monopoly in Yucatán." Admitting that as "thankless a task" as it was for a "newspaper to come to the defense of a corporation," it maintained that it was "unreasonable to charge" IH with complicity in the new fiber monopoly. "In the first place the business of the big corporation is to sell . . . machinery," it argued, and "to make the price of twine prohibitive ruins the sale of harvesters, the principal business of this concern." It also warned that "the burden . . . will fall on the ultimate consumer—the farmers of Kansas."[22] Another newspaper angrily headlined that "Price of Sisal Doubled at Farmers' Cost." The *Topeka Daily Capital* discussed how the state's penitentiary went from buying sisal fiber through dealers for as low as $3.60 per hundredweight in early 1914 to $7.35 in early 1916. It lamented the fact that the prison now had to buy only through the Reguladora without the benefit of fair market pricing afforded by competitive fiber brokers, as in the past.[23]

Enough complaints like that prompted a congressional investigation into the matter based on anti-monopoly legislation outlined in the Sherman Anti-Trust Act. Pushed by the cordage industry as a way to punish, and hopefully limit the CRMH, the Sixty-fourth Congress took up the issue in early 1916. Senator McCumber of North Dakota introduced a resolution regarding the production of binding twine, arguing that whereas "binding twine is one of the large items of expense in the production of grain" and because the "present price is exorbitant and fixed," the attorney general should be authorized "to investigate the importation of sisal and the manufacturing of twine." His home-state colleague, Sen. Asle Gronna, who had been in the farming and hardware business in Wahpeton, North Dakota, rose to speak on Senate Resolution 94: "Those of us who are familiar with the conditions of agriculture and know something about binding twine are also familiar with the fact that it is not only the price of sisal that has advanced, but also the price of twine after it has been manufactured." In support of McCumber's resolution, which passed, Gronna argued that price hikes negatively affected prison twine manufacturers in states like his.[24]

While the U.S. attorney general considered the matter, the Senate sent Resolution 94 to its Committee on Agriculture and Forestry, which formed a subcommittee to investigate "the importation of sisal and manila hemp" and the extent of price manipulation by the CRMH. The list of people called to testify, and the organizations they represented, included all the VIPs in the sisal producing and twine manufacturing worlds. Defending the CRMH were Dr. Rendón, his American secretary from the Wall Street office, bankers from New Orleans who were directors of the Pan-American Commission, and a number of henequen planters from Yucatán. Speaking against the CRMH were representatives and attorneys of IH, Plymouth Cordage, Henry W. Peabody, Hanson & Orth, and Mid-City Brokerage of Kansas City; two senators, Charles Curtis of Kansas and Asle Gronna of North Dakota; the wardens or representatives of state penitentiaries with binder twine plants in Minnesota, Wisconsin, Michigan, and North Dakota (Minnesota also sent its former warden, Henry Wolfer, who had first engineered the idea for prison twine mills); both the editor and secretary-treasurer of *Farm Implement News* of Chicago; and representatives from the American Society of Equity and the Ancient Order of Gleaners.[25]

Rendón was one of the first to testify before the subcommittee. He provided background information on the history and economics of henequen production, how seven-eighths of the state's population was "devoted" to henequen ("the life of the state"), and how debt peonage labor had been eliminated on the haciendas when the revolution "brought freedom" to the state. He also highlighted the history of the CRMH and why it had been developed "at the behest of the planters" and reiterated that the income from the increased prices was going toward schools and other social services. Other Yucatecans who testified went into greater detail on how IH had dominated the sisal trade. For example, they showed that IH controlled 67 percent of the fiber trade from Yucatán in 1912 and 60 percent in 1914, just two years before the Senate hearings. By then, as they reminded the committee, IH and Peabody together monopolized seven-eighths of the baled fiber and were able to fix prices, as they had done for many years. Worse for the henequen growers, they had to repay IH for loans on their henequen at 10 percent interest—a fee that the CRMH was not charging. The IH representatives replied in the hearings that they "resented" the accusation that their company had a monopoly on the sisal trade. In fact, they presented as evidence the *New York Times* article (mentioned above) that quoted Rendón admitting that the CRMH would in effect control the price of henequen in the same monopolistic way that the Yucatecans were accusing IH of having done. Rendón quickly countered by saying that the author of the *Times* article had taken his words out of context and that he was going to demand that the newspaper retract the statement.[26]

Senator Curtis of Kansas (later vice president under Herbert Hoover) took an active part in the proceedings and proudly cited his home as the "top wheat state," consuming between 15 million and 20 million pounds of twine per year. He discussed the importance of securing sisal and of his state's prison twine mill that had so greatly helped farmers by selling them twine for at least one cent per pound cheaper than trade brands. North Dakota's Senator Gronna repeated his stance on how the CRMH was guilty of "unduly increasing the price of twine."[27]

The hearings went on for more than two months. Yet despite hundreds of pages of statements, the subcommittee merely deemed the CRMH a "harmful monopoly" and could only state the seemingly obvious: that the government had no control over a foreign corporation.[28] However, not everyone's time was completely wasted during the proceedings. Representatives from the cordage companies complained to the committee that they foresaw a drastic shortage of sisal fiber and insufficient quantities of binder twine for the 1916 harvest, especially after twine supplies had dwindled during the record breaking wheat harvests of the previous year. Dr. Rendón and other CRMH officials denied that supply would be a problem, and to back up their argument they offered 125,000 additional bales of sisal over and above their previous commitments for export to the United States. Senator Gronna and others quickly drafted the agreement into the form of a Senate resolution (SR 170), which easily passed and directed the Federal Trade Commission (FTC) to notify manufacturers of the CRMH's intention to offer additional fiber and to distribute it to them accordingly. The FTC wired forty-three cordage companies (including eight penitentiary twine plants) that the additional sisal would be on its way should they be in need of it. The caveat attached to the resolution was that the cordage firms would agree that all additional twine to be made was for domestic consumption only. While many cordage firms were glad of the offer, the FTC received applications for only 109,000 of the 125,000 bales to be distributed.[29] Still not satisfied, in 1918 IH "and its constellation of satellite manufacturing firms" filed suit against the CRMH under the Sherman Anti-Trust Act in U.S. state and federal courts to enjoin it from operating in the United States. The suits were to no avail once again, however, because the CRMH was outside of U.S. jurisdiction.[30]

Canadians kept abreast of the CRMH situation and the U.S. Senate hearings on the matter, once again via the British ambassador to Washington, Sir Cecil Spring Rice. In a lengthy memorandum to the Canadian government in early 1916, Spring Rice explained the background of the sisal industry and of the political situation in Yucatán (regarding the "peaceful and hardworking habits of the entire population" and the state's "continued era of peace and tranquility" that had not been interrupted by all the unrest in Mexico "until lately, from the disturbed conditions" of the revolution). That kind of language set a pro-U.S. tone that the ambassador had maintained since the events surrounding the Progreso blockade a year earlier. On the CRMH matter, he somewhat deceptively wrote that "there never had been an absolute monopoly of the hemp business" until the reestablishment of the Reguladora, which was "an arbitrary action" of Governor Alvarado. "Finding the hemp business was inexhaustible mine of wealth," Spring Rice asserted, "the new authorities started a plan towards obtaining a complete monopoly of the production of hemp and at once started to force prices up of everything." He lamented how Alvarado's "immense rise in price of the hemp" fell on the "American and Canadian farmer, and the benefit of the increase in price remains . . . to be used as the Governor . . . orders, as he is the only person in the State who can dispose of the wealth." He was also critical of the price fixing, the holding back of profits for the Reguladora's "own ends," and its "costly office in New York" from which Rendón was "deluging the newspapers and magazines with his articles . . . [about] the non-existence of a monopoly."[31]

Spring Rice was perhaps most critical of the formation of the Pan-American Commission in New Orleans—the corporation that received the baled fiber from Yucatán and distributed it across North America. He believed its profits were too extreme in comparison to how the sisal growers were "not likely to receive any." Furthermore, he noted sarcastically, "No details are given as to the shareholders of this wonderful corporation!" He wrote that in all its press releases and news articles, the CRMH was "always omitting to state the real object they have, which is to make the American consumer pay an enormous price for the raw material, in order to provide for the exaggerated expenses of their business and the enormous commissions."[32] Spring Rice's concerns represented more about his (and Britain's and Canada's) propensity to side with the United States on issues concerning Mexico than they did to advocate any policy changes in Canada. There were no hearings in Canada similar to the ones the U.S. Senate had conducted on the question of a CRMH "monopoly." Instead, the Canadians followed the lead and urging of their mother country to purchase more sisal from the British Commonwealth territories in East Africa and New Zealand that were expanding fiber production. In response, the Yucatecans during the 1930s worked successfully to market their fiber directly to the Canadian cordage firms instead of using New York brokerages. Thus, while Canadians were concerned with the henequen price hikes, dealing with that matter was always more of a U.S. concern. (As for Rendón, charges of corruption ended his stint at the New York CRMH office. He then won a PSS seat as a federal congressman from Yucatán in 1927 but was later expelled from the Socialist Party when he opposed the reelection of President Álvaro Obregón later that year.[33])

It was with this Reguladora structure that the U.S. Food Administration had to work during World War I, and Herbert Hoover became very personally involved with it during his tenure as wartime food czar. The binational entities did not work well together as the CRMH officials balked at reducing prices—even for the war effort. At that point the U.S. government granted generous export licenses to individual *henequeneros*, and the cordage firms took advantage of these licenses, especially when released from their agreement to buy only through the Food Administration after the war. When negotiations failed, one of Hoover's assistants even went so far as to recommend that the United States send troops in to force better prices—an echo of Wilson's earlier fiascos in Mexico. The State Department killed the idea, claiming that intervention might only further impede fiber production. Instead of a naval blockade or military intervention, Hoover settled on an embargo of food and gold to Yucatán to squeeze a region that was incapable of producing sufficient subsistence crops until, as he advised the State Department, "the Mexican Central Government comes on its knees to receive help." But while this quid pro quo plan was being implemented, it was the U.S. cordage representatives who begged that it be discontinued even though they did not have enough sisal to produce the amount of twine needed for the anticipated bumper crops of 1918.[34] (As it did during the "Sisal Situation" of 1915 in the face of a pending agricultural disaster, the cordage industry forecast the 1918 harvest correctly. That year's 950-million-bushel wheat harvest was the highest in three years, probably making farmers and cordage manufacturers wonder why bumper crops tended to coincide with threatened supplies of fiber.) Hoover backed off, ended the food embargo to Yucatán, and accepted the CRMH's terms, which, compared to the prices of fibers such as Philippine manila, were never that high during the war. This deal, however, was to be one of the Reguladora's final successes before an eventual decline precipitated by the end of World War I.[35]

Back in the United States, the government remained involved in binder twine matters. In 1917 the Bureau of Foreign and Domestic Commerce issued a report that its agent Herbert Browne had written about the situation in Yucatán. Browne wrote that high sisal prices were translating into higher wages and better conditions for Yucatecans: "The peons, now free, have curtailed their labor to about 5 days a week, and there is a shortage of some 20,000 laborers in the henequin [*sic*] fields." That meant, he warned, that a shortage of some 400,000 bales of fiber worth fifty dollars each would occur later that year. In 1919 these concerns landed in the Senate Foreign Relations Committee, chaired by powerful New Mexico senator Albert Fall, when it conducted hearings on sisal importations. As testimonies indicated, the cordage interests remained skeptical, suspicious, and critical of Governor Alvarado and his authority within the CRMH for fiber production and price fixing. A New York "hemp merchant" named Michael Smith testified that Alvarado had "forced" henequen workers to be instructed in anarchism and that they had then not properly tended to the henequen plants, overcutting some, neglecting others, and not cleaning out the underbrush, which often caused the plants to "send up a pole"—the tall stems indicating the plant was at the end of its life. Assistant Attorney General Francis Kearful even described Alvarado as "bolshevistic." Several speakers mentioned how Alvarado's land reform policy, allowing peasants to raise henequen on small tracts, was an "absurdity"—that it was "absolutely impossible" to raise the agaves commercially in nonplantation environments. The evidence, they lamented, was that under Alvarado fiber production had dropped by 30 percent between 1900 and 1919—a real danger since "ninety percent of the binder twine which the farmers of the United States use is made of Yucatán sisal or henequen." And finally, to contest the argument that Alvarado's policies were improving social conditions in Yucatán, one speaker stated that henequen's benefits had already been felt, that "rapid strides" in education and sanitation had already improved the "well being of the people."[36]

Also of interest to committee members were the statements regarding U.S. involvement in Yucatán. Replying to Kearful's question regarding the veracity of reports that American capitalists "were engaged in exploiting the Mexican peon" of that region, Michael Smith claimed that there was "no truth at all" to the accusation, and he posited instead that U.S. intervention was a great boon for the people in Yucatán due to its "semi barbaric condition": "When Americans went in there and started to really develop Mexico, the Mexican people had neither the money nor the knowledge necessary to permit them to develop their own country." Kearful requested that Smith remind the committee "what moved the U.S. government to take steps to protect the owners of henequen" in 1915. Smith explained the "Sisal Situation" and why it was so important for twine manufacturers to secure their fiber orders. Mexico's Ambassador Arredondo argued that his country was "very anxious to avoid all appearance of any coercion on the part of the U.S. government."[37] Therefore, these proceedings, like others, were more for congressional information than for any policy changing measures, and none of the hearings was successful in forcing CRMH to lower its prices. With that in mind, IH—once the Yucatán's largest customer—refused to buy henequen from the CRMH, leaving the organization with vast quantities of baled fiber in warehouses.

The late 1910s and 1920s bore witness to the fact that policies to raise prices did not accrue their desired rewards. The CRMH's own policies thus set in motion its eventual demise. A government administrator and critic of the revolution bemoaned the fact that there had been fewer henequen plantings after the 1915 reforms than there had been before, and he prophetically stated that the industry was "being ruined at a great speed . . . going violently to its end."[38] The Reguladora's decline was precipitated by the U.S. Food Administration's overpurchase of sisal in 1918. Enraged at the CRMH's prices, Hoover's agency purchased far more sisal than the cordage firms needed for that year, stored the additional quantities for the 1919 season, and then bought none that year, leaving the Reguladora with thousands of unsold bales. The vengeful act, made in collusion with the U.S. cordage industry, was "to discipline the Reguladora," as the U.S. consul in Progreso admitted. The cordage industry also spread rumors to twine makers and farmers throughout the United States about how "socialistic" the Reguladora's policies were, with the goal of bankrupting and so discrediting the agency that it would finally collapse. By the end of that year the combined results of henequen overproduction, the accumulation of a large unsold stock of processed fiber in the United States, the post–World War I economic slump, and fierce competition from abroad forced the government to liquidate the Reguladora and to disband the Pan-American Commission.[39] Two years later, newly elected U.S. president Warren Harding rewarded Hoover's work as food czar by naming him secretary of commerce, a position in which he remained involved with the sisal trade.

In Yucatán the election of Felipe Carrillo Puerto, a well-loved local and radical socialist, as governor of Yucatán in 1922 brought a renewed emphasis on socialism that led the state to resume control of fiber production under a new entity established by the state legislature: the Comisión Exportadora. Carrillo, emulating Salvador Alvarado during the revolution, sought to diversify and collectivize the henequen industry. He also believed in supporting the *henequeneros* and in maximizing production by offering loans to those who would expand plantations and develop better decorticating equipment. In addition, he firmly maintained that one-quarter of all export profits channeled through the Exportadora be distributed to Yucatecan workers and used as credit for small growers' cooperatives.[40] Based in Mérida, the Exportadora chose the New York firm of Hanson & Orth to be its agent for selling fiber in North America. But when the Pan-American Commission found itself with 500,000 bales of sisal at its disposal, and with the CRMH out of the picture, it quickly reformulated itself as the ERIC Corporation (an acronym for Equitable Trust, Royal Bank of Canada, Interstate Trust and Banking, and the Comisión Reguladora).[41] (See Table 6.1 for the evolution of the henequen exporting arrangements.)

ERIC acquired the CRMH's surplus fiber and tried to market it to North American buyers. It failed in that respect, however, when at the same time the bottom fell out of the henequen market. The Peabody Company even recommended that Yucatecans dispose of the stock "whether as fuel or otherwise." With few choices available, ERIC sold most of its remaining stock to IH at cost, 9.9 cents per kilogram—the same price IH and Avelino Montes had worked out in 1912 that was the genesis of the first Reguladora. The deal, however, caused outrage in Mexico and in the U.S. cordage industry since it

Table 6.1 Henequen exporting arrangements, 1912–1930

Exporting Agency	Year	Financial Agency
Comisión Reguladora del Mercado de Henequén (CRMH)	1912	
Reformulated CRMH ↘	1915	Pan-American Commission ↘
Comisión Exportadora	1921	ERIC Corporation ↘
↘	1922–23	Sisal Sales Corporation
Cooperativa Henequeneros de Yucatán	1925	

gave the appearance that IH may have had an inside trade advantage. The allegation surfaced when it became known that Harold McCormick, head of IH and son-in-law of John D. Rockefeller, was a major stockholder and possible director of the Equitable Trust Company. There was enough evidence of foul play that the State Department ordered an investigation by a special agent who found plenty of evidence to prove that IH, via its alliance with two commercial banks in Chicago, had helped bankroll ERIC. The whole mess made the Exportadora seem too much like the old CRMH and quickly caused the directors of ERIC to disband and incorporate in 1922 under a new name: the Sisal Sales Corporation (see Table 6.1).[42]

By July, complaints continued pouring forth in North America against Yucatecan control of the henequen trade and pricing policies, but now they were directed at the Exportadora and the Sisal Sales Corporation. Angry at how the Yucatecans were restricting production and holding on to fiber to drive prices up, Sen. Arthur Capper of Kansas (who had been governor of that state during the "Sisal Situation" of 1915 and had lobbied for U.S. intervention in Yucatán) responded again to concerns from Kansans about "a monopoly operating in the United States" and charging "excessive and unwarranted prices for sisal . . . [causing] farmers of the country to pay outrageous prices for binding twine." "Any increase in the price they must pay," he stated, "constitutes a burden that they will no longer bear with patience." Appealing to the Harding administration to prosecute the "monopoly," he filed a complaint with the U.S. attorney general against Exportadora, its U.S. agent Hanson & Orth, and the Sisal Sales Corporation on grounds that the triad was operating in violation of the Sherman Anti-Trust Act. Capper, who chaired the Senate Agriculture Committee, also quoted a letter he had received from Secretary of Agriculture Henry Wallace on the subject, stating that Congress had plenary power to take "whatever steps may be necessary" to urge foreign governments against restricting the "production of any product which would result in unreasonably enhancing the price thereof in foreign markets."[43]

Capper's and others' concerns not only prompted the attorney general and the Department of Agriculture to look into the matter but also led the Department of State to become involved again. In 1922 Secretary of State Charles Evans Hughes (who had narrowly lost to incumbent Woodrow Wilson in the presidential election of 1916) directed his department to study the international relations aspects of the fiber trade. The study found that IH and most other cordage firms were purchasing greater amounts of fiber from East Africa, the Philippines, and Java than ever before.[44] The cordage industry, however, did appreciate that the government was remaining involved regarding Yucatecan sisal. An official at Plymouth Cordage wrote Capper saying that "the Assistant Attorney General . . . has the matter actively in charge in the Attorney General's Department, and Mr. Secretary Hughes has been kind enough to take a great deal of personal interest in the matter. . . . [And] I think that the President [Harding] himself understands the facts fairly well."[45] Many Yucatecans were opposed to the way the sisal trade was being conducted, too. The Cámara Agrícola de Yucatán (a growers' organization) believed that the Exportadora was unduly restricting production with its pricing policies and strict requirements. A delegate of the Cámara even went so far as to write U.S. Secretary of Commerce Hoover about the growers' plight and pleaded with him to have his department conduct an investigation. The reason he wrote was "because the state of Yucatán is going without fail to complete ruin; that the production of sisal that was before a million bales a year is reduced to 500,000. The fields are no longer being cultivated. Farms are being abandoned and the moment may arrive when the harvesting of wheat in the United States may not have the necessary twine for lack of the raw material."[46]

At this point the Department of Commerce did intervene, though not simply because of the Cámara delegate's letter. In the spring of 1923, the Harding administration laid the "foundation for a determined battle against the 'sisal trust,'" as the *Chicago Daily News* put it, "which yields a potent influence over the price of binder twine to the American farmer." Thus, Secretary Hoover, extremely familiar with the sisal and binder twine industries, authorized his department to conduct an investigation "into conditions surrounding the fiber supply . . . in an effort to break the hold of the Mexican sisal monopoly."[47] The purpose was to secure a long-term compact with the Yucatecans to ensure fair prices into the future. The task was taken seriously; Hoover selected a "sisal specialist" and the Department of Commerce, "ambitious to come to the point quickly," hired a "sisal staff" to mobilize, as one trade journal put it, "all the information in the hands of the government on sisal sources, sisal production, and sisal prices." Some of the "ample data on sisal" that the investigation amassed was from the Food Administration during World War I and from the U.S. Justice Department's own investigation "of the Yucatán sisal monopoly and its U.S. sales agency" that had been collected "quietly and continuously" during the two previous years and now turned over to Commerce.[48]

By April the investigation had proceeded for "a fortnight of almost continuous conference" and testimonies by many in the cordage and implement industries and by representatives in Congress, especially from "farm bloc" states. The politicians were interested to find out "just how far Congress [could] be expected to go in support or sanction of any equitable relationship that may be arranged between sisal producers and consumers." While seeking to establish fair prices, it was also made clear that there was no "desire to grind down the producer in Yucatán or to allow less than a fair margin for distribution." Instead, "a definite, mutually acceptable working plan" was what the Department of Commerce sought. To assist in that regard, Commerce commissioned "special representative" P. L. Bell to Yucatán for a number of weeks. Not an expert in the fiber trade, Bell was known as an "experienced investigator of Latin American trade and industrial conditions, with a facility for getting under the skin of any proposition in research," as he had done in Venezuela and other places for the U.S. Bureau of Foreign and Domestic Commerce.[49]

Hanson & Orth responded to Commerce's charges in a memorandum to Secretary Hoover in April 1924. The firm's "Digest of Principal Statements" listed twenty-seven points supporting the Exportadora's arrangement. Some of the main points included how Commerce's statistics on sisal consumption were incorrect, how Commerce could not prove that American consumers had been injured, and how the price of binder twine in 1922 and 1923 was actually less than it was in the five preceding years. It also stated that Commerce's suggested arrangement could be disadvantageous for state (prison) cordage industries, that the FTC had already investigated the sisal industry and found nothing remiss, and that there was "no danger of excessive prices under existing conditions."[50]

Nonetheless, the Commerce Department's investigation revealed enough data on price fixing to prompt the Department of Justice to file suit against the Sisal Sales Corporation. One of the strongest arguments in the case concerned the damaging impact of the Yucatecans' pricing policies on the farmers in the Great Plains. The court ruled in favor of the government based on antitrust legislation, and that ruling plus the continuing slump in the world fiber market caused the Sisal Sales Corporation to go out of business by 1924. As a number of entities were quick to reveal, however, the price of fiber actually *increased* after Commerce's investigations and Justice's successful lawsuit. New York's *Journal of Commerce* showed price patterns between 1923 and 1928, indicating how both "the price of sisal and of binder twine advanced substantially" and

had never been below the pre-hearings prices that, based on the standard annual consumption estimates of 250 million pounds of sisal, would have cost
American farmers an estimated additional $15.5 million. Still, that Hoover
had gone after the foreign trust and was partially responsible for its elimination was a fact used by Republicans in the election of 1928 to woo Great
Plains voters when Hoover was the Republican nominee for president. Based
on the record of post-investigation price hikes, the *Journal of Commerce* editorialized against Hoover on that issue and cautioned his campaign against making the sisal hearings a campaign issue. Some in the cordage and implement
industries, however, called the publication's accusation "pure political bunk,"
thinking that had the "trust" not been busted, prices could have climbed even
higher.[51]

Meanwhile, back in Yucatán political changes caused changes in the henequen industry. The year 1924 was one of tragedies for Yucatecans, not only
because of the decline in henequen sales and the collapse of the Exportadora
and Sisal Sales Corporation but also when popular governor Felipe Carrillo
Puerto was assassinated. By 1925, due to continued mismanagement, a drop
in production, and new state policies under Carrillo's successor, Álvaro Torres Díaz, the state government replaced the Exportadora with a state-run organization owned by *hacendados:* the Cooperativa Henequeneros de Yucatán
(see Table 6.1). The idea to establish the Cooperativa came from state and
federal authorities during the presidency of Álvaro Obregón in an attempt
to control the production of henequen and to show that the national government had the right to intervene in the public interest. However, the growers in
charge retained most of the former pricing and export policies, which resulted
in few changes or benefits to the growers at the time. Likewise, the *hacendados,*
especially the large producers, resented federal intervention when the state
instituted production decreases and stoppages and when Obregón required
henequeneros to lend him money for his reelection campaign. But when a slow
economic recovery improved market conditions and fiber sales in the late 1920s,
the *hacendados* of the Cooperativa were quicker to acknowledge the benefits of
the state's support. This support gave a certain amount of clout to some powerful *hacendados*, known as *coyotes,* which allowed them to take advantage of their
political connections and trade in the world fiber market without going through
the Cooperativa's channels. For those reasons, and because it never represented
any substantive changes to Exportadora's pricing policies, the Cooperativa did
not succeed in slowing the decline of the Yucatecan henequen industry.[52]

In the mid-1920s, however, the U.S. government sometimes seemed to be
siding with the Yucatecan growers more than the U.S. cordage industry. Studies confirmed that due to the postwar economic slump and abundant supplies
of sisal, prices for the raw fiber actually remained rather low. When the Com-

merce Department reported that 80 percent of the raw fiber used for binder
twine was still coming from Yucatán, some government officials advised that it
should remain that way—as the fiber of choice due to its proximity and thus as
the fastest, most secure, and least expensive way to ensure successful harvests.
With that in mind, the government urged IH and the rest of the manufacturers
to back off the complaints and to stick with the most readily available supply
of relatively inexpensive fiber.[53] Furthermore, officials in the cordage industry
explained to Senator Capper that while the creation of the Cooperativa caused
yet another price hike for raw sisal and the situation remained "rather critical"
since they feared that "the old monopoly" in Yucatán would be restored, it was
"the producers themselves [who] got the benefit of this increase in price . . . it
did not go to any middle-men." Thus, "we felt that the condition of affairs was
healthy, and one about which we should not complain." The Cooperativa, they
believed, would be a better entity with which to trade than the Exportadora,
since growers had to abide by a strict policy "to sell exclusively to manufacturers and not speculators at all."[54]

All of these events signaled the decline of the henequen industry by the
1930s. And then, by the middle of that decade, the severe drought that greatly
reduced grain crops in the Great Plains further diminished the demand for
binder twine and therefore henequen. Thus, growers had hoped there would
be a "great future for Mexican henequen in Europe," as *El sisal mexicano* once
proclaimed.[55] But with East Africa and Java supplying more fiber for Europe's cordage needs, that market never materialized. Global competition is
discussed at length in the next chapter, but it is important to point out here
that by 1929 the Yucatecans were providing a little more than half the world's
supply of hard fibers—a huge drop from their 100 percent supply record in
1900 and from their 88 percent during World War I. The figure would continue to drop throughout the 1930s.[56] Which persons and what policies were at
fault for the decline became widely disputed in these years; the "blame game"
began in earnest.

First, the *hacendados* stated various versions of and reasons for the decline.
One group of growers issued its own interpretation in a 1933 pamphlet entitled *Ante la ruina del henequén* (Confronting the Ruin of Henequen). There the
growers lamented not only the fact that production was almost half of what it
had been in the 1920s but also that the industry now found "itself in imminent
risk of disappearing or being reduced to insignificant proportions" and that
the low market prices "barely justified planting" any new fields. "In the long
range," the pamphlet warned, "Yucatecan production will not have any importance at all in the [fiber] trade." However, the situation was not "irremediable"
if policy changes could be made. The problem "never has been . . . the fault of
the market consumer." Instead, they explained, the problems were due to the

"erroneous policy of high prices" and the production restrictions and moratoriums placed on them by the former CRMH and Exportadora structures—the policies that placed them on "this suicidal path."[57] A different pamphlet entitled *Cuestiones henequeneras* (Henequen Questions), which the group Henequeneros Unidos (United Henequen Growers) issued in 1935, also sought to "expose the anguished situation" of the Yucatecan fiber industry. It too blamed not the market but the moratoriums and restrictions imposed on the growers by the state agencies. That those agencies were state owned caused many growers to blame the government itself for the demise. They accused state authorities and federal bureaucrats of manipulating the market for their own advantage with little thought for the growers and especially for the impoverished laborers.[58]

In other words, some growers, especially conservative ones, started to blame the revolution itself and Yucatán's revolutionaries. The always pro-grower *Diario de Yucatán* painted Salvador Alvarado as a non-Yucatecan with unrealistic visions whose revolutionary changes led only to bankruptcy and failure: "His schools and libraries have disappeared; alcohol, prostitution and idleness have returned; and so have the foreign monopolies, and corrupt governors." Worse, for the common worker "hunger and sickness are again life's daily reality for him and his family."[59]

For their part, the politicians had their own version of who was to blame. They claimed that during the good years the *henequeneros* were loath to reinvest their earlier fiber earnings and were slow to modernize the cultivation, harvesting, and rasping that would have kept the business more competitive in a changing world market. Those problems, all played out during the backdrop of the worldwide depression, were the issues on which Yucatán governor Bartolomé García Correa (1930–1934) and his supporters squarely placed the blame for the henequen decline.[60]

The Great Depression's impact on the henequen decline in Yucatán cannot be underestimated. The old adage "when the United States sneezes, Latin America gets a cold" (or, "when the United States gets a cold, Latin America gets pneumonia") was especially pertinent to Yucatán, which was so economically entwined with its North American neighbors. Historian Ben Fallaw has written, "The era of stability ended abruptly in 1929 when the Great Depression devastated the Yucatán henequen industry." It was then that the big hacendados demanded an end to the cooperative Henequeneros de Yucatán and when García Correa began his term as governor after a resounding electoral victory (having faced no opponent) in which he received the support of the wealthy growers.[61]

Not knowing exactly how to deal with the economic crisis, García Correa appointed Alberto Montes Molina, a member of the powerful Casta Divina clans who had helped fund his election, to direct the cooperative—a move that showed he was leaning toward disbanding the agency and reprivatizing the henequen industry. The thinking was based on a belief that a laissez-faire approach could help restore the industry to its former glory, and yet the governor sought additional federal loans, tax breaks, and production restrictions to get the *henequeneros* through the bad times. But García Correa came to regret these moves. In just a few months the cooperative's reserves were depleted, its debts expanded, and its markets with both North America and Europe rapidly dwindling. Montes predictably made favorable arrangements for the businesses owned by his family network, which enraged other *henequeneros* and Socialist Party stalwarts, and discredited García Correa during his four years in office. His policies and appointments worsened the Yucatán fiber situation and did not help dig Henequeneros de Yucatán out of its deep indebtedness.[62]

Growers tried to respond to the effects of the Great Depression. In 1931 *El sisal mexicano* advocated that the government work toward ameliorating the situation in this "critical moment of the world economic depression." It called on the state to intervene on fiber pricing, railroad rates, and supports for cooperatives.[63] But since there were few funds available to help the cooperatives, they too started to go under. By then the economy of Yucatán had basically collapsed.

Making matters far worse for both North American grain farmers and Yucatecan henequen growers in the 1930s were the extreme weather conditions in the United States and Canada. From 1931 to 1937 all of North America experienced some of the driest and hottest summers and some of the coldest winters in recorded history. A U.S. Weather Bureau scientist called the conditions "the worst in the climatological history of the country." The same could be said of Canada. The transnational Great Plains experienced the worst conditions of all. According to one study, the 1930s "was the worst decade in the history of prairie Canada. . . . Adding to the economic depression were the natural disasters on the prairies of drought, wind and dust storms, and grasshopper plagues."[64] The weather, described so well by Gerald Friesen, added to the truly hard times of the prairie farmers: "The dust storms began in 1931. Hot winds blew steadily day after day in the month of June." It only got worse throughout the decade, when during the summer of 1934 "soil began to blow in mid-June, to destroy gardens and crops." It was a bit better in 1935, but 1936 "was a disaster," with the "coldest winter in history . . . compounded by blizzard after blizzard . . . [and] with the longest, hottest summer yet." It was so bad then that the high winds caused "desert-like conditions," and, "like the Sahara, the prairie desert was moving and growing." The early summer of 1937 was "even hotter, drier, windier, and dirtier than the year before." Dust storms were more common, lakes dried up, and "farmers actually raced to cut

Russian thistle in order to feed starving cattle. Needless to say, there was no crop." As if that were not bad enough, the conditions were ideal for grasshoppers, or Rocky Mountain locusts, which "proliferated into a plague of biblical proportions" as early as 1930 and were followed by infestations of sawflies, army worms, cutworms, and even gophers that ravaged croplands. And when there was some moisture in 1935 and 1938, stem rust destroyed many farmers' wheat crops.[65]

In the northern U.S. plains the drought was so bad that much of eastern Montana and the Dakotas were as arid as the Sonoran Desert of northern Mexico. Investigators for the Works Progress Administration, a program in Franklin Roosevelt's New Deal, declared that more counties in South Dakota and North Dakota (forty-one and twenty-three, respectively) than elsewhere were in desperate straits as some of the poorest counties in the nation due to "intense drought and distress."[66] But farmers in the southern plains had it even worse. There, cyclical droughts were characteristic, coming at twenty-year intervals or so, but the one in the 1930s was so severe and had such consequences that a journalist coined the term "Dust Bowl" upon seeing the mountains of dust (dirt as fine as face powder), destroyed fields, and general devastation in the region. The Dust Bowl encompassed the panhandles of Texas and Oklahoma, parts of eastern New Mexico and Colorado, and most of western Kansas—the most seriously affected state. It was characterized by huge dust storms, many of which came day after day, in the springs and summers of the mid-1930s, with some of the worst storms occurring in 1936 and 1937. The storms blew millions of tons of topsoil off of plowed fields, and the dirt piled up in dunes on farms, fields, houses, and towns throughout the area. Crops were destroyed for several years in a row for many farmers. By 1935 some 33 million acres of the southern plains, or one-third of the Dust Bowl area, "lay naked, ungrassed, and vulnerable to the winds." Donald Worster has called the conditions not only "the darkest moment in the twentieth-century life of the southern plains" but also "the most severe environmental catastrophe in the entire history of white man on this continent" and "one of the three worst ecological blunders in history."[67]

The conditions had huge social repercussions as well. When depression and drought doubled up on them in the "Dirty Thirties," farm families suffered economically and emotionally. The situation in Saskatchewan was so bad that some farmers could not even afford to buy binder twine, even though they needed much less of it due to the poor crops. In 1932 the province's Relief Commission made binder twine available to struggling farmers, "provided they cannot secure twine any other way." The agency expected "the grower, the banker, the loan companies, and local authorities to take care of the twine situation in those areas." Even with such relief, many, perhaps up to 2.5 million people, left the plains (many moving to California, but most just into towns or other counties). Every plains state's population was lower at the end of the 1930s than it was at the beginning, with South Dakota's 7.2 percent loss as the highest loss in the country. In Canada, an estimated 247,000 people abandoned the Prairie Provinces between 1931 and 1941.[68]

Many historians now accept that the cause for such ecological and social disruption in both the American and Canadian plains was the great plow-up of the 1910s and 1920s. The famed ecologist Aldo Leopold referred to it as "wheating land to death."[69] As discussed earlier, prices during and after World War I were so fantastic that farmers raced to place as much "virgin" land as possible under the plow to plant and harvest grain crops. The fact that it was all conducted in a laissez-faire economy with increased mechanization and unwise farming practices is what allowed the transformation from native prairie to millions of acres of wheat to occur so quickly. Referring to Canadian farmers caught up in the wheat boom, John Herd Thompson wrote, "Western farmers neglected proper agricultural techniques during the Great War and quickly paid the price." He listed such faults as insufficient tillage, failure to summer-fallow, and excessive eagerness to mine the export market in wheat.[70] Edna Jacques, whose family farmed near Briercrest, Saskatchewan, and never sold a bushel of wheat in nine years during "drouth" times, paraphrased the situation well when she wrote in a poem:

> And now I ask, O Lord, a mother's prayer,
>> Help me to know these fields so brown and bare;
>> Art not of Thee, that all this stricken land
>> Is not because of Thine avenging hand,
>> But ours the fault; we did not farm it right
>> And now it answers us with wind and blight.[71]

Similarly, in the States the rapid mechanization of plains agriculture, along with "methods of industrial capitalism," created what Worster has called "an exploitative relationship with the earth: a bond that was strictly commercial, so that the land became nothing more than a form of capital that must be made to pay as much as possible." That was the message conveyed in the 1936 Farm Security Administration film *The Plow That Broke the Plains*. Director Pare Lorenz sought to show viewers that it was more than drought that caused the Dust Bowl; it was farmers' overzealous plow-ups without regard to cyclical weather patterns.[72] With that in mind, many scholars agree with Worster's conclusion that while the 1930s drought cycle on the plains may have been coincidental with the depression, its unusual devastation was caused by the same conditions that created the economic disaster, "that the same society produced them both, and for similar reasons." It was drought, "but natural factors did not make the storms—they merely made them possible."[73]

The matter of mechanization as part of the plains' environmental change is pertinent to the study of binders here. Did binders cause the Dust Bowl? Certainly railroads, which permitted rapid distribution of agricultural materials across wide spaces, and plows pulled by tractors were more directly responsible than binders for the "great plow-up." The tractor-pulled plow was part of the much larger picture of a machinery-dependent, industrialized agriculture on the Great Plains that binders, and later combines, also came to represent, although binders and combines often have been excluded from the discussions and literature regarding the implications of machinery in early nineteenth-century North America. The greater amount of tilled and planted acreage would not have been worth anything to the farmers if they did not have a faster, more mechanized way to harvest. Thus, it was mechanization in all its forms, for everything from sod busting to harvesting, which played a major role in the ecological disaster. That the harvest process in the American and Canadian plains was dependent on another agricultural commodity from Yucatán makes it is equally important to consider the drought's considerable effects on the demand for fiber. The Dust Bowl bore heavily on the henequen-wheat complex and was indeed severely felt in Mexico.

All the effects revolved around the production and marketing of wheat. By the end of the 1920s, and pre-dating the crash on Wall Street, fiber producers had already noticed the volatility of that market. The booming post–World War I wheat demand was by then giving way to an unstable market: exporting countries were overproducing, and France, Germany, and Italy were buying less grain from overseas as their own farms came back into operation, often with quotas and tariffs encouraging increased domestic production. This development especially hurt farmers in the Canadian prairies where they unwisely had devoted 60 percent of all field crops to wheat, 70 percent of which was exported. They felt it hard when wheat prices dropped at unprecedented rates, from more than two dollars a bushel in the mid-1920s to thirty-four cents a bushel in 1932.[74]

And then came drought. Wheat production in the Canadian prairies fell from an average of 350 million annual bushels in the 1920s (with roughly 17 bushels per acre) to 230 million bushels in the mid-1930s (with 9.5 bushels an acre). One of the worst hit areas was Saskatchewan, where in 1936 a report on the drought stated, "Practically all crops stubbled in are a complete failure. . . . The farmer will not have any purchasing power this fall, consequently businesses and professionals will likewise suffer." In 1936 harvests there yielded only 2.6 bushels per acre.[75] The rates in the American plains were equally dismal. In North Dakota production plummeted from more than 110 million bushels in 1932 to a little more than 19 million bushels in 1936 (with a mere 5.2 bushels per acre). Montana's harvest of 54.6 million bushels in 1932 was cut to almost 12 million in 1936 (at 5.3 bushels per acre), and South Dakota's near 52 million bushels in 1932 became a fraction of that in 1935 at 732,000 bushels (4.6 bushels an acre). Wheat king Kansas's harvests were nearly cut in half, from 120 million bushels in 1932 to 64.5 million in 1935 (at 9.3 bushels per acre).[76]

The implications of these figures for binder twine and henequen use are not difficult to imagine. Both the North American cordage and Yucatecan fiber industries kept abreast of the economic and climatic conditions that so profoundly and negatively affected demand for their products. Before the dust storms blew, the fiber interests were discussing the postwar market conditions that set off the downward spiral for twine demand. *The New York Times Magazine* ran a story in 1931, which was reprinted in *El sisal mexicano*, that dealt with the decline in grain prices and specifically how it was affecting farmers in Kansas. Headlined "Empire in Wheat Deeply Wounded" and repeating the lyrics to the old Protestant hymn "Bringing in the Sheaves," the article stated how in the "immense western lands they are bringing in the sheaves in great abundance without precedence," but the farmers were not "coming in rejoicing" due to the weak market and the rapidly dropping prices. By 1934 the trade journal *El sisal mexicano* was reporting that "the consumption of twine was lower than in any other years."[77]

The fiber producers also kept up with the alarming weather conditions. In 1931 *El sisal mexicano* gave detailed accounts of the "critical situation" in the Canadian wheat belt. It reported that no part of the Prairie Provinces had received "sufficient rain," how southern Saskatchewan was especially dry, and how wheat harvests were predicted to be down 3 percent in Manitoba, 5 percent in Saskatchewan, and as much as 7 percent below average in Alberta.[78] The next year, the trade journal reported similar news for the American plains. "Diminished Harvests in Five States," it warned, giving rainfall data for Kansas, Nebraska, Oklahoma, Texas, and Colorado, and predicting a harvest that would be smaller by 250 million bushels than 1931's. Worse, quoting from *Farm Implement News*, early in the summer it discussed how in various regions such as western Kansas, northwestern Oklahoma, and eastern Colorado farmers were starting to abandon unknown numbers of wheat fields, and it reported that in western Canada rainfall had reached unprecedented lows.[79]

Periodicals such as the *Cordage Trade Journal* kept tabs on how the weather in the plains would affect twine demand, often giving state-by-state accounts of weather conditions and harvest forecasts. In August 1934 it opined that irrigation would save eastern Montana's crops but that in North Dakota and parts of Minnesota the early plantings would "not be worth cutting" and that in South Dakota harvests of minor grains would amount to "complete failure." *El sisal mexicano* echoed the concerns that year, stating that the summer's harvest would be "one of the worst in the history of binder twine," especially with the intense heat in the plains that caused grains to come to a head too early. That same year, the journal was calling the drought and dust storms a "desperate situation" for both wheat growers and fiber producers. It cited a *Saturday Evening Post* article that detailed the terrible conditions.[80] Also, Mérida's *Diario de Yucatán* monitored the conditions quite closely, especially at the height of the drought in 1936. "Drought in the U.S. Wheat Zone May Eclipse the One in 1934" proclaimed an article in the newspaper, going on to report that North Carolina was the only state in the union that received above average rainfall so far that year. It was a "tenacious drought" that was producing a "highly critical situation" for plains farmers, especially in the spring wheat zones of North Dakota, which received only one-third its normal rainfall. Another article discussed the situation in South Dakota, where the value of lost wheat fields was estimated to be $140 million, almost half the wheat losses ($300 million) for the entire nation. The newspaper also kept readers alert to conditions in Canada and to the world wheat market.[81]

In 1935, however, the plains weather had improved enough to give a glimmer of hope to the cordage and fiber producers. With an air of hopefulness, *El sisal mexicano* reported that while the plains were still in the Dust Bowl (*la zona del polvo*,) crops looked better than they had in 1934. One Yucatecan wrote that "the henequen leaves will sustain new life." Mexico City's *Excélsior* even reported that 1936 would hold "brilliant prospects for Yucatán."[82] But sometimes in their optimism the newspapers missed the mark. The story in the December 1935 issue of *El sisal mexicano* declaring that there were "Good Prospects for 1936" and that twine "manufacturers and distributors were preparing for better sales than in other recent years" ended up not being accurate for the Dakotas and western Canada, where 1936 proved to be the most disastrous year. However, prospects for winter wheat in Kansas were indeed quite better (and there were better harvests in parts of the southern plains that year). And IH's purchase of 200,000 bales of sisal gave "all a good feeling for 1936." In fact, sisal sales did improve somewhat in the mid-1930s. They had a record-setting low in 1931 with slightly more than 400,000 bales and climbed back up to a fluctuating average of 500,000 bales the rest of the decade— nowhere close to the near 1.2 million bales sold in 1915 or the 900,000 bales sold in 1920. But by 1938 the Yucatecan share of the world market had slipped to 23 percent.[83]

By 1937 it looked like things would finally get better. The *Cordage Trade Journal* announced in July that grain prospects in the United States were "ex-

cellent," the best in the previous five years, and that there was "every indica-
tion now that practically all available binder twine will be required for the
several crops which are bound." The optimism, however, did not extend to
Canada, where conditions in 1937 continued in the drought and dust storm
mode. Crops in the prairies there were "far less satisfactory, and the three
provinces will not require anything like the amount of binder twine that normal crops use." More specifically, the article explained that drought in southern and central Saskatchewan and southeastern Alberta—usually one of Canada's best wheat producing regions—made crops there "practically [a] total
failure." Still, there was some cause to remain upbeat: "In June the Canadian
crop deterioration was mainly in the sections where the combined harvester-
thresher [or "combine"] is used, while there was actual improvement in the
sections where binder twine continues to be used for the bulk of the crop."
Furthermore, in Manitoba crops were doing better and presented "the brightest outlook."[84]

By the end of the decade—the dusty, dirty, and seemingly unending thirties—wheat, henequen, and twine production started to rebound. In March
1939 sisal shipments were flowing freely to New Orleans, and shipments to
New York jumped by 41 percent in 1937.[85] By then wheat production was
approaching pre–Dust Bowl yields. Things in the henequen-wheat complex
seemed to be returning to normalcy, at least in the United States and Canada.
Not so for Yucatán. The decline that had begun in the late 1910s, increased in
the postwar 1920s, and intensified during the depression and drought of the
1930s worsened to the point of the industry's demise by 1950, after only a temporary surge in sisal interests during World War II. The demise is discussed
more in detail in the following chapter, but there is one further point regarding the 1930s that merits attention here: the failed efforts to halt the decline
through political and economic actions that followed the election of Lázaro
Cárdenas as president of Mexico in 1934.

While Mexicans were suffering through their own unique consequences
of the worldwide Great Depression, they elected the populist Cárdenas. He
and the electorate were bent on reestablishing the goals of the Mexican Revolution that seemed to have faded in the 1920s and early 1930s. To a large degree, Cárdenas took the revolution to the left, with sweeping agrarian policy
reform, land reform, and an expanded system of *ejidos* (communal farm lands)
backed by the establishment of a credit bank to make loans to *ejidatarios* working the land. Like other presidents before him, Cárdenas understood the financial promise of henequen in Yucatán, although his reforms for that state did
not take effect until 1937. By then, as Ben Fallaw argues, only the La Laguna
region of northern Durango and southern Coahuila (a land of cotton and other
agricultural exports) matched the scale of agrarian reform that Cárdenas

brought to Yucatán, and only at La Laguna were more federal resources spent on his ejido policies during most of his presidency. In fact, the president's plan called for the henequen zone to follow "the example of La Laguna." But Cárdenas viewed land reform in Yucatán as part of broader social reform policy needed in that state: he sought a less *henequenero*-based patriarchal society, he advocated a more modernized society with better education and health care, and he demanded (but did not accomplish) political reform that included expunging regional bosses and the land-owning oligarchy that controlled the Socialist Party of the Southeast. Thus, in terms of the scale of change, "no state would be more affected than Yucatán."[86]

To enable him to implement the land reform program in Yucatán, Cárdenas expropriated the henequen haciendas. It was a bold move, and it hearkened to the spirit of the revolution when Salvador Alvarado spoke of agrarian reform but never did much of it. In some ways, the expropriation was the furtherance of the efforts of the president's predecessor, the all-powerful jefe máximo (maximum chief) Plutarco Elías Calles (1924–1928, but still "in charge" of other presidents from 1928 to 1935), who sought to extend federal control over the henequen industry. Calles and Yucatán governor García Correa strived to bring Yucatán more into the milieu of the national economy that would require control of the *henequenales*.[87] Along with the wealthy *henequeneros* who supported their campaigns, the two worked well together through the "willful inaction of state and national authorities" to derail the breakup and transfer of haciendas to local ejidos that Governor Carrillo Puerto began in the mid-1920s. In fact, by 1932 García Correa had announced that agrarian reform was over for Yucatán—it was too costly and technically unworkable.[88]

The Calles/García Correa system was new and caused some confusion with North American fiber brokers. Henry W. Peabody & Company notified customers in 1932 that Calles had "taken control of the sisal business" and had "decided to try new sales methods," going through any broker in New Orleans or New York (instead of just Hanson & Orth, which was used exclusively during the Carrillo years). "This is something entirely new to the trade," the company admitted, "and we do not know just how it will work out."[89] But the new system, as Fallaw has shown, was designed to continue propping up the large producers' Henequeneros de Yucatán cooperative with federal and state supports (e.g., financial credit from Mexico City) to get them through the depression, whereas the government did not deliver on similar promises to small producers and campesinos. In return, the wealthy hacendados lent their support to both Calles and García Correa while the small producers languished and suffered more during the market declines and bad times of the depression. Thousands of rural workers and unemployed peons went hungry in the early 1930s and attributed their plight to the policies that aided the wealthy. In

1931 they organized "hunger caravans" in the henequen zone and marched on Mérida, demanding changes.[90] Many henequen workers went on strike in both the field and processing sectors. A group of small producers complained to the federal government that the wealthy landowners "think they are the only producers" and therefore had too much control over henequen production, pricing, and sales. "We denounce . . . the rich hacendados . . . the eternal enemies of the Yucatecan proletariat," wrote a large number of members of the Central Committee of Workers and Campesinos to President Abelardo Rodríguez—a Calles puppet who directly preceded Cárdenas, "[and] we beg your energetic intervention."[91]

Much of the trouble, the workers claimed, stemmed from the practice of restricting or halting production of henequen as a response to declining demand and the desire to hold out for better international prices. The policy began in 1930 when García Correa announced the first production moratorium to raise prices.[92] He slapped on more limits in 1932, resulting in a 20 percent decrease in production. However, in 1933, despite the depression-reduced prices, the limits were temporarily lifted and production experienced "favorable increases," as *El nacional* reported, greatly pleasing the Liga Central de Resistencia (Central League of Resistance of the Socialist Party of the Southeast), which had advocated abolishing the limits. Restrictions were a central grievance presented in the widely distributed pamphlet *Ante la ruina del henequén* and also the reason that the Henequeneros de Yucatán cooperative sought "to oppose the production stoppages." Cooperative members wrote President Rodríguez outlining their complaints: "We reject the halts, we want the workers, peons, and all Yucatecans to have work, we want to continue producing, and we are tired of the restrictions."[93] The general secretary of the cooperative also wrote begging for the president's intervention, saying how the limits were causing the "complete ruin" of the industry. "We want to continue working," he reiterated. Others echoed the problems of the "anguishing conflict," suggested that there were many other methods of dealing with the pricing difficulties, and argued that it was "never necessary to suspend work" when the stoppages were affecting upwards of twenty-five thousand workers. The production moratoriums were causing "irreparable damage" and were not "remedying the situation."[94]

The entire situation created a scenario ripe for reform when Cárdenas was elected. While his predecessor, Calles, opposed agrarian reform in Yucatán, his role in the cooperative Henequeneros de Yucatán in the mid-1920s became, as Fallaw has written, "the key legal precedent for the subsequent expropriation of the henequen fields effected by Cárdenas in 1937."[95] Cárdenas, anointed for the presidency by Calles but falling from the jefe máximo's good graces soon thereafter, announced his vision for Yucatecan land reform before he was even elected. While campaigning in 1934 he laid out a plan that would distribute nineteen thousand hectares of henequen land to peasant villages to be worked as collective ejidos, although he allowed large landholders to keep parts of their estates and, oddly, some landowners to keep their plantations intact. Some 236 communities were eligible to receive ejidos (with each ejidatario getting four hectares of henequen), 80 of which were in the henequen zone. Cárdenas's agrarian reform expropriated roughly 70 percent of Yucatán's fiber-producing haciendas, and government surveyors delineated all the new ejido boundaries carved from the haciendas in just two weeks' time.[96] His hope was that a broader base of the population would enjoy the economic benefits of henequen production, thus creating a "new class-based consciousness," and that wealthy landowners would invest their capital in industry to help stimulate that sector of the national economy. At the same time, radically expanding the ejido system at the expense of the wealthy landowners' haciendas was part of Cárdenas's goal for the "social liberation of the Yucatecan peasantry."[97]

However, after Cárdenas was elected, it was several years before he could bring Yucatán into his national agrarian reform program. According to many, the plan did not come soon enough. One study shows that in the two decades between 1916 and 1936 the number of henequen haciendas decreased from 1,161 to 583; the amount of fiber produced dropped from 1,007,000 bales to 594,000 bales; and the number of workers employed in the henequen industry plummeted from 56,610 to 25,582.[98] By 1936, the "suffering, hunger, [and] misery" of campesinos had not abated, as the number of letters and telegrams to Cárdenas shows. Some of the suffering led to violence and sabotage against wealthy *henequeneros* as some disgruntled workers set fire to henequen fields. Arson, claimed the Agrarian Reform office in Yucatán, was reflective of "ejidatarios conquered by misery." Workers also sent several petitions to the president calling on him to consider "the extremely grave danger for henequen production" when so many laborers were cut from their jobs seeding, cultivating, harvesting, defibering, and packing henequen. The *Diario de Yucatán* reported in the summer of 1936 that strikes, riots, and railroad attacks continued as angry henequen workers tried to bring attention to their plight.[99]

Thus, Cárdenas perceived the need for agrarian reform to be great. From 1935 to 1937 the federal government created nearly 6,000 ejidos on 25 million acres of former estates for the benefit of 569,000 campesinos.[100] To announce reforms specifically for Yucatán, the president traveled to Mérida in August 1937 and decreed a twelve-point plan to incorporate the henequen zone into the national Agrarian Code. Among other things, that plan would assign 150-hectare units to various ejidal communities to be organized and farmed "in collective form." It also outlined how the government, through the secretary of finance and public credit, would provide credit for the start-up and maintenance of ejidal operations, oversight and recommendations "toward the lessening of waste in henequen," and oversight in the establishment of cordage factories. The last point mandated that the Agrarian Department would "give immediate attention" to public education, sanitary services, and other social welfare programs that would "be of ultimate benefit to the farmer population of Yucatán."[101] In his message "to the people of Yucatán" that prefaced the plan, Cárdenas rationalized his actions based on the fact that the henequen industry had suffered a 50 percent decline in the years 1917 to 1937 from its boom years of 1896 to 1916. He was critical of the "conditions of class privilege which the great landowners continued to enjoy" and cited a "lack of economic foresight" and "incomplete agrarian legislation" as reasons for the decline. He was thus committed to the new ejidal land reform system as "an imperative economic necessity" and "an undeniable act of social justice." By 1938 the program was benefiting 38,000 ejidatarios in Yucatán. The people on the ejidos, villagers or workers from a former hacienda, worked the lands collectively to deal with the massive amount of henequen to be produced.[102]

Producing henequen for sale meant rasping and defibering the crop. Cárdenas received complaints concerning the ejidatarios' lack of not only land on which to grow henequen but also the "necessary equipment" for the cooperatives to function. An editorial in Mexico City's *El nacional* even suggested that the desfibradoras be declared public utilities as a way to extend the reforms. But Cárdenas did not touch that part of the fiber production process. His agrarian reforms left the desfibradoras, considered the most valuable part of a henequen plantation, in the hands of the wealthy hacendados. Those areas and buildings of the henequen hacienda that housed all the decorticating machinery were neither expropriated nor divided up among the ejidatarios.[103] However, he did address the question of manufacturing twine—industrializing the henequen industry beyond the growing and decorticating processes—as another measure to boost Yucatán's economy. He explicitly mentioned in his expropriation plan "the need for its industrialization for the better economic exploitation of the henequen ejidos" and thus commissioned the secretary of the national economy to continue researching and developing "modern cordage works for the establishment of factories."[104]

Like any new program, Cárdenas's expropriation plan received both avid support and strong opposition. Many peasant workers in Yucatán, like their counterparts throughout Mexico who lovingly referred to the president with the fatherly term Tata Lázaro, viewed the ejido program as their economic and cultural salvation. The presidential archives of his term are overflowing with correspondence from Yucatán expressing deep appreciation. For example, a henequen worker named Enrique Núñez González wrote Cárdenas a personal note suggesting how grateful he was for the president's ejido policies and other "general labor laws." He placed Cárdenas in line as the fulfillment of Salvador Alvarado's earlier goals of "breaking forever the chains of slavery of the campesinos."[105] Telegrams and letters sent by others express gratitude for the president's "immortal work," "heroic virtue," "historic deeds," "social justice," and "great revolutionary work," and some have the handwritten words *"muy agradecido"* (very thankful) printed across the top. Much of the correspondence came from newly organized campesino labor unions, such as the Federación Regional de Obreros y Campesinos de Yucatán (Regional Federation of Workers and Peasants of Yucatán), the Unión Sindical de Empleados de Campo de Yucatán por la Defensa de Industria Henequenera (Syndicated Union of Rural Workers for the Defense of the Henequen Industry), and the Liga de Resistencia de Medianos y Pequeños Productores de Henequén (League of Resistance of Medium and Small Henequen Producers). Many letters had multiple signees with mostly Mayan surnames or that were "signed" with the fingerprints of the rural workers. Typical was a letter by Román Zavala representing the Unión Estatal Independiente de Veteranos de la Revolución en Yucatán (Independent State Union of Veterans of the Revolution in Yucatán). This correspondent promised that the workers were ready to "prevent any obstructions by reactionaries" who attempted to halt the expropriation plan, and he assured the president that they were "as united in peace as they were in war." Cárdenas also had the support of one of the nation's largest newspapers, *El nacional,* for his land reform measures in Yucatán. "It's necessary to destroy the latifundismo," an editorial in the newspaper argued in 1936. "Henequen is a plant that should be cultivated with care for the utility of all in the nation."[106]

While such statements represented a great deal of hope that the henequen industry would recuperate, in reality the demand for twine remained so low that world market prices for sisal went from six cents to three cents a pound in 1937, the first year of the expropriation. Yucatecans placed the blame squarely on the North American drought but still trusted President Cárdenas enough to seek his personal attention on the matter, specifically asking for protective pricing. Yucatecans wrote directly to the president with their concerns: "The meteorological phenomena in the principal wheat zones are completely adverse for the harvests, that is, they will be almost totally lost due to the drought; the twine buyers will not have wheat to bind."[107] However, things seemed brighter for the next season's harvest in the Great Plains. A henequen report from 1937 showed that production was up by more than 150,000 bales over preceding years and that grain harvests for 1938 looked "entirely favorable," creating a welcome "big demand for twine." This was good news, as henequen remained Yucatán's "sole source of life for the state" and since the United States was "without doubt the principal market," receiving 70 percent of henequen exports.[108]

Opposition to expropriation was equally strong. Logically, some of the first voices to speak against it were from the hacendados who stood to lose a great deal of land without compensation, especially four thousand hectares that had already been seeded. In an attempt to fight the plan, they organized the Asociación Defensora de la Industria Henequenera (Henequen Industry Defense Association) and issued a variety of reports and memoranda that they sent to the president. One, entitled "Problema agrario en la Zona Henequenera de Yucatán" ("The Agrarian Problem in the Henequen Zone of Yucatán"), was passionate: "Officials are forgetting that you can't just give land away, and much less so in Yucatán." It especially decried the suggestion that henequen fields could be used to raise corn or other grains—an "almost inconceivable idea" because it would take ten to twelve years for the land to produce corn after being used for henequen. An earlier memo by Gustavo Molina Font stated in no uncertain terms that the National Agrarian Commission had erred in thinking that corn could grow on henequen land, which was "absolutely inadequate" for grains. He suggested that henequen fields would have to be cut and burned, wasting valuable, productive lands, especially since it was so "urgent to plant henequen." "If we don't," Molina advised, "then Yucatán in just a few years will be in disaster and ruin."[109]

Later, the Defense Association issued a fifty-page "alternate plan to resolve the problem." Simply entitled "El Problema Agrario de Yucatán" ("The Agrarian Problem of Yucatán") and written by Salvador Zamudio in the summer of 1937, the report reflected the "tenacious opposition of the latifundista group" based on its historical interpretation of failed agrarian reform plans under governors Salvador Alvarado and Felipe Carrillo Puerto. Thus, the association's alternative proposed a way to avoid adversely affecting current henequen production, which they claimed Cárdenas's program would do, by forming a Henequen Agrarian Fund of 7 million pesos from state henequen profits to support a new, gradually expanding ejido system. Much of this thinking was based on the idea that it was "a grave error" to give campesinos land to farm in the henequen zone—it simply was not the best way to boost the production and export of fiber. Likewise, he argued that ejidos had always been used "as an instrument to dominate the campesino masses politically" as opposed to being an action based on a philanthropic ideology about sharing land.[110]

The problem in executing Cárdenas's agrarian reform was that it required a great deal of federal intervention in Yucatán, "a state long suspicious of the national government and jealous of its distinctive regional identity," as Fallaw has described it. The henequeneros never appreciated carpetbagging by others in Mexico, and they were not about to accept it from Cárdenas. Fallaw concluded that in Mexico City "negative views and outright stereotypes of Yucatecans coexisted with a mythical vision of the Yucatecan Mayas as a tragically oppressed 'race' in need of redemption by the national government." Cárdenas himself "clung to a romantic view of the Maya as a proud, stoic folk requiring his government's paternalistic guidance for salvation," which did not go over well in Yucatán.[111]

It was not just the large landowners who were outspoken against expropriation, however. Members of the various henequen workers' unions and the League of Resistance of Medium and Small Henequen Producers (who, as shown, also had members strongly supporting the plan) wrote to the federal Agrarian Department advising that dividing the land into ejidos would decrease Yucatán's overall henequen production by 40 percent. They argued that the ejidatarios did not have the "means to cultivate henequen efficiently," especially in the early summer when it was time to replant, "which takes special considerations."[112] In the United States many were against what critic Henry J. Allen called Cárdenas's "irrevocable decision to dispossess the rural owners of their henequen plantations and deliver the same to the peasants . . . as collective property under the patronage, tutelage and administration of an official body." Allen, a newspaper editor from wheat-dependent Kansas who toured henequen plantations in 1938, referred to expropriation as "the tragedy of Yucatán" and wrote that the ejidal credit bank "became the economic dictator of the state." According to Allen, the worker peasants reacted to Cárdenas's decision in an "unthrilled" and "bemused" sort of way—they were "stupefied" and "confused" when the president, "with the generosity of a god," gave them the sisal plantations that were previously owned by "the private citizens who, through torturous years, had wrought the miracle of capital and labor upon the desert."[113]

Allen represented the fears of others who interpreted Cárdenas's "collectivist experiment" as the beginnings of Stalinist communism in Mexico. He wrote that "communistic writers went into ecstasies over the confiscation" and that anyone who doubted "the success of the enterprise was denounced as a 'traitor to the revolution.'" He asserted that the forty-five thousand peasants said to benefit from the expropriation "would become partners of the government in what would be practically a huge communal plantation embracing all Yucatán."[114] In similar fashion, John Magoon, an American fiber merchant in Yucatán, wrote IH about "a big meeting here of the Communist Party" that included "five or six foreign communists as speakers." He recalled that they said "workmen" would seize sisal fields and cordage mills, that all farms would be "operated under the collective system," and that all factories would be "owned and operated by the workers." Thus it was "only a matter of a few years" before

Mexico would be "more communistic than Russia." Magoon's prediction never materialized, but the anti-socialist sentiment lingered. Even a former mayor of Mérida in the 1990s blamed Yucatán's problems on Cárdenas: "This was a very rich state until 1937," asserted Ana Rosa Payán, "when the all-powerful Mr. Lázaro Cárdenas came to destroy the wealth of this state, and since then things have only gotten worse."[115]

In the end, Cárdenas's expectations for the expropriated henequen fields did not materialize. The demand for fiber continued to slump in the late 1930s, causing any cardenista advances to dwindle. When that happened, the ejidal bank, in charge of distributing henequen profits, was unable to make payments to the "hungry and infuriated workers," which launched them back into the streets to protest in 1938. "When do we get paid?" and "Death to the Banco Ejidal!" they shouted. As one newspaper account put it, "The revolt against the administration of the communal banks became so violent that the federal government ordered these institutions to cease operations in all the henequen zones." Still, new Yucatán governor Humberto Canto called on the peasants to subject themselves to a "regimen of sacrifice" because government pay advances would "have to be limited."[116] He was on record early in his term in 1938 supporting the agrarian reforms against the "feudalistic monopoly" and regretting how the "low prices" of the "calculating capitalist, cold, unpitying, blind" world market worked to "extinguish a just and humane idea."[117]

Some people translated that kind of sentiment as an indictment of IH. Plymouth Cordage field representative Ellis Brewster noted from Mérida, "Whenever you see 'speculators,' 'capitalists,' and 'imperialists' mentioned in the sisal news reports from here, you can well bet they are talking about IHCO." He wrote that he had tried to combat that mentality but explained that there were other economic forces at work: "These people just can't seem to understand that there is such a thing as too much fibre in the world nor that there can be over-production or under-consumption. Neither can I seem to get it through their thick skulls that we, as sellers working on commission, want high prices."[118] Henry Allen posited that the workers' "misery" was from "forcing them to become owners of properties which they [could] not manage" and that the "collectivist operations" had "seriously crippled" the industry. He worried that it would take nine years to restore the henequen fields to the level that could produce their pre-expropriation yields. In a conclusion ringing of environmental declension, Allen wrote that the "failure of the plan" had caused the growers and workers "to sacrifice that which made the state great, and with that sacrifice to send the hard-earned land of Yucatán back toward the state of barrenness which it knew when it was the unyielding home of the struggling natives one hundred years ago, and on back into countless centuries."[119]

In retrospect, the conservative Allen can be considered correct in his assessment that the agrarian reform plan failed in Yucatán, but there are other reasons, visible perhaps only in hindsight. For example, Fallaw has explained convincingly that the "serious delays" in getting the plan off the ground—waiting those several years after Cárdenas's election and promises—planted the germ of its demise. Likewise, the long-standing difficulties in "forging horizontal linkages to overcome factionalism, caciques [regional bosses] and landowners, and peasant-peon antipathy" became too insurmountable for Cárdenas and his followers. The Cardenistas made the fatal mistake of making "key concessions to regional politicos," thus circumventing the hoped-for reforms, and the wealthy *henequeneros* strongly resisted the plan for more than two years, damaging the timing and efficacy of the plan. Tata Lázaro also failed to allocate sufficient funds to implement the reforms in Yucatán, working on other national priorities first. The welcomed oil industry nationalization and heavily funded cotton projects in the La Laguna region received vastly more federal attention and funding than did the henequen project in Yucatán. Agrarian reform simply could not have worked without the concomitant political reform needed in Yucatán. What Cárdenas really needed was a plan to break the stronghold of the ruling elites and to work more closely with the urban labor movement, but such policies never made it onto his agenda.[120]

To make things even worse, by the end of the decade a plague of flies hit Yucatán and damaged the already ailing henequen industry. A Secretariat of Agriculture and Development official reported to President Cárdenas in 1939 that the flies "suck the juices from the pulp of the leaves making the fiber worthless."[121] But perhaps the insects were no more than harbingers of the greater ills that would quickly befall the industry. While the years 1916 to 1929 brought serious declines in the industry and the depression and drought cast their evil shadows over Yucatán in the 1930s, it was competition from abroad (both in fibers from other regions and in synthetic twines) and the adoption of the combine harvester on the American and Canadian plains that sucked the remaining strands of life from henequen in the 1940s.

CHAPTER 7

Competition and Combines

The End of the Henequen-Wheat Story

> There was one more apparatus that completed the industrialization of
> the grasslands: the combined harvester-thresher, or, as it was called more
> simply, the combine. . . . The grain, threshed as it was cut, poured like a
> golden stream into the bed of a truck driven alongside; then off it went to
> the elevators and flour mills of the world.
>
> *—Donald Worster*

THE end of the henequen-wheat story can be attributed to a variety of factors. Price hikes on Yucatecan fiber during the Mexican Revolution and exogenous economic factors, especially the one-two punch of the Great Depression and drought in North America in the 1930s that reduced the demand for binder twine, played significant roles in the decline of both the henequen and twine industries. However, it was competition from other fiber-producing regions and later from synthetic twines developed by the plastics industry that forecast a deadly decline for Yucatán's henequen industry. This study argues that the real harbinger of doom for the Yucatecan henequen and North American twine industries was the development and adoption of the combined harvester-thresher (or combine). All of these dimensions are critical to an understanding of the henequen-wheat complex's demise. Easy access to and relatively low prices for the raw fiber that the cordage industry and particularly International Harvester (IH) needed to meet the binder twine needs of North American farmers was interrupted in a big way in 1915. The Mexican Revolution, the various dimensions of the "Sisal Situation," and the significant increase in prices imposed by the state when Salvador Alvarado reactivated and strengthened the Comisión Reguladora del Mercado de Henequén (CRMH) not only halted IH's monopsony on sisal importation but also forced the North American cordage industry to look to alternative sources for its fiber needs. By the late 1910s and 1920s a variety of places raised sisal and other hard fibers, even though up to this point the North Americans had always preferred Yucatán henequen because of its high quality and relative proximity to U.S. ports, especially those at New Orleans and Mobile. In the Philippines, growers of abacá (manila) had always competed with Yucatán, but the distance to ship the raw fiber across the Pacific and then by rail from West Coast ports to faraway twine plants inland made it an expensive operation. But although abacá's long-length fibers (often blended with henequen) made the strongest and highest grades of twine, it was also the most expensive binder twine on the market, and demand for it was considerably lower among most farmers on the Great Plains.[1]

Meanwhile, growers in less distant locations in the Caribbean saw the potential for profit in the North American fiber market and began planting sisal. Some Mexicans believed that as early as 1890 foreigners took henequen seeds from Yucatán, perhaps clandestinely, as in the case of Brazilian rubber trees, to start new plantations in Florida, from which the agave plant was then dispersed to various Caribbean islands and from there to East Africa.[2] Although sisal did not grow well in Florida, it could be cultivated successfully in Cuba, Puerto Rico, Haiti, the British West Indies, and the Netherlands Antilles. Investors and planters, taking advantage of those islands' Yucatán-like climate and conditions, began preparations for sisal planting in the 1910s, and after the requisite seven-year wait to cut the *pencas* (spiny fibrous leaves), they began to enter the market. Fiber dealers such as Henry Peabody and IH were eager to exploit the Caribbean sisal and market it to the twine making industry and penitentiary clients. In the early 1930s, officials at the North Dakota State Prison claimed that they were "very well satisfied" with the Haitian sisal, that it made "wonderful twine," and that they would be most interested in ordering more of it should the price remain below that of the Yucatecan fiber.[3]

By then, Brazil, Jamaica, Hawaii, and Portuguese East Africa (which later became Mozambique) had also begun producing sisal and competing aggressively in the world market. In addition, growers of other fibers, such as jute in India and phormium (*Phormium tenax*) in New Zealand, started to compete with sisal producers in the international hard fiber market. To a lesser extent growers on the island of Mauritius were raising a fibrous aloe plant with the same name (mauritius, *Furcraea foetida*), and in El Salvador and Costa Rica farmers raised cabuya (*Furcraea cabuya*), which was often called Central American sisal.[4] José "Pepe" Figueres, who later fomented a revolution in Costa Rica in 1948 and became its president for three different terms, raised Central American sisal on his farm in the central valley of that country. The U.S. Department of Commerce in its investigations of the sisal industry in 1923 had recommended Costa Rican sisal as a viable alternative to the

Yucatecan fiber. In fact, Costa Rican growers had even sent Commerce Secretary Herbert Hoover proposals for expanding their sisal production to meet U.S. agricultural needs. The Commerce Department found out, however, that Costa Rica and other interested Central American nations needed greater financial backing to produce the quantities needed in North America, although one report asserted that the banana exporting giant United Fruit Company was "probably" assisting the nascent Costa Rican cabuya fiber industry.[5]

However, the Yucatecans faced their strongest competition from the British East African colonies of Kenya, Uganda, and Tanganyika (now Tanzania) and from Java in the East Indies (now Indonesia). A point that assuredly would come back to haunt the Yucatecans was that some of the growers in these competing regions had purchased sisal shoots or bulbils from the Yucatecan *henequeneros* who at the time were happy to make the extra profits. Some of the bulbils had arrived via Florida or London's Kew Gardens. Sisal production in East Africa quadrupled in just eight years, increasing from twenty thousand tons in 1923 to eighty-three thousand tons by 1931.[6] Before World War I, Tanganyika was a colony of Germany and instrumental in supplying the fiber needs of Europe. But the war interrupted the flow of fiber from East Africa, causing Yucatecan henequen to be in particularly high demand and causing Yucatán to reemerge as the world's leading fiber producer. But after the war, when Tanganyika was transferred to British rule, Europeans once again started to use more East African sisal because it did not have to be transported as far. At the same time, North Americans discovered that the East African and Asian prices were lower than Yucatán's, primarily due to cheaper labor and the absence of state control mechanisms such as Yucatán's Reguladora.[7] Plymouth Cordage responded to charges in 1923 that it was "not friendly to the planters in Yucatán" when the company reduced its henequen purchases. "If this were a free market," responded a Plymouth official in an open letter to the growers that was printed in a Mérida newspaper, "we would willingly buy sisal. . . . Unfortunately the price which the monopoly [the Exportadora at that time] asks for sisal delivered in this country is so high that we and other binder twine manufacturers have been obliged to buy large quantities of other suitable fibres . . . at relatively lower prices than henequen." The Yucatecan growers' response argued that Plymouth's letter ("laughable indeed . . . with its vows of repentant love") and its charges could not be "allowed to pass without refutation," especially since the company's "only interest has been speculation (and) to come and sow discord among the [henequen] farmers." It stated that claims of prices being too high were "ridiculous"—that the North Americans should be willing and able to pay the slight increases as a way to support an industry on which they had depended for so long. Plymouth could then actively "aid us in reaching the end for which we are striving, namely, to continue to consume slowly the stocks in the United States without affecting the normal production of the State."[8]

Overstocking and pricing were all legitimate concerns for the North Americans, however, whose sisal demand had dropped considerably by the 1920s. Also, news came that the East African sisal was "cleaner" than the Yucatecan (a result of less retting during a water shortage on the peninsula in the 1930s), making it more appealing to the European market that desired fewer impurities in fibers to be spun.[9] Still, in 1923 government reports indicated that 80 percent of all sisal imported into the United States came from Yucatán, and due to its proximity, the government urged cordage firms to continue relying on Yucatecan fiber to avoid a possible interruption of flow from faraway producers.[10]

The year 1929, however, was the first year of many to follow in which the East African, Javanese, and Cuban sisal industries produced more fiber than Yucatán's *henequeneros* (125,000 tons versus 101,000 tons). Non-Yucatecan production continued apace. By 1934 this production figure was almost double that of the Yucatecan sisal (203,000 tons to 108,000 tons), and one year later it was more than double the Yucatecan production (230,000 tons to 100,200 tons).[11] A pie chart prepared by Plymouth Cordage in 1937 showed that for that year's nearly 2-million-bale world sisal production, East Africa's represented almost 44 percent compared to Mexico's 30.6 percent, with sisal from the East Indies (mainly Java) at 20 percent and from the Caribbean (Cuba, Haiti, and the British West Indies), 5.5 percent. By 1960 a full 50 percent of the world's sisal production was coming from Tanganyika, Kenya, and Uganda.[12]

Much to the chagrin of the Yucatecans, growers in other parts of Mexico started to raise henequen as well. Farmers in Chiapas (southern Mexico), Tamaulipas (northeast Mexico on the border with Texas), Sonora and Sinaloa (northwest Mexico), and on the peninsula of Baja California began experimenting with various fiber crops in the 1920s. However, by 1927 most of those regions were showing negligible results. In Tamaulipas growers primarily raised istle and zapupe (*Agave zapupe*) and produced only 1.52 percent of the national fiber total, and Sinaloa (with its mescal agaves, primarily used for the fermented liquor tequila, but also for some fiber cultivation), produced even less of the national fiber output, with 0.16 percent.[13] Most of this non-Yucatecan fiber production was for use in local mills. By 1929 in all of these places combined, including Yucatán's neighboring state of Campeche, which had grown henequen in its northern regions since the beginning of the fiber boom, henequen production equaled a mere 4.2 percent of Mexico's total—with the remaining 95.8 percent coming from Yucatán.[14] *El henequenero* may have alarmed readers in 1927 when it showed pictures of Mexican president Álvaro Obregón on his hacienda in Sonora asserting that henequen was "the only thing that would grow" in the desert environment around Ensenada, Baja California. But northwest Mexico never became a strong contender in the fiber producing industry, even though some growers in Baja raised it until the mid-1960s.[15]

Although competition from East African, Caribbean, and Asian fiber producers and the effects of the Great Depression and simultaneous drought in North America all extracted a heavy toll on the Yucatecan henequen industry, they pale in comparison to the one thing that put an end to the world's heavy demand for all fiber: the combine. The combined harvester-thresher was not really a new invention in the mid-1920s through the 1940s, when farmers in the North American wheat belt adopted it. In fact, nearly one hundred years earlier, in 1838, Hiram Moore of Kalamazoo, Michigan, perfected a harvesting machine he had patented two years earlier that could not only reap or cut crops but also thresh (separate kernels from chaff), clean, and even bag the harvested grain. Interestingly, this invention came at about the same time that Cyrus McCormick developed his much simpler reaper that transformed agriculture for small-scale farmers. The combine, however, was a huge machine powered by a team of twenty horses that required six workers to operate and others to haul the sacked grain. At first Moore only made and sold a few of the combined harvesters to farmers in his area, but in 1853 he shipped one of the giant contraptions around Cape Horn to California, where it quickly became popular and was later adapted by inventors in the Central Valley for the drier West Coast conditions and the large-scale grain operations there. Many of the machines were headers (which harvested only the grain heads and did not cut the straw) combined with separators and storage tanks. Some estimates suggest that by the 1880s farmers in California and the inland Northwest were using more than five hundred of these early combines, many with enormous steam engines in place of horse teams, especially as modifications were made for the hillside harvesting that took place on the large wheat farms in the Palouse region of eastern Washington.[16]

The very nature of these enormous combines prevented them from being readily adopted by wheat farmers in the Great Plains. Costing around five hundred dollars in the mid-nineteenth century and between two thousand and three thousand dollars by the 1920s, the initial investment was just too expensive for many small farmers, let alone the additional workers' wages and horse care involved. Certainly most farmers did not have twenty or more draft horses at their disposal. Likewise, the big and bulky combines with up to twenty-foot headers were not suited for the smaller farms and fields of the Midwest and eastern Plains. Nor were they conducive to harvesting in the more humid regions that required cut grain to dry before being threshed, especially in spring wheat areas of the northern Plains and Prairie Provinces where grain fields often had many weeds.[17] Canadians were especially loath to adopt the combine, believing it was not conducive to their usual nonuniform ripening of spring wheat. For those reasons, implement firms such as IH and Massey-Harris (a Canadian firm, no less) did not even attempt to market their combines in the Prairie Provinces in the early 1920s.[18] The four-horse, two-man binders worked just fine for farmers in these regions from the end of the nineteenth and start of the twentieth centuries and through the World War I grain boom, all of which accelerated the robust demand for binder twine and kept the Yucatecan fiber producers happily busy during those decades.

The postwar slump in agriculture in the 1920s and of course the depression and droughts of the 1930s also prevented a great many farmers from being able to switch to combines. Although during that time the demand for twine fibers certainly fell, it did not disappear, and Yucatecan growers adjusted their production and market strategies accordingly. But it was also by the late 1910s and 1920s when, flush with wartime profits, many winter wheat farmers in the southern and central Great Plains (from Texas to Nebraska) and in eastern Montana started to mechanize their operations more fully, making greater use of gasoline-powered tractors and switching from binders to combines.[19] While wheat farmers on big spreads in those regions were the first to start using combines, the machines became increasingly popular on medium-sized and smaller farms by the mid-1920s. This shift was made possible when the implement manufacturing industry designed a combine more suited to the Great Plains. Called the "prairie model," "prairie combine," or "baby combine," the new model was much smaller, with only ten- to twelve-foot headers. It was designed to be pulled by gasoline tractors (first with the combine's own auxiliary gasoline engine and later, by the 1930s, some with power take-offs, or PTOs, to run the combine's engine) and was thus more manageable for a variety of farm sizes. Combine use in Kansas rose dramatically, from 4,700 in 1920 to more than 24,000 by 1925. The next year, more than 8,000 were added to the Kansas agricultural landscape. In Oklahoma the figure climbed from 3,189 combines in 1926 to 5,182 in 1927, and in Texas, from 2,684 up to 3,681 for the same years. Nationally, combine sales rose steadily in the 1920s, reaching a peak in 1929 of almost 20,000 sales of all brands—a bellwether year in which 75 percent of all winter wheat in the Great Plains was harvested with combines. By 1940, there were 43,000 combines in use in Kansas.[20]

One of the biggest selling points for combines was their labor savings. Harvesting with binders required farmers to hire local or itinerant workers in addition to using their own family members to ensure that crops got cut and threshed at the proper time. Running binders required one person to drive the team of horses or tractor, another to run the binder (before power take-offs were used in the 1930s), another to follow the binder to shock the bundles, and later bundle haulers and threshing crews, all working for three to five dollars a day (up to eight dollars a day by the 1940s) and requiring hearty harvest meals and field "lunches," usually provided by the farmer's wife. Often wages were driven up due to the scarcity of harvest hands in less populated rural areas, raising farmers' overall expenses and threatening to delay the harvest. The central wheat belt annually required an additional 100,000 workers with tens of thousands more for harvests in the northern plains and the Canadian prairies.[21] Many of the itinerant workers were "Harvest Wobblies," members of the Industrial Workers of the World (IWW), who traveled by rail or by thumb following winter wheat harvests in Texas, Oklahoma, and Kansas, then north to Nebraska and the spring wheat harvests of the Dakotas, Montana, and western Canada. Many eastern Canadian laborers seeking harvest work also traveled by rail to the grain-rich Prairie Provinces.[22]

Harvesting with combines required no bundle haulers or threshing crews. As historian Douglas Hurt explains, "At most, the farmer needed one man to drive the tractor, another to ride the combine, operate the cutter bar, and monitor the gasoline engine, and one to haul the threshed grain to a storage

Figure 7.1. Harvesting grain with a McCormick-Deering No. 41 harvester-thresher combine, 1932. Courtesy Wisconsin Historical Society (McCormick–International Harvester Collection, Whi-25458).

bin or grain elevator. If a farmer had sons, he did not need to hire help, and his labor costs could be absorbed by the family." Thus, once past the initial investment in the combine, the savings could be dramatic. Hurt continued, "If a wheat field, for example, averaged 15 bushels per acre, 4.6 man-hours were required to bind, shock, and thresh it. A similar crop required 3.8 man-hours to harvest with a header. In contrast, only .75 man-hours were needed to harvest that grain with a combine." And as combine proponents were quick to point out, the reduced number of harvest hands saved farm women from preparing those huge meals for the crew. Hurt noted, "Like threshing machines of the late nineteenth century, the twentieth-century combine lightened the work of the wheat farmer's wife. With fewer hands needed at harvest time, her cooking responsibilities lessened considerably, but she might become the [grain] truck driver. For her, the combine made life easier in the summertime."[23] As a Canadian trade journal described it, the combine was a "a great boon to the farmer and his wife," or as a Mexican one more bluntly put it, combines were "better for women" as "harvest time was no longer a nightmare"—implying, as historians Bruce Shepard and Thomas Isern have argued, that "farm women rejoiced at the departure of hungry, rude harvest hands."[24]

Labor savings meant financial savings. By 1925 farmers using combines figured their labor and implement expenses came to about five cents per bushel harvested, compared to the eighteen cents a bushel that threshing crews charged. Hurt calculated that even including fuel and repairs, a fifteen-foot combine could cut grain for $1.50 an acre, or ten cents a bushel, while harvesting with a binder cost $4.22 an acre, or twenty-two cents a bushel, and using a header, $3.36 an acre, or twenty-two cents a bushel.[25] Combines also earned their keep by harvesting more efficiently, with less grain lost in the process. Results from a 1928 test in Swift Current, Saskatchewan, published in a booklet by the Canadian federal government revealed that there was only a 1.6 percent grain loss with straight combining, compared to more than 3.5 percent using binders and threshing machines. Across the American plains, various studies concluded that combines averaged a 2.6 percent loss, or thirty-two pounds of grain per acre, compared to the binder/thresher, which lost 6 percent, or seventy-four pounds of grain per acre.[26]

Less labor meant more savings, and since time is money, a quicker harvest also meant more savings. Combines sped the harvest; farmers could cut thirty-five to forty acres of wheat a day with a combine, compared to fifteen to twenty acres a day with a binder. For large farms with vast acreage of wheat ripening at the same time, harvesting as quickly as possible was of maximum importance. For example, in 1929 a prominent farmer in Alberta using a giant California-style combine that cut thirty-four-foot swaths could harvest an acre of grain every seven and one-half minutes. Around the same time, custom cutters in Kansas using combines with twenty-foot reels could, under good conditions, average eighty acres a day per combine. While those examples were hardly the norm, even smaller scale combine harvesting represented a considerable time savings. According to Hurt, the speed then "reduced the risk from bad weather at harvest and encouraged farmers to expand their production," which in good market years produced still more profit and helped the farmers pay off their investments in the new implement. Thus, some farmers maintained that they could pay off their combines in a year or soon thereafter. The data led the Canadian study to conclude that the savings to farmers could be as high as 50 percent over binder harvested grain.[27]

Trade journals carried testimonials from farmers and implement dealers about the time and labor savings of the combine. A farmer wrote of how on his big spread in Kansas he could harvest with four combines and twenty-five men what used to take sixteen binders and seventy-five workers hauling bundles and manning the threshing machine. An International Harvester representative from Calgary, Alberta, boasted in 1928 about how one of his customers harvested his whole 200 to 300 acres of wheat by himself using an IH combine. A counterpart of his from Regina, Saskatchewan, had similar success stories, including one about his customer who harvested his entire 340 acres with a combine in twelve days and saved thirteen hundred dollars over the old binder harvesting method.[28] All in all, the combine came to embody savings in labor, time, and money, as spelled out in the advertisements the implement manufacturers used to promote it in trade journals and farm magazines. For example, 1930s-era ads for Case combines boasted how the machine's "absence of manpower" could "save time, labor, grain, and money" for farmers. International Harvester ran an ad for its McCormick-Deering No. 60 Harvester-Thresher extolling it as a "one-man machine" that "makes harvest a family affair—cutting and threshing small grains and seed crops in one field operation at the rate of 15 to 20 acres a day." The ad then listed all the combine's other virtues: "no twine to buy, no shocking, no stacking, no waiting your turn in the thresher 'ring,' no thresher bills to pay, no crew to feed, no extra work for your wife."[29]

The testimonials and advertisements, however, did not detail the disadvantages involved with combine harvesting. While a speedy harvest was good for many farmers, it could pose problems in areas prone to uneven ripening of grain. Binding allowed the grain to mature and dry in shocks before being threshed, whereas combining too soon when the grain was still damp often resulted in rejected loads at the elevator. Also, harvesting in moist conditions could cause the spread of smut, a cereal-infecting fungus disease, which could also ruin a load of wheat. Smut was particularly bad in 1927 when there was a great deal of wet weather in the Great Plains, causing many farmers that year

Figure 7.2. Discarded binder along a fence line (from *Harvester World*, April 1915).

to stick with binders. Using binders required an earlier harvest than when using combines; to avoid shattering the kernel, grain had to be cut when still damp and then dried in shocks before being threshed. In that way binders helped get the crop in as early as possible, reducing the risk of bad weather during harvest. But with combines, the harvest was later, when the wheat kernels were dead ripe and could be threshed right in the machine's separator. At first, farmers were not aware of the mechanical difficulties that combines often had. Repairs could be costly and time consuming—a loathsome curse during the rush of harvest.[30]

Finally, switching to combines was just not financially sound for many farmers. With the machines costing an average of two thousand dollars in the 1920s—and many of them projected to last a mere eight years—farmers figured that a ten-foot combine would be worth its investment if one had at least 100 acres in wheat, or for a fifteen-foot combine, more than 100 acres of wheat. Logically, the more gas-powered equipment one had, the more acreage of wheat one needed to pay off the machine. For example, a ten-foot combine run with a power take-off would require nearly 200 acres of wheat to pay for itself; a fifteen-foot tractor-drawn combine with its own gasoline engine needed 276 acres of wheat, and so forth. Using combines also meant needing a tractor (if the farm had not yet made the switch from animal traction) and grain trucks, all of which added to implement and fuel investments as well as farmers' heavy indebtedness—often more than they could pay off in a lifetime. Those with smaller farms, then, found it less expensive to keep harvesting with binders and threshing machines, especially since the stationary threshers could separate and hold more grain than the small tanks on many of the early combines. Many chose to hire custom cutters, who had their own combines, for about three dollars an acre.[31]

Nonetheless, the momentum was growing so strongly, and the advantages becoming so well known, that farmers in the Dakotas and western Canada gradually came to adopt the combines. However, the adoption was predicated on the development of yet another farm implement that made it possible for the unevenly ripened and later-harvested spring wheat in those regions to dry before being combined. A South Dakota farmer named August Hovland invented a machine in 1907 called the central delivery reaper, or swather, that cut grain crops and laid them in windrows to dry. To complete the harvest, a few days later a combine with a pick-up attachment could then go through the windrows without disruptions due to grain being too moist or weeds being too green. Hovland's neighbors picked up the idea, and when they moved to Saskatchewan to farm, they began developing and promoting the machine to others, including manufacturing representatives. International Harvester was impressed enough with the idea to start making swathers by 1927, and other manufacturers followed in subsequent years. Some farmers feared using swathers would run the risks of kernel-sprouting that could occur while the grain was drying in windrows or that damage to the windrow from windstorms or to the grain from hailstorms could ruin the swathed crops. But by 1929 swathing had gained significant popularity in the northern plains to advance the use of combines in the region, although the method meant expending the extra time and fuel for two harvesting trips through the fields.[32] Swathers were also used for cutting hay to dry in windrows before being baled.

With these innovations, Prairie Province farmers began to invest in combines, slowly at first; only 200 were sold in 1926 (and only two in Manitoba, where adoption was consistently slower than other provinces), but sales rose steadily thereafter. The region's farmers purchased 600 in 1927, 3,600 in 1928 (a 2000 percent increase in just two years), and 3,500 in 1929. Sales everywhere in North America dropped in the early 1930s due to the depression and drought (the low year for U.S. sales was 1933, with a total of 870, and in Canada the low was in 1934, with a total of only 68), although New Deal farm programs in the States helped spawn a mini boom in implement sales later in the decade. Sales recovered and expanded greatly in the 1940s with another wartime boom and increased mechanization of agriculture in general. A *Canadian Farm Implements* report showed that there were 36,734 combines on Prairie Province farms by 1946, nearly two-thirds of which were in Saskatchewan. And a Department of Agriculture memo from that province in 1950 showed a steady increase in sales of combines (both self-propelled and tractor-pulled) there throughout the 1940s, climbing from nearly 2,000 in 1941 to nearly 6,000 by 1950. The figures certainly worried twine-manufacturing officials in Canada. Sales managers from IH-Canada of Hamilton and Brantford Cordage of Winnipeg wrote letters to E. H. Evans of the Saskatchewan Department of Agriculture in 1945 requesting as much statistical information as they could get on combine use to help plan their own marketing of twine. To gather these data, Evans relied on information from a commodities and manufacturing agency in Winnipeg that showed that between the late 1920s and 1946 combines had harvested some 97 billion pounds of grain in the three Prairie Provinces, therefore displacing some 97,000 tons of binder twine.[33]

In Yucatán, reaction to this type of news was overtly one of fear and trepidation. Henequen industry representatives began worrying about the looming economic changes due to combines in the mid- to late 1920s and used articles in trade journals to alert sisal growers. For example, front-page articles in *El sisal mexicano*, published by the Cooperative of Yucatán Henequen Growers, practically every month in 1927 warned readers of the dangers lurking in combines. In its very first issue, the publication's major story, which carried the headline "Fiber Commerce Threatened by Combines That Could Eliminate Binder Twine," discussed the "important influence" combines would have on the cordage industry. "We don't know its full impact," the article admitted, "but it's necessary to be ready for any emergencies." It also ensured that "the management of this cooperative is looking at this issue with all care."[34]

In its next issue (March 1927), *El sisal mexicano* offered a more informational and ominous article on the topic, proclaiming in enormous, bold headlines, "The Harvesting Machine Called the Combine Will Eliminate the Use of Binder Twine." It reported that the combines were then in use in the United States and Mexico "at a level that worries twine manufacturers." It also suggested that while combines had been in use quite a while in Argentina and California, it was not until recently that farmers had started to adopt them in the U.S. Midwest and Great Plains, especially in Illinois and Kansas. It also spoke to the reasons that farmers had been somewhat reluctant to adopt them, for example, problems with the implement's turning radius, and how engineers at farm machine factories were working to address the flaws. The article prophesied, "It's something to watch for now and be much more concerned about for the future."[35]

The publication detailed other dimensions of the combine in its next issue as part of its "promise to keep . . . readers informed of all the news regarding the combine." Next to a large photo of a combine harvester, the article listed advantages and disadvantages of the implement. Combines could harvest a wide variety of grains (wheat, barley, oats, milo, soybeans) in many agricultural climates because it included a drying process; it was not, "as was first thought,

[that] it would be used only for wheat in semi-arid regions." Combines also provided not only a much quicker harvest but also better soil fertilization with the chopped-up chaff and straw being blown out of the combine's separator onto the ground. The most revolutionary aspect advantage of the combines, the paper reported, was that is saved labor and thus saved the farmer money. At the same time, the article related in very hopeful language how farmers in North Dakota, with more humid conditions, were reluctant to adopt the combine. It also listed the disadvantage of mechanical breakdowns—more moving parts meant potentially more trouble out in the field, especially with inexperienced combine operators. Nonetheless, the paper warned that combines were fast becoming popular in the United States and that wheat farmers in western Canada were beginning to "recognize their enormous advantages."[36]

Each issue of *El sisal mexicano* added more information and fear about combines in the Great Plains. "A Revolution in Wheat: More Than 8,000 Combines in Use in 1926" was the warning it sounded in its issue for the summer of 1927. The article quoted the Kansas agricultural commissioner's praise for how the implement could harvest 1,538 bushels a wheat a day and get the grain to the elevator more quickly. At a cost of around a penny a bushel to harvest, compared to the binder's fifteen to twenty-five cents a bushel, he argued that it could save farmers money. In the 1920s, however, he suggested that the combine was primarily of use on very large wheat farms like those in the panhandle of Oklahoma, western Kansas, and eastern Colorado ("separated only by an imaginary line")—giving some strands of hope to the henequen growers that small farmers would continue harvesting with binders. The article concluded by asserting that it was just "a few years ago that it seemed like wheat production in the United States would have to yield its [prominent] place in the world to other countries. But the combine now says 'no,'" as it continued moving fast into the grain growing southern plains. Not surprisingly, the combine's growing popularity caused a dramatic reduction in demand for twine in the mid-1920s, and that coupled with the fierce twine market competition in Minnesota, North Dakota, South Dakota, and the Prairie Provinces forced the price of twine to drop in those years.[37]

The news got somewhat better for the henequen growers that fall. It was certainly a front-page matter when word came that during the harvest of 1927 grain elevators and flour mills in some states were rejecting a great deal of combine-harvested wheat. "Bad Year for Combines," screamed the headlines in *El sisal mexicano*, adding that the wheat from combines was arriving at elevators too moist to be acceptable or ruined by smut. Also assuredly welcome was the news that use of sisal binder twine was up that harvest season in the western United States and Canada. Later the paper ran an article on the economic importance of henequen. It showed how export of henequen from

Yucatán climbed from 113,000 bales in 1880 up to 555,000 bales in 1926 and that in the six months before the article was written, the United States had imported more than 275,000 bales of the Yucatecan raw fiber. Sales to Canada, France, and other parts of Mexico were also continuing. Adding to the good news, the paper announced that "insects that have been destroying twine made with other fibers are not attacking the Yucatecan henequen."[38]

The good news was short-lived, as combines continued to rise in popularity the next year. In the summer of 1928 the trade journals continued alerting their readers to any breaking news regarding combine use in the Great Plains. Such was the case in July when *El sisal mexicano* headlined that "In Western Canada They Like the Combine Harvester." The article cited interviews from IH sales agents in Saskatchewan and Alberta who both sang the wondrous praises of combine harvesters. "The use of the harvester-thresher in this territory can be considered absolutely advantageous," stated the Alberta agent, who predicted that end-of-year sales totals for the machine would show a great increase. They described how farmers growing spring wheat in the Prairie Provinces benefited from the quicker harvests that combines provided before the first frosts set in, especially when ripening of the grain came later due to weather conditions like those they had been experiencing there the last few years. Thus, as the Saskatchewan sales agent exclaimed, probably to the chagrin of the *El henequenero* readers, combines soon "will be as popular as binders are now." The agents, however, may have been a bit premature in their forecast. Binder twine sales were up in the Prairie Provinces in 1928, even with bad hail damage in Saskatchewan and Alberta. The trade journal relayed the news of the "magnificent harvests" across North America that fall and a "decreased scale" of combine use.[39]

By 1930, however, combine production had gone into full swing across the world. *El sisal mexicano* reported in early 1932 that nearly 117,000 combines had been sold in the United States between 1926 and 1930, which was steadily cutting the demand for binder twine in that country by 5 percent a year. Canadians by then were harvesting with more than 5,000 combines. They were rapidly growing in popularity in wheat-growing Argentina and Australia, and by 1930 they were starting to be used somewhat in Great Britain. A whopping 55,000 combines had already been manufactured in the Soviet Union (very rarely a customer of Yucatecan fibers, however), with 100 being used on an enormous collective farm on the Russian steppes.[40] Worse for the Yucatecan growers, their wheat-raising counterparts in northern Mexico had started to use combines in 1926. The *henequeneros* were so alarmed at this news that they sent a representative to the northern border states to investigate the matter. His observations, reported in *El henequenero*, showed that the wheat farmers of the La Laguna region in Coahuila would be ordering only half the amount of binder twine in 1928 that they had used in 1927. In next-door Chihuahua, combines were introduced in 1927, causing henequen producers to expect reductions in twine orders. As for Sonora, he reported that combines were in use "but will not completely take over for twine use." He was quick to point to one farm he observed where a combine's mechanical problems prevented a successful harvest. However, in the Yaqui Valley farmers were "every day using less twine," and in the Altar and Magdalena Rivers region, where they used to order "a car and a half or two car loads of twine a year," twine use had already ceased.[41] Ten years later the *henequeneros* sent a commission to visit bankers and industry representatives in the United States "to learn the true situation" of combines. The group received plenty of information on how the "'baby combine' . . . added to the diminished consumption of binder twine."[42]

Such data worried not only henequen growers but also Mexican bankers and investors. R. F. DeGeorge, a New York representative of Mexico's Banco Nacional, wrote to IH offices in Chicago in late 1937 requesting information about the combine's impact. "Mexico is naturally interested in this question," he began, "as you know, the twine which is widely utilized to harvest wheat is not needed when the combine is put to use." Thus, he inquired about the extent of small combine use during the past harvest and "the prospects for the next and future harvests." H. L. Boyle, IH's director of economic research, responded with a list comparing combine and binder sales in the United States from 1923 to 1936. It showed steady climbs for combines (except in the early 1930s), with the best sales year being 1929, with nearly twenty thousand combines sold, but the list also showed how grain binders continued averaging sales of more than thirty thousand a year in the same time period. Saying that it was "a little too early to state how great an effect the small combines will eventually have on the harvesting of grain crops," Boyle tended to downplay the implement's impact since "they have done little more than to harvest the additional acres put into small grain by United States farmers since the advent of the smaller type machines."[43]

That all changed, however, in the 1940s, giving *henequeneros* and Mexican bankers more reason to worry. The combine's labor saving advantage became especially useful to farmers during World War II, when there was a significant shortage of harvest hands. By then, implement companies were making self-propelled combines that were more efficient and quicker than the tractor-drawn models and that eliminated the need for one more person now that the combine operator could do it all. So, as they could afford to do so, many Great Plains farmers purchasing self-propelled combines reduced their harvest labor needs even more. As Hurt puts it, "They did not have to endure the agony of waiting" for itinerant workers or custom combiners and harvest crews, or the agony of "worrying whether their already dead-ripe wheat would be lost to a hail-storm or shatter from the heads in the wind."[44] The war had made combines even more attractive to farmers in western Canada, where earlier sales had been less robust than in the central plains of the United States. The Shepard and Isern study argues that in the Prairie Provinces the war "rekindled interest in combines" not only because of the labor shortage "but also because it restored farmers' purchasing power." Combine sales climbed to a new Canadian high of 4,756 in 1940 and steadily increased for the next decade. Keeping up with demand then became a problem, especially in Saskatchewan, where farmers reportedly needed more than 18,000 combines during their conversion from binders.[45] In 1944, however, the Canadian implement firm Massey-Harris sold 500 fourteen-foot self-propelled combines to farmers and custom cutters who pledged to harvest two thousand acres of wheat each as they traveled north from Texas with the wheat harvests. The buyers, known as the Massey-Harris Harvest Brigade, became a large part of the company's wartime sales push, representing the dual patriotic and profit-minded goals of cutting 1 million acres of wheat and saving 300,000 man-hours for an estimated 60 percent labor savings.[46]

Even with the increase in combine sales, the war also provided a boost to henequen producers in Yucatán. Sales reached more than 600,000 bales by 1943, the highest they had been for twenty years, as a result of the heightened demand for rope and binder twine in areas still using binders to harvest more crops and thus provide food for the Allies. Also boosting henequen sales was the fact that importing manila hemp (abacá) across the Pacific from the Philippines was too risky during the war. For that reason, in June 1942 Floyd Ransom of the Defense Supplies Corporation signed a three-year contract for henequen imports from Yucatán, and in September the U.S. Office of War Production ordered that all henequen be used for the manufacture of essential cordage products. At that point the United States had contracted for almost all of Yucatán's estimated production from 1941 through 1945—the kind of boost the Mexicans needed, albeit for unfortunate reasons in the face of world war and albeit for only a short time. Mexico's principal journal of economics even praised Yucatán's wartime "reorganization of the henequen economy" and forecast that demand would "always be up."[47]

After the war, when industry reverted to peacetime industrialization, combines were made more available and became even more popular. By 1950 conversion to combines was complete across the American and Canadian plains.[48] After that, only a very few farmers anywhere continued using twine binders, with most farmers selling them for scrap iron (popular during World War II, especially in Canada) or relegating them, along with other discarded, rusting implements, to farmyard corners, fence lines, or scrap heaps (see Figure 7.2,

p. 206). As Saskatchewan farmer/poet Hugh Duddridge wrote in "A Last Farewell to the Bucking Binder,"

> Old friend, I thought to find a nook
>   For your old age requirement,
>   Some quiet corner where you'd rest
>   In honourable retirement.
>
> But now there comes from Ottawa
>   The call, "Your country needs you,"
>   And you must leave your home, old gal,
>   To go where duty leads you.
>
> Perchance some fragment of your frame,
>   A ball or roller bearing,
>   On some far field may be the end
>   Of Hitler or of Goering.[49]

It may not have ended fascism in Europe, but the end of the binder hastened very quickly the demise of Yucatán's once great henequen industry. Seeing the end in sight, the *henequeneros* by the late 1920s did what any business leaders would do to try to salvage their industry: diversify marketing and industrialize their own raw material. As early as 1917 *El henequén* listed thirty non-twine manufacturing uses for "the great Yucatecan treasure." It advocated the fiber's use in making carpet, drapes, tapestries, hammocks, packsaddles, straps, ropes and cables, cots, baskets, whips, and a wide variety of burlap bags, among other things.[50] As for marketing, the Yucatecans sought to sell more henequen directly to Canada so that cordage mills there would not have to deal with brokers in New York. In 1927 the Mexican consulate in Toronto made "persevering gestures" to secure direct sales to the Canadians, and as *El henequenero* reported hopefully, "Assuredly with a little more understanding and better reciprocal trust, we can succeed in having the advantages of direct control of those rich markets." The plan must have worked; Canadians went from purchasing no fiber directly from Yucatán in 1930 to purchasing 75,450 bales in 1936.[51] Also, by 1940 some Mexicans believed that Chile could be a potentially excellent market for Yucatecan fiber due its copper mining boom, which required more food production for an influx of miners, and due to the fact that the country would have more funds for imports. Unfortunately for the *henequeneros*, however, a Chilean market never materialized.[52]

More importantly, the henequen growers wanted to increase fiber sales to Europe, which had been such a good customer during World War I when

Tanganyikan sisal had been blocked. *El sisal mexicano* proclaimed in 1927 that there would be a "great future for Mexican henequen in Europe."[53] By 1931 the *Wall Street Journal* was reporting that France and Sweden had become Yucatán's second and third biggest sisal customers (after the United States), with Cuba being fourth and Germany and Denmark following behind it. And in 1936, one of the worst harvest years in North America due to drought, especially in the northern plains, the Yucatecans pushed sisal sales to Europe. And sales indeed increased to Sweden, Finland, the Netherlands, Belgium, Germany, France, and Spain, accounting for more than ninety-five thousand bales. France, the biggest European customer at the time, purchased thirty-seven thousand bales, and Germany doubled its sisal orders from Yucatán between 1930 and 1936. A few years later (1941), the Soviet Union, which had started importing Yucatecan sisal in 1930, increased its purchases.[54] Sales to Europe dropped during World War II, however, when practically all of the Yucatecan fiber was contracted to the United States.

It was industrialization—establishing Yucatán's own cordage plants (called *cordelerías*) using the region's henequen—that Yucatecans and the Mexican government viewed as the region's economic salvation. As early as 1916, revolutionary governor Salvador Alvarado pushed to reorganize and expand La Industrial, Yucatán's small *cordelería*, to convert more homegrown fiber into twine instead of exporting so much of it. But despite his efforts and his continual sloganeering, "Henequen must be industrialized in our own land," the majority of *henequeneros* were content to maintain the status quo export relationship with North American fiber dealers. Alvarado even devised a plan in 1918 to finance a twine factory in grain-rich Argentina that would be supplied with Yucatecan fiber. That plan was cut short, however, by a strategy engineered by H. L. Daniels, the former head of IH's Fiber Department who led the U.S. Food Administration's wartime Division of Chemicals, Sisal, and Jute. Daniels used U.S. control of shipping in the region during the war to prevent shiploads of sisal from being sent to any non-U.S. destinations. Thus, efforts to diversify the industry were stymied until the 1930s.[55]

Several studies in that decade supported the need for industrialization. Efraim Buenrostro, sub-secretary of the Mexican Federal Treasury, who visited Yucatán in 1935 as a member of a presidential special committee to study the conditions of the henequen industry, conducted one investigation. His suggestions for the "reconstruction" of the industry included the improvement of social and sanitary conditions along with the industrialization of henequen. He recommended the development of an agricultural school for the study of the henequen zone's specific soil, chemical, and climatic needs; the creation of an "experimental analytical laboratory for studying forms of utilizing henequen waste"; the establishment of two models "for henequen preparation" for the "cheaper, more uniform, and more rapid transformation of the fibre (including such processes as classification, cleaning, drying, brushing, whitening, and baling); and a campaign to increase domestic consumption of henequen products such as burlap bags.[56]

Another widely distributed report was written in 1938 by industry representative Humberto Canto (later governor of Yucatán), who met with President Cárdenas to argue for support for henequen industrialization. Canto maintained that the *cordelerías* were "of vital importance for the sisal industry;" that they represented "the most important question we have at the present time." He reported that Cárdenas promised half a million pesos for growers to expand planting that would help sustain the flow of fiber to the Yucatecan cordage plants.[57] Finally, a study conducted in the late 1930s by Manuel Cirerol suggested that because "the culture of henequen is found to be in decline," the search for new uses of the fiber was of paramount importance. He advocated that the decorticating and industrialization processes be co-operatized.[58]

The local print media jumped on the industrialization bandwagon, too. *El diario del sureste* argued that the plan to diversify would not only help Yucatán but also be, as it boldly headlined in December 1931, the "economic salvation of the entire country." The article dealt with the serious competition henequen was facing from fibers grown in other parts of the world. It offered as evidence a recent British Commonwealth economic conference in Ottawa that had actively promoted increased sales of jute from India for member nations' cordage factories. Yucatecan industrialization, therefore, "would help assure henequen's place as a fountain of wealth for the country."[59] The Mérida-based cordage trade journal *Cooperation* agreed. "Yucatán producers, prepare to industrialize all your production or die!" it emotionally warned readers in the summer of 1937. *El yucatanista* echoed the sentiment a few weeks later: "Industrialization of henequen is the salvation of our local economy. . . . The public agreed that to industrialize is the best course for safeguarding this resource . . . thereby giving employment to many Yucatecans."[60] The next year, Martín Díaz de Cossío published his book *Henequén: riqueza yucateca* (*Henequen: The Wealth of Yucatán*) in which he proclaimed that the "new organization of the henequen industry in all its aspects" would be the "solution to the agrarian problem in Yucatán." He affirmed his conviction "that Yucatán will reappear in a new era of general well-being, the likes of which it has never known before."[61]

As the Buenrostro study had urged, one important facet of the industrialization plan was to increase domestic consumption of henequen products. For that end, perhaps the Yucatecan cordage firms drew on Mexican national and regional iconography to help market their products. For example, the Compañía Cordalera Mayapán's logo was the Mexican eagle holding up the world with sisal rope and that of the Cordelería San Juan was of the plumed snake god Quetzalcóatl formed of the Yucatán-made rope. Products manufactured for domestic and foreign sales included rope, burlap, gunny sacks, mats, hammocks, curtains, and rigging lines for ships. Sisal bagging seemed to offer especially sound prospects for the *cordelerías*. And some firms, such as Mérida's San Juan mills, started to manufacture binder twine.[62]

That Yucatecan cordage companies began to produce binder twine in the 1930s is surprising in light of the much-reduced demand for the product in those years. It would be easy to wonder what they were they thinking, but the move represents in a large way the growers' do-whatever-it-takes approach to compete aggressively in the world market and save their industry and livelihood. They likewise knew that there were plenty of farmers still using binders and that they needed to get their twine business. They then had to petition strongly for the right to have their own cordage mills, which the cooperative structure had legally denied them in the 1920s.[63] Once established and spinning their own products, they found their best twine market in Argentina, where they sold an average of 268,000 pounds a year from 1928 to 1933. By 1934 they were selling twine primarily to European nations and were expanding production.[64] As the journal *Cooperation* editorialized, "If Yucatán does not increase twine production, there will be the most terrible crisis in history." The Cordelería San Juan had already heeded that advice by installing "more multiple spinners . . . than in all of the plants of the International Harvester Company," according to *Cooperation*'s exaggerated boast.[65] By 1930, then, these local *cordelerías* were consuming 10 percent of all Yucatecan fiber production and were manufacturing a wide assortment of cordage and bagging products for local and national markets. They also started to market their goods abroad, including the United States, which at the time did not have a tariff on imported cordage products.[66]

To help stimulate production, the sisal growers sold their fiber (often surplus amounts not sold on the international market) to local Yucatecan twine mills at below world market prices because Mexican state and federal governments did not impose taxes on the sale of fiber to local mills. It was Yucatán governor Florencio Palomo who on November 24, 1936, issued the decree suspending the three-cent per kilo state tax on sisal sales to local mills "to alleviate the difficult position of these manufacturers, largely brought on by the serious drought and to help prevent widespread unemployment in these industries, adding to the economic difficulties of the state."[67] The federal tax break was in part the result of a strong lobbying campaign by the Yucatecan cordage industry. In the summer of 1936 four such companies (Mayapán, Cordelería La Guadalupana, Antilano González, and Cordelería de Sisal, S.A.) wrote directly to President Cárdenas regarding their difficulty competing in the European market due to the strong competition of jute from India and sisal from East Africa, and in North America due to the drought and to industry stockpiles there that created a "disastrous price" for twine.[68]

The incentives outraged American manufacturers, who paid higher prices and tariffs on the Mexican sisal. They complained to the U.S. Tariff Commission that Yucatecan twine mills had a vastly unfair advantage by purchasing raw fiber untaxed and at below market rates and by paying their workers far less than North Americans did.[69] Their concern was accentuated by the fact that in 1923 the Yucatecans started to export their more inexpensive twine to the United States. The export figures grew from more than 309,000 pounds of twine (worth $30,800) in 1923 to nearly 9 million pounds (worth $553,200) in 1932. In those ten years the amount of twine exported to the United States totaled more than 34,256,000 pounds (worth almost $3 million).[70] Even more alarming for the industry was the fact that imports of Mexican twine were growing faster than any other. When the amount reached 20 million pounds in 1936 (27 percent of all imports), cordage representatives protested directly to the Roosevelt administration. By that year, all imported twine combined was equal to 35 percent of the total amount of twine consumed in the United States. And with penitentiaries producing 25 percent of the total with inmate labor, it left only 40 percent of the nearly 250 million pounds annually consumed in the country that was produced by free labor in U.S. cordage mills.[71] As Table 7.1 shows, between 1925 and 1936 Mexico and Canada were the largest exporters of binder twine to the United States, with the Netherlands, Cuba, Belgium, and Great Britain following. That Canada had become such a large twine exporter is also of note, since even as late as 1929 it was also *importing* large amounts of U.S. twine. In fact, Canada was the U.S. cordage industry's fifth largest customer. Thus, it too had a two-way flow of twine in

Table 7.1 Total imports of binder twine into the United States by country of origin, 1925–1936

Mexico	88,037,000 pounds
Canada	82,000,000 pounds
Netherlands	66,577,000 pounds
Cuba	43,000,000 pounds
Belgium	20,553,000 pounds
United Kingdom	18,617,000 pounds

Note: numbers rounded to nearest thousand.
Source: U.S. Bureau of Foreign and Domestic Commerce, M95-262, folder 2, box 19, McCormick–International Harvester records, State Historical Society of Wisconsin.

ARM IMPLEMENT NEWS COMPANY—E. J. BAKER, PRESIDENT; C. A. LUKENS, VICE-PRESIDENT; E. J. BAKER, JR., SECRETAR'

7OL. 57 No. 4   CHICAGO, ILL., FEBRUARY 13, 1936 $2.00 PER YEA:

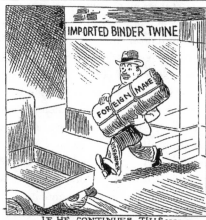

"The Prudent Man Looketh Well to His Going"

Figure 7.3. A cartoon used in the campaign against imported twine (from *Farm Implement News,* February 13, 1936)

and out of the country. And the Yucatecans kept track of all such trade. In 1932, *El sisal mexicano* reported on the development of the Canadian cordage industry, suggesting that it "seemed logical in a country with such great wheat production which requires such great amounts of twine" that more mills be established there. It also mentioned how U.S. cordage firms had at first built twine mills in Canada (for example, IH's in Hamilton, Ontario) but how by the 1920s Canadians were developing their own, resulting in reduced twine imports from the United States (down from 47.6 million pounds in 1926 to 10.6 million pounds in 1932). However, the journal lamented, just as part of the Commonwealth Canada was importing more raw fiber from British East Africa and New Zealand, the droughty 1930s stymied demand for Canadian twine in the Prairie Provinces, causing the nation's cordage industry to decline rather than flourish.[72]

Those kinds of figures spurred the U.S. cordage industry to seek protective tariffs against foreign-made twine, especially the lower-priced twine from Mexico. As one 1937 intraindustry memo put it, "The increase in imports from Mexico has become the most serious problem . . . the domestic industry has had to face," adding that the imports could "threaten the existence of the twine manufacturing industry in the United States." U.S. manufacturers complained about the lower wages the Yucatecans paid their mill workers, opposed the *henequeneros'* policy of selling surplus fiber at below-market value to Yucatecan cordage mills, argued that the sisal growers should reduce their price for raw sisal "to encourage wider use in the United States," and maintained that the state of Yucatán should stop encouraging the manufacture of twine within its borders.[73] But they did not put the same kind of pressure on other countries that exported twine to the United States, especially Canada. As a letter from Plymouth Cordage to Secretary of State Cordell Hull (of the second Roosevelt administration) explained, "A particularly unfair and dangerous situation exists with respect to Mexico." The company reminded the administration that trade with Yucatán had been made easier due to proximity to New Orleans and due to the free trade zone established there for sisal imports, the terms of which would take executive branch action to repeal. Therefore, since "a healthy Binder Twine industry in the United States is decidedly in the interest of the public welfare," Plymouth pleaded on behalf of the cordage industry in general that the State Department approach Mexican officials "with a view to some change in the situation" and that Secretary Hull "permit cooperative consideration between his Department and the industry to further explore the matter."[74]

To help clarify the manufacturers' concerns and other related matters for the State Department, Plymouth sent a "supplementary memorandum" a week later. Its stated purpose in reference to importations from Mexico was "to discuss the possibilities of ameliorating the situation through diplomatic action." Plymouth first spelled out the background: "[P]rior to the World War the industry was resourceful enough to meet this situation and also to meet the competition of a number of State prison twine mills. . . . Following the world war, however, European nations . . . adopted policies of encouraging development of new sources of fiber supply and also of encouraging production of binder twine within their borders by protective tariffs. . . . [T]his has resulted in . . . other countries supplying not only their own needs, but taking away from American manufacturers a great part of their former American trade and practically all of the foreign trade."[75]

But having stated that, there was no lobbying for direct protective tariffs. While the "time has come to reconsider this policy with a view of protecting the national interests under new and radically changed conditions," the memo continued, the industry at this point made clear it did not want "to suggest a duty on imported twine, but rather the exploration of the possibilities of relief through diplomatic channels." The main point was that "for reasons of national interest it [the United States] cannot afford to become dependent on a supply of fiber from the other side of the world, nor on the operation of foreign factories to convert such fiber into binder twine." And to assure the State Department that the appeal was not solely for U.S. interests, the memo argued for the welfare of Mexico: "A vicious spiral is in operation under which it would seem that the national interests of both countries are suffering and the only gainers are the European mills and the Far East fiber producers. If the present tendencies go on, the volume of American twine manufactured will continue to shrink, and . . . the demand for Yucatán fiber will shrink. On the other hand, if American manufacturers could regain the American market lost to European manufacturers, Yucatán at the same time could regain its lost sisal market and the national interests of both nations would be maintained." Thus, it urged diplomatic talks to try to work out an arrangement, which as it admitted "may not be sufficient alone to adequately protect America's national interests" but which would be "a first step toward a fair and logical solution to the problem." However, if further action were needed "to enable the American binder twine industry to survive against the European onslaught," the U.S. manufacturers suggested the "incorporation of quotas in reciprocal treaties under which the exports of twine to the United States would be limited," not the immediate introduction of outright tariffs. The memo ended with an emotional appeal for the support of "American farmers to enable them to buy the products of American labor."[76]

The State Department listened to the cordage industry's concerns. Secretary Hull passed the matter along to Raleigh Gibson, the foreign services officer in the Division of American States who by the summer of 1937 had contacted the American embassy in Mexico about what course of action to pursue. The U.S. ambassador to Mexico at the time was none other than Josephus Daniels—the former secretary of navy during the Wilson administration who had been in charge of the U.S. naval attack on Veracruz in 1914 and of sending gunboats to Progreso during the "Sisal Situation" of 1915. His undersecretary at the time was a young Franklin Roosevelt, who upon becoming president in 1933 had appointed his old boss to the ambassadorship, a move that did not sit well with many Mexicans who remembered the attack and occupation of Veracruz during their revolution. Nonetheless, Daniels sought good relations between the two countries and showed interest in this new round of twine diplomacy. Gibson pressed on him the same kind of nationalistic emotionalism that the cordage industry had used on him. In a memo dated August 24, Gibson wrote, "During the World War, we heard the slogan 'Food will win the War.' Our domestic grain crops are tied with binder twine made chiefly from Mexican fibre. The destruction of the fibre business in Mexico and the binder twine business in the United States might seriously affect our food supplies during any national emergency, because it would make us dependent upon distant sources of supply." He then urged Daniels to discuss "this important subject" with authorities in Mexico, including President Cárdenas.[77]

The reaction in Yucatán to the American pressure was predictable. Weary of their years of having been exploited by U.S. cordage interests, the Yucatecans responded harshly to this set of complaints about their binder twine being imported to the United States. For example, Humberto Canto's report examined what he called the "true situation of binder twine," lamenting how "our friends of North America" had worked with Mexican government officials for the "reduction and suppression" of Mexican-made twine, how they had conspired to spread their poorer quality product at below-market prices to drive out the "first-class" twine made in Yucatán.[78] An editorial in *El yucatanista* went even further in its criticism of the "foreign potentates" who were trying to prevent the Yucatecans from making twine from their own sisal. It stated how "by iniquitous combinations" the North American cordage industry worked to "standardize the price of twine, . . . place prohibitive tariffs on the entry of twine into the United States" and was involved in "hindering the making of twine in our own cordage factories."[79]

Nonetheless, the Americans did succeed in getting the Mexicans to agree to discuss the matter further at a series of binder twine conferences held in 1937 and 1938 in Mexico City. Several U.S. cordage firm representatives (from IH, Plymouth, Columbian Rope of Auburn, New York ["the Cordage City"], Peoria Cordage, and the Hooven & Allison Company) brainstormed the idea at their own meeting in Chicago in June of that year, the purpose of which was to formulate plans for a conference between representatives of the

Cooperativa de Henequeneros and the U.S. twine manufacturers. The representatives selected Ellis W. Brewster of Plymouth as their chairperson and welcomed the idea for the summit in Mexico, "believing that it should be helpful in developing sound economic and national policies for both nations," as it was explained in a memo to Ambassador Daniels in Mexico City. Brewster had even conducted his own research on the Mayapán Cordage Company in Yucatán to check the quality of the twine it exported to the United States. The representatives also exchanged notes regarding President Cárdenas's agrarian reform policies in Yucatán. But the main point of the international meeting was to discuss "the great and grave concern" regarding "the rapidly increasing importation of binder twine" into the United States. On that matter, they recommended two main agenda points. The first broadly stated that "having in mind that the United States is the logical nearby market for Mexican fibre, and Mexico is the logical nearby source of fibre supply for the United States, what joint measures can be taken by producers and manufacturers to recover the United States binder twine market from European competitors who use Eastern Hemisphere fibre?" The second point more specifically concerned "the manufacture and sale of binder twine by Mexican mills" and whether such activity was in "the long range national interests of Mexico and the development of mutually profitable trade relations with the United States."[80]

The conferences began in July 1937 in the Mexican capital. Yucatán governor Florencio Palomo presided over the meetings, whose attendees included such representatives as Mexico's minister of the economy and delegates from the Cooperativa de Henequeneros, U.S. and Mexican cordage firms and banks, and the U.S. embassy. W. E. Worth, the IH delegate, wrote that the goal of the meeting was "to acquaint all the interested parties with the problems that must be worked out if we are to produce in the Western Hemisphere the fibre and binder twine necessary for the harvest of our grain crops." In his welcoming remarks, Governor Palomo indicated that the Mexicans had studied the cordage firms' information, agreed that all parties would have to work together against "the common threat" of the European manufacturers, and that the Yucatecans would continue to give the matter their "most earnest endeavor . . . and closest study."[81] Representing the U.S. cordage firms, Ellis Brewster delivered the opening address, greeting the Mexicans "as a neighbor, in the spirit of friendship and good will" and thanking the Mexican government for its "friendly and cooperative and serious study" of a "problem of mutual interest." He said that the Americans had also given it "a long and careful study" and indicated that the hope of the conference was that "a solution [could] be had," while recognizing "the impossibility of immediate action." Voicing the hoped-for spirit of mutuality, Brewster continued, "We have all gathered here today to find out [how] . . . we can improve our positions in the fibre and binder twine markets of the world or if we must continue to lose ground in competition . . . from other parts of the world. Our committee believes that by working together we may successfully compete with any nation . . . in the world."[82] The attending conferees then discussed the "most serious" and potentially "disastrous" situation of imported twine and non-Yucatecan fibers, as well as the possibility of standardized twine pricing. The Mexican government also proposed forming a binder twine cooperative similar to the henequen cooperative in Yucatán. Brewster later confided that the meetings were "friendly in nature" but came to no "definite conclusions."[83]

Given that the conferences took place in the late 1930s, it was probably too late to salvage the fiber and twine industries completely, although it was logical to try to come to a meeting of the minds on how to compete with East African sisal and European twine. World War II did not supply much of a boost in the market for Yucatecan fibers, although the U.S. government did decree a moratorium on purchasing any non-Mexican or non-Cuban sisal for binder twine production to avoid any concerns farmers or twine manufacturers may have had about transatlantic shipping.[84] But even that measure came too late. A prophetic *El universal* newspaper headline after the war ended captured the scenario well: "Henequen: Green Gold—The Wealth and Tragedy of the Mayan Land." The accompanying article described how almost 40 percent of the state of Yucatán and 70 percent of its seeded surface was still devoted to henequen. The state, it continued, and 23,800 *ejidatarios* "lived and were [still] completely dependent on the henequen industry," even as the postwar demand for hard fibers rapidly dwindled.[85] Certainly for Yucatán, the economic tragedy was developing very quickly at that point.

By then the shift from binders to combines was also signaling a rapid decline in the binder twine industry throughout North America. This shift did not mean that there were not kitchen and packaging twines to be made, and there were certainly many other types of rope and fiber products to sustain the cordage industry in a much reduced form. But all of those products together did not come close to equaling the hundreds of millions of pounds of twine that grain farmers throughout the United States and Canada had consumed each year. Twine demand dropped so precipitously by the late 1940s and 1950s that it forced the cordage and implement industries, like their counterparts in Yucatán's henequen industry, to find alternative uses and markets for fiber. The penitentiary twine plants shut down completely. International Harvester, always by far the largest manufacturer of binder twine, was forced to reduce production significantly at its four large twine mills in North America. (It also had plants in France, Germany, and Sweden that eventually closed.) Officials at IH admitted that total twine consumption had been fast decreasing "due to the rapid introduction of the small combine."[86]

Figure 7.4. Brochure from the International Harvester binder and baler twine sales campaign, 1949. Courtesy Wisconsin Historical Society (International Harvester Company Records, Blue Box Series, folder 2, box 73).

Interestingly enough, however, IH made some desperate attempts to sustain a binder twine market. As late as 1949 the company's cordage marketing department launched a new ad campaign for its dealers. Perhaps befitting the popular culture of the times, the promotional program was based on the cartoon characters "Homer Hemp" and "Susie Sisal" whose marriage ("carefully selected hard fibers, scientifically blended and spun") produced the "superchild"—"Tillie Twine" (Figure 7.4). The promotional literature told dealers that they would be "'pleased to make the acquaintance of Homer, Susie, and Tillie.' They're 'quality folks' . . . especially created to help you sell high-quality International twine . . . that's full-strength, full-length, and uniform . . . that makes binding a smooth, trouble-free operation!" The brochure also stressed that there were "still thousands of grain binders in use the country over. Thousands of corn binders, too." True, in the late 1940s and early 1950s there were still many farmers using binders, especially in the northern plains. Saskatchewan had an all-time record wheat crop in 1952 (with nearly 400 million bushels harvested, "the greatest wheat harvest in history," as one newspaper remarked) that required great amounts of sisal twine, and at prices farmers still complained about. The president of the Saskatchewan Farmers' Union mentioned how the twine price increases kept making it "more and more difficult for farmers."[87] Thus, the dealers were enjoined to "put Homer, Susie, and Tillie to work" to "set up store traffic, build good will, and keep [the] cash register jingling!"[88]

What is curious about this campaign is that it competed directly against another IH entity, the division that was making combines and thus making binder twine obsolete. However, the promotion also was geared toward selling *baler* twine for haying operations. "More and more farmers are using twine-tying pick-up balers," the brochure explained. "There are between 50,000 and 60,000 of them," with each using "50 bales of twine a year." "Go after this repeating and growing market!"[89] Baler twine, also made of sisal (often blended with other fibers), did for a while become the next boom for Yucatán's and other regions' sisal exports. It certainly had the potential to replace the fast disappearing binder twine market, and the *henequeneros* knew it; the prospect was often mentioned in their trade journals from the 1950s and 1960s. And some prisons manufactured it for a few years, notably the North Dakota State Penitentiary with its NODAK brand baler twine. Thus, a mini boom in baler twine caused henequen to pick up by the end of the decade, rising from 408,000 bales in 1950 to 750,000 bales ten years later.[90] But the adoption of the combine as the preferred harvesting machine by the vast majority of Great Plains farmers had already planted the seed of destruction so deeply by 1950 that even the scintilla of hope offered by the much smaller baler twine market could not have rescued Yucatecan henequen.

New technologies such as the combine made grain harvesting easier and hurt the cordage industry, but other types of technology soon came to the aid of the cordage industry. In the 1950s the burgeoning plastics industry developed the synthetic fibers polyethylene and polypropylene, which began to replace organic fibers in the manufacture of baler twine. Synthetic twines were durable, relatively inexpensive, performed well in the baler's knotter, and were resistant to grasshopper damage. According to one study from Alberta, the synthetic twine was cheaper than sisal and not at the mercy of weather conditions or price fluctuations.[91] By the mid-1960s synthetic twine had all but eliminated organic twine from the commercial twine market. Mexico City's *El nacional* reported in 1966 that "the decline in henequen use was paradoxically the result of the great advances in science that create and devour, construct and destroy with the imperturbability of being fatal." It cited how Yucatán's once great henequen industry had made it "one of the most prosperous states" in Mexico but how by then the state was in its "worst crisis ever due to synthetic fibers" and how henequen was "at the point of becoming completely replaced." Historian Ben Fallaw called the synthetic fiber "the coup-de-grace": "When henequen finally died in Yucatán, it was plastics that killed it . . . and federal subsidies had already prolonged its life artificially."[92] The wonders of polyethylene notwithstanding, the baler twine industry in general started to dim by the 1970s when many farmers and ranchers resorted to using giant round bales that required less twine. Also, soon thereafter many hay raisers reverted to the old tried and true method of hay stacking that requires no twine baling at all.

But even these developments did not signal the *complete* end of the henequen industry, although it never was restored to its boom-year heights. Another hopeful boost came in the mid-1950s with increased oil exploration in Mexico that upped the demand for cables. One Mexican newspaper reported that the oil boom was putting "Yucatecan henequen back in demand" and that the industry would become "a brilliant business again."[93] Of course the Mexican cordage industry continued to rely on Yucatecan fibers. In fact, in 1954 local cordage mills absorbed a full 50 percent of all Yucatecan henequen for the manufacture of rope, twines, rugs, hammocks, sacks, and other products. To assist with the diversification, interested parties formed the Asociación Productores de Artefactos de Henequén (Association of Producers of Henequen Goods) "to safeguard quality, study pricing, and correct irregularities" in the various products. Still, as the industry entered the 1960s in a slump, henequen workers joined together to request government subsidies to support their work until the market could improve.[94] The government went one step further: in 1964 it nationalized the Yucatecan cordage mills under one publicly owned corporation named Cordemex. It was the largest measure of federal involvement in Yucatán's industry since the days of President Cárdenas in the 1930s. According to one study, by 1970 the federal government "exercised almost total control over Yucatán's henequen industry, the state's premier source of both income and employment."[95]

Other countries had continued to develop sisal plantations, however. Brazil, which established plantations in the northeastern states of Bahía and Paraíba that employed some 120,000 workers, became the world's leading sisal producer and exporter. Mexico remained somewhat strong in that decade, employing 100,000 people in the sisal industry, but with most of the production staying within Mexico for national cordage needs. Brazil and Mexico together accounted for nearly 70 percent of sisal production in 1977. Angola, Mozambique, Kenya, and Madagascar had joined Tanzania in putting Africa in the heart of the sisal-producing world by this time, and Haiti continued to grow the crop to a limited degree. A United Nations study, however, warned that all of these places would have to learn to compete with the synthetic cordage industry. "Price competition between sisal and polypropylene twines is a factor which sisal exporting countries have to incorporate in[to] their commercial

Figure 7.5. Remnant of a dying industry: drying henequen fiber in Yucatán in the 1970s. Photograph by Roderic A. Camp.

and pricing strategies," it advised, "if they want to counter the penetration of synthetics in the world twine market."[96]

By 1981, however, due to some changes in agricultural priorities in Yucatán, Mexico's rank among the world's largest henequen producers dropped to third, and it was employing only half the number of people in the industry that it had

Figure 7.6. Worker baling henequen fiber in Yucatán in the 1970s. Photograph by Roderic A. Camp.

in the 1970s. So low was production in 1980 that Cordemex actually had to *import* sisal from Brazil to keep up with cordage orders. In 1982, production hit an all-century low at sixty-one thousand tons.[97] It was then that the state government petitioned President José López Portillo for federal assistance to "diversify and reorient" the henequen economy. The government agreed to help, and the next president, Miguel de la Madrid, continued the "henequen reordering march," giving the governor of Yucatán greater authority over Cordemex and henequen production in general. Those policies endured for about a decade, when in 1992 the government completely stopped subsidizing the industry, causing its final collapse. Still, even at the end of the twentieth century many Yucatecans continued trying to promote henequen as the *oro verde* (green gold) of the land. A Mérida newspaper reported that a state government report in July 1996 promised that henequen would be a "great source of employment" with forty-five hundred hectares of abandoned henequen fields replanted with the fiber crop.[98]

The radical drop in henequen production overall, however, has had a beneficial impact on the ecology of north central Yucatán. In an almost textbook case of ecological restoration, native flora and fauna are returning to the henequen zone. One study cites how abandoned henequen fields are rich in pioneer and late successional species, although original native mature forests are practically nonexistent in the area.[99] The change is visible and important to local residents. One older local official near the slowly decaying San Antonio Tehuitz plantation told the author that in six years after the hacienda's abandonment the locals were seeing "much more of nature" and that many "plants and animals were returning to the area."[100] Perhaps nature will bat last in Yucatán. But the abandoned *henequenales* are also the site of ongoing efforts to continue diversifying the state's agricultural economy. Studies show that Yucatán's climate and soil (thin as it is atop the limestone karst) can be productively used for the production of aloe vera (with its host of commercial products in the health and cosmetic industries), Italian limes (for consumption and oil extract), a variety of other orchard and vegetable crops (including fruit trees and, in some areas, tomatoes), and finally, chaya, a green vegetable gaining quickly in popularity.[101] All of the products have local, national, and international market potential. Most would be part of an export commodity scenario but would never be in demand to the degree that Yucatecan henequen was needed during the binder twine years.

Thus it is with technological developments that replace one another, and thus it is with the power of a machine. As a replacement for binders, combines were at the heart of many social, economic, and transnational changes beyond their perceived agricultural benefits. Socially, they transformed the agricultural labor landscape and gendered divisions of farm work on the American and Canadian plains. Ending the need for bindlestiffs, bundle haulers, and threshing crews (many of whom, but certainly not all, "drank heavily, frightened the children, required the [farmer's] wife to feed them, and sometimes demanded higher wages," as Donald Worster has described them), the combine thus ended the seasonal flow of workers to the plains states and Prairie Provinces, forcing those individuals to look for work elsewhere. The social composition of the farm workplace became more family-focused, with women serving less as cooks for large harvest crews and more as seasonal truck drivers and machinery operators along with their other year-round homemaking roles. However, as Bruce Shepard and Thomas Isern have pointed out, "The combine also destroyed the cooperative threshing ring, thereby eroding neighborliness."[102]

Economically, as Douglas Hurt has shown, combines were the very "symbol of capital-intensive, technological change in the Great Plains and Far West." As such, they "contributed to the problem of surplus production of wheat which, in turn, kept prices low and taxed the ability of the railroads to move the grain to market in a timely fashion."[103] The overproduction was often focused on paying off the loan for the machine; farmers went deeply into debt to keep up with the increased mechanization, as well as pay for the additional fuel and maintenance that combines require. This indebtedness was always made considerably worse when grain prices fell due to exogenous factors far outside farmers' control but to which they were forever beholden. "In every county," Worster has written, "there were those who could not survive the crunch and went under. On the other hand, as the survivors saw it, their salvation depended on more, not fewer, machines, so that they could achieve greater economies of scale." The economic and environmental results of that experience led Worster to conclude that "the machine made possible, and common, an exploitative relationship with the earth: a bond that was strictly commercial, so that the land became nothing more than a form of capital that must be made to pay as much as possible."[104]

Finally, the changes brought about by combines were transnational in nature. Worster's analysis can be applied to the areas in Mexico where combines replaced binders (primarily in the northern states of Coahuila, Chihuahua, and Sonora) and to western Canada. Isern and Shepard have argued that the combine was "key to the completion of mechanization on the Canadian plains" and that its "technical and economic importance was matched by its psychological consequence in regional culture."[105] The combine's heaviest impact, however, was on the Yucatecan fiber industry, ensuring and hastening its end.

In many ways the adoption of the combine affected four different, but intrinsically related, industries: the implement manufacturing industry, the transborder Great Plains agricultural industry, the North American cordage industry (including that of prison-made twine, which it ended), and the Yucatecan henequen industry. Economic indicators and world market factors reflected each of these industries like a four-way mirror. Booms from both world wars caused all four to produce more; postwar declines and the Great Depression caused all four to produce less, and so forth. But the adoption of combines broke the rule. That development caused a redirection and increase in the farm implement business, an increase in agricultural production, but a decrease in the cordage industry, and the virtual death of the henequen in-

Figure 7.7. McCormick-Deering 123-SP combine (typical of the combined harvester-threshers used in the late 1940s and 1950s), 1947. Courtesy Wisconsin Historical Society (McCormick–International Harvester Collection, Whi-7651).

dustry. As diligent as the *henequeneros* were in trying to diversify their line of products and expand the markets for their versatile fibers, nothing they tried even approached the successes achieved during the reign of the binder, with its insatiable demand for twine. With the adoption of the combine, Yucatán went from being one of Mexico's wealthiest states in the early twentieth century to one of its poorest by the late twentieth century. Nobody in the cordage, agricultural, or implement sectors seemed to notice or care, and certainly none of those industries proffered any kind of alternative market, insurance, or remuneration to the industry and labor pool in Yucatán on which they had been so completely dependent and from which they had profited so greatly for so many years. It was a classic case study of the dependency = underdevelopment theory—a textbook model of the *dependista* school's teachings. Even by 1938, Henry J. Allen, that Topeka, Kansas, editor and critical American observer, wrote in the *New York Herald Tribune,* "Meanwhile a confused and penniless population [in Yucatán] still puts on its hunger marches, while an indifferent world goes by, hunting and finding substitutes for sisal." And as a Mérida newspaper so poignantly put it, it was "those American interests . . . with their 'combines' [that] brought starvation to Yucatán."[106]

Conclusion

Bound in Twine

The interests of the American farmers are intimately
bound up in the preservation of the sisal market.

—*Editorial*, Bismarck Daily Tribune, *March 31, 1915*

AWKER City, Kansas, is home to what residents there claim is the world's
largest ball of twine. Many travelers and tourists motoring on U.S. Highway 24 in north central Kansas may not take the time to stop and admire
this landmark that is preserved under a metal pavilion complete with park
benches on which guests can relax and ponder the enormous ball, but if they
do, they learn little of the history of twine. The plaques and the brochures at
the site tell us it is "sisal twine" and that local resident Frank Stoeber started
rolling it on his farm back in 1953 and then donated it to the town of Cawker
City in 1961 (Figure C.1). Local residents have added to it ever since so that
by 2005 it was estimated to weigh nearly nine tons, have a circumference of
forty feet, and, if unraveled, would extend more than a thousand miles although, according to Harold Reling, the ball's unofficial "keeper," the diameter
from time to time shrinks when local pranksters set it on fire to see how much
of it will burn.

Cawker City residents occasionally have staged Labor Day "twine-a-
thons" to add girth to the ball's dimensions. One source cites how the giant
ball was used in a tongue-in-cheek article to promote tourism in Kansas by
saying the twine is long enough to unwind all the way to Carrollton, Missouri,
going east, but that the westward limit would be unknown, because the ball is
"too heavy to roll uphill."[1] And interestingly enough, Cawker City came to be

Figure C.1. World's largest ball of twine, Cawker City, Kansas. Photograph by the author.

the home of the Richardson Manufacturing Company, a business that made special windrow pick-up attachments for combines—the machines that helped make binders and binder twine obsolete.[2]

Meanwhile, Cawker City is in a stiff survival-of-the-fittest competition with Darwin, Minnesota, where another landmark ball of twine claims to be the world's largest, or at least the largest rolled by a single individual, and is also protected from the weather by a rain- and snow-deflecting metal pavilion (Figure C.2). Also nearly forty feet around, standing eleven feet tall, but weighing 8.7 tons (just under the weight of the ball in Kansas), the Darwin ball of twine was the brainchild of Francis A. Johnson, son of U.S. Senator Magnus Johnson, who began winding the ball in 1950. The date of both of the balls' beginnings and development indicate that they are primarily made of baler twine for hay bales, which is similar to binder twine and made of the same sisal fiber but came into use after farmers discontinued using binders to harvest grain crops. They were both created in states where grain farmers were dependent for decades on sisal fiber to harvest their crops and where two of the nation's largest penitentiary twine mills garnered state subsidies to produce lower priced twine for their farmers, which popularized the commodity even more. Also, both have been somewhat disparaged in U.S. popular culture as vapid icons of Americana, perhaps most tellingly in a song by "Weird Al" Yankovic entitled "The Biggest Ball of Twine in Minnesota." The song compares the Darwin attraction with other roadside wonders, such as the Boll Weevil Monument, Cranberry World, the Shuffleboard Hall of Fame, and

Figure C.2. World's largest ball of twine hand-rolled by one person, Darwin, Minnesota. Photograph by the author.

Poodle Dog Rock. Yankovic explains that this great ball of twine if it could, *would* roll west, "all the way to Fargo, North Dakota." Cawker City's ball of twine has borne the brunt of jokes about Kansas, including ones by syndicated columnist Dave Barry in his essay "Stating Your Case for the Stupidest State." There, Barry writes, residents "not only built a public gazebo to display the ball as a tourist attraction, but also created an annual festival to celebrate it"—the Twine-a-Thon, matched only by Darwin's "Twine Ball Days."[3] The Kansas site was made a bit more famous from a one-line comment about it in the 1983 comedy film *National Lampoon's Vacation* when the inimitable Griswold family was charting its westward summer vacation.

Twenty-one years later, National Public Radio (NPR) investigated to see if such an unusual tourist attraction really existed and, upon learning that it does, ran a short program on *Morning Edition* entitled "Unraveling the Story behind a Big Ball of Twine."[4] But similar to the International Harvester Company's brochure "The Story of Twine" from nearly a century before, the NPR program did not go into the *full* story of twine. It did not discuss where sisal was grown, the transnational interconnections involved, the extent to which the Great Plains and other grain producing areas of the United States and Canada were dependent on sisal, that it was so vital to harvesting cereal crops in the late nineteenth and early twentieth centuries, the questionable labor practices on which the henequen industry depended, how an indigenous nation was brutally fractured and removed to work in henequen fields, how ten different state and provincial governments subsidized at taxpayer expense the manufacture of twine in penitentiaries, how the United States once threatened military action to secure the flow of sisal, and what happened to the industry when the fiber was no longer in demand. No, NPR hardly unraveled much of a story at all, relying instead on about the same amount of information one can get about the dimensions of the Cawker City ball of twine while reading the marker at its pavilion. Even its keeper did not know that sisal primarily came from Mexico's Yucatán Peninsula.[5]

The larger history of the henequen-wheat complex merits attention as a case study of a trinational commodities-trade relationship on which American and Canadian agriculture depended, on which Yucatán came to rely exclusively, and from which the government of greater Mexico often derived major financial benefits. These factors suggest a more international context, one befitting the late twentieth- and early twenty-first-century term "globalization"— hardly a new phenomenon—especially in the degree to which Yucatecan fibers were used in Europe, Argentina, and elsewhere, and in the development of competition from fiber growers in the Philippines, East Africa, Java, Brazil, and the Caribbean. For a good many years, the whole world was bound in twine. (Figure C.3).

This study has traced the growth in demand for sturdy and rot- and insect-resistant fiber for binder twine, how Yucatán stepped up to the plate to provide such a resource, and how a labor force was provided from Sonora to cultivate that resource. In these three points of the henequen-wheat complex there were social, political, economic, and environmental transformations that emanated from the need for twine. This history, I believe, is useful for a historical analysis of latter-day projects such as the Mexican/U.S./Canadian North American Free Trade Agreement (NAFTA), which has had, and will continue to have, implications beyond what its proponents perceive as economic growth. Richard Kiy and John Wirth noted this dimension in the introduction to their book *Environmental Management on North America's Borders*: "The increasing integration of the countries of North America is causing important changes in economic, social, and environmental relationships among Canada, the United States, and Mexico. The increased volume of trade that NAFTA both facilitates and promotes is focusing attention on complex environmental challenges, including transboundary impacts. . . . [The] accord has provided the occasion for considering a range of discrete phenomena as an integrated whole. . . . [It] is nothing less than a new way of looking at things from a continental, or regional, perspective."[6]

NAFTA continues to trigger questionable labor practices (e.g., sweatshop *maquiladoras* in Mexico) while providing less expensive products to U.S. and

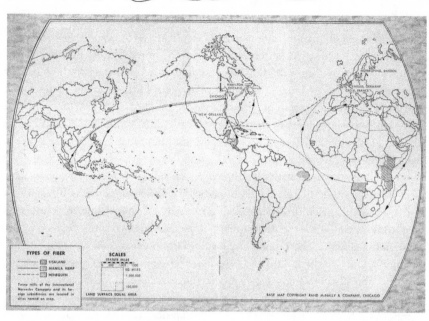

Figure C.3. Map of the globalized fiber trade during the binder twine boom (from International Harvester Company booklet, *The Story of Twine in Agriculture,* n.d., Navistar International Transportation Corp.) Courtesy Wisconsin Historical Society, McCormick-International Harvester Collection, WHi 44010.

Canadian markets. It continues Mexico's dependence on trade with its North American neighbors and in an export-dependent scenario, in place of focusing on local or regional trade with long-term economic development. It continues to create environmental changes that have social effects that should not be ignored. For example, with the increased free-trade market in agricultural products, places in Mexico such as the Yaqui Valley in Sonora continue to mass produce vegetables for export in a process heavily dependent on limited water resources and on fertilizers and chemical pesticides (including DDT, which cannot legally be used in the United States but can still be manufactured for export), with poor labor conditions, and low pay for workers, many of whom are indigenous people from other parts of Mexico who have been pushed out of their regional economy and who suffer the effects of working with chemical pesticides.[7] The demand for Mexico's agricultural products has increased with NAFTA, worsening the situation for Yaqui Indians trying to reclaim land that is legally theirs, much of which was confiscated during the henequen boom years. Meanwhile, NAFTA continues to cause millions of Mexicans to immigrate (legally and illegally) to the United States to seek work, since the free-trade economy has not stimulated local development to provide incentives for people to stay.[8] Yet many of the same lawmakers in the United States who support NAFTA also support anti-immigration initiatives.

In the twelve years since the passage of NAFTA at the time this book went to press, economic opportunities have worsened, not improved, for the majority of Mexicans, especially in rural Mexico.[9] With NAFTA's focus on ending agricultural tariffs, Mexico now allows wheat, rice, barley, potatoes, pork, beef, and twenty other agricultural imports from the United States to enter Mexico tariff free. Even with protective tariffs still remaining on imports of corn and beans into Mexico (which Mexico will eliminate in 2008), American farmers enjoy a very real advantage since they often receive government subsidies and other federal crop supports and have better access to irrigation, fertilizers, and equipment to stabilize yields. Mexican farmers, not being able to compete against this subsidized agribusiness, often leave their rural areas and head either to cities in search of factory jobs (often with little success since thousands and thousands compete for a few jobs) or to the border for jobs in *maquilas* (which are already starting to decline due to even cheaper wages being paid in El Salvador, the Dominican Republic, China, and Vietnam), or they try to immigrate to the United States.[10] Thus, are free-trade agreements benefiting the source (Mexico) of so many of the modes of production (labor and raw materials) at the beginning of the twenty-first century any better than the free-trade zone for henequen shipments at the beginning of the last century? Others have wondered this same thing. Allen Wells and Gilbert Joseph, for example, prefaced *Summer of Discontent, Seasons of Upheaval,* their 1996 book on elite politics and rural insurgency in Yucatán, with valid points for consideration: "Today . . . the 'New World Order' busily entrenches itself on both sides of the Rio Grande. . . . however the tune being played in Washington and Mexico City is one that was heard almost a century ago. . . . Will the campesinos of Yucatán and southern Mexico ultimately find more of a place in the 'new North American economy' than they did in its previous incarnation?"[11]

More recently, Steven Winter has written that the steps that the Mexican government took to prepare for a NAFTA-based economy were predicated on agricultural restructuring, economic liberalization, austerity measures, and the enactment (during the presidency of Carlos Salinas de Gortari) of the 1992 Agrarian Law, which amended Article 27 of the Mexican Constitution to discontinue distribution of communal *ejido* lands. Later Mexico cut rural credit programs, privatized some of the federal agricultural agencies, and worked to reduce the rural labor force of the country, all of which has resulted in a national agricultural crisis. "Latin American trade negotiators should not dismiss the severity of the . . . crisis," Winter writes, "since it clearly demonstrates the risks inherent in an unbalanced trade accord with the United States."[12]

These thoughts, and others pondering the Canadian connections, come to mind when contemplating the henequen-wheat complex from 1880 to 1950. Walking through the rows of henequen in Yucatán's receding plantations today (some of which are experiencing a kind of ecological restoration), one feels the weight of this history and can almost see the field workers harvesting the *pencas*, shipping the cut leaves on the remains of the tram tracks at one's feet. The remnants of the rasping sheds and drying lines, some of which are still in use for limited fiber production, stand as monuments to former times, economies, dreams, and labor brutality on the Yucatecan landscape. One could follow the bales of henequen to the port of Progreso (recalling Carranza's blockade and Wilson's gunboat response in 1915), all the way to a twine mill in Chicago, Saint Paul, or Winnipeg, or to a penitentiary in Sioux Falls, Waupon, or Bismarck, and eventually to a hot harvest day on the Great Plains, with farmers sweating away on the slow-moving, clanking binder, happy to be getting the crop in before a hailstorm or an early frost could ruin it.

One could perhaps wonder if all of these connections were well known to farmers at the time. Many assuredly just wanted their twine, just as we today often do not consider the background and history of our imported goods. But the diplomatic experience of the "Sisal Situation" and the great angst exhibited when twine prices increased after the Mexican Revolution were all well reported in local and regional newspapers and farm trade journals, showing that many indeed knew of the connections and were very intent upon maintaining favorable trade agreements for sisal. Local newspapers knew of these dimensions and reported the government's handling of the situations.

Policy makers in all three countries were even more keenly aware of the fiber's importance to their agricultural economies. In the first half of the twentieth century, the list of politicians who involved themselves (by choice or not) in matters dealing with sisal or binder twine reads like a "who's who" in North American politics; Woodrow Wilson, William Jennings Bryan, Herbert Hoover, Josephus Daniels, Albert Fall, Warren Harding, Charles Evans Hughes, Henry Wallace, Franklin Roosevelt, Cordell Hull, Arthur Capper, Sir Cecil Spring Rice, Sir Robert Laird Borden, Sir Edward Grey, William Richard Motherwell, Venustiano Carranza, Salvador Alvarado, Felipe Carrillo Puerto, Plutarco Elías Calles, and Lázaro Cárdenas are but a few who spring to mind. Many others, including members of the U.S. Congress, members of Canada's Parliament, penitentiary wardens, and Mexican *diputados* and governors could be listed. Hoover and Alf Landon both made campaign issues out of sisal-related events. And a wide variety of government agencies had various responsibilities in dealing with and investigating fiber matters. In the United States those included the Office of the President, the Department of State, the Department of Agriculture, the Department of Commerce, the Office of the Attorney General, the U.S. Food Administration, the Department of Justice, the U.S. Navy, Congress (including House and Senate subcommittees), and various state governors' offices and corrections boards; and in Canada it included the Ministry of Foreign Affairs, the Ministry of Trade and Commerce, the Ministry of Agriculture, Parliament, the Federal Corrections Board, the Office of the Governor General, a royal commission to investigate twine inspections, and the Ontario provincial government—all for fiber or twine. Combined, they clearly illustrate in no small way the significance that sisal fiber and binder twine had on North America for many years. It is no exaggeration to suggest that the whole scenario represented a strong, interconnected, and continental-dependency model.

Twine matters, however, were hardly limited to Washington and Ottawa. A whole popular culture of twine emerged that was a solid part of the larger farming scene of the United States and Canada. It was sold at most hardware stores, implement dealers, and farmers' co-ops. It was advertised in local newspapers and farmers' magazines. Some farmers made seasonal trips to their state prisons to buy twine; others ordered it via hardware distributors. The North Dakota penitentiary even entered binder twine floats in parades and exhibited its twine in the state products booth at the Great Exposition in San Francisco in 1915. The International Harvester Company was there too with its own booth, where its binder twine won the Grand Prize for quality.[13] IH also had elaborate twine booths and displays (including a clock tower made of balls of binder twine) at the Paris Exhibition in 1935. Binder twine also found its way into many kitchens and workshops as a fastener and fixer-upper of choice for hundreds of thousands of North Americans. Even today, bundles of twine-tied wheat are visible as symbolic icons across the Great Plains. A sheaf of wheat tied with twine is the provincial symbol of Saskatchewan, appearing on provincial highway signs and welcoming signs at its borders; the University of Saskatchewan campus newspaper is even called *The Sheaf.* The symbol of Brandon, Manitoba—"the Wheat City"—is a sheaf of wheat tied with twine. The nickname for sports teams at Wichita State University in Kansas remains the "Shockers."

In the years around the turn of the twentieth century many Yucatecans likewise seemed keenly interested in all things related to binder twine up north. The henequen trade journals were packed with stories on such remote-seeming issues as weather conditions in North Dakota, wheat yields in Kansas, harvest records in Saskatchewan, the prison twine plant in Minnesota, combine sales in Oklahoma, drought in South Dakota, sisal exports to Ontario, and binder usage in Alberta. Where else in Latin America could that have possibly occurred? Yucatecan henequen growers understood their North American connections well, and with good reason they feared for their well-being during the drought years in the Great Plains and during the advent of the combine harvester. They also feared the stiff competition from the growing fiber trade in other parts of the world, which the journals followed closely.

Thus, scholars should be aware of the complete history of binder twine not only as a case study of the social and cultural biography-of-things model recently advanced by anthropologists but also as an example of continental dependency and transnational interactions based on commodity exports.[14] Perhaps we can be reminded of some of these lessons inherent in the story that I have attempted to tell here. Perhaps the "world's largest" balls of twine in Kansas and Minnesota should stand as monuments to the interdependent nature of agricultural production—symbols not only of how late nineteenth- and early twentieth-century grain production in the American and Canadian plains was tied very tightly to a commodity from Mexico but also how the world is truly linked together for raw materials and markets. Perhaps the symbols should represent just how far governments will go to protect those flows of material— gunboat diplomacy and ultimatums then, and "free-trade" agreements such as NAFTA and the FTAA today—and the social results of those policies. Likewise, they should represent the nature of subsidized industry in a supposedly free-market economy, in terms of state governments using low-wage convict labor to benefit farmers, especially as that remains a controversial point today when corporations are fast exploiting inmates at extremely low wages. Finally, perhaps they should stand for the lessons that could be gleaned from this henequen-wheat experience: the social, economic, and environmental results of an increasingly mechanized agriculture, the ups and downs of dependence on foreign raw materials, and the boom/bust development patterns that occur as a result in places like Yucatán. Thus, all of these twists and turns in the complete story of binder twine, and the transformations they both reflected and instigated, should be recognized in the larger telling of North America's agricultural history.

NOTES

Abbreviations Used in Notes

AGES, Archivo General del Estado de Sonora (Hermosillo)

AGEY, Archivo General del Estado de Yucatán (Mérida)

AGN, Archivo General Nacional (Mexico City)

CONDUMEX, Centro de Estudios de Historia de México (Mexico City)

IHCA/Navistar, Archives of the International Harvester Company, Navistar International Transportation Corporation Documents Management and Knowledge Center (Chicago)

KSHS, Kansas State Library and Archives Division, Kansas State Historical Society (Topeka)

MHS, Minnesota State Archives, Minnesota Historical Society (Saint Paul)

NAC, National Archives of Canada / Archives Nationales du Canada (Ottawa)

NARA II, National Archives and Records Administration (College Park, Md.)

NSHS, Nebraska State Historical Society, Archives and Manuscripts (Lincoln)

SAB-R, Saskatchewan Archives Board–Regina (Regina)

SAB-S, Saskatchewan Archives Board–University of Saskatchewan (Saskatoon)

SDSHS, South Dakota State Historical Society, South Dakota Archives (Pierre)

SHSND, State Historical Society of North Dakota, North Dakota Archives (Bismarck)

SHSW, State Historical Society of Wisconsin (Madison)

Introduction

1. Appadurai, ed., *The Social Life of Things*, 3, 6; Kopytoff, "The Cultural Biography of Things," 64.

2. Walsh et al., *The Social Relations of Mexican Commodities*, 1.

3. See, for example, Kurlansky, *Salt*; Mintz, *Sweetness and Power*; Jack Turner, *Spice*; Kurlansky, *Cod*; Dean, *Brazil and the Struggle for Rubber*; Pendergrast, *Uncommon Grounds*; Allen, *The Devil's Cup*; Clarence-Smith and Topik, eds., *The Global Coffee Economy in Africa, Asia, and Latin America, 1500–1989*; Pettigrew, *A Social History of Tea*; Moxham, *Tea*; Cox, *The True History of Chocolate*; Zuckerman, *The Potato*; Harvey, Quilley, and Beynon, *Exploring the Tomato*; Soluri, *Banana Cultures*; Valenzuela-Zapata and Nabhan, *¡Tequila!*; Hebdige, "Object as Image"; Miller, *The Panama Hat Trail*; and Rybczynski, *One Good Turn*. See also Robbins, "Commodity Histories." On the social history of industrialization and technology, see Noble, *America by Design*; Noble, *Forces of Production*; Purcell, *The Machine in America*; and Cowan, *A Social History of American Technology*.

4. Wolf, *Europe and the People without History*, 3–4.

5. Thelen, "The Nation and Beyond," 968.

6. Truett and Young, "Making Transnational History," 1; Bukowzcyk et al., *Permeable Border;* Evans, ed., *The Borderlands of the American and Canadian Wests;* and Johnson and Graybill, eds., *Bridging National Borders in North America.* For more on the theoretical nexus between transnational and borderlands history, see Adelman and Aron, "From Borderlands to Borders."

7. See Truett, "Neighbors by Nature"; Truett, *Fugitive Landscapes;* White, "The Nationalization of Nature"; Tyrrell, "American Exceptionalism in the Age of International History," 1031. Crosby's works in this regard include *America, Russia, Hemp, and Napoleon; The Columbian Exchange;* and *Ecological Imperialism.* For a critique of the progress in transnational environmental history, see the paper "Boundary Terminology" by Joseph Taylor III.

8. Worster, "World without Borders," 662.

9. Soluri, *Banana Cultures,* 242.

10. For a comprehensive overview of this literature, see Joseph, "From Caste War to Class War."

11. The continentalist nature of this story is in tune with what the late Stanford historian John D. Wirth advocated in his pathbreaking essay, "Pike's Progress: A North American Agenda for Environmental History," which he presented at a conference of the American Society for Environmental History in Baltimore, Maryland, in March 1997. For further elaboration, see Wirth, "Advancing the North American Community"; and Earle and Wirth, eds., *Identities in North America.* For applying the continentalist concept to the study of North American pollution, see Kiy and Wirth, *Environmental Management on North America's Borders,* especially their introduction to the book.

Chapter 1

1. Worster, *Dust Bowl,* 87. For a standard account of the history of the region, see Webb, *The Great Plains.*

2. On the evolution of the farm machinery and grain production industries, see Partridge, *Farm Tools across the Ages;* Blanchard, *Old Farm Tools and Machinery;* Quick and Buchele, *The Grain Harvesters;* Hurt, *American Farm Tools;* Schlebecker, *Whereby We Thrive;* Shepard, "The Mechanized Agricultural Frontier of the Canadian Plains"; and Isern, *Bull Threshers and Bindlestiffs.*

3. Rasmussen, ed., *Readings in the History of American Agriculture,* 79; International Harvester Co., *Saving the World from Starvation,* 14.

4. Casson quoted in International Harvester Co., *Saving the World from Starvation,* 4. See also Casson, *Cyrus Hall McCormick;* and Casson, *The Romance of the Reaper.*

5. International Harvester Co., *Saving the World from Starvation,* 6.

6. Casson quoted in ibid., 4.

7. Quoted in *Harvester World* 22 (May 1931): 8.

8. Quick and Buchele, *The Grain Harvesters,* 74; *Itinerary: Deering Works & Deering Twine Mill* (booklet), 3 (Chicago: International Harvester Co., 1913), IHCA/Navistar.

9. Quick and Buchele, *The Grain Harvesters*, 75.

10. McCormick, *Century of the Reaper*, 69.

11. Hutchinson, *Cyrus Hall McCormick*, 539–41, 622–27, 724–25; Denison, *Harvest Triumphant*, 79, 81; Carstensen and Roazen, "Foreign Markets, Domestic Initiatives, and the Emergence of a Monocrop Economy," 570–71.

12. Sayre, "The Manufacture of Binding Twine," 19–20.

13. For further history, analysis, and illustrations of straw binders, see Quick and Buchele, *The Grain Harvesters*, 77.

14. McCormick, *Century of the Reaper*, 70.

15. Quick and Buchele, *The Grain Harvesters*, 78–79; Denison, *Harvest Triumphant*, 80. The image of Wisconsin native John Appleby holding his bill-hook knotting device, representing the importance of the invention to North American agriculture, is part of a wall-sized mural hanging in a stairwell at the Wisconsin State Historical Society's building in Madison.

16. Quick and Buchele, *The Grain Harvesters*, 78–79.

17. Wendel, *One Hundred Fifty Years of International Harvester*, 398; Appleby quoted in Quick and Buchele, *The Grain Harvesters*, 79.

18. Quoted in Denison, *Harvest Triumphant*, 80.

19. Ibid., 77.

20. See Denison, *Harvest Triumphant*, chap. 5; McCormick, *Century of the Reaper*, chap. 6.

21. Carstensen and Roazen, "Foreign Markets, Domestic Initiatives, and the Emergence of a Monocrop Economy," 570–71; Hutchinson, *Cyrus Hall McCormick*, 725; Quick and Buchele, *The Grain Harvesters*, 81.

22. McCormick, *Century of the Reaper*, 71; Carstensen and Roazen, "Foreign Markets, Domestic Initiatives, and the Emergence of a Monocrop Economy," 571.

23. Quick and Buchele, *The Grain Harvesters*, 79; Crossette, "Sisal," 2.

24. McCormick, *Century of the Reaper*, 72; MacEwan, *Between the Red and Rockies*, 206.

25. MacEwan, *Between the Red and Rockies*, 206; Denison, *Harvest Triumphant*, 77.

26. International Harvester Co., *Saving the World from Starvation*, 3. Per-hour harvest rate information is from "Farm Machinery," R-260, file I-30, SAB-R. Sales information is from Marsh, *A Corporate Tragedy*, 42; U.S. Department of Labor, Bureau of Labor Statistics, "Formulation of Industrial Wage and Price Policies," 5; *Harvester World* 6 (Aug. 1915): 13; 23 (July/Aug. 1932): 8; 6 (Sept. 1915): 26.

27. Dewey, "Fibers Used for Binder Twine," 193.

28. A. E. McKinstrey to U.S. Rep. Henry C. Luckey, Apr. 24, 1935, M95–262, folder 10, box 19, SHSW.

29. Casson, *Romance of the Reaper*, 176–77.

30. Quoted in Wilkins and Wilkins, *North Dakota*, 83.

31. Hammer, "Bonanza Farming," 56. For more on the history of the bonanza farms, see Drache, *The Day of the Bonanza*; Briggs, "The Great Dakota Boom, 1879–1886"; Tweton, "The Golden Age of Agriculture"; Hunter, "The Bonanza Farms"; and S. N. Murray, *The Valley Comes of Age*.

32. Hammer, "Bonanza Farming," 56–57.

33. Casson, *Romance of the Reaper*, 178.

34. Edwards, "'The Greatest Hazard of All Is the 'Human Element,'" 26–31 (including quotation).

35. Voisey, *Vulcan*, xvii, xvi, 144.

36. McCormick, *Century of the Reaper*, 111.

37. Ibid., 112.

38. Ibid., 113, and 111–28 for the complete history of the merger. See also Cronon, *Nature's Metropolis*.

39. Sales brochures, RG: Stillwater State Prison, Series: Prison Industries, 118. B.11, box 1, MHS. For more on binders, headers, and early combines, see Hurt, "Combine Harvesters," 43–62; and Isern, "The Adoption of the Combine on the Northern Plains."

40. Ward, "Farming Technology and Crop Area on Early Prairie Farms," 24; Hutchinson, *Cyrus Hall McCormick*, 647–51; Denison, *Harvest Triumphant*, 84. For more on Canadian implement industry development, see Cook, *Massey at the Brink*.

41. Canada, *House of Commons Debates*, 12th Parliament (George V), 5th sess., 1915, 1649–50.

42. Quotations from Hutchinson, *Cyrus Hall McCormick* , 647–51, 685.

43. International Harvester Co., *The Story of Twine* (booklet), 60, IHCA/Navistar; Farm Machinery Act records (1913), file II-9, SAB-S.

44. Massey-Harris Co., *M-H High Grade Farm Machinery* (1917), 1; *M-H Farmers Handy Catalogue, 1937*, 32; *M-H Farmers Handy Catalogue, 1939*, 33, all in SAB-R.

45. Denison, *Harvest Triumphant*, 85; Casson, *Romance of the Reaper*, 103.

46. Ward, "Farming Technology and Crop Area on Early Prairie Farms," 24; MacEwan, *Between the Red and Rockies*, 207. See also Thomas, "A History of Agriculture on the Prairies," 31–45.

47. Fieguth, *Flour Sacks and Binder Twine*, 48.

48. Duddridge, "The Rime of the Bucking Binder," in *Seen from My Seeder Step*, 21–22.

49. Denison, *Harvest Triumphant*, 85; *Harvester World* 1 (June 1910): 12; *Nebraska Farmer* 57 (Aug. 18, 1915): 799.

50. International Harvester Co., *Saving the World from Starvation*, 3; Casson, *Romance of the Reaper*, 125; "You were wrong, Dr. Malthus" ad campaign, file 10876, IHCA/Navistar.

51. G. Friesen, *The Canadian Prairies*, 329. For more on how farmers of the Prairie Provinces were "eager to take advantage" of the international market during and after World War I, see Thompson, *The Harvests of War*, 23–70.

52. U.S. Department of Agriculture, *Wheat*, 2; Canada, Dominion Bureau of Statistics, *Wheat Review* (1956), as quoted in Vernon C. Fowke, *The National Policy and the Wheat Economy*, 75; Canada, Dominion Bureau of Statistics, *The Prairie Provinces in Their Relation to the National Economy of Canada*, 30; Bukowczyk et al., *Permeable Border*, 66.

53. *Regina Leader*, June 27, 1892, 4; University of Saskatchewan, *Farm Business in Saskatchewan*, June 1927, 11, 45; Waiser, *Saskatchewan*, 130.

54. Joseph and Wells, "Corporate Control of a Monocrop Economy," 73. Per acre twine statistics are from Ward, "Farming Technology and Crop Area," 33; and W. G. McMahon, Ltd. (Winnipeg) to Secretary, Statistics Branch, Saskatchewan Department of Agriculture, Sept. 28, 1945, R-266, file IV-8, SAB-R.

55. IH Department Managers Conference, minutes, Aug. 1, 1923, file 01605, IHCA/Navistar; Owen, *Prosperity without Progress*, 48; Canadian Department of Statistics as cited in *Canadian Farm Implements* editor to E. H. Evans, Sept. 15, 1945, R-266, file IV-8, SAB-R.

56. *Harvester World* 5 (Aug. 1914): 30; "Report of Joint Meeting of Twine Mill and Twine and Fibre Committee," Jan. 27, 1903, file 02148, IHCA/Navistar; International Harvester Co., *The Story of Twine*, 25–30; Wendel, *One Hundred Fifty Years of International Harvester*, 399.

57. Joseph, "Revolution from Without," 101; Casson, *Romance of the Reaper*, 104.

58. *Harvester World* 5 (Aug. 1914): 30.

59. Fibre Committee to Charles Deering, May 9, 1903, file 02148, IHCA/Navistar; *Harvester World* 5 (May 1914): 10.

60. Casson, *Romance of the Reaper*, 104; International Harvester Co., *The Story of Twine*, 28–40; Wendel, *One Hundred Fifty Years of International Harvester*, 399.

61. International Harvester Co., *Saving the World from Starvation*, 10.

62. Joseph, *Revolution from Without*, 319; Dewing, *A History of National Cordage Company*, 50; Plymouth Cordage advertisement in *Canadian Farm Implements* 43 (Jan. 1947): 18.

63. The brochure is in Plymouth Cordage, record 04847, envelope 1, IHCA/Navistar.

64. *Harvester World* 1 (Mar. 1910): 4–5.

65. For the complete history of the National Cordage Company and its relation with other twine manufacturers, see Dewing, *History of National Cordage Company*.

66. P. R. Pounder and Brantford Cordage Co., Ltd., to Board of Railway Commissioners, Aug. 1, 1918; and Brantford Cordage Co., Ltd., to Board of Railway Commissioners, Aug. 3, 1918, RG 30, series V-A-9-h, Vol. 9263, file 10436–3–80, NAC.

67. *Canadian Farm Implements* 31 (Dec. 1935): 1, 5, 13, 23.

68. Quoted in Joseph, "Revolution from Without," 101.

69. *Cordage Trade Journal* 95 (July 15, 1937): 22. Information about different grades of IH twine is from G. Detzer, Assistant Manager, Fibre Department, to Harold F. McCormick, Oct. 10, 1904, file 02148, IHCA/Navistar.

70. *Harvester World* 1 (Mar. 1910): 29; and 7 (May 1916): 6; *Washington Post* editorial, Apr. 19, 1916, reprinted in *Harvester World* 7 (May 1916): 7.

71. Dewey, "Fibers Used for Binder Twine," 193–200 (quotation, 200). I thank Paul Sutter for bringing this government report to my attention.

72. *El henequén* 1 (Oct. 15, 1916): 3–6; Oakley, *Long Vegetable Fibres*, 135–45. For more information on fibrous plants, see Kirby, *Vegetable Fibres*; Maiti, *World Fiber Crops*; and Catling and Grayson, *Identification of Vegetable Fibres*.

73. Carstensen and Roazen, "Foreign Markets, Domestic Initiatives, and the Emergence of a Monocrop Economy," 582.

74. *The Binder Twine Steal* (anonymous pamphlet), 1–5, NAC; *Regina Leader,* June 27, 1892, 4; Apr. 7, 1892, 2; May 2, 1892, 2, 4; *Farmer's Sun,* Feb. 3, 1898, 3.

75. Ward, "Farming Technology," 24. The information about prices in Qu'Appelle is in the *Regina Leader,* Oct. 4, 1894, 4.

76. Fieguth, *Flour Sacks and Binder Twine,* 47–48. She also related this story: "Henry Peters, a prankster of the community, found another use for the sturdy twine. One Sunday while sitting in church he couldn't resist the idea of tying the worshipper ahead of him to the pew. . . . When the preacher said, "Lasset uns aufstehn zum gebet" (Let us arise for prayer), [the worshipper] unaware that he was tied tried to get to his feet. He lifted the pew part way then fell back with a terrible clatter!" (47–48).

77. Joseph, *Revolution from Without,* 319.

78. Carstensen and Roazen, "Foreign Markets, Domestic Initiatives, and the Emergence of a Monocrop Economy," 558; Joseph and Wells, "Corporate Control of a Monocrop Economy," 84–86; Joseph, *Revolution from Without,* 54; *El agricultor* 1 (June 1, 1907): 95. The "oligopsony" argument is from Brannon and Baklanoff, *Agrarian Reform and Public Enterprise in Mexico,* 42.

79. Joseph and Wells, "Corporate Control of a Monocrop Economy," 72, 89–91.

80. Wells, "Henequen and Yucatan," 39, 57.

81. International Harvester Fibre and Twine Department memo, ca. 1904, file 02148, IHCA/Navistar.

82. Cámara Zavala, *Reseña histórica de la industria henequenera,* 47; Joseph and Wells, "Corporate Control of a Monocrop Economy," 90. For more on Fordlândia, see Hecht and Cockburn, *The Fate of the Forest,* 97–100.

83. Reported in *El agricultor* 1 (July 1, 1907): 105.

84. Joseph, *Revolution from Without,* 176, 177 (quotation from special agent R. S. Sharpe).

85. *El agricultor* reported on Aug. 1, 1908, that IH of Canada held the same kind of monopoly on fiber sales in Canada as it did in the United States.

86. Benjamin, "International Harvester and the Henequen Marketing System in Yucatan, 1898–1915," 4.

87. *El agricultor* 2 (Aug. 1, 1908): 114–15; 4 (June 1, 1910): 160.

88. Fornaro, "Yucatan and the International Harvester Company," 337–38, 343.

89. For further information, see Herer, *The Emperor Wears No Clothes.* For more on hemp cultivation, see Dempsey, *Fiber Crops;* Bosca and Karus, *The Cultivation of Hemp;* and Pollan, *The Botany of Desire,* chap. 3, "Marijuana."

90. Sayre, "The Manufacture of Binding Twine," 19.

91. Wells, "Henequen and Yucatan," 91. For more on the history of industrial hemp in the United States, see Hopkins, *A History of the Hemp Industry in Kentucky;* and Crosby, *America, Russia, Hemp, and Napoleon.*

92. Wendel, *One Hundred Fifty Years of International Harvester,* 398; Nelson, " 'The Greatest Single Industry'?" I thank Paul Nelson for hastening this aspect of twine history to my attention. Farmers' statements are from a Minnie Binder ad in an AGT catalogue, 1901, McCormick–International Harvester Collection, Documented Series, file 13941, box 263, SHSW.

93. International Harvester Company, annual Reports of the International Harvester Company (1907–15), IHCA/Navistar. Saskatoon flax plant information is from *Saskatoon Phoenix*, Mar. 15, 1915, 1.

94. T. E. Mitchell to W. R. Motherwell, Feb. 12, 1907; and Motherwell to Mitchell, Feb. 18, 1907, both in file II.117, Motherwell Papers, SAB-S.

95. Dewey, "Fibers Used for Binder Twine," 200.

96. *El henequén* 4 (Feb. 15, 1919): 47. The article in which this information was found was entitled "El cultivo del henequén en el estado de North Dakota." The word *henequén*, as used elsewhere in Mexican literature at the time, was used to mean the generic "hemp" as well as the specific *Cannabis sativa*. Neither sisal nor henequen can grow outside of tropical or subtropical climates and could never survive a harsh Red River Valley winter. The *El henequén* article cited an article in the Williston (North Dakota) *Herald* but unfortunately without providing the date.

97. Saskatchewan Department of Agriculture, Statistics Branch, "Hemp" (memo), R-266, file IV-39, SAB-R.

98. *El sisal mexicano* 3 (Nov. 1929): 9. Information on flax was also derived from Records of the Kingston Penitentiary, NAC, and from documents relating to the Saint Paul Twine Plant, found in IHCA/Navistar.

99. Information on Van Allen is in J. Bruce Walker to W. R. Motherwell, Minister of Agriculture, Dec. 8, 1917, file II.117, Motherwell Papers, SAB-S.

100. Joseph, *Revolution from Without*, 181; Wells, *Yucatan's Gilded Age*, 57.

101. Plymouth Cordage, record 0484, envelope #6, IHCA/Navistar.

102. *Chicago Daily News*, Mar. 14, 1923, 5; *Farm Implement News*, Mar. 29, 1923, 1.

103. Morlan, *Political Prairie Fire*,119–20. I thank my colleague George Hoffman for alerting me to this citation.

104. *Farm Implement News*, Mar. 29, 1923, 1.

105. Quoted in *El diario de Yucatán*, July 3, 1936, 3.

Chapter 2

1. Joseph, "Revolution from Without," 27; Wells, "From Hacienda to Plantation," 115.

2. Wells, *Yucatan's Gilded Age*, 13–14. European quotations are cited in Chardon, *Geographic Aspects of Plantation Agriculture in Yucatan*, v; and Wells, *Yucatan's Gilded Age*, 13. For more on Yucatan's physical setting, see Foster, "Sisal Production in Semi-Arid Karst Country of Yucatan," 16–21.

3. Landa, *Yucatan before and after the Conquest*, 1, 93.

4. *New York Herald Tribune*, Aug. 27, 1938, 5.

5. Fitchen, "Self-Determination or Self-Preservation?" 33.

6. *El sisal mexicano* 6 (Aug. 1932): 6; 6 (Sept. 1932): 3. Soils quotation from Rasmussen, ed., *Readings in the History of American Agriculture*, 75.

7. E. M. Wilson, "Physical Geography of the Yucatan Peninsula," 7.

8. Chardon, *Geographic Aspects of Plantation Agriculture in Yucatan*, 10, v (quotation).

9. Irigoyen, *¿Fue el auge del henequén producto de la Guerra de Castas?* 43. Oakley (*Long Vegetable Fibres*, 138) argues for *nequen*, and Manero (*La anarquía henequenera de Yucatán*, 9) argues for *jeniquén*.

10. International Harvester, *The Story of Twine in Agriculture*, Educational Series #3, 15, IHCA/Navistar; U.S. Senate, Subcommittee on Agriculture and Forestry, "Hearings on Importation of Sisal and Manila Hemp."

11. Fornaro, "Yucatan and the International Harvester Company," 337; Escoffié, *Yucatán en la cruz*, 33, 27, respectively.

12. Orellana, "Agave, Agavaceae y familias afines en la Península de Yucatán," 83.

13. Benítez, *Ki*, 55; Irigoyen, *Los mayas y el henequén*, 8. The alternative version of the legend was published in *El henequén* 3 (Mar. 15, 1918): 4.

14. Irigoyen, *Los mayas y el henequén*, 8; Chardon, *Geographic Aspects of Plantation Agriculture in Yucatan*, 14–15. See also Manero, *La anarquía henequenera de Yucatán*, 9.

15. Chardon, *Geographic Aspects of Plantation Agriculture in Yucatan*, 15; Oviedo source and Landa quoted in Manero, *La anarquía henequenera de Yucatán*, 15–17, which cites many other sources as well. For more on the general history of the Spanish invasion of Yucatán, see Clendinnen, *Ambivalent Conquests*.

16. Wells, *Yucatan's Gilded Age*, 18–21; Brockway, *Science and Colonial Expansion*, 170.

17. Chardon, *Geographic Aspects of Plantation Agriculture in Yucatan*, 15; Brockway, *Science and Colonial Expansion*, 171.

18. Suárez Molina, *La evolución económica de Yucatán a través del siglo XIX*, 1:132–33.

19. Wells, *Yucatan's Gilded Age*, 21.

20. Fitchen, "Self-Determination or Self-Preservation?" 33–35.

21. Rugeley, *Yucatan's Maya Peasantry and the Origins of the Caste War*, xiv.

22. Wells, *Yucatan's Gilded Age*, 25–26. For further information and analysis see Reed, *The Caste War of Yucatan*; González Navarro, *Raza y tierra*; Rugeley, *Yucatan's Maya Peasantry and the Origins of the Caste War*; and Remmers, "Henequen, the Caste War, and the Economy of Yucatan, 1846–1883."

23. Carstensen and Roazen, "Foreign Markets, Domestic Initiative and the Emergence of a Monocrop Economy," 555.

24. *La razón del pueblo*, Oct. 23, 1869, quoted in Irigoyen, *¿Fue el auge del henequén producto de la Guerra de Castas?* 38; Orosa Díaz, *Felipe Carrillo Puerto (Estudio biográfico)*, 15 (export figures); Chardon, *Geographic Aspects of Plantation Agriculture in Yucatan*, 29.

25. Fornaro, "Yucatan and the International Harvester Company," 338; *Diario yucateco*, Jan. 10, 1911, 5; Pasos Peniche, *Historia de la industria henequenera desde 1945 hasta nuestros días*, app. I; Brannon and Baklanoff, *Agrarian Reform and Public Enterprise in Mexico*, 43.

26. Chardon, *Geographic Aspects of Plantation Agriculture in Yucatan*, 4, 5. For further clarification of definitions, see Waibel, "The Tropical Plantation System," 157; and Chardon, *Geographic Aspects of Plantation Agriculture in Yucatan*, 8. For further analysis, see Wells, "Henequen," 85–124.

27. Chardon, *Geographic Aspects of Plantation Agriculture in Yucatan*, 13; Joseph, *Revolution from Without*, 46; Baklanoff and Brannon, "Forward and Backward Linkages in a Plantation Economy," 83.

28. For more on the theoretical differences between haciendas and plantations, see Wolf and Mintz, "Haciendas and Plantations in Middle America," 380–412.

29. Chardon, *Geographic Aspects of Plantation Agriculture in Yucatan*, 13. For a case study of this phenomenon on the Santo Domingo Xcuyum hacienda, see Wells, "From Hacienda to Plantation"; and Wells, *Yucatan's Gilded Age*, chap. 5.

30. *El henequenero* 1 (Nov. 1927): 222.

31. On the 1825 colonization law, see Suárez Molina, *La evolución económica de Yucatán a través del siglo XIX*, 1:111. Information on other state laws and the quotations are in Orosa Díaz, *Legislación henequenera en Yucatán (1833–1955)*, 145, 9 (respectively). Federal decree information is from Chardon, *Geographic Aspects of Plantation Agriculture in Yucatan*, 33–34.

32. Wells, "Henequen," 93; Chardon, *Geographic Aspects of Plantation Agriculture in Yucatan*, 30; Fornaro, "Yucatan and the International Harvester Company," 338; President of the *Cámara Agrícola* to Yucatán governor Enrique Muñoz, Apr. 1, 1910, series: Poder Ejecutivo, file: Fomento, box 641, AGEY.

33. Carstensen and Roazen, "Foreign Markets, Domestic Initiatives, and the Emergence of Monocrop Economy," 569; Joseph, "Revolution from Without," 28.

34. Baklanoff, "The Diversification Quest," 209. Most economists credit David Ricardo for establishing the basis for comparative trade economics in 1817 in his book *On the Principles of Political Economy and Taxation.*

35. Editorial in *El henequén* 1 (July 15, 1916): 2.

36. Wells, "Henequen and Yucatan," 2, 35; Baklanoff, "The Diversification Quest," 209.

37. Reed, *Caste War of Yucatan*, 232; Joseph and Wells, "Corporate Control of a Monocrop Economy," 71; Fornaro, "Yucatan and the International Harvester Company," 344.

38. González Navarro, *Raza y tierra*, 172.

39. Department of Agriculture and Commerce (Yucatán) to M. E. Boyle of Austin, Tex., Apr. 4, 1916, series: Poder Ejecutivo, box 522, AGEY.

40. Joseph, "Revolution from Without," 61; John Kenneth Turner, *Barbarous Mexico*, 8; Wells, "From Hacienda to Plantation," 135–36. For further details on the aristocratic lifestyle, see Wells, *Yucatan's Gilded Age*, 61–88.

41. Villanueva Mukul, *Así tomamos las tierras*, 124. Employment data are from the statement of Víctor Rendón in U.S. Senate, Subcommittee on Agriculture and Forestry, "Hearings on Importations of Sisal and Manila Hemp," 6. For a contemporary critique of the aristocracy's monopoly, see Juan Miguel Castro, "El henequén de Yucatán y el monopolio."

42. Baklanoff, "The Diversification Quest," 214.

43. For complete discussion and analysis, see Wells, "Family Élites in a Boom-Bust Economy," 224–53; Wells, *Yucatan's Gilded Age*, chap. 3; Joseph, *Revolution from Without*, 37–41; and Wells and Joseph, *Summer of Discontent, Seasons of Upheaval*, chap. 4.

44. Benítez, *Ki*, 83.

45. Joseph, *Revolution from Without*, 49; Cámara Zavala, *Reseña histórica de la industria henequenera de Yucatán*, 68; Wells, *Yucatan's Gilded Age*, 56.

46. Wells, *Yucatan's Gilded Age*, 74–75; Joseph, *Revolution from Without*, 36.

47. Wells, "Henequen and Yucatan," 72; Fornaro, "Yucatan and the International Harvester Company," 338; Wells, *Yucatan's Gilded Age*, 50; Joseph and Wells, "Corporate Control of a Monocrop Economy," 71–72. The contract between IH and Montes is in IH to Montes, Oct. 2, 1906, file 021–48, IHCA/Navistar.

48. Agreement quoted in Escoffié, *Yucatán en la cruz*, 48. See also, Irigoyen, *Ensayos henequeneros*, 104; and Joseph and Wells, "Corporate Control of a Monocrop Economy," 80.

49. Carstensen and Roazen-Parrillo, "International Harvester, Molina y Compañía, and the Henequen Market," 197, 201.

50. Benjamin, "International Harvester and the Henequen Marketing System in Yucatan, 1898–1915," 16; Brannon and Baklanoff, "Corporate Control of a Monocrop Economy," 193–94.

51. Joseph and Wells, "Collaboration and Informal Empire in Yucatan," 209, 213.

52. Wells, "Henequen and Yucatan," vi, 1; *El henequén* 2 (July 31, 1917): 1.

53. *El agricultor* 2 (Feb. 1, 1908): 32; Benítez, *Ki*, 55.

54. José Salvador Flores, "Caracterización de la vegetación en la zona henequenera de México," 78–79.

55. Joseph and Wells, "Corporate Control of a Monocrop Economy," 70; data from Secretaría de Agricultura y Ganadería, Estado de Yucatán, as reported in Pasos Peniche, *Historia de la industria henequenera desde 1945 hasta nuestros días*, app. I; *El universal*, Apr. 19, 1946, 15.

56. Benítez, *Ki*, 26, 47–49.

57. Joaquín Lanz Trueba, "En un henequenal," reprinted in *El henequén* 3 (Jan. 1, 1918): 17; Joseph and Wells, "Corporate Control of a Monocrop Economy," 70.

58. Benítez, *Ki*, 26.

59. *El henequén* 2 (Nov. 15, 1917): 8.

60. González Navarro, *Raza y tierra*, 191–94; announcement about the passage of laws allowing conversion of "vacant" lands from local Socialist Party, Agrarian Commission, Dec. 2, 1916, series: Poder Ejecutivo, box 537, AGEY.

61. Faustino Escalante to Salvador Alvarado, Nov. 6, 1916, series: Poder Ejecutivo, box 537, AGEY. As would likely happen today, the governor promised the farmer that he would turn the matter over to a "local agricultural commission" to mediate any problems (Alvarado to Escalante, Nov. 10, 1916, series: Poder Ejecutivo, box 537, AGEY).

62. Crossett, "Sisal," 5. On rail concessions and growth of the rail system, see Orosa Díaz, *Legislación henequenera en Yucatán (1833–1955)*, 53–188; and Joseph, *Revolution from Without*, 34.

63. Wells, "From Hacienda to Plantation," 125; Benítez, *Ki*, 64.

64. For details on the history of decorticator development, see Benítez, *Ki*, 64–70. For more on specific rasping machine patents, see Orosa Díaz, *Legislación henequenera en Yucatán (1833–1955)*, 25–53.

65. *El henequén* 2 (Oct. 15, 1917): 4; Joseph, *Revolution from Without*, 247.

66. Joseph, *Revolution from Without*, 3–4.

67. Quoted (without reference to the author's name) in Suárez Molina, *La evolución económica de Yucatán a través del siglo XIX*, 1:210–11.

68. Eugenio Frey, "Utilidad de los bosques" (1882), reprinted in *El agricultor* 2 (Apr. 1, 1908): 57. For more on the history of conservationist thought in Mexico at this time, see Simonian, *Defending the Land of the Jaguar*, chap. 4.

69. Suárez Molina, *La evolución económica de Yucatán a través del siglo XIX*, 1:211–12.

70. *El henequén* 3 (Feb. 15, 1918): 5.

71. *El henequén* 3 (Nov. 15, 1918): 10–11.

72. *El agricultor* 1 (Mar. 1, 1907): 37; 10 (June 1, 1923), 5.

73. Suárez Molina, *La evolución económica de Yucatán a través del siglo XIX*, 1:125, 209. For a pertinent comparison of forest destruction due to the chicle industry in Yucatán's neighboring state, Quintana Roo, see Konrad, "De la subsistencia forestal tropical a la producción para exportación."

74. González Navarro, *Raza y tierra*, 179; Katz, "El sistema de plantación y esclavitud," 118; Fallaw, "The Economic Foundations of Bartolismo," 19.

75. Wells, "From Hacienda to Plantation," 131–32.

76. *El henequenero* 1 (Apr. 1927): 60.

77. Benítez, *Ki*, 49.

78. Wells, "Yucatan," 228; Benítez, *Ki*, 49; *El agricultor* 1 (Mar. 1, 1907): 37.

79. Suárez Molina, *La evolución económica de Yucatán a través del siglo XIX*, 1:164–65.

80. Wells, "Yucatan," 214–16, 224; *El henequén* 2 (Sept. 15, 1917): 6; *El agricultor* 1 (Mar. 1, 1907): 37, 49; Wells and Joseph, *Summer of Discontent, Seasons of Upheaval*, 149.

81. González Navarro, *Raza y tierra*, 195; Joseph, *Revolution from Without*, 72; Wells and Joseph, *Summer of Discontent, Seasons of Upheaval*, 149.

82. Suárez Molina, *La evolución económica de Yucatán a través del siglo XIX,*: 1:155–56; Chardon, *Geographic Aspects of Plantation Agriculture in Yucatan*, 37; Joseph, *Revolution from Without*, 73.

83. Suárez Molina, *La evolución económica de Yucatán a través del siglo XIX*, 1:158.

84. Ibid., 1:29.

85. Wells and Joseph, *Summer of Discontent, Seasons of Upheaval*, 154. For further details, see Cámara Zavala, *Reseña histórica de la industria henequenera de Yucatán*, 59; Betancourt Perez, *Revoluciones y crisis en la economía de Yucatán*, 73; González Navarro, *La colonización en México, 1877–1910*, 223.

86. Quoted in Joseph, *Revolution from Without*, 72.

87. Wells, "Yucatan," 227.

88. Chardon, *Geographic Aspects of Plantation Agriculture in Yucatan*, 33.

89. Suárez Molina, *La evolución económica de Yucatán a través del siglo XIX*, 1:160; Chardon, *Geographic Aspects of Plantation Agriculture in Yucatan*, 13, 33; Wells and Joseph, *Summer of Discontent, Seasons of Upheaval*, 149. See also Katz, "Labor Conditions on Haciendas in Porfirian Mexico," 15. For a breakdown and analysis of workers from individual Mexican states, excepting Sonora, see Suárez Molina, *La evolución económica de Yucatán a través del siglo XIX*, 2:316–17.

90. From series of letters and reports in series: Poder Ejecutivo 1909, file: Sanidad, box 642, AGEY.

91. Suárez Molina, *La evolución económica de Yucatán a través del siglo XIX*, 1:159–60; Wells, "Henequen and Yucatan," 286.

92. Jorge D. Flores, "La vida rural en Yucatán en 1914," 479–80. (This journal article is based on Esteban Flores's unfinished report, which his son Jorge discovered years later.)

93. Ibid., 481, 483.

94. Antochiw, "El enganche de peones huastecos para las haciendas de Yucatán," 21. See also, "Peones huastecos enganchados para las haciendas de Yucatán, 1893," Documentos Históricos Peninsulares, vol. 12, 1995, Centro de Apoyo a la Investigación Histórico de Yucatán, Mérida.

95. See John Kenneth Turner, *Barbarous Mexico*. For more on the background history of Turner and the impact of his writings, see Sinclair Snow's introduction to the University of Texas Press edition of *Barbarous Mexico*.

96. Snow, introduction to *Barbarous Mexico*, 18–23.

97. See Channing and Frost, *The American Egypt*; and *American Magazine*, Apr. 1910, 829–35.

98. Chandler and Frost, *The American Egypt*, 332–33.

99. Baerlein, *Mexico, the Land of Unrest*, 143, 175, 185.

100. Wells and Joseph, *Summer of Discontent, Seasons of Upheaval*, 206.

101. Wells, "*Yucatan:* Violence and Social Control," 231; Wells and Joseph, *Summer of Discontent, Seasons of Upheaval*, 206.

102. Shuman, "The Town Where Luck Fell," 24; Chandler and Frost, *The American Egypt*, 325–26.

103. Chandler and Frost, *The American Egypt*, 326–29.

104. Letters between the society secretary and the British Foreign Office worker, reprinted in the London *Morning Post*, Sept. 5, 1910, 1.

105. Quotations from Smith's telegram in Snow, introduction to *Barbarous Mexico*, xv–xvii. For more analysis about the denial, see Joseph, *Rediscovering the Past at Mexico's Periphery*, 59.

106. *Harvester World*, Mar. 1910, 30.

107. Ruz Menéndez, "Los yaquis en las haciendas henequeneras de Yucatán," 59–61.

108. "Contrato celebrado entre C. Manuel Fernández Leal, Secretario del Estado y del Despacho de Fomento y el C. Manuel Arrigunaga," series: Poder Ejecutivo, Gobierno 1916, box 515, AGEY. See Ruz Menéndez, "Los yaquis en las haciendas henequeneras de Yucatán," 63–67, for his analysis on the document.

109. Antochiw, "El enganche de peones huastecos para las haciendas de Yucatán," 21, 22.

110. Michel Antochiw, interview by author, June 6, 1999, Mérida, Yuc. The legal document is *Constancias judiciales que demuestran que no existir esclavitud en Yucatán y que son falsas las imputaciones hechas en el libelo difamatorio.*

111. Baerlein, *Mexico, the Land of Unrest*, 148.

112. Benítez, *Ki*, 63; Gruening, *Mexico and Its Heritage*, 138.

113. Joseph, *Revolution from Without*, 78–79. See also, Joseph, *Rediscovering the Past at Mexico's Periphery*, 67–68.

114. Brannon and Baklanoff, *Agrarian Reform and Public Enterprise in Mexico*, xi. The Yucatecan saying is quoted in Joseph, "Revolution from Without," 25.

115. Quotations from Benítez, *Ki*, 38.

Chapter 3

1. Wells and Joseph, *Summer of Discontent, Seasons of Upheaval*, 45.

2. For the complete anthropological history of the Yaquis, see Spicer, *The Yaquis;* Fabila, *Las tribus yaquis de Sonora;* García Wikit, *Tribu yaqui;* Dabdoub, *Historia de el Valle del Yaqui;* Figueroa, "Derechos políticos y organización social"; Zavala Castro, *El indio Tetabiate y la nación de los ocho pueblos del Río Yaqui.* For a more condensed work, see Spicer, "Highlights of Yaqui History."

3. On Yaqui agriculture, see Valencia Jusacamea, "Agricultura tradicional ya-qui"; Dabdoub, *Historia de el Valle del Yaqui;* Spicer, *The Yaquis;* and Evans, "Yaquis vs. Yanquis."

4. Kelley, introduction to *The Tall Candle*, by Moisés, Kelley, and Holden, xiii–xvi. For more on the history of Yaqui resistance and resilience, see Velasco Toro, *Los yaquis;* Hu-deHart, "Development and Rural Rebellion"; Hu-deHart, *Yaqui Resistance and Survival;* Gouy-Gilbert, "Los yaquis de Sonora"; and *Tres procesos de lucha por la sobrevivencia de la tribu yaqui.*

5. C. Ramón Corral, "Informe dado a la Legislatura," 1888, 33, Collección del Noroeste, AGES.

6. "La yaqui hermosa" in Nervo, *Obras completas de Amado Nervo*, 20:34.

7. For further information on the colonization policy, see González Navarro, *La colonizacíon en México, 1877–1910.*

8. For more on the commission, see Huarte, *Eclipse total de la constitución para la tribu yaqui*, 14; and Evans, "Yaquis vs. Yanquis," 383.

9. Hu-deHart, "Development and Rural Rebellion," 76; Kelley, introduction to *The Tall Candle*, xv.

10. Lorenzo Torres, "Expediente General Campaña del Yaqui," 1901, doc. 1, vol. 1632, AGES.

11. Hu-deHart, "Development and Rural Rebellion," 79. For contemporary ac-counts, see Troncoso, *Las guerras con las tribus yaqui y mayo del estado de Sonora* (a report commissioned by the Mexican Department of War); and Balbás and Hernández, *Crónica de la guerra del Yaqui.* For more on Tetabiate, see Zavala Castro, *El indio Tetabiate y la nación de los ocho pueblos del Río Yaqui.* For further details, see Huarte, *Eclipse total de la constitución para la tribu yaqui.*

12. Quotations from Henry Lane Wilson to Secretary of State Philander Knox, July 5, 1910, in U.S. State Department, Records Relating to the Internal Affairs of Mexico, microfilm roll 206, 812/333, NARA II.

13. W. D. King to Alberto Cubillas, Sept. 4, 1908; and Cubillas to Corral, Sept. 14, 1908, both in CONDUMEX; Padilla Ramos, *Yucatán, el fin del sueño yaqui,* 118–19.

14. Ruiz, *The People of Sonora and Yankee Capitalists*, 178.

15. See, for example, Hu-deHart, *Yaqui Resistance and Survival;* Savala, *The Autobi-ography of a Yaqui Poet;* John Kenneth Turner, *Barbarous Mexico;* Zavala Castro, *El indio Tetabiate y la nación de los ocho pueblos del Río Yaqui;* and Padilla Ramos, *Yucatán, el fin del sueño yaqui.*

16. Izábal correspondence in 1905 and 1906, as quoted in Hu-deHart, "Develop-ment and Rural Rebellion," 83; and Ruiz, *The People of Sonora and Yankee Capitalists*, 181.

17. Izábal to Los Nueve Capitanes Yaquis, Apr. 19, 1904, in Izábal, *Memoria de la administración pública del Estado de Sonora durante el período constitucional de 1903–1907*, 157.

18. Spicer, *The Yaquis*, 160; Padilla Ramos, *Yucatán, el fin del sueño yaqui*, 46. For more on Kosterlitzky, see Truett, "Transnational Warrior"; and C. C. Smith, *Emilio Kosterlitzky*.

19. Spicer, *The Yaquis*, 160; Hu-deHart, "Development and Rural Rebellion," 89; Padilla Ramos, *Yucatán, el fin del sueño yaqui*, 118.

20. Louis Hostetler to Robert Bacon, Assistant Secretary of State, Mar. 16, 1906, Despatches from U.S. Consulate in Hermosillo, M293, Roll 1, RG 59, NARA II.

21. Ibid., Jan. 9, Jan. 12, 1906.

22. Spicer, *The Yaquis*, 158.

23. González Navarro, *La colonización en México, 1877–1910*, 34.

24. Zavala Castro, *El indio Tetabiate y la nación de los ocho pueblos del Río Yaqui*, 186.

25. Troncoso, *Las guerras con las tribus yaqui y mayo del estado de Sonora*, 22, 24.

26. Quotation from Fabila, *Las tribus yaquis de Sonora*, 191; Hu-deHart, "Development and Rural Rebellion," 89.

27. Hu-deHart, *Yaqui Resistance and Survival*, 156.

28. García y Alva, *México y sus progresos*, 12–13.

29. Ruiz, *The People of Sonora and Yankee Capitalists*, 181.

30. Spicer, *Cycles of Conquest*, 80.

31. Savala, *The Autobiography of a Yaqui Poet*, 7.

32. Cosío Villegas, *Historia moderna de México*, vol. 4, *La vida política interior*, 681. See also Hu-deHart, "Sonora," 182.

33. Hu-deHart, "Development and Rural Rebellion," 84, 91. For the earlier annihilation argument, see Savala, *The Autobiography of a Yaqui Poet*, 25.

34. Díaz decree paraphrased in English by John Kenneth Turner, *Barbarous Mexico*, 35. Regarding the 1900 start date, see Padilla Ramos, *Yucatán, el fin del sueño yaqui*, 47; and Cosío Villegas, *Historia moderna de México*, vol. 4, *La vida política interior*, 258–59. Others, such as James C. Carey (*The Mexican Revolution in Yucatán, 1915–1924*, 12), argue for the 1880s; Evelyn Hu-deHart (*Yaqui Resistance and Survival*, 163, 181) states that it was the 1890s for "the most incorrigible of Yaqui leaders" but 1902 for most others. Eduardo Huarte (*Eclipse total de la constitución para la tribu yaqui*, 12) says the slave "experience to Yucatán" started in 1908 with Díaz's decree.

35. Communications quoted in Hu-deHart, "Development and Rural Rebellion," 88.

36. Hu-deHart, "Development and Rural Rebellion," 89; Padilla Ramos, *Yucatán, el fin del sueño yaqui*, 43.

37. Hu-deHart, "Development and Rural Rebellion," 72; John Kenneth Turner, *Barbarous Mexico*, 35.

38. *La revista de Mérida*, June 20, 1900, as quoted in Wells, "*Yucatán:* Violence and Social Control on Henequen Plantations," 227.

39. Zavala Castro, *El indio Tetabiate y la nación de los ocho pueblos del Río Yaqui*, 194.

40. Padilla Ramos, *Yucatán, el fin del sueño yaqui*, 43, 46; *henequenero* statement from *La revista de Mérida*, June 20, 1900, quoted in Wells, *"Yucatán:* Violence and Social Control,"* 227. See also, Wells and Joseph, *Summer of Discontent, Seasons of Upheaval*, 164.

41. Padilla Ramos, *Yucatán, el fin del sueño yaqui*, 116.

42. Quotations from John Kenneth Turner, *Barbarous Mexico*, 36–37. See also Hu-deHart, "Development and Rural Rebellion," 92.

43. Hu-deHart, "Development and Rural Rebellion," 83.

44. John Kenneth Turner, *Barbarous Mexico*, 37.

45. Document 1, vol. 1, 983, Archivo Histórico del Gobierno de Sonora, 1903–1907, AGES; Hu-deHart, "Development and Rural Rebellion," 83.

46. John Kenneth Turner, *Barbarous Mexico*, 36–37; British Anti-Slavery Society information as reported in London *Morning Post*, Aug. 5, 1910, 1.

47. Spicer, introduction to *The Autobiography of a Yaqui Poet* by Savala, xiv; Spicer, *The Yaquis*, 160; Spicer, "Highlights of Yaqui History," 7.

48. Cosío Villegas, *Historia moderna de México*, vol. 4, *La vida social*, 259.

49. Padilla Ramos, *Yucatán, el fin del sueño yaqui*, 81–92, 130; Wells, *Yucatán's Gilded Age*, 165.

50. Joseph, *Revolution from Without*, 66.

51. Document 1, vol. 1, 983, Archivo Histórico del Gobierno de Sonora, 1905, AGES.

52. John Kenneth Turner, *Barbarous Mexico*, 33; Dominga Tava, as told to Kelley, *Yaqui Women*, 78–125.

53. Josefa Morena, as told to Kelley, *Yaqui Women*, 126–53, with quotation from 134.

54. Moisés, Kelley, and Holden, *The Tall Candle*, 25, 30, 31.

55. Velázquez testimony in *Tres procesos de lucha por la sobrevivencia de la tribu yaqui*, 57–63, 85–89; Ramírez testimony in Kelley, *Yaqui Women*, 154–96.

56. Martínez Valdéz testimony in *Tres procesos de lucha por la sobrevivencia de la tribu yaqui*, 109–15.

57. Quoted in John Kenneth Turner, *Barbarous Mexico*, 15–16, 44–47.

58. John Kenneth Turner, *Barbarous Mexico*, 54.

59. Newspaper quoted in Chandler and Frost, *The American Egypt*, 161–62; John Kenneth Turner, *Barbarous Mexico*, 24.

60. Moisés, Kelley, and Holden, *The Tall Candle*, 27. See also, Spicer, *The Yaquis*, 161.

61. Morena quoted in Kelley, *Yaqui Women*, 134.

62. For more on the Catmís uprising, see Chacón, "Yucatán and the Mexican Revolution," 99–100.

63. John Kenneth Turner, *Barbarous Mexico*, 11.

64. For further analysis, see Hu-deHart, "Development and Rural Rebellion," 85; and Joseph, *Rediscovering the Past at Mexico's Periphery*, 80, 106.

65. Huarte, *Eclipse total de la constitución para la tribu yaqui*, 12.

66. Alfredo Breceda to Venustiano Carranza, Feb. 3, 1915, Papers of Venustiano Carranza, fondo XXI-4, CONDUMEX; the Ávila statement is quoted in Chacón,

"Yucatán and the Mexican Revolution," 179–80; Wells and Joseph, *Summer of Discontent, Seasons of Upheaval*, 273, 362n.85.

67. Padilla Ramos, *Yucatán, el fin del sueño yaqui*, 94–95; *Mexican Herald*, Apr. 17, 1915, 4.

68. Hu-deHart, "Development and Rural Rebellion," 85.

69. González Navarro, *Raza y tierra*, 229.

70. Series: Poder Ejecutivo, Gobierno, 1913, box 485, AGEY; Spicer mentions 1910 as the beginning of the end of Yaqui slavery (Spicer, introduction to *The Autobiography of a Yaqui Poet*, by Savala, iv); others like Carey (*Mexican Revolution in Yucatán*, 12) suggest it was more like 1915, the year that Carranza's forces invaded Yucatán.

71. See "Liberacion de los servientes endeudados, 11 de septiembre de 1914" in the documentary appendix of González Navarro, *Raza y tierra*, 329–33.

72. The 1914 document is in series: Poder Ejecutivo, Gobierno 1914, box 462, AGEY. (I thank Paul Eiss for bringing it to my attention.)

73. Padilla Ramos, *Yucatán, el fin del sueño yaqui*, 100, 156. Spicer writes that by the 1930s there was no trace of Yaquis left in Yucatán. Many had died, others reportedly had fled to the jungles of Tabasco, and some had made their way back to Sonora (Spcier, *The Yaquis*, 161).

74. *Tombstone Prospector*, July 26, 1911, 1.

75. Statement of Dr. Víctor A. Rendón in U.S. Senate Subcommittee on Agriculture and Forestry, "Hearings on Importation of Sisal and Manila Hemp," Feb. 17, 1916, 5.

76. *Mexican Herald*, Mar. 11, 1915, 4.

77. *Excélsior*, Jan. 4, 1918, 1, 4.

78. González Navarro, *Raza y tierra*, 239; *Excélsior*, Jan. 9, 1918, 2.

79. *Excélsior*, Jan. 12, 1918, 8; Jan. 29, 1918, 1; *El diario de Yucatán*, Aug. 4, 1936, 1.

80. Guzmán, *The Eagle and the Serpent*, 46–47.

81. Spicer, *The Yaquis*, 160–61; Ramírez quoted in Kelley, *Yaqui Women*, 194–95; Hu-deHart, "Development and Rural Rebellion," 92, 83, respectively; Hu-deHart, *Yaqui Resistance and Survival*, 155.

82. Wording of the common thought is from Zavala Castro, *El indio Tetabiate y la nación de los ocho pueblos del Río Yaqui*, 188. Some scholars might question that logic, however. Ramón Ruiz has argued that "Yankee speculation, the railroad particularly, and the lure of markets across the border affected the Yaqui wars but did not cause them. Sooner or later the *yori's* [the Yaqui term for Mexicans] hunger for fertile, well-watered lands would have led him to take them by force" (Ruiz, *The People of Sonora and Yankee Capitalists*, 181–82).

83. Hart, *Revolutionary Mexico*, 351; Hu-deHart, "Sonora," 182; Ruiz, *The People of Sonora and Yankee Capitalists*, 181; McGuire, *Politics and Ethnicity on the Río Yaqui*, 31. For a more thorough discussion of U.S. investments in the Yaqui Valley, see Dabdoub, *Historia de el Valle del Yaqui*. For the long-range environmental implications in comparative context, see Evans, "Yaquis vs. Yanquis." Baerlein's quote is from *Mexico, the Land of Unrest*, 157.

84. Troncoso, *Las guerras con las tribus yaqui y mayo del estado de Sonora*, 22.

85. The various plans and promotional literature for Yaqui Valley development are in the Papers of the Compañía Constructora Richardson, University of Arizona Special Collections, Tucson. For further information and analysis, see Evans, "Yaquis vs. Yanquis."

86. Ruiz, *The People of Sonora and Yankee Capitalists*, 144; Bassols Batalla, *El noroeste de México*, 610; Sanderson, *The Transformation of Mexican Agriculture*, 5. For more on the agricultural history of Sonora, see Sanderson, *Agrarian Populism and the Mexican State*. For more on the impact of the dams, see Dozier, "Mexico's Transformed Northwest," and Evans, *Damming Sonora*.

87. Sevilla Mascarenas, *Aquí Sonora, S.O.S*, 109–10; Ruiz, *The People of Sonora and Yankee Capitalists*, 146; Dabdoub, *Historia de el Valle del Yaqui*, 3. See also García y Alva's *México y sus progresos* for a contemporary account of Sonora's agricultural modernization.

88. Departamento de Estadística Nacional, *Sonora, Sinaloa, y Nayarit: estudio estadístico y económico social, 1927–28*, 151–52.

89. "Annual Report, Despatches from U.S. Consulate in Guaymas, Mexico," Dec. 31, 1888, M284, roll 4, RG 59, NARA II.

90. Alexander A. Willard, U.S. Consul in Guaymas, to U.S. Department of State, Nov. 25, 1890, M284, roll 4, RG 59, NARA II.

91. García y Alva, *México y sus progresos*, 174.

92. I thank Terry Rugeley for making this facet of the henequen-wheat complex triangle more obvious to me.

93. Valentín Gaubeca (IH Mexico, S.A.) to John Dierbeck (IH, Chicago), Oct. 15, 1973, and pamphlet, "Harvester in Mexico," both in file 08850, International Harvester records, IHCA/Navistar; Swift, "Farm Machines in Mexico," 27.

94. Hu-deHart, "Development and Rural Rebellion," 91.

95. Casson, *Romance of the Reaper*, 159.

96. For further analysis on this contradiction, see Ramos Padilla, *Yucatán, el fin del sueño yaqui*, 158.

97. See especially Wells, *Yucatán's Gilded Age*, 164; Chardon, *Geographic Aspects of Plantation Agriculture in Yucatán*, 33; Askinasy, *El problema agrario de Yucatán*, 100–103; and Betancourt Pérez, *Revoluciones y crisis en la economía de Yucatán*, 73; also, Antochiw interview by author.

98. Snow, introduction to *Barbarous Mexico*, ix.

99. See Ruiz, *The People of Sonora and Yankee Capitalists*, 178, and Snow, introduction to *Barbarous Mexico*, xvii–xix, for more information and examples.

100. Marc M. Reynolds, "The Scourge of the Yaquis," undated article from *Harper's Weekly*, a portion of which was reproduced in Padilla Ramos, *Yucatán, fin del sueño yaqui*, 126–27.

101. For more on this incident in 1918, see Katz, *The Secret War in Mexico*, 502.

Chapter 4

1. The 90 percent figure is in the deposition of Horace Daniels, manager of International Harvester Fibre Department, in a statement for *International Harvester*

Company vs. Republic of Mexico before the General Claims Commission, July 3, 1926, 1, file 04192, IHCA/Navistar. The 200 million pounds figure was stated by Secretary of Agriculture David Houston and reported in the *Sioux Falls Argus Leader,* Mar. 15, 1915, 1.

2. Joseph, *Revolution from Without,* 6, 13.

3. See Joseph, *Revolution from Without,* 6.

4. Venustiano Carranza to Toribio de los Santos, Feb. 11, 1915; Carranza to Gabriel Calzada, Feb. 11, 1915, in Papers of Venustiano Carranza, fondo XXI-4, CONDUMEX (hereafter cited as Carranza Papers, CONDUMEX).

5. For the complete records of how IH accomplished these maneuvers, see the statements and depositions of their agents in file 04192, IHCA/Navistar.

6. Carranza to Alvarado, Feb. 16, 1915, file 04192, IHCA/Navistar.

7. The authoritative work on the topic is Joseph's *Revolution from Without.* See also Carey, *The Mexican Revolution in Yucatán, 1915–1924.*

8. Ignacio Magallón et al. to Carranza, Feb. 3, 1915; Luis Andrade to Carranza, Feb. 3, 1915; Calzada to Carranza, Feb. 5, 1915; Heriberto Barrón to Carranza, Feb. 6, 1915, all in Carranza Papers, CONDUMEX.

9. *New York Times,* Mar. 21, 1915, 11.

10. Salvador Alvarado to Carranza, Feb. 13, 1915, Carranza Papers, CONDUMEX. See also Joseph, *Revolution from Without,* 8.

11. Alvarado to Carranza, Feb. 11, 1915; Carranza to Alvarado, Feb. 12, 1915, both in Carranza Papers, CONDUMEX.

12. Alvarado to Carranza, two different communiqués, Feb. 13, 1915, Carranza Papers, CONDUMEX.

13. Carranza to Alvarado, Feb. 14, 15, 1915, both in Carranza Papers, CONDU-MEX.

14. Carranza to Alvarado, Feb. 17, 1915; Alvarado to Carranza, Feb. 17, 1915, both in Carranza Papers, CONDUMEX.

15. Carranza to Alvarado, Mar. 8, 10, 13, 1915; Carranza to Arturo Lapham, Mar. 26, 1915, all in Carranza Papers, CONDUMEX.

16. Carranza to Alvarado, Mar. 13, 1915, Carranza Papers, CONDUMEX.

17. Deposition of Eduardo Robleda, former manager for House of Montes, as testimony in *International Harvester Company vs. Republic of Mexico* before the General Claims Commission, Aug. 15, 1925, 2, file 04192, IHCA/Navistar.

18. Various messages from Royal Bank of Belgium to Carranza, Feb. 20 and 21, 1915; Belgian governor Wilfrid Collet to Carranza, Mar. 17, 1915, both in *International Harvester Company vs. Republic of Mexico,* file 04192, IHCA/Navistar.

19. Link, *Wilson: The Struggle for Neutrality, 1914–1915,* 462; Clements, "'A Kindness to Carranza,'" 483.

20. *Topeka Daily Capital,* Feb. 14, 1915, 10–11; Feb. 16, 1915, 3; *Manitoba Free Press,* Mar. 22, 1915, 10.

21. *New York Times,* Mar. 24, 1915, 7.

22. *Topeka Daily Capital,* Mar. 2, 1915, 1; *New York Times,* Mar. 24, 1915, 1.

23. Joseph, *Revolution from Without,* 154; Link, *Wilson: The Struggle for Neutrality, 1914–1915,* 457.

24. *Topeka Daily Capital,* Mar. 2, 1915, 1; Mar. 7, 1915, 2; *Grand Forks Weekly Times-Herald,* Mar. 11, 1915, 1, 4.

25. Depositions of Michael J. Smith, June 2, 1926, 6–7, and William R. O'Dell Jr., Feb. 10, 1954, 1, respectively, taken by the General Claims Commission for *International Harvester Company vs. Republic of Mexico,* in file 04192, IHCA/Navistar.

26. Willis Brown, quoted in *Topeka Daily Capital,* Feb. 4, 1915, 12.

27. J. N. Amador to Carranza, Mar. 6, 1915; Carranza to Amador, Mar. 7, 1915; Carranza to Aristarco Acereto, Mar. 6, 1915, Carranza Papers, CONDUMEX.

28. The standard biographies of Bryan are by LeRoy Ashby, Donald K. Springen, Robert Cherney, David D. Anderson, Paxton Hibben, Lawrence W. Levine, Paolo E. Coletta, and Kendrick A. Clements. See also Merle Eugene Curti's *Bryan and World Peace* and *The Memoirs of William Jennings Bryan,* by Bryan with Mary Baird Bryan.

29. Kaplan, *U.S. Imperialism in Latin America,* 25; quotations from Link, *Wilson the Diplomatist,* 26, 28, 22, 23, respectively.

30. Kaplan, *U.S. Imperialism in Latin America,* 25. Another historian, however, gives Bryan much more credit. Louis W. Koenig asserts that "Bryan was the architect of American policy toward Mexico in the administration's early years" (*Bryan,* 517).

31. Clements, "'A Kindness to Carranza,'" 479, 480. For the campaign contribution information, see Link, *Wilson: The Road to the White House,* 403.

32. Clements, "'A Kindness to Carranza,'" 479.

33. The meeting of cordage industry representatives in Washington was reported in the *Topeka Daily Capital,* Mar. 7, 1915, 2. See also Joseph, *Revolution from Without,* 154. Statement about the Michigan prison twine plant is from Clyde Bennett to Preston Clark, Mar. 26, 1915, Plymouth Cordage Records, envelope 1, IHCA/Navistar. Capper information is from Arthur Capper to Woodrow Wilson, Mar. 2, 1915, Records of the Governor's Office, Arthur Capper Administration (cited hereafter as Governor's Records–Capper), folder 264, box 4, KSHS. After two terms as governor (1915–1919) during which Capper headed a Belgian relief movement in Kansas, urged people to plant a vegetable garden in every yard and vacant lot, asked all state citizens to conserve food, and appointed a State Agricultural Defense Council to work with the U.S. Department of Agriculture on the war conservation effort, he was elected to five terms as U.S. senator from Kansas (1919–1949).

34. William Jennings Bryan to Capper, Mar. 12, 1915, Governor's Records–Capper, folder 264, box 4, KSHS.

35. Link, *Wilson: The Struggle for Neutrality,* 462.

36. Link, *Wilson the Diplomatist,* 24.

37. Bryan and Wilson correspondence quoted in Clements, "'A Kindness to Carranza,'" 482.

38. For more details, see Link, *Wilson: The Struggle for Neutrality,* 460–63.

39. Cabinet meeting details reported in the *Sioux Falls Argus Leader,* Mar. 15, 1915, 1.

40. Wilson to Bryan, Mar. 12, 1915, Letters 1914–1915, box 45, Papers of William Jennings Bryan, Manuscript Collections, Library of Congress (cited hereafter as Bryan Papers, LC).

41. Bryan to Wilson, Mar. 13, 1915, Bryan Papers, LC.

42. Link, *Wilson: The Struggle for Neutrality*, 462–63; Clements, "'A Kindness to Carranza,'" 485–86.

43. Wilson statement quoted in Kaplan, *U.S. Imperialism in Latin America*, 26.

44. Ibid., 28–29.

45. All quotations from Kaplan, *U.S. Imperialism in Latin America*, 27, 30.

46. Clements, *William Jennings Bryan*, 47, 49.

47. Link, *Wilson: The Struggle for Neutrality*, 463.

48. Quotations from *New York Times*, Mar. 18, 1915, 5.

49. Carranza to General Arturo Garcilazo, Mar. 18, 1915, Carranza Papers, CONDUMEX.

50. *New York Times*, Mar. 16, 1915, 1; Mar. 18, 1915, 5; Mar. 17, 1915, 1 (respectively).

51. *Sioux Falls Argus-Leader*, Mar. 15, 1915, 1; Mar. 16, 1915, 1; *Topeka Daily Capital*, Mar. 15, 1915, 1; Mar. 16, 1915, 9; *Wichita Daily Eagle*, Mar. 16, 1915, 2.

52. *Kansas City Star*, Mar. 15, 1915, 1; *Fargo Forum*, Mar. 15, 1915, 1; *Bismarck Daily Tribune*, Mar. 16, 1915, 1; *Grand Forks Weekly Times-Herald*, Mar. 18, 1915, 6.

53. *Calgary Daily Herald*, Mar. 15, 1915, 1.

54. *Nebraska Farmer*, Mar. 24, 1915, 383.

55. Joseph, *Revolution from Without*, 155; H.W. Peabody Co. to Arturo Price (in Mérida), Mar. 31, 1915, envelope 8, H.W. Peabody Files, IHCA/Navistar.

56. Peoria Cordage Co. to William Jennings Bryan, Mar. 19, 1915; Hooven and Allison Company to Bryan, Mar. 19, 1915; John Rausehenberger Company to Bryan, Mar. 19, 1915, U.S. State Department, Records Relating to the Internal Affairs of Mexico 1910–1929, microfilm roll 206 (hereafter cited as USSD), 812.61326/12–18, 26, 33, NARA II.

57. Warden J. D. Botkin to Bryan, Mar. 19, 1915; Warden E. J. Fogarty to Bryan, Mar. 19, 1915; Warden C. S. Reed to Bryan, Mar. 19, 1915; Whitlock Cordage Co. to Bryan, Mar. 19, 1915; Whitlock Cordage Co. to Bryan, Mar. 22, 1915; Columbian Rope Co. to Bryan, Mar. 19, 1915, all in USSD, 812.61326/12–18, 26, 33.

58. Hatfield and Palmer Co. to U.S. State Department, Mar. 19, 1915; Wall Rope Works to Bryan, Mar. 19, 1915; New Bedford Cordage Co. to Bryan, Mar. 19, 1915, USSD, 812.61326/20–23.

59. Bryan to Peoria Cordage Co., Mar. 20, 1915; Bryan to U.S. Consul in Progreso, Mar. 20, 1915; Alvey A. Adee to Hatfield and Palmer Co., Mar. 20, 1915, all in USSD, 812.61326/12, 42a, 20.

60. Bryan to Silliman, Mar. 20, 1915; Silliman to Bryan, Mar. 24, 1915, both in USSD, 812.61336/29a, 45; Arredondo to Carranza, Mar. 24, 1915, Carranza Papers, CONDUMEX.

61. Alvarado to Carranza, Mar. 24, 1915, Carranza Papers, CONDUMEX; Joseph, *Revolution from Without*, 155.

62. Edward H. Filler Co. to Bryan, Mar. 16, 1915, USSD, 812.61326/19.

63. *New York Times*, Mar. 18, 1915, 5; Mar. 19, 1915, 6. Wilson's message is from State Department records cited in Joseph, *Revolution from Without*, 155.

64. Joseph writes that "this episode of gunboat diplomacy was prompted less by a fear of burned fields and more by Alvarado's takeover of the railroad system and his obvious intention to oust Montes-Harvester and Peabody from the state." He concluded that "the Wilson government's haste in summoning a gunboat gave credence to Montes's claim of influence and suggests the effectiveness of Harvester's brand of informal empire based on tested collaborator networks" (*Revolution from Without*, 155, 156).

65. *Washington Post*, Mar. 24, 1915, 1; International Harvester to Bryan, Mar. 23, 1915; Bryan to Silliman, Mar. 22, 1915; International Harvester to Bryan, Mar. 25, 1915, all in USSD, 812.61326/32, 24, 51 (respectively).

66. *Washington Post*, Mar. 24, 1915, 1.

67. From reports in the *New York Herald*, Mar. 24, 1915, 1; *Washington Post*, Mar. 24, 1915, 1; *New York Times*, Mar. 24, 1915, 7; *Bismarck Daily Tribune*, Mar. 24, 1915, 1; *Fargo Forum*, Mar. 24, 1915, 5.

68. *Bismarck Daily Tribune*, Mar. 31, 1915, 4.

69. *New York Sun*, Mar. 26, 1915, 1.

70. Spring Rice to the Right Honourable Sir Edward Grey, Apr. 1, 1915, and Mar. 24, 1915, Ministry of External Affairs, RG 25, series A-3-a, vol. 1161, file 1915–572-c, NAC.

71. Spring Rice to Bryan, Mar. 24, 1915, Ministry of External Affairs, RG 25, series A-3-a, vol. 1161, file 1915–572-c, NAC.

72. *Bismarck Daily Tribune*, Mar. 23, 1915, 1; *Toronto Globe*, Mar. 23, 1915, 13.

73. Spring Rice to Governor General, Mar. 23, 1915, Ministry of External Affairs, RG 25, series A-3-a, vol. 1161, file 1915–572-c, NAC.

74. Miscellaneous telegrams to Bryan, Mar. 18–April 1, 1915, USSD, 812.61326/56, 55, 43, 67, 30, 31, 56a (respectively).

75. Spring Rice to Grey, Mar. 24, 1915, Mar. 26, 1915, Mar. 31, 1915, Ministry of External Affairs, RG 25, series A-3-a, vol. 1161, file 1915–572-c, NAC.

76. Spring Rice to Gray, Apr. 1, 1915, Ministry of External Affairs, RG 25, series A-3-a, vol. 1161, file 1915–572-c, NAC.

77. Arredondo quoted in Joseph, *Revolution from Without*, 156; Clements, "'A Kindness to Carranza,'" 485.

78. Arredondo quoted in Joseph, *Revolution from Without*, 156; Joseph, *Revolution from Without*, 155.

79. Bryan to American Legation in Havana, Mar. 25, 1915, USSD, 812.61326/55a; Bryan to American Legation in Havana, Mar. 22, 1915, Letters 1914–1915, box 45, Bryan Papers, LC.

80. American Legation in Havana to Bryan, Apr. 3, 1915, USSD, 812.61326/71.

81. Carranza statement reported in the Mérida newspaper *La voz de la revolución*, Mar. 29, 1915, 1; Carranza to Arturo Lapham, Mar. 26, 1915, Carranza Papers, CONDUMEX; Bryan to Gronna, Apr. 5, 1915; Bryan to Redfield, Mar. 31, 1915, both in USSD, 812.61326/69, 104.

82. Bryan to Wilson, Apr. 8, 1915; Wilson to Bryan, Apr. 8, 1915, both in Letters 1914–1915, box 45, Bryan Papers, LC.

83. *Syracuse Journal*, Apr. 3, 1915, 1; Alex Legge to Bryan, Apr. 14, 1915, USSD, 206, 812.61326/80.

84. Memorandum, Apr. 20, 1915, USSD, 206.61326/81.

85. *New York Times*, July 18, 1915, 1; *New York Herald*, July 18, 1915, 1.

86. U.S. Navy to Secretary of State, n.d., USSD, 812.61326/126.

87. U.S. Department of Agriculture, *Wheat*, 2, 10–11.

88. Fowke, *The National Policy and the Wheat Economy*, 78; Thompson, *Harvests of War*, 68. Crop figures are from Statistics Canada as reprinted in Charles F. Wilson, *A Century of Canadian Grain*, 182.

89. M. N. Campbell to Motherwell, Aug. 20, 1915; Brink and Agar to Motherwell, Aug. 24, 1915; Motherwell to Brink and Agar, Aug. 24, 1915; and IH to Motherwell, Aug. 24, 1915, file II.117, Motherwell Papers, SAB-R.

90. IH request quoted in Joseph, *Revolution from Without*, 343n.15.

91. Link, *Wilson the Diplomatist*, 4.

92. William Jennings Bryan, "On Food Conservation" (speech delivered in Houston, Tex., Oct. 29, 1917), MS464, series 6, folder 13, box 3, William Jennings Bryan Papers, NSHS.

93. Bryan to Wilson, May 22, 1915; Wilson to Bryan, May 23, 1915, Letters of 1914–1915, box 45, Bryan Papers, LC.

94. Kaplan, *U.S. Imperialism in Latin America*, 1, 4. Louis Koenig surprisingly named his chapter on the history of Bryan in the State Department, "A Pacifist Secretary of State" (*Bryan*, 502). Bryan never used the term pacifist to describe himself, and his policies were more pacifistic in theory than in practice. For more on Bryan's contradictory philosophies, see Curti, *Bryan and World Peace*.

95. Bryan to Wilson, June 14, 1914, Letters of 1913–1914, box 45, Bryan Papers, LC. In the letter, Bryan suggested that the additional ships might be necessary for evacuating Americans from the area if the crisis worsened, but having more warships off the coast of Mexico could very well have worsened the scenario if the Mexicans perceived that Americans were saber rattling.

96. Bryan to Wilson, Mar. 23, 1915, Letters 1914–1915, box 45, Bryan Papers, LC.

97. *The Commoner*, Sept. 1915, 1.

98. Levine, *Defender of the Faith, William Jennings Bryan*, vii–viii.

99. Clements, "'A Kindness to Carranza,'" 487.

100. Link, *Wilson the Diplomatist*, 6–7, 20.

101. Wilson quoted in *New York Times*, June 3, 1915, 1.

102. Ibid. Arthur Link described this statement as Wilson's "tendency to take insufficient account of hard realities and to oversimplify the complexities of international life." It was his "Pharasaism," as Link called it: "too much introspective concern about standards, right conduct . . . [so that] his motives and purposes were purer than those of the men with whom he happened to be contending" (*Wilson the Diplomatist*, 20).

103. Katz, "Pancho Villa and the Attack on Columbus, New Mexico," 102.

104. For the best American accounts, see Katz, *The Life and Times of Pancho Villa*; Katz, "Pancho Villa and the Attack on Columbus, New Mexico"; Harris and Sadler,

"Pancho Villa and the Columbus Raid"; Braddy, *Pershing's Mission in Mexico;* Clendenen, *The United States and Pancho Villa;* and Vandiver, *Black Jack.*

105. Levine, *Defender of the Faith, William Jennings Bryan,* 79.

106. As Joseph has pointed out, "Gunboat diplomacy was falling into disrepute, even among the British, who found it simply no longer got the job done. Overt displays of violence were now regarded as admissions of failure, anachronistic nineteenth-century tactics inadequate in the management of twentieth-century empires that often did not include formally annexed colonies" (*Revolution from Without,* 157).

107. For an authoritative analysis on the legal history of "no duty to retreat" and how the concept had been applied to U.S. foreign relations, see Richard Maxwell Brown's *No Duty to Retreat,* chap. 4.

108. *Bismarck Daily Tribune,* Mar. 30, 1915, 1.

Chapter 5

1. See Miller and Greiser, "The Evolution of Prison Industries," 1–2.

2. For additional analysis besides Foucault, *Discipline and Punish: The Birth of the Prison,* see Melossi and Pavarini, *The Prison and the Factory;* van Zyl Smit and Dünkel, eds., *Prison Labour;* L. N. Robinson, *Should Prisoners Work;* and Simon, *Prisoners' Work and Vocational Training.* For a specifically sociological analysis of prison labor in Canada, see R. Evans Jr., *Prison Industries in the Canadian Penitentiary Service: A Survey Prepared for the Honourable George J. McIlraith, Solicitor General of Canada;* and Foucauld, "Prison Labour, Punishment, or Reform."

3. For analysis on how prison industries' marketplace activity squares with the "capitalist industrial system" through "exploitation of prisoners," see Melossi and Pavarini, *The Prison and the Factory,* 137, and Lightman, "Industrial Work by Inmates in Correctional Facilities."

4. For more information, see Mancini, *One Dies, Get Another;* Walker, *Penology for Profit;* and Lichtenstein, *Twice the Work of Free Labor.* For analysis of a western state's prison labor, see McGinn, *At Hard Labor.*

5. See Gildemeister, "Prison Labor and Convict Competition with Free Workers in Industrializing America, 1840–1890" (cited hereafter as "Prison Labor and Convict Competition"). For analysis of the differentiation between different types of contract and lease systems, including the "piece price" method, see Miller and Greiser, "The Evolution of Prison Industries," 4.

6. See Shapiro, *A New South Rebellion.*

7. For further information, see Gildemeister, "Prison Labor and Convict Competition," 249. On the end of the contract lease system in Canada, see Hennessy, *Canada's Big House,* 69.

8. Berkovits, "'Us Poor Devils,'" 90, 97. See also Gildemeister, "Prison Labor and Convict Competition," 1.

9. The policy was further solidified in 1920 when a royal commission recommended to the federal government that prison-made products be marketed only at other government institutions and that they not compete against private industry in the free market. The cabinet passed an order to that effect in 1921 (Berkovits, "'Us

Poor Devils,'" 110n.1; Hennessy, *Canada's Big House,* 69). For more on union opposition, see Melossi and Pavarini, *The Prison and the Factory,* 138–41; and Gildemeister, "Prison Labor and Convict Competition." For more on the Kingston mailbag repair service, see Curtis et al., *Kingston Penitentiary,* 67.

10. L. N. Robinson, *Should Prisoners Work?* 1; and Lightman, "Industrial Work by Inmates," 7

11. National Center for Policy Analysis, "Factories behind Bars," 3.

12. Lightman, "Industrial Work by Inmates," 8.

13. Albert Garvin (warden, Stillwater State Prison) to James Moylan (Inspector of Prisons, Ottawa), Apr. 25, 1892; Henry Wolfer (warden, Stillwater State Prison) to Moylan, Jan. 21, 1893, Binder Twine Kingston Penitentiary, RG: 13, series D-1, vol. 1027, file 39, NAC.

14. Minnesota Farm Machinery Catalog, 1915, 36, RG Stillwater State Prison, series: Prison Industries, 118.B.11.2F, box 1, MHS.

15. Minnesota Prison Industries, Statement of Profits Transferred to Revolving Fund, RG Stillwater State Prison, Annual Statements, MHS; legislative manual statement quoted in McMahon, "Industrial Training," 21; *pencas* information from Minutes of the Twine Conference, July 23, 1915, RG Stillwater State Prison, series: Prison Industries, 118.B.11.2F, box 1, MHS.

16. Letters are in Minnesota Farm Machinery Catalogs, 1914–1917; labeling information is from Minutes of the Twine Conference, Mar. 19, 1915, RG Stillwater State Prison, series: Prison Industries, 118.B.11.2F, box 1, MHS.

17. *El henequén* 1 (Dec. 31, 1916): 10–12.

18. Quotations from L. N. Robinson, *Should Prisoners Work?* 77, 50, 229 (respectively).

19. Christianson quoted in L. N. Robinson, *Should Prisoners Work?* 130; L. N. Robinson, *Should Prisoners Work?* 276.

20. Berkovits, "'Us Poor Devils,'" 100. See also Berkovits, "Prisoners for Profit."

21. *Peterborough Daily Examiner,* Sept. 13, 1894, 1.

22. Berkovits, "'Us Poor Devils,'" 94, 100. For more on the harshness of the Central Prison, see Oliver, *"Terror to Evil-Doers."*

23. Oliver, *"Terror to Evil-Doers,"* 114; Berkovits, "'Us Poor Devils,'" 104–106; limestone saying quoted in Hennessy, *Canada's Big House,* 11. For more on Kingston, see Neufeld, "A World within Itself"; and Curtis et al., *Kingston Penitentiary.*

24. Foucauld, "Prison Labour, Punishment, and Reform," 116; Curtis et al., *Kingston Penitentiary,* 62.

25. Garvin to Moylan, Apr. 25, 1892; Wolfer to Moylan, Jan. 23, 1893, both in Binder Twine Kingston Penitentiary, RG 13, series D-1, vol. 1027, file 39, NAC.

26. Lavell to Moylan, May 18, 1893, Binder Twine Kingston Penitentiary, RG 13, series D-1, vol. 1027, file 39, NAC; Berkovits, "'Us Poor Devils,'" 100, 109–110n.1.

27. Correspondence, notices, and clippings are in Binder Twine Kingston Penitentiary, RG 13, series D-1, vol. 1027, file 39, NAC.

28. Berkovits, "'Us Poor Devils,'" 109n.1. For more on the inquiry, see Canada, Parliament, *The Action of the Government in Respect to the Manufacture and Sale of Twine Produced by Convict Labour,* Sessional Paper No. 18a.

29. Warden's statement quoted in Berkovits, "'Us Poor Devils,'" 109n.1.

30. Reported in *El agricultor* 1, no. 4 (Apr. 1, 1907): 54.

31. Production information from "Production (Approximate) State Prison Binder Twine Plants," International Harvester Co. Records, M95–262, folder 3, box 20, McCormick–International Harvester Collection, SHSW; spinner information from correspondence included in Gov. Robert Williams, "State of the State Message to the Fifth Legislature of the State of Oklahoma," Jan. 17, 1916, www.odl.state.ok.us./oar/governors/addresses/williams1916, 18–23 (cited hereafter as Williams, "State of the State Message").

32. I thank Geoff Cunfer at the University of Saskatchewan for bringing this point to my attention.

33. The Iowa and Nebraska "preparations" were mentioned in *El agricultor* 1, no. 4 (Apr. 1, 1907): 56.

34. *Regina Leader,* June 27, 1892, 4.

35. Quotation from Evans, "Prison-Made Binder Twine," 22–23.

36. Correspondence in Williams, "State of the State Message," 18–23. For more on the history of Oklahoma prisoners at the Kansas prison and why Oklahomans were in such a hurry to get them back to their state, see Hougen, "The Impact of Politics and Prison Industry in the General Management of the Kansas State Penitentiary, 1883–1909."

37. Kansas governor's quotation and other information from www.kslib.info/ref/message/bailey/1903/html;Warden, South Dakota State Penitentiary, to Robert Williams, Governor of Oklahoma, Oct. 2, 1915, in Williams, "State of the State Message," 23; Oklahoma information is from *Lingo-Leeper Lumber Co. v. Carter, State Auditor,* 1932 OK 735 17, p. 2d 365, Case #: 23825, decided Nov. 15, 1932, Supreme Court of Oklahoma.

38. Carlson, "Prison Industries," 12.

39. Warden's Report of Installation of Cordage and Twine Plant at State Penitentiary, Dec. 31, 1900; John J. Lee, "A General Description of the North Dakota Twine and Cordage Plant," 1925, both in North Dakota Archives, 365.65, N814tr, 1900, 1925, SHSND; C. F. Fein to Davis, June 21, 1923, Governor's Records–Davis, folder 5, box 6, KSHS.

40. Minnesota figures reported in *El agricultor* 1, no. 4 (Apr. 1, 1907): 56; Warden, South Dakota State Penitentiary, to Robert Williams, Governor of Oklahoma, Oct. 20, 1913, and Warden, Kansas State Penitentiary to Williams, Oct. 9, 1913, both in Williams, "State of the State Message," 19–20.

41. Warden's Report of Operation of Twine and Cordage Plant at State Penitentiary, Biennial Period 1901–1902; Lee, "A General Description of the North Dakota Twine and Cordage Plant"; Biennial Report of the North Dakota Twine and Cordage Plant, 1920–22, all in North Dakota Archives, 365.65 N814tr 1900, 1925, 1920–22, SHSND.

42. Information and brochure quotations are from Evans, "Prison-Made Binder Twine," 25.

43. Warden J. D. Botkin to Greeley Milling Co., June 17 1914, Governor's Records–Hodges, folder 1, box 6; Willis Brown, in Proceedings of the Board of

Corrections, 1915, Governor's Records–Capper, folder 179, box 3, both in KSHS; L. N. Robinson, *Should Prisoners Work?* 280.

44. O. S. Swenson, Twelfth Biennial Report, June 30, 1912, 16; Swenson, Thirteenth Biennial Report, June 30, 1914, 153–54, in South Dakota State Board of Charities and Corrections Biennial Reports: Reports of the State Penitentiary (Sioux Falls), South Dakota Archives, SDSHS.

45. *El agricultor* 1, no. 4 (Apr. 1, 1907): 54; 1, no. 10 (Oct. 1, 1907): 157; *El henequén* 1, no. 24 (Jan. 31, 1916): 10.

46. Warden's Report of Operation of Twine and Cordage Plant at State Penitentiary, Biennial Period 1901–1902, North Dakota Archives, 365.65, N814tr 1901–02, 7–9, SHSND.

47. Hougen, "The Impact of Politics and Prison Industry," 313.

48. The letters are compiled in a file of prison records: Minutes of Farm Machinery Conference, Mar. 15, 1915, RG Stillwater State Prison, series: Prison Industries, 118.B.11.2F, box 2, MHS.

49. L. N. Robinson, *Should Prisoners Work?* 54, 71. Robinson reported that other minor industries adversely affected included furniture, farm machinery (from Minnesota), boots and shoes, brooms and brushes, harnesses and whips, cooperage, hosiery, and inexpensive clothing.

50. Information and quotations from Hennessy, *Canada's Big House,* 76–77.

51. "Prisoners' Insurrection in the Twine Shop," report in RG Stillwater State Prison, series: Prison Industries, 118.B.11.2F, box 1, MHS.

52. Berkovits, "'Us Poor Devils,'" 96.

53. Greening, "The Making of a Community"; "City Started Century with Era of Change," *Michigan City News-Dispatch,* Nov. 17, 2004, at www.michigancityin.com/articles/2004/11/17/a_look_back/back1900.txt.

54. *Kansas City Star,* Apr. 12, 1913, 1; Hodge quoted in *Topeka Daily Capital,* Apr. 12, 1913, 1. I have analyzed this incident more thoroughly in Evans, "From Kanasín to Kansas."

55. *Topeka Daily Capital,* Apr. 12, 1913, 1. The damage account is from J. D. Botkin, "Facts about the Prison Twine Mill," June 30, 1915, Governor's Records–Capper, folder 264, box 4, KSHS.

56. J. K. Codding to Governor Hodges, Apr. 15, 1913; Hodges to James Orr, May 28, 1914; Codding to Purchasers, Apr. 16, 1913, all in Governor's Records–Hodges, folder 1, box 6, KSHS.

57. *Star* article quoted in R. C. Haskins (IH president) to W. L. Brown (Board of Corrections member), Apr. 16, 1913, Governor's Records–Hodges, folder 1, box 6, KSHS.

58. Haskins to Brown, Apr. 16, 1913; George L. Rice to R. C. Haskins, Apr. 16, 1913, both in Governor's Records–Hodges, folder 1, box 6, KSHS.

59. Codding to Hodges, Apr. 16, 1913; Hodges to Codding, May 22, 1913, both in Governor's Records–Hodges, folder 1, box 6, KSHS.

60. Socolofsky, *Kansas Governors,* 142.

61. Executive Clerk to Codding, May 14, 1913; Codding to Hodges, June 6, 1913, both in Governor's Records–Hodges, folder 1, box 6, KSHS.

62. Cashier, Kansas State Penitentiary Twine Plant, to Robert Williams, Governor of Oklahoma, Oct. 9, 1913, in Williams, "State of the State Message," 20.

63. Botkin to Hodges, Dec. 29, 1913, and Jan. 19, 1914, in Williams, "State of the State Message," 20; factory output figures from Botkin, "Facts about the Prison Twine Mill."

64. U.S. Department of Agriculture, *Wheat,* 11; Federal Writers' Project, Work Projects Administration, *Kansas,* 70.

65. Botkin, "Facts about the Prison Twine Mill."

66. Ibid.; Botkin to Manager, Greeley Milling Co., June 17, 1914, Governor's Records–Hodges, folder 1, box 6, KSHS.

67. Richmond, *Kansas,* 205–206.

68. Board of Corrections Proceedings, 1915, folder 179, box 3; Official Report of State Accounts Relating to the State Penitentiary, June 1914–July 1916, folder 33-A, box 7; J. K. Codding to Capper, July 28, 1916, folder 301, box 9, all in Governor's Records–Capper, KSHS.

69. John Ellenbecker to Capper, Apr. 13, 1914; and J. W. Hazen to Capper, Jan. 28, 1915, folder 264, box 4, both in Governor's Records–Capper, KSHS.

70. Richmond, *Kansas,* 205–206; Evans, "From Kanasín to Kansas," 295. For more on Kansas as the "Wheat State," see Dean, ed., "Wheat Culture in Kansas."

71. Testimony of Mr. Ringsrud, (no first name given), Papers of the Committee to Investigate the State Penitentiary (cited hereafter as Papers of the Investigation)], 1921, vol. III, 32, Manuscript Collection H74.24, South Dakota Archives, SDSHS. For the complete history surrounding this incident, see Evans, "Entwined in Conflict," from which parts of this chapter were extracted.

72. J. T. Belk to Charles Eyeler, Aug. 12, 1920, Papers of the Investigation, vol. IV, 18–19.

73. Belk quoted in Papers of the Investigation, vol. III, 8–9.

74. Lars Larson to Eyeler, n.d.; Gayle Snedacar to Eyeler, Feb. 24, 1920; and statement of Charles Eyeler, all in Papers of the Investigation, vol. IV, 9–10, 5–6, 71 (respectively).

75. John Halverson to Eyeler, Jan. 27, 1921; T. W. Stillwell to Eyeler, Feb. 23, 1920, both in Papers of the Investigation, vol. III, 2, 21–22.

76. From correspondence between Eyler and Norbeck, February–July 1920, Papers of the Investigation, vol. V, 6–12.

77. Testimonies of George Jameson (warden) and A. H. Muchow, Papers of the Investigation, vol. I, 3–6.

78. Testimony of J. S. Noyes, Papers of the Investigation, vol. I, 47.

79. Testimony of Mr. Day (no first name given), Papers of the Investigation, vol. III, 17.

80. Schell, *History of South Dakota,* 272.

81. Testimonies of various convicts and Superintendent Noyes are from Papers of the Investigation, vol. I, 33–34, 99, 107, 171–72.

82. Statements of State Examiner Leonard Shagar and Samuel Torgeson, Papers of the Investigation, vol. IV, 70–71, 78–79.

83. *Sioux Falls Argus-Leader,* Feb. 7, 1921, 1.

84. Minutes of Farm Machinery Conference, Feb. 17, 1925, Minnesota State Archives, RG: Stillwater State Prison, series: Prison Industries, 118.B.11.2F, box 2, MHS.

85. Quotation from Penitentiary Twine and Cordage Plant Credit Report Files, 1919–1926, North Dakota Archives, series 30377, box 1, SHSND.

86. Ibid.

87. State Penitentiary, Twine and Cordage Plant Misc. Correspondence, North Dakota Archives, series 30374, box 2, SHSND.

88. C. Detzer to Harold McCormick, Oct. 10, 1904, file 02148, IHCA/Navistar; *El agricultor* 4, no. 1 (Apr. 1, 1907): 57.

89. L. N. Robinson, *Should Prisoners Work?* 71–72.

90. Memo "Production (Approximate) State Prisons Binder Twine Plants," Mar. 13, 1933, International Harvester Co. Records, M95–262, folder 3, box 20, McCormick–International Harvester Co. Collection, SHSW.

91. Inspection and Sale Act, misc. letters from Brantford Cordage Co. to G. H. Clarke, Canadian Department of Agriculture (Ottawa) from early 1925; R. L. Brown to Hon. W. R. Motherwell, Nov. 28, 1928, both in RG 17, vol. 3088, file 47–2, NAC; International Harvester Co., *The Story of Twine*, 31.

92. E. D. Mikesell to Reed, June 18, 1930; M. F. Amrine to Lacy M. Simpson, June 29, 1930, both in Governor's Records–Reed, folder 20, box 17, KSHS.

93. Lacy M. Simpson to Reed, July 3, 1930; M. F. Amrine to E D. Mikesell, June 29, 1930, both in Governor's Records–Reed, folder 20, box 17, KSHS.

94. J. D. Botkin to Greeley Milling Co., June 17, 1914, Governor's Records–Hodges, folder 1, box 6, KSHS.

95. Warden, South Dakota State Penitentiary, to Williams, Oct. 2, 1915, in Williams, "State of the State Message," 23.

96. G. K. Gerdes to Capper, Apr. 30, 1917; G. A. Grove to Capper, June 1, 1917; and Bales Bros. Mfg. to Capper, June 3, 1917, all in Governor's Records–Capper, folder 118, box 12, KSHS.

97. USSD, 812.61326/229.

98. Capper to J. K. Codding, Mar. 15, 1918; Codding to Capper, Mar. 15, 1918, both in Governor's Records–Capper, folder 118, box 12, KSHS.

99. Botkin, "Facts about the Prison Twine Mill," 1.

100. Hodges to Botkin, May 28, 1914; Executive Clerk (of the prison) to Alfred Docking (of the governor's office), June 10, 1914, both in Governor's Records–Hodges, folder 1, box 6, KSHS.

101. Board of Corrections member quoted in *Topeka Daily Capital*, Feb. 4, 1915, 12; Office of Governor Capper to F. E. Ertel, Apr. 5, 1915, Governor's Records–Capper, folder 264, box 4, KSHS.

102. Biennial Report of the North Dakota Twine and Cordage Plant, 1920–22, North Dakota Archives, 365.65 N814tr, 1920/22, 72, 56, SHSND.

103. Warden's Report of Operation of Twine and Cordage Plant at State Penitentiary, Biennial Period 1901–1902, and 1903–1904, North Dakota Archives, 365.65, N814tr 1901/02, SHSND.

104. F. W. Dixon to Hodges, Apr. 20, 1914; Botkin to Grant Harrington, Apr. 29, 1914, both in Governor's Records–Hodges, folder 1, box 6, KSHS.

105. D. W. Batdorf to Capper, Mar. 2, 1915; Capper to Batdorf, Mar. 4, 1915; J. L. Mellor to Capper, Apr. 15, 1915, all in Governor's Records–Capper, folder 264, box 4, KSHS.

106. Minutes of Farm Machinery Conference, Mar. 15, 1915, Minnesota Archives, RG: Stillwater State Prison, series: Prison Industries, 118.B.11.2F, box 2, MHS.

107. Minutes of Farm Machinery Conferences, Mar. 22, 1915, Nov. 21, 1922, Minnesota Archives, RG: Stillwater State Prison, series: Prison Industries, 118. B.11.2F, box 2, MHS.

108. Minutes of Farm Machinery Conference, Nov. 21, 1922, Minnesota Archives, RG: Stillwater State Prison, series: Prison Industries, 118.B.11.2F, box 2, MHS; Evans, "From Kanasín to Kansas," 297.

109. USSD, 812.61326/229.

110. Wisconsin Division of Corrections, State Prison Financial Reports, Binder Twine Plant Financial Statements, fiscal year 1924, SHSW.

111. Warden G. T. Jameson to Farmers Elevator Company of Bryant, S.Dak., Jan. 15, 1919, Papers of the Investigation, vol. V., 27.

112. Farmers Elevator Company of Bryant, S.Dak., to Jameson, Oct. 8, 1918; Jameson to Farmers Elevator Company, Jan. 15, 1919, both in Papers of the Investigation, vol. V., 24–26, 28.

113. Minutes of Farm Machinery Conference, Nov. 11, 1922, Minnesota Archives, RG: Stillwater State Prison, series: Prison Industries, 118.B.11.2F, box 2, MHS.

114. E. L. Barrier, Budget Director of the State of Kansas, to Henry Caulfield, June 18, 1930, Governor's Records–Reed, folder 18, box 7, KSHS.

115. Barrier to Reed, Aug. 29, 1930, and Sept. 11, 1930; H. R. Rhodes to Reed, Sept. 8, 1930, both in Governor's Records–Reed, folder 20, box 17, KSHS.

116. McMillan to Turner, Apr. 12, 1932; Wagar to McMillan, Apr. 14, 1932, both in series 30374, box 2, SHSND.

117. Jameson to Wagar, Apr. 18, 1932, series 30374, box 2, SHSND; and Jameson testimony in Papers of the Investigation, vol. I, 11.

118. Wagar to Jameson, May 22, 1933; Jameson to Wagar, May 24, 1933, both in series 30374, box 2, SHSND.

119. Wagar to McMillan, May 23, 1933; McMillan to Wagar, May 26, 1933, both in series 30374, box 2, SHSND.

120. Battcher to Michigan State Prison Warden, June 26, 1934; C . L. Stebbins to Battcher, July 3, 1934, both in series 30374, box 2, SHSND.

121. Walter Conway to John J. Lee, Jan. 25, 1935; Lee to Conway, Jan. 28, 1935, both in series 30374, box 2, SHSND.

122. *El sisal mexicano* 9, no. 92 (Mar. 1935): 5.

123. *El henequenero*, May 1933, 4.

124. L. F. Craig, "Twenty-fourth Biennial Report of the South Dakota State Prison," June 30, 1936; G. E. Wheelen, "Twenty-fifth Biennial Report of the South Dakota State Prison," June 30, 1938; G. N. Jameson, "Twenty-sixth Biennial Report

of the South Dakota Prison," June 30, 1940, all in State Board of Charities and Corrections Biennial Reports, SDSHS.

125. Miller and Greiser, "The Evolution of Prison Industries," 6.

126. Wisconsin Division of Corrections, State Prison Financial Reports, Binder Twine Plant Financial Statements, fiscal years 1924, 1940, SHSW; G. N. Jameson, Thirty-first Biennial Report, June 30, 1950, 91, South Dakota State Board of Corrections Biennial Reports, SDSHS.

127. Mills, *The Struggle for Existence*, 524–25.

128. "Production of Binder Twine in the United States," International Harvester Co. Records, M95–262, folder 4, box 20, SHSW.

129. Evans, "From Kanasín to Kansas," 282–83.

130. See Burton-Rose, ed. *The Celling of America*. For information on the Prison Activist Research Center and its attention to the problems of prison labor, visit their website at www.prisonactivist.org/prison.labor/#state. For legislation and policy implications, see National Center for Policy Analysis, "Factories behind Bars."

131. Information from Washington County (Minnesota) Historical Society, www.wchsmn.store/.

Chapter 6

1. G. Friesen, *The Canadian Prairies*, 328. For more on how Canadian prairie farmers were "eager to take advantage" of the international market during and after World War I, see Thompson, *The Harvests of War*, 23–70.

2. From Canadian government reports as compiled by Shepard in "The Mechanized Agricultural Frontier of the Canadian Plains," 2.

3. Worster, *Dust Bowl*, 89. For more detail specifically on Kansas, see Dean, ed., "Wheat Culture in Kansas."

4. U.S. Department of Agriculture, *Wheat*, 8, 10, 20, 21.

5. Worster, *Dust Bowl*, 89; *Wichita Daily Eagle*, Mar. 4, 1915, 1.

6. International Harvester Company, *Report of the International Harvester Company*, 1916, 15, IHCA/Navistar.

7. Per acre twine figures are from Ward, "Farming Technology and Crop Area on Early Prairie Farms," 33. Kansas figure is from Evans, "From Kanasín to Kansas," 287. American and Canadian figures are from the British Ambassador to the United States, Sir Cecil Spring Rice, to Governor General of Canada, Sir Edward Grey, Mar. 23, 1915, Ministry of External Affairs, RG 25, series A-3-a, vol. 1161, file 1915–572-c, NAC.

8. Chardon, *Geographic Aspects of Plantation Agriculture in Yucatan*, 29.

9. Statement of Eliseo Arredondo (Mexican representative to Washington) in U.S. Senate, *Investigation of Mexican Affairs*, 891; Canada, Dominion Bureau of Statistics, *Report on Cordage, Rope, and Twine Industry in Canada, 1919 and 1920*, 1–5.

10. Joseph, *Revolution from Without*, 158–59, 167.

11. *Farm Implement News*, Mar. 26, 1923, 12; Joseph, *Revolution from Without*, 159, 173.

12. *La voz de la revolución*, Apr. 7, 1915, 1. For more on Alvarado's role in agrarian reform in Yucatán, see Irigoyen, *Salvador Alvarado*.

13. For further information, see Joseph, *Revolution from Without*, 125–30.

14. Fallaw, *Cárdenas Compromised*, 11.

15. Ancona quoted in Benítez, *Ki*, 144.

16. Joseph, *Revolution from Without*, 137–38.

17. Ibid., 141. Railroad and warehouse rate increases are in "Memorandum on the Yucatan Hemp Industry," Mar. 20, 1916, Ministry of External Affairs, RG 25, series A-3-a, vol. 1161, NAC.

18. *Cordage Trade Journal* to Secretary of State William Jennings Bryan, Mar. 31, 1915, USSD, 812.61326/62; *Harvester World*, Dec. 1915, 2.

19. *New York Times*, Dec. 30, 1915, 14.

20. Ibid.

21. Senator McCumber directed the Senate secretary to read the letter from A. O. Sather, as recorded in *Congressional Record*, 64th Cong., 1st sess., Jan. 6, 1916, 587.

22. *Concordia Daily Kansan*, Mar. 16, 1916, reprinted in *Harvester World* 7 (Apr. 1916): 4–5.

23. *Topeka Daily Capital*, Feb. 28, 1916, reprinted in *Harvester World* 7 (Apr. 1916): 4.

24. Quotations from *Congressional Record*, 64th Cong., 1st sess., Jan. 6, 1916, 587–88.

25. U.S. Senate, Subcommittee on Agriculture and Forestry, "Hearings on Importation of Sisal and Manila Hemp."

26. Ibid., 6–8, 46, 55, 260.

27. Ibid., 79 (quotation), 257–259.

28. Joseph, *Revolution from Without*, 153; *Chicago Daily News*, Mar. 14, 1923, 1.

29. Letter of the Chairman of the Federal Trade Commission Transmitting in Response to Senate Resolution of Apr. 17, 1916; SR 170; List of Manufacturing Concerns to Which Was Sent Telegram of Apr. 21, 1916; and Memorandum of Compliance, all in U.S. Senate, Subcommittee on Agriculture and Forestry, "Hearings on Importation of Sisal and Manila Hemp," 1–7.

30. Joseph, *Revolution from Without*, 153.

31. "Memorandum on the Yucatan Hemp Industry" by Sir Cecil Spring Rice, Mar. 20, 1916, 1–3, Ministry of External Affairs, RG 25, series A-3-a, vol. 1161, NAC.

32. Ibid., 3–4.

33. Fallaw, "The Economic Foundations of Bartolismo," 7.

34. Joseph, *Revolution from Without*, 145–46, 159–60, 173. The Hoover quotation is cited in Joseph, *Revolution from Without*, 160.

35. U.S. Department of Agriculture, *Wheat*, 2; Joseph, *Revolution from Without*, 160, 163, 178.

36. The Browne report was released by the Congressional Information Bureau in a letter to Plymouth Cordage, Sept. 21, 1917, in Plymouth Records, envelope 6, IHCA/Navistar. Quoted testimony from the Senate committee hearing is in U.S. Senate, *Investigation of Mexican Affairs*, 873–74, 880, 889–91.

37. U.S. Senate, *Investigation of Mexican Affairs*, 886, 888.

38. Torre, *La ruina del henequén en Yucatán*, 75, 84.

39. Chardon, *Geographic Aspects of Plantation Agriculture in Yucatan*, 37; Joseph, *Revolution from Without*, 162–63, 172–73.

40. Joseph, *Revolution from Without*, 246–47, 261. For more on the changes inaugurated by Carrillo Puerto, see Irigoyen, *Felipe Carrillo Puerto*.

41. *New York Journal of Commerce*, Jan. 4, 1922, 1.

42. Joseph, *Revolution from Without*, 175–77.

43. Quotations from *New York Times*, July 25, 1922, 26.

44. Joseph, *Revolution from Without*, 256.

45. Plymouth Cordage to Arthur Capper, Dec. 26, 1924, International Harvester Records, Plymouth Cordage File 1923–24: Sisal Monopoly, IHCA/Navistar.

46. Copy of E. Robledo to Hoover, July 18, 1922, IHCA/Navistar.

47. All quotations from *Chicago Daily News*, Mar. 14, 1923, 1.

48. *Farm Implement News*, Mar. 26, 1923, 12.

49. All quotations from *Farm Implement News*, Apr. 16, 1923, 12.

50. Hanson & Orth Company, "Digest of Principal Statements in Letter to Secretary Hoover," Apr. 1924, International Harvester Records, Plymouth Cordage File 1923–24: Sisal Monopoly, IHCA/Navistar.

51. *Journal of Commerce*, Sept. 19, 1928, 4; F. H. Lindsay (Lindsay Bros., Inc., Milwaukee) to F. C. Holmes (Plymouth Cordage), Oct. 5, 1928, International Harvester Records, Plymouth Cordage File, envelope 9, IHCA/Navistar.

52. Chardon, *Geographic Aspects of Plantation Agriculture in Yucatan*, 39–40; Fallaw, "The Economic Foundations of Bartolismo," 8–9.

53. Joseph, *Revolution from Without*, 256.

54. Plymouth Cordage to Arthur Capper, Dec. 26, 1924, International Harvester Records, Plymouth Cordage File 1923–24: Sisal Monopoly, IHCA/Navistar.

55. *El sisal mexicano* 1 (Mar. 1927): 1, 8.

56. Echegaray Bablot, *Irrigación, crisis henequenera y condiciones agrícolas y económicas de Yucatán*, 49.

57. *Ante la ruina del henequén*, i, ii, 5, 9.

58. *Cuestiones henequeneras*, 2, 7; Fallaw, "The Economic Foundations of Bartolismo," 18.

59. *El diario de Yucatán*, Mar. 19, 1920, as quoted in Joseph, *Revolution from Without*, 180.

60. Fallaw, "The Economic Foundations of Bartolismo," 19.

61. Fallaw, "Bartolocallismo," 12, 17.

62. Fallaw, "The Economic Foundations of Bartolismo," 11–12, 19, 30.

63. *El sisal mexicano*, 5 (Sept. 1931): 3.

64. Scientist quoted in Worster, *Dust Bowl*, 12; Francis and Palmer, eds., *The Prairie West*, 535. See also Sears, *Deserts on the March*.

65. Gerald Friesen, *The Canadian Prairies*, 386–387. For more on the Prairie Provinces in the 1930s, see Gray, *Men against the Desert*; and D. C. Jones, *Empire of Dust*.

66. Quotation from Worster, *Dust Bowl*, 35.

67. Worster, *Dust Bowl*, 12, 94, 35, 4, 24 (respectively).

68. Twine relief announcement as reported in *Regina Leader-Post*, July 30, 1932, 2. Demographic information from Worster, *Dust Bowl*, 48–49; Gray, *Men against the Desert*, 190. For a thorough account of the federal policy implications for those who ended up staying on their farms in the U.S. plains during the drought and depression, see Grant, *Down and Out on the Family Farm*.

69. Leopold, *A Sand County Almanac*, 15.

70. Thompson, *Harvests of War*, 68.

71. Edna Jacques, "A Farmer's Wife (in the Drouth Area)," reprinted in Gray, *Men against the Desert*, ix.

72. Worster, *Dust Bowl*, 93. For a critique of New Deal and Farm Security Administration (FSA) policies and programs like *The Plow That Broke the Plains*, see Malin, *Winter Wheat in the Golden Belt of Kansas* and *The Grassland of North America*. For additional critique of New Deal agricultural propaganda, see Ganzel, *Dust Bowl Descent*. I thank Geoff Cunfer for alerting me to these critiques. His book *On the Great Plains: Agriculture and Environment* likewise offers a revisionist approach, or rather a retroanalysis of "environmental determinism," on the causes of the Dust Bowl; he agrees with Malin that cyclical drought patterns along with high winds were responsible for the Dust Bowl. He also argues that only one-third of the Great Plains was ever plowed up and that some areas that suffered Dust Bowl conditions, especially in eastern New Mexico, were unplowed rangelands used only for cattle grazing. For more on the drought cycles over time, see Malin, "Dust Storms, 1850–1900." For information on the return of drought conditions in the 1950s, see Hurt, "Return of the Dust Bowl."

73. Worster, *Dust Bowl*, 5, 13. For differing analyses on the history of the Dust Bowl, see Webb, *The Great Plains*; Cunfer, *On the Great Plains*; Lookingbill, *Dust Bowl, U.S.A.*; Riney-Kehrberg, *Rooted in Dust*; Hurt, *The Dust Bowl*; Bonnifield, *Dust Bowl*. William Cronon has masterfully compared the theoretical differences between Worster's and Bonnifield's books in "A Place for Stories." For a variety of primary accounts of Dust Bowl experiences, see Svobida, *Farming the Dust Bowl*; Low, *Dust Bowl Diary*; Henderson, *Letters from the Dust Bowl*; Wunder, Kaye, and Carstensen, eds. *Americans View Their Dust Bowl Experience*; and Miner, *Next Year Country*.

74. G. Friesen, *The Canadian Prairies*, 386; Francis and Palmer, eds., *The Prairie West*, 535.

75. "The Present Drought Situation," PFRA, 1936, R-266, file IV-60-PFRA, SAB-R; G. Friesen, *The Canadian Prairies*, 387–88. For more on the drought effects in Saskatchewan, see Waiser, *Saskatchewan*, chap. 14.

76. U.S. Department of Agriculture, *Wheat*, 10, 11, 20.

77. *El sisal mexicano* 5 (Sept. 1931): 1; 8 (Sept. 1934): 5.

78. Ibid., 5 (Jan. 1931): 6; 5 (May 1931): 5.

79. Ibid., 6 (Apr. 1932): 3, 5; 6 (June 1932): 1.

80. *Cordage Trade Journal*, Aug. 3, 1934, 1; *El sisal mexicano* 8 (Aug. 1934): 5; 8 (July 1934): 5. See also *Saturday Evening Post*, July 21, 1934.

81. *El diario de Yucatán*, July 7, 1936, 1; July 10, 1936, 1; July 11, 1936, 1.

82. *El sisal mexicano* 9 (May 1935): 3; 9 (June 1935): 4; *Excélsior*, Sept. 14, 1935, 25.

83. *El sisal mexicano* 9 (Dec. 1935): 1, 4; 10 (Jan. 1936): 1, 5. Sisal sales are from Chardon, *Geographic Aspects of Plantation Agriculture in Yucatan*, 29; and Echegaray Bablot, *Irrigación, crisis henequenera y condiciones agrícolas y económicas de Yucatán*, 49.

84. *Cordage Trade Journal*, July 15, 1937, 1, 18, 22.

85. *Revista del comercio exterior*, Mar. 1939, 3.

86. Fallaw, *Cárdenas Compromised*, 2, 3, 12; English translation copy of decree issued by President Cárdenas, Mérida, Yuc., Aug. 3, 1937, in McCormick–International Harvester Collection, M95–262, folder 4, box 20, SHSW.

87. Fallaw, "Bartolocallismo," 1, 2.

88. Fallaw, "The Economic Foundations of Bartolismo," 29, 30.

89. Henry W. Peabody & Co. (Boston) to North Dakota Twine and Cordage Plant (Bismarck), Apr. 1, 1932, State Penitentiary, Twine and Cordage Factory Misc. Correspondence, series 30374, box 2, SHSND.

90. Fallaw, "The Economic Foundations of Bartolismo," 19.

91. Cooperativa Henequeneros de Yucatán to President Rodríguez, Oct. 6, 1934; Members of the Comité Central de Obreros y Campesinos to Rodríguez, Oct. 7, 1934, both in Colección Abelardo Rodríguez, 562.011–11, AGN.

92. Fallaw, "The Economic Foundations of Bartolismo," 26.

93. *El nacional*, Aug. 14, 1933, 15; *Boletín mensual de Departamento de Economía y Estadística*, Aug. 16, 1933, 2; Henequeneros de Yucatán to Rodríguez, Oct. 6, 1934, all in Colección Abelardo Rodríguez, 562.011–11, AGN.

94. Quotations from miscellaneous letters to Rodríguez in Colección Abelardo Rodríguez, 562.011–11, AGN.

95. Fallaw, "Bartolocallismo," 19.

96. Brannon and Baklanoff, *Agrarian Reform and Public Enterprise in Mexico*, 3; Chardon, *Geographic Aspects of Plantation Agriculture in Yucatan*, 41, 43.

97. Fallaw, *Cárdenas Compromised*, 12, 15. For more on *ejidos* in Yucatán during this period, see Brannon and Baklanoff, *Agrarian Reform and Public Enterprise in Mexico*, 10.

98. Manero, *La anarquía henequenera de Yucatán*, 24.

99. Miscellaneous correspondence to Cárdenas, 1935–1936, Colección Lázaro Cárdenas, 404.1–12, folder 1: Ejidos Yucatán, AGN; *El diario de Yucatán*, July 14, 1936, 1.

100. As reported in the *New York Times*, Oct. 24, 1937, 33.

101. Decree issued by President Cárdenas, Mérida, Yuc., Aug. 3, 1937, in Mc-Cormick–International Harvester Collection, M95–262, folder 4, box 20, SHSW. For analysis on the expropriation of the henequen fields, see Fallaw, *Cárdenas Compromised*; Paoli Bolio, *Cárdenas y el reparto de los henequenales*; and Orthón Baños Ramírez, "El trasfondo político de la reforma agraria: El caso de Yucatán, 1933–1937."

102. As reprinted in *El diario de Yucatán*, Aug. 9, 1937, 1. *Ejidatario* information is from Brannon and Baklanoff, *Agrarian Reform and Public Enterprise in Mexico*, 67, 192.

103. Juan Guerrero, Secretary General of the Cámara Nacional de Trabajo, to Cárdenas, Aug. 17, 1936, Colección Lázaro Cárdenas, 404.1–1-12, folder 1: Ejidos Yucatán, AGN; *El nacional*, May 8, 1935, 35; Fallaw, *Cárdenas Compromised*, 165.

104. Decree issued by President Cárdenas, Mérida, Yuc., Aug. 3, 1937, in Mc-Cormick–International Harvester Collection, M95–262, folder 4, box 20, SHSW.

105. Núñez González to Cárdenas, Oct. 15, 1935, Colección Lázaro Cárdenas, 404.1–12, folder 1: Ejidos Yucatán, AGN. For a detailed contemporary study of the agrarian reforms and how they related to Yucatán, see Molina Font, *El problema agrario en la Zona Henequenera de Yucatán,* which was published in 1934.

106. Miscellaneous correspondence to Cárdenas, summer 1937, Colección Lázaro Cárdenas, 404.1–12, folder 4: Ejidos Yucatán, AGN; *El nacional,* June 4, 1936, 1.

107. Cordelería "La Guadalupana" (and various other cordage firms in Mérida) to Cárdenas, June 30, 1936, Colección Lázaro Cárdenas, 404.1–12, folder 2: Ejidos Yucatán, AGN.

108. Memorandum sobre la Producción, Comercio, Financimiento y Consumo de la Industria Henequenera, June 1937, Colección Lázaro Cárdenas, 404.1–12, folder 4: Ejidos Yucatán, AGN.

109. "Problema argrario en la Zona Henequenera de Yucatán," Feb. 10, 1936, 2–3, folder 2; Memorandum written by Gustavo Molina Font, "Afectaciones para ejidos en la Zona Henequenera de Yucatán," Mar. 27, 1934, 2, 4, folder 1, both in Colección Lázaro Cárdenas, 404.1–12, AGN.

110. Salvador Zumudio M., "El problema agrario de Yucatán," July 5, 1937, 2, 6, folder 3; Luis Cabrera to Carlos M. Peralta, n.d. 1936, folder 2, both in Colección Lázaro Cárdenas, 404.1–12, AGN.

111. Fallaw, *Cárdenas Compromised,* 13.

112. Memorandum, Poder Ejecutivo Federal, Departamento Agrario, June 1934, folder 1, Colección Lázaro Cárdenas, 404.1–12, AGN.

113. From one of Allen's guest articles, *New York Herald,* Aug. 27, 1938.

114. Ibid.

115. Magoon (Mérida) to Brewster (Mexico City), Oct. 12, 1937, McCormick–International Harvester Collection, M95–262, folder 4, box 20, SHSW; Payán quoted in Fallaw, *Cárdenas Compromised,* 3.

116. Quotations from article by Allen, *New York Herald,* Aug. 27, 1938.

117. "Message of the New Governor," quoted in *El diario del sureste,* Feb. 2, 1938, 1.

118. Ellis Brewster to Plymouth Cordage, Feb. 12, 1938, International Harvester Records, Brewster File, Plymouth Cordage, IHCA/Navistar.

119. From Allen's guest article, *New York Herald,* Aug. 27, 1938.

120. Fallaw, *Cárdenas Compromised,* 5, 6, 160–62.

121. Fernando Foglio M. to Cárdenas, Dec. 12, 1939, folder 4, Colección Lázaro Cárdenas, 404.1–12, AGN.

Chapter 7

1. For the complete history of the abacá (manila hemp) industry, see Owen, *Prosperity without Progress.*

2. The story is discussed in *El nacional,* May 10, 1955, 10.

3. Secretary of the North Dakota Twine and Cordage Plant to Henry W. Peabody & Co., Mar. 17, 1932, Miscellaneous Correspondence, State Penitentiary, Twine and Cordage Plant, series 30374, box 2, SHSND.

4. For more on these fibers, see Dewey, "Fibers Used for Binder Twine," 193–203; and Díaz de Cossío, *Henequen: riqueza yucateca,* 103–104.

5. *Farm Implement News,* Apr. 16, 1923, 12; *El henequén* 1 (Nov. 30, 1916): 1.

6. Joseph, *Revolution from Without,* 181; Brockway, *Science and Colonial Expansion,* 178–79. Production figures are from *Ante la ruina del henequén,* 5.

7. I thank Allen Wells for making these points clearer to me.

8. Office of Treasurer and General Manager, Plymouth Cordage, in statement to "Farmers of Yucatan," Feb. 10, 1923, International Harvester Records, file: Plymouth Cordage Company, 1922–23, Sisal Monopoly, IHCA/Navistar. The response was printed in *La revista de Mérida,* Mar. 3, 1923, 1.

9. *El nacional,* Mar. 10, 1937, 1.

10. Joseph, *Revolution from Without,* 256.

11. From data entered in W. B. Worth of McLeod and Company, Inc., to E. W. Brewster of Plymouth Cordage, Jan. 2, 1940, International Harvester Co. Records, file 00798, IHCA/Navistar.

12. Plymouth Cordage, "Principal Sources of Sisal Supply," sent to International Harvester, International Harvester Co. Records, M95–262, folder 4, box 19, McCormick–International Harvester Collection, SHSW. The 1960 figure is as reported in *Excélsior,* Aug. 4, 1960, 14.

13. See Dewey, "Fibers Used for Binder Twine," 199.

14. "Producción de Henequén, 1927," *Boletín mensual del Departamento de Economía y Estadística,* Oct. 15, 1927, 145; "Producción de Henequén, 1929," *Boletín mensual del Departamento de Economía y Estadística,* Oct. 15, 1929, 459.

15. *El henequenero* 1 (July 1927): 128, 136; *El nacional,* Oct. 3, 1966, 9.

16. Ray E. Smith, International Harvester Company Advertising Department, to Erskine Caldwell, in response to a question on the history of combines, July 14, 1939, International Harvester Records, file 00798, IHCA/Navistar; Quick and Buchele, *The Grain Harvesters,* 90; Hurt, "Combine Harvesters," 43. For the complete story of the invention of the first combine, see Quick and Buchele, *The Grain Harvesters,* chap. 10; and Hill, "The First Combine."

17. Hurt, "Combine Harvesters," 45.

18. Shepard and Isern, "The Adoption of the Combine on the Canadian Plains," 457.

19. Hurt, "Combine Harvesters," 45.

20. Figures are from *El sisal mexicano* 1 (Apr. 1927): 1, 6; Self, *Environment and Man in Kansas,* 101; International Harvester Co. records, M95–262, box 20, McCormick-International Harvester Collection, SHSW; and Hurt, "Combine Harvesters," 52.

21. Hurt, "Combine Harvesters," 49. On itinerant harvesters in Canada, see Thompson, "Bringing in the Sheaves." For a complete analysis of the harvest labor experience in the transboundary Great Plains, see Isern, *Bull Threshers and Bindlestiffs.*

22. For further information, see Hall, *Harvest Wobblies.* For more on the transboundary aspect of the Harvest Wobblies, see Pickett, "Hoboes across the Border."

23. Hurt, "Combine Harvesters," 49, 50, 52, 61.

24. From *Western Producer,* quoted in Shepard and Isern, "The Adoption of the Combine on the Canadian Plains," 461; *El henequenero* 1 (Feb./Mar. 1927): 37; Shepard and Isern, "The Adoption of the Combine on the Canadian Plains," 461.

25. Hurt, "Combine Harvesters," 50, 52.

26. These studies are cited in Shepard and Isern, "The Adoption of the Combine on the Canadian Plains," 457; and Hurt, "Combine Harvesters," 51–52.

27. Hurt, "Combine Harvesters," 51, 52; Shepard and Isern, "The Adoption of the Combine on the Canadian Plains," 457, 458.

28. Quoted in *El sisal mexicano* 1 (Apr. 1927): 6; 1 (July 1928): 10. For more on the use of combines in western Canada, see Thomas, "Early Combines in Saskatchewan;" R. J. Friesen, "The Combine Harvester in Alberta"; Shepard, "The Mechanized Agricultural Frontier of the Canadian Plains"; and Shepard and Isern, "The Adoption of the Combine on the Canadian Plains."

29. Case ads are in Erb and Brumbaugh, *Full Steam Ahead,* 292, 299; the IH ad is from the McCormick–International Harvester Company Archives, Blue Book Series, folder 2, box 73, McCormick–International Harvester Collection, SHSW.

30. Shepard and Isern, "The Adoption of the Combine on the Canadian Plains," 457; Hurt, "Combine Harvesters," 61; *El henequenero* 1 (Oct. 1927): 196; *El sisal mexicano* 1 (Apr. 1927): 6.

31. Hurt, "Combine Harvesters," 51, 61. See also, Isern, *Custom Combining on the Great Plains.*

32. Shepard and Isern, "The Adoption of the Combine on the Canadian Plains," 460–61; Hurt, "Combine Harvesters," 52–54.

33. Shepard and Isern, "The Adoption of the Combine on the Canadian Plains," 456–57; International Harvester Co. records, M95–262, box 20, McCormick–International Harvester Collection, SHSW; *Canadian Farm Implements* 43 (Jan. 1947): 7; Government of the Province of Saskatchewan, Department of Agriculture Memo, R-266, file IV-27 "Farm Implements," SAB-R. Letters from cordage firms to Evans are in R-266, file IV-8, SAB-R. For more on the combines in the Dakotas, see Isern, "The Adoption of the Combine on the Northern Plains." For more on U.S. federal farm programs in the late 1930s, see Clarke, *Regulation and Revolution in United States Farm Productivity,* and Clarke, "New Deal Regulation and the Revolution in American Farm Productivity."

34. *El sisal mexicano* 1 (Feb. 1927): 1.

35. *El sisal mexicano* 1 (Mar. 1927):1.

36. *El sisal mexicano* 1 (Apr. 1927): 1, 6.

37. *El sisal mexicano* 1 (May–July 1927): 1, 6; 1 (Aug. 1927): 5.

38. *El sisal mexicano* 1 (Oct. 1927): 1; 1 (Dec. 1927): 7, 9.

39. *El sisal mexicano* 2 (July 1928): 10; 2 (Sept. 1928): 2.

40. *El sisal mexicano* 6 (Mar. 1932): 7; 4 (Oct. 1930): 7.

41. *El henequenero* 1 (Oct. 1927): 196.

42. *El diario del sureste,* Sept. 15, 1938, 1.

43. Boyle to DeGeorge, Jan. 3, 1938, International Harvester Co. records, M95–262, box 20, McCormick–International Harvester Collection, SHSW.

44. Hurt, "Combine Harvesters," 56. For more on custom cutters, see Isern, *Custom Combining on the Great Plains*.

45. Shepard and Isern, "The Adoption of the Combine on the Canadian Plains," 461.

46. Quick and Buchele, *The Grain Harvesters*, 140–41; Hurt, "Combine Harvesters," 56–57.

47. *Revista del comercio exterior*, Nov. 20, 1942, 1; *El nacional*, June 2, 1942, 3; Oct. 15, 1941, 15; Chardon, *Geographic Aspects of Plantation Agriculture in Yucatan*, 29, 44; *Revista de economía*, June 1, 1945, 3.

48. International Harvester Co. records, M95–262, box 20, McCormick–International Harvester Co. Collection, SHSW; Shepard and Isern, "The Adoption of the Combine on the Canadian Plains," 461; Hurt, "Combine Harvesters," 61. Curiously, Hurt's quotation is, "By 1950, the combine had mechanized the wheat harvest from the Canadian border to Texas." The 49th parallel in no way prevented wheat harvests or the spread of combines to the Prairie Provinces.

49. From "A Last Farewell to the Bucking Binder," in Duddridge, *Seen from My Seeder Step*, 24.

50. *El henequén* 2 (Mar. 15, 1917): 10–11.

51. *El henequenero* 1 (July 1927): 137; *Boletín mensual del Departamento de Economía y Estadística*, June 10, 1932, 1; "Mexican Sisal Exports, 1936," Brewster File, envelope 6, IHCA/Navistar.

52. *Revista del comercio exterior*, Apr. 10, 1940, 1.

53. *El sisal mexicano* 1 (Mar. 1927): 1.

54. *Wall Street Journal*, Oct. 9, 1931, 3; "Mexican Sisal Exports, 1936," Brewster File, envelope 6, IHCA/Navistar; *Boletín mensual del Departamento de Economía y Estadística*, June 10, 1932, 1; *El nacional*, May 9, 1941, 13.

55. Joseph, *Revolution from Without*, 146, 167.

56. Study quoted in Henry W. Peabody & Co.'s *Yucatan Sisal Bulletin*, Dec. 7, 1936, 1–2, M95–262, folder 4, box 19, McCormick–International Harvester Collection, SHSW.

57. The report was printed in *El diario del sureste*, Sept. 15, 1938, 1.

58. Manuel Cirerol S., "Apuntes sobre un proyecto para la resuelta del problema henequenero de Yucatán," Oct. 6, 1939, in Colección Lázaro Cárdenas, 404.1–12, legajo 4, ANM.

59. *El diario del sureste*, Dec. 11, 1931, 1.

60. *Cooperation*, June 15, 1937, 1; *El yucatanista*, July 10, 1937, 1.

61. Díaz de Cossío, *Henequén*, 111.

62. *El sisal mexicano* 1 (Mar. 1927): 8.

63. Fallaw, "The Economic Foundations of Bartolismo," 23.

64. Preliminary Report of Binder Twine Committee Meeting, July 17, 1937, International Harvester Co. records, M95–262, folder 1, box 20, McCormick–International Harvester Co. Collection, SHSW.

65. *Cooperation*, June 15, 1937, 1.

66. Baklanoff, "The Diversification Quest," 225.

67. As reported in Henry Peabody & Co.'s *Yucatan Sisal Bulletin*, Dec. 7, 1936, 1.

68. Cordelería La Guadalupana et al. to Cárdenas, June 30, 1936, Collección Lázaro Cárdenas, 404.1–12, folder 2, ANM.

69. H. L. Boyle to Sidney Morgan, U.S. Tariff Commission, Feb. 11, 1937, International Harvester Co. records, M95–262, folder 2, box 20, McCormick–International Harvester Co. Collection, SHSW.

70. From data in a chart included in W. E. Worth (McLeod & Co.) to Ellis Brewster (Plymouth Cordage), Jan. 2, 1940, Brewster File, IHCA/Navistar.

71. C. W. Leach (Plymouth Cordage) to Secretary of State Cordell Hull, Feb. 25, 1937, International Harvester Co. records, M95–262, folder 2, box 20, McCormick–International Harvester Co. Collection, SHSW.

72. *El sisal mexicano* 3 (Nov. 1929): 3; 6 (July 1932): 1; 6 (Oct. 1932): 6.

73. Quotations from Plymouth Cordage memos to International Harvester, n.d., 1937, International Harvester Co. records, M95–262, folder 2, box 20, McCormick–International Harvester Co. Collection, SHSW.

74. Plymouth Cordage to Secretary Hull, Feb. 20, 1937, International Harvester records, M95–262, folder 4, box 20, McCormick–International Harvester Collection, SHSW.

75. Plymouth Cordage to U.S. State Department, "Supplemental Memorandum Re. the Importation of Foreign Binder Twine," Mar. 3, 1937, 1, International Harvester records, M95–262, folder 4, box 20, McCormick–International Harvester Collection, SHSW.

76. Ibid., 1–2.

77. Copy of the Memorandum, Gibson to Daniels, Aug. 24, 1937, International Harvester records, M95–262, folder 1, box 20, McCormick–International Harvester Collection, SHSW.

78. Canto quoted in *El diario del sureste*, Sept. 15, 1938, 1.

79. *El yucatanista*, July 10, 1937, 1.

80. Various correspondence, "Mexican Binder Twine Conferences"; and Memorandum of the United States Manufacturers of Binder Twine to Josephus Daniels, U.S. Ambassador to Mexico, June 9, 1937, all in International Harvester records, M95–262, folder 1, box 20, McCormick–International Harvester Collection, SHSW.

81. Statement of Governor Florencio Palomo Valencia, in International Harvester records, M95–262, folder 4, box 20, McCormick–International Harvester Collection, SHSW.

82. Copy of "Opening Address by E. W. Brewster," July 12, 1937, International Harvester records, M95–262, folder 4, box 20, McCormick–International Harvester Collection, SHSW.

83. Worth to Brewster, Dec. 13, 1938; Memorandum, Gibson to Daniels, Aug. 24, 1937; Memorandum by E. W. Brewster, July 23, 1937, all in International Harvester records, M95–262, folder 2, box 20, McCormick–International Harvester Collection, SHSW; *Cordage Trade Journal* 45 (July 15, 1937): 20.

84. *Revista del comercio exterior*, Mar. 1943, 3.

85. *El universal*, Apr. 19, 1946, 5.

86. *El henequenero* 1 (Apr. 1927): 116; H. L. Boyle (IH Economic Research Division) to Royal Netherlands Legation, Washington, D.C., Aug. 9, 1938, International Harvester records, M95–262, folder 1, box 20, McCormick–International Harvester Collection, SHSW.

87. *Regina Leader-Post*, Aug. 14, 1952, 1; Aug. 14, 1952, 1, 3.

88. Promotional brochure (1949) in International Harvester Co. Records, Blue Book Series, folder 2, box 73, McCormick–International Harvester Collection, SHSW.

89. Ibid.

90. *Excélsior*, Jan. 8, 1958, 23; Pasos Peniche, *Historia de la industria henequenera desde 1945 hasta nuestros días*, app. I. For more on the hope that baler twine would stimulate Yucatán's henequen industry, see Menéndez Rodríguez, *Yucatán o el genocidio*, 204.

91. Elmer C. Allen, "The Story of Twine," report for Alberta Rural Development Studies, series B: For Information, January 1975, Glenbow Archives, Calgary, Alta., 1, 3.

92. *El nacional*, Oct. 3, 1966, 9; Fallaw, *Cárdenas Compromised*, 164 (quotations). See also Fallaw, "The Economic Foundations of Bartolismo."

93. *Novedades*, Mar. 17, 1954, 10.

94. *El universal*, Aug. 12, 1954, 7; Pasos Peniche, *Historia de la industria henequenera desde 1945 hasta nuestros días*, 42; *Excélsior*, Feb. 10, 1965, 22.

95. Brannon and Baklanoff, *Agrarian Reform and Public Enterprise in Mexico*, 5.

96. United Nations Conference on Trade and Development (UNCTAD), "The Marketing of Hard Fibres (Sisal and Henequen)," 3–4, 47.

97. *Novedades*, Mar. 8, 1981, 6; Brannon and Baklanoff, *Agrarian Reform and Public Enterprise in Mexico*, 138.

98. *Excélsior*, July 30, 1981, 15; *El sol*, May 31, 1984, 23. For more on the "sweeping reforms" of the López Portillo and de la Madrid administrations, see Brannon and Baklanoff, *Agrarian Reform and Public Enterprise in Mexico*, 149–50. The 1996 report information is in *¡Por Esto!* (Mérida, Yuc.), July 30, 1996, 3.

99. Mizrahi et al., "Composition, Structure, and Management Potential of Secondary Dry Tropical Vegetation in Two Abandoned Henequen Plantations of Yucatan, Mexico," 273–74.

100. Egidio López López, interview by author, San Antonio Tehuitz, Yuc., June 6, 1999.

101. For more on these alternative crops, see the section on "Cultivos de diversificación" in Peniche Rivero and Santamaría Basulto, eds. *Memorias de la Conferencia Nacional sobre el Henequén y la Zona Henequenera de Yucatán*, 484–580.

102. Worster, *Dust Bowl*, 91–92; Shepard and Isern, "The Adoption of the Combine on the Canadian Plains," 461.

103. Hurt, "Combine Harvesters," 62, 61.

104. Worster, *Dust Bowl*, 92, 93.

105. Shepard and Isern, "The Adoption of the Combine on the Canadian Plains," 462.

106. *New York Herald Tribune*, Aug. 28, 1938; *El yucatanista*, July 10, 1937, 1.

Conclusion

1. Bader, *Hayseeds, Moralizers, and Methodists*, 171.

2. See ad for the Cawker City–based Richardson combine attachments in Hurt, "Combine Harvesters," 54.

3. Lyrics to Al Yankovic's "The Biggest Ball of Twine in Minnesota" can be found at www.com-www.com/weirdal/thebiggestballoftwineinminnesota.html. Dave Barry, "Stating Your Case for the Stupidest State," syndicated column printed in the *Anderson (Indiana) Herald Bulletin*, Oct. 20, 2002, D3. I thank my mother-in-law Betty Little for seeing the article and sending it to me.

4. The program, which aired on NPR on Nov. 29, 2003, is archived at www.npr.org/templates/story/storyphp?/storyID=4189959.

5. Harold Reling, interview by author, May 27, 1996, Cawker City, Kans.

6. Kiy and Wirth, eds., *Environmental Management on North America's Borders*, 3, 12. For deeper economic analysis, see P. H. Smith, "From NAFTA to FTAA?" For NAFTA's impact on a range of issues, see Chambers and Smith, eds., *NAFTA in the New Millennium*. For further information on and analysis of a variety of international aspects relating to NAFTA, see Randall and Konrad, eds., *NAFTA in Transition;* and Chambers and Smith, eds., *NAFTA in the New Millennium*.

7. For further analysis, see Wright, *The Death of Ramón González;* Weir and Shapiro, *The Circle of Poison;* and D. L. Murray, *Cultivating Crisis*.

8. I have worked to establish this argument more fully in my forthcoming book *Damming Sonora*. On immigration, see *Migration News*, May 2002. For more on the environmental effects of NAFTA, see Gallagher, *Free Trade and the Environment;* and Davidson and Mitchell, "Environmental Challenges to International Trade."

9. See for example, Faux, "How NAFTA Failed Mexico"; Celia Dugger, "Report Finds Few Benefits for Mexico in NAFTA," *New York Times*, Nov. 19, 2003; Mary Jordan and Kevin Sullivan, "Trade Brings Riches, But Not to Mexico's Poor," *Washington Post*, Mar. 22, 2003; and Tim Weiner, "Free Trade Accord at 10: Growing Pains Are Clear," *New York Times*, Dec. 27, 2003. For an opposing view that suggests that NAFTA has been a "huge success," see Nevaer, *NAFTA's Second Decade*.

10. Tim Weiner, "In Corn's Cradle: U.S. Imports Bury Family Farms," *New York Times*, Feb. 26, 2002. For more on the agricultural implications of NAFTA, see Michelle M. Veeman, Terrence S. Veeman, and Ryan Hoskins, "NAFTA and Agriculture: Challenges for Trade and Policy." Regarding the impact of NAFTA on labor and *maquilas*, see Bacon, *The Children of NAFTA;* Kopinak, ed., *The Social Costs of Industrial Growth in Northern Mexico;* Kopinak, *Desert Capitalism;* John Warnock, *The Other Mexico* (especially chap. 3, "Maquila Mexico"); and U.S. Congress, GAO, "International Trade." On immigration, see *Migration News*, Jan. 2002; and Cornelius, "Impacts of NAFTA on Mexico-to-U.S. Migration."

11. Wells and Joseph, *Summer of Discontent, Seasons of Upheaval*, vi.

12. Winter, "Towards a Fair FTAA," 60–76, 79 (quotation).

13. *Fargo Forum*, Mar. 27, 1915, 1; Wendel, *One Hundred Fifty Years of International Harvester*, 399.

14. See Appadurai, ed., *The Social Life of Things*.

BIBLIOGRAPHY

Archives, Special Collections, Unpublished Reports

Alberta Provincial Archives. Edmonton, Alta.

Archivo General del Estado de Sonora. Hermosillo, Son.

Archivo General del Estado de Yucatán. Mérida, Yuc.

Archivo General Nacional. Mexico City.

Centro de Apoyo a la Investigación Histórica de Yucatán. Mérida, Yuc.

Centro de Estudios de Historia de México. Mexico City.

Glenbow Archives. Calgary, Alta.

Kansas State Library and Archives Division. Kansas State Historical Society. Topeka, Kans.

Library of Congress. Manuscript Collections. Washington, D.C.

Minnesota State Archives. Minnesota Historical Society. Saint Paul, Minn.

National Archives of Canada / Archives Nationales du Canada. Ottawa, Ont.

National Archives and Records Administration. College Park, Md.

Navistar International Transportation Corp. Documents Management and Knowledge Center. Chicago, Ill.

Nebraska State Historical Society. Archives and Manuscripts. Lincoln, Nebr.

Saskatchewan Archives Board–Regina. Regina, Sask.

Saskatchewan Archives Board–University of Saskatchewan. Saskatoon, Sask.

South Dakota State Historical Society. South Dakota Archives. Pierre, S.Dak.

State Historical Society of North Dakota. North Dakota Archives. Bismarck, N.Dak.

State Historical Society of Wisconsin. Madison, Wisc.

United States Congress. General Accounting Office. "International Trade: Mexico's Maquiladora Decline Affects U.S.-Mexico Border Communities and Trade." GAO Report #03–891, July 2003. www.gao.gov/cgi-bin/getrpt?GAO-03–891.

United States. Department of Commerce. Supplement to Commerce Reports.

United States. Department of Labor. Bureau of Labor Statistics. "Formulation of Industrial Wage and Price Policies, Vol. I: The International Harvester Company." December 1939.

United States. State Department. Records Relating to the Internal Affairs of Mexico, 1910–1929. Microfilm Roll 206. National Archives and Records Administration. College Park, Md.

University of Arizona Special Collections. Tucson, Ariz.

Periodicals and Trade Journals

The Appeal to Reason (Girard, Kansas)
Bismarck Daily Tribune (Bismarck, North Dakota)
Boletín Mensual de la Dirección de Economía Rural, Secretaría de Agricultura y Fomento (Mexico City)
Calgary Albertan (Calgary, Alberta)
Calgary Daily Herald (Calgary, Alberta)
Canadian Farm Implements (Winnipeg, Manitoba)
Chicago Daily News (Chicago, Illinois)
The Commoner (Lincoln, Nebraska)
Concordia Daily Kansan (Concordia, Kansas)
Cordage Trade Journal (New York)
Cordage World (London)
Daily Examiner (Peterborough, Ontario)
Diario de Yucatán (Mérida, Yucatan)
Diario Oficial (del Gobierno del Estado de Yucatán) (Mérida)
Diario yucateco (Mérida, Yucatán)
Diario del sureste (Mérida, Yucatán)
El agricultor (Mérida, Yucatán)
El economista (Mexico City)
El henequén (Mérida, Yucatán)
El henequenero (Mérida, Yucatán)
El noticioso (Guaymas, Sonora)
El sisal mexicano (Mérida, Yucatán)
Edmonton Bulletin (Edmonton, Alberta)
Excélsior (Mexico City)
Fargo Forum (Fargo, North Dakota)
Farm Implement News (Chicago, Illinois)
Farmer's Sun (Ottawa, Ontario)
The Gazette (Montreal, Quebec)
Grain Growers' Guide (Calgary, Alberta)
Grand Forks Weekly Times Herald (Grand Forks, North Dakota)
Hardware and Metal (Toronto, Ontario)
Harvester World (Chicago, Illinois)
International Harvester Farm Magazine (Chicago, Illinois)
Journal of Commerce of New York (New York)
Kansas City Star (Kansas City, Missouri)
Leavenworth Times (Leavenworth, Kansas)
Manitoba Free Press (Winnipeg, Manitoba)
Medicine Hat News (Medicine Hat, Alberta)
Mexican Herald (Mexico City)
Michigan City News-Dispatch (Michigan City, Indiana)
Migration News (Davis, California)
Minnesota Agricultural Catalog (Stillwater, Minnesota)

Morning Post (London)

Nebraska Farmer (Lincoln, Nebraska)

New York Herald Tribune (New York)

New York Times (New York)

Regina Leader (Regina, Northwest Territories)

Regina Leader Post (Regina, Saskatchewan)

Regina Morning Leader (Regina, Saskatchewan)

Saskatoon Phoenix (Saskatoon, Saskatchewan)

Saskatoon Star-Phoenix (Saskatoon, Saskatchewan)

Sioux Falls Argus-Leader (Sioux Falls, South Dakota)

Tombstone Prospector (Tombstone, Arizona)

Topeka Daily Capital (Topeka, Kansas)

Toronto Globe (Toronto, Ontario)

La unión yucateca (Mérida, Yucatan)

La voz de la Revolución (Mérida, Yucatán)

Wichita Eagle (Wichita, Kansas)

Books and Articles

Adelman, Jeremy, and Stephen Aron. "From Borderlands to Borders: Empires, Nation-States, and the Peoples in Between in North American History." *American Historical Review* 104 (June 1999): 814–41.

Allen, Stewart Lee. *The Devil's Cup: A History of the World according to Coffee.* New York: Ballantine Books, 2003.

Anderson, David D. *William Jennings Bryan.* Boston: Twayne Publishers, 1981.

Ante la ruina del henequén: documentos relativos a los labores efectuados en defensa de la industria henequenera por un grupo de productores. Mérida, Yuc.: Compañía Tipográfica Yucateca, 1933 (anonymous pamphlet).

Antochiw, Michel. "El enganche de peones huastecos para las haciendas de Yucatán." *Revista de la Universidad Autónoma de Yucatán* 10 (July–September 1995): 18–22.

Appadurai, Arjun, ed. *The Social Life of Things: Commodities in Cultural Perspective.* Cambridge: Cambridge University Press, 1986.

Ashby, LeRoy. *William Jennings Bryan: Champion of Democracy.* Boston: Twayne Publishers, 1987.

Askinasy, Siegfried. *El problema agrario de Yucatán.* Mexico City: Ediciones Botas, 1936.

Bacon, David. *The Children of NAFTA: Labor Wars on the U.S.-Mexico Border.* Berkeley: University of California Press, 2004.

Bader, Robert Smith. *Hayseeds, Moralizers, and Methodists: The Twentieth-Century Images of Kansas.* Lawrence: University Press of Kansas, 1988.

Baerlein, Henry. *Mexico, the Land of Unrest: Being Chiefly an Account of What Produced the Outbreak in 1910.* Philadelphia: J. B. Lippincott, 1913.

Baklanoff, Eric N. "The Diversification Quest: A Monocrop Export Economy in Transition." Pp. 202–44 in *Yucatan: A World Apart,* edited by Edward H. Moseley and Edward D. Terry. Tuscaloosa: University of Alabama Press, 1980.

————, and Jeffrey Brannon. "Forward and Backward Linkages in a Plantation Economy: Immigrant Entrepreneurship and Industrial Revolution in Yucatan, Mexico." *Journal of Developing Areas* 19 (October 1984): 83–94.

Balbás, Manuel, and Fortunato Hernández. *Crónica de la guerra del Yaqui.* 1927. Hermosillo: Gobierno del Estado de Sonora, 1985.

Baños Ramírez, Othón. "Crisis henequenera y estrategias de vida." Pp. 349–59 in *Memorias de la Conferencia Nacional sobre el Henequén y la Zona Henequenera de Yucatán,* edited by Piedad Peniche Rivero and Felipe Santamaría Basulto. Mérida: Estado de Yucatán, 1993.

————. "El trasfondo político de la reforma agraria: el caso de Yucatán, 1933–1937." *Revista de la Universidad Autónoma de Yucatán* 172 (January–March 1990): 80–95.

————. *Yucatán: ejidos sin campesinos.* Mérida: Universidad Autónoma de Yucatán, 1989.

Bassols Batalla, Angel. *El noroeste de México: un estudio geográfico-económico.* Mexico City: UNAM, 1972.

Benítez, Fernando. *Ki: el drama de un pueblo y de una planta.* Mexico City: Fondo de Cultura Económica, 1962.

Benjamin, Thomas. "International Harvester and the Henequen Marketing System in Yucatan, 1889–1915: A New Perspective." *Inter-American Economic Affairs* 31 (winter 1997): 3–20.

————, and William McNellie, eds. *Other Mexicos: Essays on Regional Mexican History, 1876–1911.* Albuquerque: University of New Mexico Press, 1984.

Berkovits, Joseph A. G. "Prisoners for Profit: Convict Labour at the Ontario Central Prison, 1874–1914." In *Essays in the History of Canadian Law.* Vol. 5, *Crime and Criminal Justice,* edited by Jim Phillips, Tina Loo, and Susan Lewthwaite. Toronto: University of Toronto Press, 1994.

Betancourt Pérez, Antonio. *Revoluciones y crisis en la economía de Yucatán.* Mérida, Yuc.: Talleres Gráficos del Sureste, S.A., 1953.

The Binder Twine Steal. Ottawa: n.p., 1899 (anonymous pamphlet).

Binnema, Theodore. *Common and Contested Ground: A Human and Environmental History of the Northwestern Plains.* Norman: University of Oklahoma Press, 2001.

Blanchard, Percy W. *Old Farm Tools and Machinery: An Illustrated History.* Fort Lauderdale, Fla.: Gale Research, 1976.

Bonnifield, Matthew Paul. *Dust Bowl: Men, Dirt, and Depression.* Albuquerque: University of New Mexico Press, 1979.

Bosca, Ivan, and Michael Karus. *The Cultivation of Hemp: Botany, Varieties, Cultivation, and Harvesting.* White River Junction, Vt.: Chelsea Green Publishing, 1998.

Braddy, Haldeen. *Pershing's Mission in Mexico.* El Paso: Texas Western Press, 1966.

Brannon, Jeffery, and Eric Baklanoff. *Agrarian Reform and Public Enterprise in Mexico: The Political Economy of Yucatan's Henequen Industry.* Tuscaloosa: University of Alabama Press, 1987.

————. "Corporate Control of a Monocrop Economy: A Comment." *Latin American Research Review* 72 (November 1983): 193–96.

Briggs, Harold. "The Great Dakota Boom, 1879–1886." *North Dakota Historical Quarterly* 4 (January 1930): 78–108.

Brockway, Lucile H. *Science and Colonial Expansion: The Role of the British Royal Botanic Gardens.* New York: Academic Press, 1979.

Brown, Richard Maxwell. *No Duty to Retreat: Violence and Values in American History and Society.* New York: Oxford University Press, 1991.

Brumfield, Kirby. *The Wheat Album: A Picture and Story Scrapbook of Wheat Harvests in Years Gone By.* Seattle: Superior Publishing, 1974.

Bryan, William Jennings, and Mary Baird Bryan. *The Memoirs of William Jennings Bryan.* Philadelphia: John C. Winston Company, 1925.

Bukowczyk, John J., Nora Faires, David R. Smith, and Randy William Widdis. *Permeable Border: The Great Lakes Basin as Transnational Region, 1650–1990.* Pittsburgh, Pa.: University of Pittsburgh Press; and Calgary: University of Calgary Press, 2005.

Burton-Rose, Daniel, ed. *The Celling of America: An Inside Look at the U.S. Prison Industry.* Monroe, Me.: Common Courage Press, 1998.

Cámara Zavala, Gonzalo. *Reseña histórica de la industria henequenera de Yucatán.* Mérida, Yuc.: Imprenta Oriente, 1936.

Canada. Dominion Bureau of Statistics. *The Prairie Provinces in Their Relationship to the National Economy.* Ottawa: Ministry of Trade and Commerce, 1934.

———. Census of Industry. *Report on the Cordage, Rope, and Twine Industry in Canada, 1919 and 1920.* Ottawa: Ministry of Trade and Commerce, 1922.

Canada. Parliament. *The Action of the Government in Respect to the Manufacture and Sale of Twine Produced by Convict Labour (for the Information of Members of Parliament).* Sessional Paper No. 18a. Ottawa: Queen's Printer, 1899.

Carey, James C. *The Mexican Revolution in Yucatan, 1915–1924.* Boulder, Colo.: Westview Press, 1984.

Carlson, Norman A. "Prison Industries." *American Journal of Corrections* 35 (November/December 1977): 12.

Carstensen, Fred, and Diane Roazen. "Foreign Markets, Domestic Initiative, and the Emergence of a Monocrop Economy: The Yucatecan Experience." *Hispanic American Historical Review* 72 (November 1992): 555–92.

———, and Diane Roazen-Parrillo. "International Harvester, Molina y Compañía, and the Henequen Market: A Comment." *Latin American Research Review* 18 (November 1983): 197–203.

Casson, Herbert N. *Cyrus Hall McCormick: His Life and Work.* Chicago: A. C. McClurg and Company, 1909.

———. *The Romance of the Reaper.* New York: Doubleday, Page, 1908.

Castro, Juan Miguel. *El henequén de Yucatán y el monopolio.* Mérida, Yuc.: Imprenta del "Comercio" de Néstor Rubio Alpuche, 1876.

Catling, Dorothy, and John Grayson. *Identification of Vegetable Fibres.* London: Chapman and Hall, 1982.

Chambers, Edward J., and Peter H. Smith, eds. *NAFTA in the New Millennium.* La Jolla, Calif.: Center for U.S.-Mexican Studies, University of San Diego; and Edmonton: University of Alberta Press, 2002.

Channing, Arnold, and Frederick J. Tabor Frost. *The American Egypt: A Record of Travel in Yucatan.* London: Hutchinson and Company, 1909.

Chardon, Roland. *Geographic Aspects of Plantation Agriculture in Yucatan.* Washington, D.C.: National Academy of Science, 1961.

Cherney, Robert W. *A Righteous Cause: The Life of William Jennings Bryan.* Boston: Little, Brown, 1985.

Chester, Charles C. *Conservation across Borders: Biodiversity in an Interdependent World.* Covelo, Calif.: Island Press, 2006.

Clarence-Smith, William Gervase, and Steven Topik, eds. *The Global Coffee Economy in Africa, Asia, and Latin America, 1500–1989.* New York: Cambridge University Press, 2003.

Clarke, Sally. "New Deal Regulation and the Revolution of American Farm Productivity: A Case Study of the Diffusion of the Tractor in the Corn Belt, 1920–1940." *Journal of Economic History* 51 (March 1991): 101–23.

———. *Regulation and the Revolution in United States Farm Productivity.* New York: Cambridge University Press, 1994.

Clements, Kendrick. "'A Kindness to Carranza': William Jennings Bryan, International Harvester, and Intervention in Yucatan." *Nebraska History* 57 (winter 1976): 479–90.

———. *William Jennings Bryan: Missionary Isolationist.* Knoxville: University of Tennessee Press, 1982.

Clendenen, Clarence. *The United States and Pancho Villa: A Study in Unconventional Diplomacy.* Ithaca, N.Y.: Cornell University Press, 1961.

Clendinnen, Inga. *Ambivalent Conquests: Maya and Spaniard in Yucatan, 1517–1570.* New York: Cambridge University Press, 1997.

Cline, Howard. "The Henequen Episode in Yucatan." *Inter-American Economic Affairs* 2 (autumn 1948): 30–51.

Coletta, Paolo E. *William Jennings Bryan.* Vol. 2, *Progressive Politician and Moral Statesman, 1909–1915.* Lincoln: University of Nebraska Press, 1969.

Congressional Record. 63rd Congress, 3rd session, 1914–15. Washington, D.C.: Government Printing Office, 1916.

Congressional Record. 64th Congress, 1st session, 1915–16. Washington, D.C.: Government Printing Office, 1916.

Constancias judiciales que demuestran que no existir esclavitud en Yucatán y que son falsas las imputaciones hechas en el libelo difamatorio. Mérida, Yuc.: Imprenta de la Lotería del Estado, 1905.

Cook, Peter. *Massey at the Brink: The Story of Canada's Greatest Multinational and Its Struggle to Survive.* Toronto: Collins, 1981.

Cornelius, Wayne A. "Impacts of NAFTA on Mexico-to-U.S. Migration." Pp. 287–304 in *NAFTA in the New Millennium,* edited by Edward J. Chambers and Peter H. Smith. La Jolla, Calif.: Center for U.S.-Mexican Studies, University of California, San Diego; Edmonton: University of Alberta Press, 2002. .

Cosío Villegas, Daniel. *Historia moderna de México: el porfiriato.* Vol. 4, *La vida social.* Mexico City: Editorial Hermes, 1957.

———. *Historia moderna de México: el porfiriato.* Vol. 9, *La vida política interior,* part 2. Mexico City: Editorial Hermes, 1972.

Cowan, Ruth Swartz. *A Social History of American Technology.* New York: Oxford University Press, 1977.

Cox, Sophie. *The True History of Chocolate.* London: Thames and Hudson, 1996.

Cronon, William. "A Place for Stories: Nature, History, and Narrative." *Journal of American History* 78 (March 1992): 1347–76.

———. *Nature's Metropolis: Chicago and the Great West.* New York: Norton, 1991.

Crosby, Alfred W., Jr. *America, Russia, Hemp, and Napoleon: American Trade with Russia and the Baltic, 1783–1812.* Columbus: Ohio State University Press, 1965.

———. *The Columbian Exchange: Biological and Cultural Consequences of 1492.* Westport, Conn.: Greenwood Press, 1972.

———. *Ecological Imperialism: The Biological Expansion of Europe, 900–1900.* New York: Cambridge University Press, 1993.

Crossette, Louis. "Sisal: Production, Prices, and Marketing." Trade Information Bulletin No. 200, Textile Division Supplement to Commerce Reports, U.S. Department of Commerce, Bureau of Foreign and Domestic Commerce, Prepared as Part of the Investigation of Essential Raw Materials Authorized by the Sixty-seventh Congress, February 25, 1924.

Cuestiones henequeneras. Mérida, Yuc.: Henequeneros Unidos, 1935 (anonymous pamphlet).

Cunfer, Geoff. *On the Great Plains: Agriculture and Environment.* College Station: Texas A&M University Press, 2005.

Curti, Merle Eugene. *Bryan and World Peace.* New York: Octagon Books, 1969.

Curtis, Dennis, et al. *Kingston Penitentiary: The First Hundred and Fifty Years, 1835–1985.* Ottawa: Correctional Services of Canada, 1985.

Dabdoub, Claudio. *Historia de el Valle del Yaqui.* Mexico City: Manuel Porrua, S.A., 1964.

Davidson, Debra J., and Ross E. Mitchell. "Environmental Challenges to International Trade." Pp. 265–86 in *NAFTA in the New Millennium*, edited by Edward J. Chambers and Peter H. Smith. La Jolla, Calif.: Center for U.S.-Mexican Studies, University of California, San Diego; Edmonton: University of Alberta Press, 2002.

Dean, Virgil, ed. "Wheat Culture in Kansas." Special double edition of *Kansas History* 23 (spring/summer 2000).

Dean, Warren. *Brazil and the Struggle for Rubber: A Study in Environmental History.* New York: Cambridge University Press, 1987.

Dempsey, James. *Fiber Crops.* Gainesville: University of Florida Press, 1975.

Denison, Merrill. *Harvest Triumphant: The Story of Massey-Harris.* Toronto: McClelland and Stewart, 1948.

Departamento de la Estadística Nacional. *Sonora, Sinaloa, y Nayarit: estudio estadística y económica social.* Mexico City: Imprenta Mundial, 1928.

de Teresa Ochoa, A. P. *Crisis agrícola y económica campesina: el caso de los productores de henequén en Yucatán.* Mexico City: Miguel Angel Porrua, 1992.

Dewey, Lyster H. "Fibers Used for Binder Twine." Pp. 193–200 in Yearbook of the Department of Agriculture, 1911. Washington, D.C.: U.S. Department of Agriculture, Government Printing Office, 1912.

Dewing, Arthur S. *A History of the National Cordage Company.* Cambridge, Mass.: Harvard University Press, 1913.

Díaz de Cossío, Martín. *Henequén: riqueza yucateca.* Mexico City: Editorial El Mundo, 1938.

Dozier, Craig. "Mexico's Transformed Northwest: The Yaqui, Mayo, and Fuerte Examples." *Geographical Review* 53 (October 1963): 548–71.

Drache, Hiram. *The Day of the Bonanza: A History of the Bonanza Farming in the Red River Valley of the North.* Fargo: North Dakota Institute for Regional Studies, 1964.

Duddridge, Hugh. *Seen from My Seeder Step.* Prince Albert, Sask.: n.p., 1950.

Dunlap, Thomas. *Nature and the English Diaspora: Environment and History in the United States, Canada, Australia, and New Zealand.* New York: Cambridge University Press, 1999.

Earle, Robert L., and John D. Wirth, eds. *Identities in North America: The Search for Community.* Stanford, Calif.: Stanford University Press, 1995.

Echegaray Bablot, Luis. *Irrigación, crisis henequenera y condiciones agrícolas y económicas de Yucatán.* Mexico City: n.p., 1956.

Edwards, Douglas M. "'The Greatest Hazard of Them All Is the "Human Element":' Manning the Machines of the World's Greatest Wheat Farm." *Montana* 51 (winter 2001): 26–37.

Erb, David, and Eldon Brumbaugh. *Full Steam Ahead: J. I. Case Tractors and Equipment, 1842–1955.* Saint Joseph, Mich.: American Society of Agricultural Engineers, 1993.

Escoffié, Manuel María. *Yucatán en la cruz.* Mérida, Yuc.: n.p., 1957.

Evans, Robert. *Prison Industries in the Canadian Penitentiary Service: A Survey Prepared for the Honourable George J. McGrath, Solicitor General of Canada.* Ottawa: Canadian Welfare Council, 1970.

Evans, Sterling. *Damming Sonora: Water, Agriculture, and Environmental Change in Northwest Mexico* (forthcoming).

———. "Dependent Harvests: Grain Production on the American and Canadian Plains and the Double Dependency with Mexico in the Early Twentieth Century." *Agricultural History* 80, no. 1 (Winter 2006): 35–63.

———. "Entwined in Conflict: The History of the South Dakota State Prison Twine Factory and the Controversy of 1919–1921." *South Dakota History* 35, no. 2 (Summer 2005): 95–124.

———. "From Kanasín to Kansas: Mexican Sisal, Binder Twine, and the State Penitentiary Twine Factory, 1890–1940." *Kansas History* 24 (Winter 2001–2002): 276–99.

———. "Prison-Made Binder Twine: North Dakota's Connection with Mexico in the Early Twentieth Century." *North Dakota History* 68 (2001): 20–36.

———. "Yaquis vs. Yanquis: An Environmental and Historical Comparison of Coping with Aridity in Southern Sonora." *Journal of the Southwest* 40 (Autumn 1998): 363–96.

———, ed. *The Borderlands of the American and Canadian Wests: Essays on Regional History of the 49th Parallel.* Lincoln: University of Nebraska Press, 2006.

Fabila, Alfonso. *Las tribus yaquis de Sonora: su cultura y anhelada autodeterminación.* Mexico City: Instituto Nacional Indigenista, 1978.

Fallaw, Ben W. "Bartolocallismo: Calles, García Correa, y la Cooperativa Henequenera de Yucatán, 1925–1933." *Boletín (Fideocomiso Archivos Plutarco Elías Calles y Fernando Torreblanco)* 27 (January–April 1998): 1–32.

———. *Cárdenas Compromised: The Failure of Reform in Post-Revolutionary Yucatán.* Durham, N.C.: Duke University Press, 2001.

———. "The Economic Foundations of Bartolismo: García Correa, the Yucatecan Hacendados, and the Henequen Industry, 1930–1933." English translation of "Los fundamentos económicos del bartolismo: García Correa, los hacendados yucatecos, y la industria henequenera, 1930–1933." *Unicornio: suplemento cultural de* ¡Por Esto! 7 (October 9 and 27, 1997): 3–9 (manuscript copy).

Faux, Jeff. "How NAFTA Failed Mexico." *American Prospect,* July 1, 2003, www.prospect.org/print/V14/7/faux-j.html.

Federal Writers' Project. Work Projects Administration. *Kansas: A Guide to the Sunflower State.* New York: Viking Press, 1939.

Fieguth, Joyce. *Flour Sacks and Binder Twine.* North Battleford, Sask.: McIntosh Publishing, 1973.

Figueroa, Alejandro. "Derechos políticos y organización social: el caso de los Yaquis." *Nueva antropología* 44 (August 1993): 43–60.

Fitchen, Edward D. "Self-Determination or Self-Preservation? The Relations of Independent Yucatán with the Republic of Texas and the United States, 1847–1849." *Journal of the West* 18 (January 1979): 32–40.

Fite, Gilbert. "The Transformation of South Dakota Agriculture: The Effects of Mechanization, 1939–1964." *South Dakota History* 19 (fall 1989): 278–305.

Flores, Dan. "Place: An Argument for Bioregional History." *Environmental History Review* 18 (Winter 1994): 1–18.

Flores, Jorge D. "La vida rural en Yucatán en 1914." *Historia mexicana* 10 (January–March 1961): 470–83.

Flores, José Salvador. "Caracterización de la vegetación en la zona henequenera de México." Pp. 77–81 in *Memorias de la Conferencia Nacional sobre el Henequén y Zona Henequenera de México,* edited by Piedad Peniche Rivero and Felipe Santamaría Basulto. Mérida: Estado de Yucatán, 1993.

Fontes, Montserrat. *Dreams of the Centaur.* New York: Norton, 1996.

Fornaro, Carlo de. "Yucatan and the International Harvester Company." *Forum* 54 (July–December 1915): 337–44.

Foster, Alice. "Sisal Production in Semi-Arid Karst Country of Yucatan." *Journal of Geography* 29 (January 1930): 16–25.

Foucault, Michel. *Discipline and Punish: The Birth of the Prison.* New York: Vintage Books, 1979.

Fowke, Vernon C. *The National Policy and the Wheat Economy.* Toronto: University of Toronto Press, 1957.

Francis, R. Douglas, and Howard Palmer, eds. *The Prairie West: Historical Readings.* Edmonton, Alta.: Pica Pica Press, 1985.

Friesen, Gerald. *The Canadian Prairies: A History.* Toronto: University of Toronto Press, 1987.

Friesen, Richard. "The Combine Harvester in Alberta: Its Development and Use, 1900–1950." Background Paper No. 9, Reynolds-Alberta Museum, Edmonton, 1983.

Gallagher, Kevin. *Free Trade and the Environment: Mexico, NAFTA, and Beyond.* Stanford, Calif.: Stanford University Press, 2004.

Ganzel, Bill. *Dust Bowl Descent.* Lincoln: University of Nebraska Press, 1984.

García Wikit, Santos. *Tribu yaqui.* Ciudad Obregón, Son.: Impresora y Editora de Occidente, 1964.

García y Alva, Federico. *México y sus progresos: album directorio del estado de Sonora.* Hermosillo: Imprenta Oficial, Gobierno del Estado de Sonora, 1905–1907.

Glad, Paul W. *The Trumpet Soundeth: William Jennings Bryan and His Democracy, 1896–1912.* Lincoln: University of Nebraska Press, 1960.

González Navarro, Moisés. *La colonización en México, 1877–1910.* Mexico City: n.p., 1960.

———. *Raza y tierra: la Guerra de Castas y el henequén.* Mexico City: Colegio de México, 1970.

Gouy-Gilbert, Cécile. "Los yaquis de Sonora: aculturación y resistencia." *La palabra y el hombre* 56 (October–December 1985): 21–28.

Grant, Michael Johnston. *Down and Out on the Family Farm: Rural Rehabilitation in the Great Plains, 1929–1945.* Lincoln: University of Nebraska Press, 2002.

Gray, James H. *Men against the Desert.* Saskatoon, Sask.: Western Prairie Producer Books, 1978.

Greening, Elwin G. "The Making of a Community: A History of Michigan City, Indiana." *Michigan City News-Dispatch,* March 7, 1976, available at www.mclib .org/ourherl.htm.

Grove, Richard. *Green Imperialism: Colonial Expansion, Tropical Island Edens, and the Origins of Environmentalism, 1600–1860.* New York: Cambridge University Press, 1996.

Gruening, Ernest. *Mexico and Its Heritage.* New York: Appleton-Century, 1928.

Guzman, Martín Luis. *The Eagle and the Serpent.* London: Knopf, 1930.

Hall, Greg. *Harvest Wobblies: The Industrial Workers of the World and Agricultural Laborers in the American West, 1905–1930.* Corvallis: Oregon State University Press, 2001.

Ham, George E., and Robin Higham, eds. *The Rise of the Wheat State: A History of Kansas Agriculture, 1861–1986.* Manhattan, Kans.: Sunflower University Press, 1987.

Hammer, Kenneth M. "Bonanza Farming: Forerunner of Modern Large-Scale Agriculture." *Journal of the West* 18 (October 1979): 52–61.

Harris, Charles, III, and Louis R. Sadler. "Pancho Villa and the Columbus Raid: The Missing Documents." *New Mexico Historical Review* 50, no. 4 (October 1975): 335–47.

Hart, John Mason. *Revolutionary Mexico: The Coming and Process of the Mexican Revolution.* Berkeley: University of California Press, 1987.

Harvey, Mark, Steve Quilley, and Huw Beynon. *Exploring the Tomato: Transformations of Nature, Society, and Economy.* Cheltenham, England: Edward Elgar Publishing, 2002.

Hebdige, Dick. "Object as Image: The Italian Motor Scooter." Pp. 77–115 in *Hiding in the Light*, edited by Dick Hebdige. New York: Routledge, 1989.

Hecht, Susanna, and Alexander Cockburn. *The Fate of the Forest: Developers, Destroyers, and Defenders of the Amazon*. New York: Harper Perennial, 1990.

Henderson, Caroline. *Letters from the Dust Bowl*. Norman: University of Oklahoma Press, 2001.

Hennessy, Peter H. *Canada's Big House: The Dark History of the Kingston Penitentiary*. Toronto: Dundora Group, 1999.

Herer, Jack. *The Emperor Wears No Clothes: The Authoritative Historical Record of Cannabis and the Conspiracy against Marijuana*. Van Nuys, Calif.: HEMP Publishing, 1985.

Hibben, Paxton. *The Peerless Leader: William Jennings Bryan*. New York: Russell and Russell, 1929.

Hill, Charles. "The First Combine." *Wisconsin Magazine of History* 35 (Summer 1952): 263–66.

Hopkins, James F. *A History of the Hemp Industry in Kentucky*. Lexington: University of Kentucky Press, 1951.

Hougen, Harvey R. "The Impact of Politics and Prison Industry on the General Management of the Kansas State Penitentiary, 1883–1909." *Kansas History* 43 (Autumn 1977): 297–318.

Huarte, Eduardo. *Eclipse total de la constitución para la tribu yaqui*. Mexico City: Tipográfico Mercantil, 1957.

Hu-deHart, Evelyn. "Development and Rural Rebellion: Pacification of the Yaquis in the Late *Porfiriato*." *Hispanic American Historical Review* 54 (February 1974): 72–93.

———. "Sonora: Indians and Immigrants on a Developing Frontier." Pp. 177–211 in *Other Mexicos: Essays on Regional Mexican History, 1876–1911*, edited by Thomas Benjamin and William McNellie. Albuquerque: University of New Mexico Press, 1984.

———. *Yaqui Resistance and Survival: The Struggle for Land and Autonomy, 1821–1910*. Madison: University of Wisconsin Press, 1984.

Hunter, William C. "The Bonanza Farms." *North Dakota History* 33 (Fall 1966): 399–419.

Hurt, R. Douglas. "Agricultural Technology in the Dust Bowl, 1932–40." Pp. 139–56 in *The Great Plains: Environment and Culture*, edited by Brian W. Blout and Frederick C. Luebke. Lincoln: University of Nebraska Press, 1979.

———. *American Farm Tools: From Hand Power to Steam Power*. Manhattan, Kans.: Sunflower University Press, 1987.

———. "Combine Harvesters." *Journal of the West* 30 (April 1991): 43–62.

———. *The Dust Bowl: An Agricultural and Social History*. Chicago: Nelson-Hall Publishers, 1981.

———. "Return of the Dust Bowl: The Filthy Fifties." *Journal of the West* 18 (October 1979): 85–93.

Hutchinson, William T. *Cyrus Hall McCormick: Harvest, 1856–1884*. New York: Appleton-Century, 1935.

International Harvester Company. *Saving the World from Starvation: The Miracle of Modern Farm Machinery*. Rev. ed. Chicago: International Harvester Company, 1929 (booklet).

Irigoyen, Renán. *El comercio de henequén a través del tiempo*. Mérida, Yuc.: Centro Regional de Estudios Políticos, Económicos, y Sociales, 1966.

———. *El comercio en Yucatán: reseña histórica*. Mérida, Yuc.: Editores Zamná, 1951.

———. *Ensayos henequeneros*. Mérida: Cordemex, 1975.

———. *Felipe Carrillo Puerto: primer gobernante socialista en México*. Mérida: Ediciones de la Universidad de Yucatán, 1974.

———. *¿Fue el auge del henequen producto de la guerra de castas?* Mérida, Yuc.: n.p., 1947.

———. *Los mayas y el henequén*. Mérida: Henequeneros de Yucatán, 1950.

———. *Salvador Alvarado: extraordinario estadista de la Revolución*. Mérida, Yuc.: Ediciones del Gobierno del Estado, 1973.

Isern, Thomas D. "The Adoption of the Combine on the Northern Plains." *South Dakota History* 10 (Spring 1980): 1–6.

———. *Bull Threshers and Bindlestiffs: Harvesting and Threshing on the North American Plains*. Lawrence: University Press of Kansas, 1990.

———. *Custom Combining on the Great Plains: A History*. Norman: University of Oklahoma Press, 1981.

———. "Folklife of the Threshing Outfit." *South Dakota History* 16 (Winter 1986): 18–34.

Izábal, Rafael. *Memorias de la administración pública del Estado de Sonora durante el período constitucional de 1903–1907*. Hermosillo, Son.: Imprenta Oficial, 1907.

Johnson, Benjamin, and Andrew Graybill, eds. *Bridging National Borders in North America*. Durham, N.C.: Duke University Press, forthcoming.

Jones, David C. *Empire of Dust: Settling and Abandoning the Prairie Dry Belt*. Edmonton: University of Alberta Press, 1987.

Jorgenson, Lloyd P. "Agricultural Expansion into the Semi-Arid Lands of the West North Central Plains during the First World War." *Agricultural History* 23 (January 1949): 30–40.

Joseph, Gilbert M. "From Caste War to Class War: The Historiography of Modern Yucatan (c. 1750–1940)." *Hispanic American Historical Review* 65 (February 1985): 111–34.

———. *Rediscovering the Past at Mexico's Periphery: Essays on the History of Modern Yucatan*. Tuscaloosa: University of Alabama Press, 1986.

———. *Revolution from Without: Yucatan, Mexico, and the United States, 1880–1924*. New York: University Press Cambridge, 1982.

———, and Jeffrey Brannon, eds. *Land, Labor, and Capital in Modern Yucatan*. Tuscaloosa: University of Alabama Press, 1991.

———, and Allen Wells. "Collaboration and Informal Empire in Yucatan: The Case for Political Economy." *Latin American Research and Review* 18 (November 1983): 204–18.

———. "Corporate Control of a Monocrop Economy: International Harvester and Yucatan's Henequen Industry during the *Porfiriato*." *Latin American Research Review* 17, no. 1 (1982): 69–100.

Kaplan, Edward S. *U.S. Imperialism in Latin America: Bryan's Challenges and Contributions, 1900–1920.* Westport, Conn.: Greenwood Press, 1998.

Katz, Friedrich. "Labor Conditions on Haciendas in Porfirian Mexico: Some Trends and Tendencies." *Hispanic American Historical Review* 54 (February 1974): 1–47.

———. *The Life and Times of Pancho Villa.* Stanford, Calif.: Stanford University Press, 1998.

———. "Pancho Villa and the Attack on Columbus, New Mexico." *American Historical Review* 83 (February 1978): 101–30.

———. *The Secret War in Mexico: Europe, the United States, and the Mexican Revolution.* Chicago: University of Chicago Press, 1981.

———. "El sistema de plantación y la esclavitud." *Ciencias políticas y sociales* 8 (January–March 1962): 103–35.

Kelley, Jane Holden. Introduction to *The Tall Candle: The Personal Chronicle of a Yaqui Indian,* by Rosalio Moisés, Jane Holden Kelley, and William Curry Holden. Lincoln: University of Nebraska Press, 1971.

———. *Yaqui Women: Contemporary Life Histories.* Lincoln: University of Nebraska Press, 1978.

Kirby, R. H. *Vegetable Fibres: Botany, Cultivation, and Utilization.* London: Leonard Hill, 1963.

Kiy, Richard, and John D. Wirth, eds. *Environmental Management on North America's Borders.* College Station: Texas A&M University Press, 1998.

Koenig, Louis W. *Bryan: A Political Biography of William Jennings Bryan.* New York: G. P. Putnam's Sons, 1971.

Konrad, Herman W. "De la subsistencia forestal tropical a la producción para exportación: la industria chiclera y la transformación de la economía maya de Quintana Roo de 1890 a 1935." Pp. 161–82 in *Etnohistoria e historia de las Américas,* edited by the International Congress of Americanists 1985. Bogotá: Ediciones Uniandes, 1988.

———. "North American Continental Relationships: Historical Trends and Antecedents." Pp. 15–35 in *NAFTA in Transition,* edited by Stephen J. Randall and Herman W. Konrad. Calgary: University of Calgary Press, 1995.

Kopinak, Kathryn. *Desert Capitalism: What Are the Maquiladoras?* Montreal: Black Rose Books, 1997.

———, ed. *The Social Costs of Industrial Growth in Northern Mexico.* La Jolla, Calif.: Center for U.S.-Mexican Studies, University of California, San Diego, 2004.

Kopytoff, Igor. "The Cultural Biography of Things: Commoditization as Process." Pp. 64–94 in *The Social Life of Things: Commodities in Cultural Perspective,* edited by Arjun Appadurai. Cambridge: Cambridge University Press, 1986.

Krauze, Enrique. *Puente entre siglos: Venustiano Carranza.* Mexico City: Fondo de Cultura Económica, 1987.

Kurlansky, Mark. *Cod: A Biography of the Fish That Changed the World.* New York: Walker Publishing, 1997.

———. *Salt: A World History.* New York: Walker Publishing, 2002.

Landa, Friar Diego de. *Yucatan before and after the Conquest.* 1566. Translated by William Gates. New York: Dover Publications, 1978.

Leopold, Aldo. *A Sand County Almanac.* 1949. New York: Ballantine, 1990.

Levine, Lawrence W. *Defender of the Faith, William Jennings Bryan: The Last Decade, 1915–1925.* New York: Oxford University Press, 1965.

Lichtenstein, Alex. *Twice the Work of Free Labor: The Political Economy of Convict Labor in the New South.* New York: Verso, 1996.

Lightman, Ernie S. "Industrial Work by Inmates in Correctional Facilities." Report no. 7903, Centre for Industrial Relations, University of Toronto, January 1979.

Link, Arthur S. *Wilson the Diplomatist: A Look at His Major Foreign Policies.* Baltimore, Md.: Johns Hopkins University Press, 1957.

———. *Wilson: The Road to the White House.* Princeton, N.J.: Princeton University Press, 1947.

———. *Wilson: The Struggle for Neutrality, 1914–1915.* Princeton, N.J.: Princeton University Press, 1960.

———, ed. *The Papers of Woodrow Wilson.* Vol. 32, *January 1–April 16, 1915.* Princeton, N.J.: Princeton University Press, 1980.

———, ed. *The Papers of Woodrow Wilson.* Vol. 33, *April 17–July 21, 1915.* Princeton, N.J.: Princeton University Press, 1980.

Lookingbill, Brad. *Dust Bowl, U.S.A.: Depression America and the Ecological Imagination, 1929–1941.* Athens: Ohio University Press, 2001.

Low, Ann Marie. *Dust Bowl Diary.* Lincoln: University of Nebraska Press, 1984.

Lyons, Norbert. *The McCormick Reaper Legend: The True Story of a Great Invention.* New York: Exposition Press, 1965.

MacEwan, Grant. *Between the Red and Rockies.* Toronto: University of Toronto Press, 1952.

Maiti, Ratikanta. *World Fiber Crops.* Enfield, N.H.: Science Publishers, 1997.

Malin, James C. "Dust Storms, 1850–1900." *Kansas Historical Quarterly* 14 (May, August, and November 1946): 129–44, 265–96, 391–413 (respectively).

———. *The Grassland of North America: Prolegomena to Its History.* Lawrence, Kans.: n.p., 1961.

———. *Winter Wheat in the Golden Belt of Kansas: A Study in Adaptation to Subhumid Geographical Environment.* Lawrence: University of Kansas Press, 1944.

Mancini, Matthew J. *One Dies, Get Another: Convict Leasing in the American South, 1866–1928.* Columbia: University of South Carolina Press, 1996.

Manero, Enrique. *La anarquía henequenera de Yucatán.* Mexico: n.p., 1966.

Marsh, Barbara. *A Corporate Tragedy: The Agony of the International Harvester Company.* Garden City, N.Y.: Doubleday, 1985.

McCormick, Cyrus Hall. *A Century of the Reaper.* Boston: Houghton-Mifflin, 1931.

McGinn, Elinor Myers. *At Hard Labor: Inmate Labor and the Colorado State Penitentiary, 1871–1940.* New York: Peter Lang Publishing, 1993.

McGuire, Thomas R. *Politics and Ethnicity on the Río Yaqui: Potam Revisited.* Tucson: University of Arizona Press, 1986.

McMahon, Brian. "Industrial Training: An Historical Perspective." *Minnesota Works* 1 (spring 1999): 2–30.

McNeill, J. R. *The Mountains of the Mediterranean World: An Environmental History.* New York: Cambridge University Press, 2003.

Meinig, D. W. *The Shaping of America: A Geographic Perspective on 500 Years of History.*
    Vol. 2, *Continental America, 1800–1867.* New Haven, Conn.: Yale University Press,
    1993.

Melossi, Dario, and Massimo Pavarini. *The Prison and the Factory: Origins of the Peni-
    tentiary System.* Translated by Glynis Cousin. Totowa, N.J.: Barnes and Noble
    Books, 1981.

Menéndez Rodríguez, Mario. *Yucatán o el genocidio.* Mexico City: FCE, 1964.

Miller, Neal, and Robert C. Greiser. "The Evolution of Prison Industries." Pp. 1–18
    in *A Study of Prison Industry: History, Components, and Goals.* College Park, Md.:
    American Correctional Association, 1986.

Miller, Tom. *The Panama Hat Trail.* Washington, D.C.: Adventure Press/National
    Geographic, 1986.

Mills, Walter Thomas. *The Struggle for Existence.* Chicago: International School of
    Social Economy, 1904.

Miner, Craig. *Next Year Country: Dust to Dust in Western Kansas, 1890–1940.* Lawrence:
    University Press of Kansas, 2006.

———. *West of Wichita: Settling the High Plains of Kansas, 1865–1890.* Lawrence:
    University Press of Kansas, 1986.

Mintz, Sidney W. *Sweetness and Power: The Place of Sugar in Modern History.* New York:
    Viking, 1985.

Mizrahi, Aliza, et al. "Composition, Structure and Management Potential of Sec-
    ondary Dry Tropical Vegetation in Two Abandoned Henequen Plantations of
    Yucatan, Mexico." *Forest Ecology and Management* 96 (September 1997): 273–82.

Moisés, Rosalio, Jane Holden Kelley, and William Curry Holden. *The Tall Candle: The
    Personal Chronicle of a Yaqui Indian.* Lincoln: University of Nebraska Press, 1971.

Molina Font, Gustavo. *El problema agrario en la Zona Henequenera de Yucatán.* Mexico
    City: Imprenta Varona, 1934.

Morlan, Robert L. *Political Prairie Fire: The Nonpartisan League, 1915–1922.* Minneapo-
    lis: University of Minnesota Press, 1955.

Moseley, Edward H., and Edward D. Terry, eds. *Yucatan: A World Apart.* Tuscaloosa:
    University of Alabama Press, 1980.

Moxham, Roy. *Tea: Addiction, Exploitation, and Empire.* New York: Carroll and Graf,
    2003.

Murray, Douglas L. *Cultivating Crisis: The Human Cost of Pesticides in Latin America.*
    Austin: University of Texas Press, 1994.

Murray, Stanley N. *The Valley Comes of Age: A History of Agriculture in the Valley of the Red
    River of the North.* Fargo: North Dakota Institute for Regional Studies, 1967.

National Center for Policy Analysis. "Factories behind Bars." www.ncpa.org/studies/
    s206/s206rw.html.

Nelson, Paul D. "'The Greatest Single Industry'? Crex: Created Out of Nothing."
    Ramsey County (Minnesota) History 40 (Winter 2006): 4–15.

Nervo, Amado. *Obras completas de Amado Nervo.* Vol. 20, *Cuentos misteriosos.* Madrid:
    Biblioteca Nueva, 1921.

Nesbitt, Leonard D. *The Story of Wheat.* Calgary: Alberta Wheat Pool, 1949 (pamphlet).

Nevaer, Louis E. V. *NAFTA's Second Decade: Assessing Opportunities in the Mexican and Canadian Markets.* Mason, Ohio: South-Western Educational Publications, 2004.

Noble, David F. *America by Design: Science, Technology, and the Rise of Corporate Capitalism.* New York: Oxford University Press, 1977.

———. *Forces of Production: A Social History of Industrial Automation.* New York: Oxford University Press, 1986.

Oakley, F. I. *Long Vegetable Fibres.* London: Ernest Benn, 1928.

Oliver, Peter. *"Terror to Evil-Doers": Prisons and Punishment in Nineteenth-Century Ontario.* Toronto: University of Toronto Press, 1998.

Orellana, Roger. "Agave, Agavaceae y familias afines en la Península de Yucatán." Pp. 82–91 in *Memorias de la Conferencia Nacional sobre el henequén y la Zona Henequenera de Yucatán,* edited by Piedad Peniche Rivero and Felipe Santamaría Basulto. Mérida: Estado de Yucatán, 1993.

Orosa Díaz, Jaime. *Felipe Carrillo Puerto (Estudio biográfico).* Mérida: Fondo Editorial de Yucatán, 1982.

———, ed. *Legislación henequenera en Yucatán (1833–1955).* Mérida: Editores Fomento de Yucatán, 1956.

Owen, Norman G. *Prosperity without Progress: Manila Hemp and the Material Life in the Colonial Philippines.* Berkeley: University of California Press, 1984.

Padilla Ramos, Raquel. *Yucatán, el fin del sueño yaqui: el tráfico de los yaquis y el otro triunvirato.* Hermosillo: Gobierno del Estado de Sonora, la Secretaría de Educación y Cultura, 1995.

Paoli, Francisco José. *Yucatán y los orígenes del nuevo estado mexicano: gobierno de Salvador Alvarado, 1915–1918.* Mexico City: Ediciones Era, 1984.

Paoli Bolio, José Antonio. *Cárdenas y el reparto de los henequenales.* Mérida: Gobierno del Estado de Yucatán, 1986.

Partridge, Michael. *Farm Tools across the Ages.* Reading, England: Osprey Publishing, 1973.

Pasos Peniche, Manuel. *Historia de la industria henequenera desde 1945 hasta nuestros días.* Mérida, Yuc.: n.p., 1974.

Patch, Robert W. "Agrarian Change in Eighteenth-Century Yucatan." *Hispanic American Historical Review* 65 (February 1985): 21–49.

Pendergrast, Mark. *Uncommon Grounds: The History of Coffee and How It Transformed Our World.* New York: Basic Books, 2000.

"Peones huastecos enganchados para las haciendas de Yucatán, 1893." Reprinted in *Documentos históricos peninsulares,* vol. 12. Mérida: Instituto de Cultura de Yucatán, 1995.

Pettigrew, Jane. *A Social History of Tea.* London: National Trust, 2002.

Pickett, Evelyn Stitt. "Hoboes across the Border: A Comparison of Itinerant Cross-Border Laborers between Montana and Western Canada." *Montana* 49 (Spring 1999): 18–31.

Pollan, Michael. *The Botany of Desire: A Plant's-Eye View of the World.* New York: Random House 2001.

Pomfret, Richard. "The Mechanization of Reaping in Nineteenth-Century Ontario." *Journal of Economic History* 36 (June 1976): 399–415.

Purcell, Carroll W. *The Machine in America: A Social History of Technology.* Baltimore, Md.: Johns Hopkins University Press, 1995.

Quick, Graeme, and Wesley Buchele. *The Grain Harvesters.* Saint Joseph, Mich.: American Society of Agricultural Engineers, 1978.

Randall, Stephen J., and Herman W. Konrad, eds. *NAFTA in Transition.* Calgary: University of Calgary Press, 1995.

Rasmussen, Wayne D. "The Impact of Technological Change on American Agriculture, 1862–1962." *Journal of Economic History* 22 (December 1962): 578–91.

———, ed. *Readings in the History of American Agriculture.* Urbana: University of Illinois Press, 1960.

Reed, Nelson. *The Caste War of Yucatan.* Stanford, Calif.: Stanford University Press, 1964.

Ricardo, David. *On the Principles of Political Economy and Taxation.* London: John Murray, 1819.

Richmond, Robert W. *Kansas: A Land of Contrasts.* Saint Louis, Mo.: Forum Press, 1980.

Rikoon, J. Stanford. *Threshing in the Midwest, 1820–1940: A Study of Traditional Culture and Technological Change.* Bloomington: Indiana University Press, 1988.

Riney-Kehrberg, Pamela. *Rooted in Dust: Surviving Drought and Depression in Southwestern Kansas.* Lawrence: University Press of Kansas, 1994.

Robbins, Bruce. "Commodity Histories." *PMLA* 120 (Mar. 2005): 454–63.

Robbins, William. *Colony and Empire: The Capitalist Transformations of the American West.* Lawrence: University Press of Kansas, 1994.

Robinson, Elwyn B. *History of North Dakota.* Lincoln: University of Nebraska Press, 1966.

Robinson, Louis N. *Should Prisoners Work?: A Study of the Prison Labor Problem in the United States.* Chicago: John C. Winston Co., 1931.

Rodríguez, Antonio. *El henequén: una planta calumniada.* Mexico City: B. Costa-Amic, 1966.

Rogin, Leo. *The Introduction of Farm Machinery in Its Relation to the Productivity of Labor in the Agriculture of the United States during the Nineteenth Century.* Berkeley: University of California Press, 1931.

Rugeley, Terry. *Yucatan's Maya Peasantry and the Origins of the Caste War.* Austin: University of Texas Press, 1996.

Ruiz, Ramón Eduardo. *The People of Sonora and Yankee Capitalists.* Tucson: University of Arizona Press, 1988.

Ruz Menéndez, Rodolfo. "Los yaquis en las haciendas henequeneras de Yucatán." *Revista de la Universidad de Yucatán* 22 (January/February 1980): 58–72.

Rybczynski, Witold. *One Good Turn: A Natural History of the Screwdriver and Screws.* New York: Touchstone, 2000.

Sanders, Thomas. *Henequen: The Structure of Agrarian Frustration.* Hanover, N.H.: American Universities Field Staff, 1977.

Sanderson, Steven E. *Agrarian Populism and the Mexican State: The Struggle for Land in Sonora.* Berkeley: University of California Press, 1981.

———. *The Transformation of Mexican Agriculture: International Structure and the Politics of Rural Change.* Princeton, N.J.: Princeton University Press, 1986.

Savala, Refugio. *The Autobiography of a Yaqui Poet.* Tucson: University of Arizona Press, 1980.

Sayre, L. E. "The Manufacture of Binding Twine." In *Transactions of the Kansas Academy of Science, 1889.* Topeka: Kansas Publishing House, 1890.

Schell, Herbert S. *History of South Dakota.* 3rd ed. Lincoln: University of Nebraska Press, 1975.

Schlebecker, John T. *Whereby We Thrive: A History of American Farming, 1607–1972.* Ames: Iowa State University Press, 1975.

Sears, Paul. *Deserts on the March.* 1935. Norman: University of Oklahoma Press, 1980.

Self, Huber. *Environment and Man in Kansas: A Geographical Analysis.* Lawrence: Regents Press of Kansas, 1978.

Sevilla Mascarenas, Mario. *Aquí Sonora, S.O.S.* Mexico City: Ciclo Ediciones Calpuleque, 1977.

Shapiro, Karin. *A New South Rebellion: The Battle against Convict Labor in the Tennessee Coalfields, 1871–1896.* Chapel Hill: University of North Carolina Press, 1998.

Shepard, R. Bruce. "The Mechanized Agricultural Frontier of the Canadian Plains." *Material History Bulletin of the Museum of Man* 7 (Spring 1979): 1–22.

———, and Thomas D. Isern. "The Adoption of the Combine on the Canadian Plains." *American Review of Canadian Studies* 16 (Winter 1986): 455–64.

Simon, Frances H. *Prisoners' Work and Vocational Training.* London: Routledge, 1999.

Simonian, Lane. *Defending the Land of the Jaguar: A History of Conservation in Mexico.* Austin: University of Texas Press, 1995.

Smith, Cornelius C. *Emilio Kosterlitzky: Eagle of Sonora and the Southwest Border.* Glendale, Calif.: Arthur H. Clark Co., 1970.

Smith, Peter H. "From NAFTA to FTAA: Paths toward Hemispheric Integration." Pp. 471–95 in *NAFTA in the New Millennium,* edited by Edward J. Chambers and Peter H. Smith. La Jolla, Calif.: Center for U.S.-Mexican Studies, University of San Diego; and Edmonton: University of Alberta Press, 2002.

Snow, Sinclair. Introduction to *Barbarous Mexico,* by John Kenneth Turner. Austin: University of Texas Press, 1969.

Socolofsky, Homer. *Kansas Governors.* Lawrence: University Press of Kansas, 1990.

Soluri, John. *Banana Cultures: Agriculture, Consumption, and Environmental Change in Honduras and the United States.* Austin: University of Texas Press, 2005.

Spector, David. "Agriculture on the Prairies, 1870–1940." *History and Archaeology / Histoire et archéologie* 65 (1983): 215–60.

Spicer, Edward. *Cycles of Conquest: The Impact of Spain, Mexico, and the United States on the Indians of the Southwest, 1533–1960.* 1962. Tucson: University of Arizona Press, 1992.

———. "Highlights of Yaqui History." *The Indian Historian* 7 (Spring 1974): 2–9.

———. Introduction to *The Autobiography of a Yaqui Poet,* by Refugio Savala. Tucson: University of Arizona Press, 1980.

———. *The Yaquis: A Cultural History*. Tucson: University of Arizona Press, 1980.

Stabler, Edward. *A Brief Narrative of the Invention of Reaper Machines*. Chicago: W. B. Conkey, 1897.

Suárez Molina, Víctor. *La evolución económica de Yucatán a través del siglo XIX: apuntes históricos*. 2 vols. Mexico City: Ediciones de la Universidad de Yucatán, 1977.

Svobida, Lawrence. *Farming the Dust Bowl: A First-Hand Account from Kansas*. Lawrence: University Press of Kansas, 1986.

Swift, Edgar F. "Farm Machines in Mexico." *Harvester World* 3 (November 1911): 27–28.

Swift, Rodney. *Who Invented the Reaper?* Chicago: n.p., 1897.

Thelen, David. "The Nation and Beyond: Transnational Perspectives on United States History." *Journal of American History* 86 (December 1999): 965–75.

Thomas, Lewis H. "Early Combines in Saskatchewan." *Saskatchewan History* 8 (Winter 1955): 1–15.

———. "A History of Agriculture on the Prairies." *Prairie Forum* 1 (April 1976): 31–44.

Thompson, John Herd. "Bringing in the Sheaves: The Harvest Excursionists, 1890–1929." *Canadian Historical Review* 59 (summer 1978): 467–89.

———. *The Harvests of War: The Prairie West, 1914–1918*. Toronto: McClelland and Stewart, 1978.

———. "'Permanently Wasteful but Immediately Profitable': Prairie Agriculture and the Great War." *Historical Papers* (Canadian Historical Association), 11, no. 1 (1976): 193–206.

"Thresher Sales in Western Canada, 1928–1946." *Canadian Farm Implements* 43 (January 1947): 6–7.

Thwaites, Reuben Gold. *Cyrus Hall McCormick and the Reaper*. Madison: State Historical Society of Wisconsin, 1909.

Torre, Manuel A. *La ruina del henequén*. Mérida, Yuc.: Imprenta Universal, 1918.

Tres procesos de lucha por la sobrevivencia de la tribu yaqui: testimonios. Hermosillo, Son.: PACMYC, 1994.

Troncoso, Francisco P. *Las guerras con las tribus yaqui y mayo del estado de Sonora*. Mexico City: Departamento de Estado Mayor, 1905.

Truett, Samuel. *Fugitive Landscapes: The Forgotten History of the U.S.-Mexico Borderlands*. New Haven, Conn.: Yale University Press, 2006.

———. "Neighbors by Nature: Rethinking Region, Nation, and Environmental History in the U.S.-Mexico Borderlands." *Environmental History* 2 (April 1997): 160–78.

———. "Transnational Warrior: Emilio Kosterlitzky and the Transformation of the U.S.-Mexico Borderlands." Pp. 241–70 in *Continental Crossroads: Remapping U.S.-Mexico Borderlands History*, edited by Samuel Truett and Elliott Young. Durham, N.C.: Duke University Press, 2004.

———, and Elliott Young. "Making Transnational History: Nations, Regions, and Borderlands." Pp. 1–32 in *Continental Crossroads: Remapping U.S.-Mexico Borderlands History*, edited by Samuel Truett and Elliott Young. Durham, N.C.: Duke University Press, 2004.

Turner, Jack. *Spice: The History of a Temptation.* New York: Knopf, 2004.

Turner, John Kenneth. "American Capitalism's Official Executioners." *Appeal to Reason,* July 30, 1910.

————. *Barbarous Mexico.* 1911. Austin: University of Texas Press, 1969.

Tweton, Jerome. "The Golden Age of Agriculture." *North Dakota History* 37 (winter 1970): 41–56.

Tyrrell, Ian. "American Exceptionalism in the Age of Internationalism." *American Historical Review* 96 (October 1991): 1031–55.

United Nations Conference on Trade and Development (UNCTAD) Secretariat. "The Marketing of Hard Fibres (Sisal and Henequen): Areas for International Co-operation." A report in Studies in the Processing, Marketing and Distribution of Commodities series. New York: United Nations, 1984.

United States. Department of Agriculture. *Wheat: Acreage Yield Production by States, 1866–1943.* Statistical Bulletin No. 158, February 1955. Washington, D.C.: U.S. Department of Agriculture, Agricultural Marketing Service, 1955.

United States. Senate. Committee on Foreign Relations. *Investigation of Mexican Affairs: Preliminary Report and Hearings of the Committee on Foreign Relations, U.S. Senate.* Washington, D.C.: Government Printing Office, 1920.

————. Subcommittee on Agriculture and Forestry. "Hearings on Importation of Sisal and Manila Hemp." 64th Congress, 1st session, 1915–16. Washington, D.C.: Government Printing Office, 1916.

University of Saskatchewan. College of Agriculture. *Farm Business in Saskatchewan.* Agricultural Extension Bulletin No. 37, June 1927.

Valencia Jusacamea, Arturo. "Agricultura tradicional yaqui." *Cuadernos de trabajo* 4 (November/December 1985): 1–61.

Valenzuela-Zapata, Ana G., and Gary Paul Nabhan. *¡Tequila! A Natural and Cultural History.* Tucson: University of Arizona Press, 2003.

van Zyl Smit, Dirk, and Frieder Dünkel, eds. *Prison Labour: Salvation or Slavery? International Perspectives.* Aldershot, England: Dartmouth Publishing, 1999.

Vandiver, Frank E. *Black Jack: The Life and Times of John J. Pershing.* Vol. 2. College Station: Texas A&M University Press, 1977.

Veeman, Michelle M., Terrence S. Veeman, and Ryan Hoskins. "NAFTA and Agriculture: Challenges for Trade and Policy." Pp. 305–30 in *NAFTA in the New Millennium,* edited by Edward J. Chambers and Peter H. Smith. Edmonton: University of Alberta Press; and La Jolla, Calif.: Center for U.S.-Mexican Studies, University of California, San Diego, 2002.

Velasco Toro, José. *Los yaquis: historia de una activa resistencia.* Xalapa, Ver.: Editorial Biblioteca Universidad Veracruzana, 1988.

Villanueva Mukul, Eric. *Así tomamos las tierras: henequén y haciendas en Yucatán durante el porfiriato.* Mérida, Yuc.: Maldonado Editores, 1984.

————. *Crisis henequenera, reconversión económica y movimientos campesinos en Yucatán.* Mérida, Yuc.: Maldonado Editores, 1993.

————. "La reordenación henequenera en Yucatán: 1984–1991." Pp. 360–79 in *Memorias de la Conferencia Nacional sobre el Henequén y la Zona Henequenera de Yucatán,* edited by Piedad Peniche Rivero and Felipe Santamaría Basulto. Mérida: Estado de Yucatán, 1993.

———, et al., eds. *El henequén en Yucatán: industria, mercado y campesinos*. Mérida, Yuc.: Maldonado Editores, 1990.

Voisey, Paul. *Vulcan: The Making of a Prairie Community*. Toronto: University of Toronto Press, 1988.

Waibel, Leo. "The Tropical Plantation System." *Scientific Monthly* 52 (February 1941): 156–60.

Waiser, Bill. *Saskatchewan: A New History*. Calgary, Alta.: Fifth House, 2005.

Walker, Donald R. *Penology for Profit: A History of the Texas Prison System, 1876–1912*. College Station: Texas A&M University Press, 1988.

Walsh, Casey, et al., eds. *The Social Relations of Mexican Commodities: Power, Production, and Place*. La Jolla, Calif.: Center for U.S.-Mexican Studies, University of California, San Diego, 2003.

Ward, Tony. "Farming Technology and Crop Area on Early Prairie Farms." *Prairie Forum* 20 (Spring 1995): 19–36.

Warnock, John. *The Other Mexico: The North American Triangle Completed*. Montreal: Black Rose Books, 1995.

Webb, Walter Prescott. *The Great Plains*. Boston: Ginn, 1931.

Weir, David, and Mark Shapiro. *The Circle of Poison*. San Francisco: Institute for Food and Development Policy, 1981.

Wells, Allen. "Family Élites in a Boom and Bust Economy: The Molinas and Peóns of Porfirian Yucatan." *Hispanic American Historical Review* 62 (May 1982): 224–53.

———. "From Hacienda to Plantation: Transformation of Santo Domingo Xcuyum." Pp. 114–37 in *Land, Labor, and Capital in Modern Yucatan*, edited by Gilbert Joseph and Jeffrey Brannon. Tuscaloosa: University of Alabama Press, 1991.

———. "Henequen." Pp. 85–124 in *The Second Conquest of Latin America: Coffee, Henequen, and Oil during the Export Boom, 1850–1930*, edited by Steven C. Topik and Allen Wells. Austin: University of Texas Press, 1998.

———. "El henequén y el mercado de fibras duras: duras lecciones de la 'Epoca Dorada.'" Pp. 184–221 in *Memorias de la Conferencia Nacional sobre el Henequén y la Zona Henequenera de Yucatán*, edited by Piedad Peniche Rivero and Felipe Santamaría Basulto. Mérida: Estado de Yucatán, 1993.

———. "Yucatan: Violence and Social Control on Henequen Plantations." Pp. 213–41 in *Other Mexicos: Essays on Regional Mexican History, 1876–1911*, edited by Thomas Benjamin and William McNellie. Albuquerque: University of New Mexico Press, 1984.

———. *Yucatan's Gilded Age: Haciendas, Henequen, and International Harvester, 1860–1915*. Albuquerque: University of New Mexico Press, 1985.

———, and Gilbert Joseph. *Summer of Discontent, Seasons of Upheaval: Elite Politics and Rural Insurgency in Yucatan, 1876–1915*. Stanford, Calif.: Stanford University Press, 1996.

Wendel, C. H. *One Hundred Fifty Years of International Harvester*. Sarasota, Fla.: Crestline Publishing, 1981.

White, Richard. "The Nationalization of Nature." *Journal of American History* 86 (December 1999): 976–86.

Wilkins, Robert P., and Wynona Huchette Wilkins. *North Dakota: A Bicentennial History*. New York: Norton, 1977.

Wilson, Charles F. *A Century of Canadian Grain: Government Policy to 1951*. Saskatoon, Sask.: Western Producer Prairie Books, 1978.

Wilson, Eugene M. "The Physical Geography of the Yucatan Peninsula." Pp. 5–40 in *Yucatan: A World Apart*, edited by Edward H. Moseley and Edward D. Terry. Tuscaloosa: University of Alabama Press, 1980.

Wirth, John D. "Advancing the North American Community." *American Review of Canadian Studies* 26 (summer 1996): 261–73.

Wolf, Eric R. *Europe and the People without History*. Berkeley: University of California Press, 1982.

———, and Sidney Mintz. "Haciendas and Plantations in Middle America." *Social and Economic Studies* 7 (1957): 380–412.

Worster, Donald. *Dust Bowl: The Southern Plains in the 1930s*. New York: Oxford University Press, 1979.

———. "World without Borders: The Internationalizing of Environmental History." Pp. 661–70 in *Environmental History: Critical Issues in Comparative Perspective*, edited by Kendall Bailes. Lanham, Md.: University Press of America, 1985.

Wright, Angus. *The Death of Ramón González: The Modern Agricultural Dilemma*. Austin: University of Texas Press, 1990.

Wunder, John R., Frances W. Kaye, and Vernon Carstensen, eds. *Americans View Their Dust Bowl Experience*. Boulder: University Press of Colorado, 1999.

Zavala Castro, Palemón. *El indio Tetabiate y la nación de los ocho pueblos del Río Yaqui*. Hermosillo: Gobierno del Estado de Sonora, 1991.

Zinn, Howard. *A People's History of the United States, 1492 to the Present*. New York: HarperCollins, 1980.

Zuckerman, Larry. *The Potato: How the Humble Spud Rescued the World*. New York: North Point Press, 1998.

Dissertations, Theses, and Conference Papers

Barber, Gerald. "Horizons of Thorns: Yucatan at the Turn of the Century." M.A. thesis, University of the Americas, 1974.

Berkovits, Joseph A. G. "'Us Poor Devils': Prison Life and Culture in Ontario, 1874–1914." Ph.D. dissertation, University of Toronto, 2000.

Chacón, Ramón D. "Yucatan and the Mexican Revolution: The Pre-Constitution Years, 1910–1918." Ph.D. dissertation, Stanford University, 1982.

Denton, James Larry. "The Adaptation and Diffusion of the Combined Harvester-Thresher in the United States." Ph.D. dissertation, North Carolina State University, 1977.

Foucauld, Deirdre. "Prison Labour, Punishment, or Reform: The Canadian Penitentiary System, 1867–1960." M.A. thesis, University of Ottawa, 1982.

Gildemeister, Glen A. "Prison Labor and Convict Competition with Free Workers in Industrializing America, 1840–1890." Ph.D. dissertation, Northern Illinois University, 1977.

Hartman, Keith. "The Henequen Empire in Yucatan, 1870–1910." M.A. thesis, University of Iowa, 1966.

Joseph, Gilbert Michael. "Revolution from Without: The Mexican Revolution in Yucatan, 1915–1924." Ph.D. dissertation, Yale University, 1978.

Montalvo, Enrique. "Imperialismo y henequén: estudio de las clases sociales en Yucatán, 1900–1919." Thesis, Universidad Iberoamericana (Mexico City), 1976.

Neeley, Michael. "The Henequen Industry of Yucatan." M.A. thesis, University of Texas, 1967.

Neufeld, Roger E. "A World within Itself: Kingston Penitentiary and Foucauldian Panopticism, 1834–1914." M.A. thesis, Queens University, 1993.

Raymond, Nathaniel. "The Impact of Land Reform in the Monocrop Region of Yucatan, Mexico." Ph.D. dissertation, Brandeis University, 1971.

Remmers, Lawrence James. "Henequen, the Caste War, and the Economy of Yucatan, 1846–1883: The Roots of Dependence in a Mexican Region." Ph.D. dissertation, UCLA, 1981.

Shuman, Malcolm K. "The Town Where Luck Fell: The Economics of Life in a Henequen Zone Pueblo." Ph.D. dissertation, Tulane University, 1974.

Taylor, Joseph, III. "Boundary Terminology." Paper presented at the conference of the American Society for Environmental History, Saint Paul, Minn., March 31, 2006.

Wells, Allen. "Henequen and Yucatan: An Analysis in Regional Economic Development, 1876–1915." Ph.D. dissertation, State University of New York–Stony Brook, 1979.

Winter, Steven B. "Towards a Fair FTAA: Brazil and Agricultural Trade in the Americas." M.A. thesis, University of Kansas, 2003.

Wirth, John D. "Pike's Progress: A North American Agenda for Environmental Historians." Paper presented at the Ninth Biennial Conference of the American Society for Environmental History, Baltimore, Md., March 1997.

Interviews

Antochiw, Michel (historian, anthropologist). June 6, 1999, Mérida, Yuc.

López López, Egidio (*comisario ejidal,* or commissioner of communal lands). June 6, 1999, San Antonio Tehuitz, Yuc.

Reling, Harold (keeper of the "World's Largest Ball of Twine"). May 27, 1996, Cawker City, Kans.

INDEX

abacá fiber (manila), 6–7, 21–24, 41–42, 106, 113, 126–28, 135, 153, 164, 172, 198
Adee, Alvey A., 108
Africa, 30, 111, 135, 147, 158, 171, 176, 198, 226; *see also* East Africa
agaves, xvii, 22, 34–35, 48, 200
agriculture, North American, xvii, xviii, 5, 40, 115, 181, 229–30, 240; transformations of, xix, 1, 201; historiography of, xix, xx, xxii, xxiii, 121
Akron Twine and Cordage Co., 22
Alaska, 63
Alberta, 10, 11, 106, 131, 161, 185, 187, 204, 210, 239
Allen, Henry J., 194–95, 196, 231
Alvarado, Salvador, 45, 48, 66, 238; as revolutionary leader in Yucatán, 82–83, 93–96, 104, 108–109, 113, 116, 180, 188, 192, 193; agrarian policies of, 165–66, 171–73, 197, 214
Amador, Juan, 97
Amarillo, Texas, 8
American Chicle Co., 95
American Correctional Association, 133
American Grass Twine Co., 28
Ancient Order of Gleaners, 169
Angola, 226
Anslinger, Harry, 27
Apache Indians, 68
Appleby, John F., 5–6, 7
Argentina, 47, 101, 120, 208, 210, 214, 216, 235
Arizona, 67, 71–73, 77, 79, 82, 83, 85
Arizona Rangers, 72
Arredondo, Eliseo, 108, 113, 173
Ashurst-Sumners Act of 1935, 123
Asia, 27, 28, 30, 56–57
Australia, 210
Austria-Hungary, 47
Ávila, Eleuterio, 92

Baerlein, Harry, 59, 85
Bailey, Willis, 133
Baja California, 201
balers, baler twine, 158, 225, 226, 233
Banderas, Juan, 69
banana industry, xxii, 40
Barry, Dave, 234
Battle of Celaya, 119
Behel, Jacob, 5
Belgium, 47, 95, 116, 214
binder twine, xvii, xviii, xxii, 98, 101, 212–13; demand for, 27, 92, 102, 113, 115, 120, 162–63, 179, 181, 197, 202–204, 208, 231; kinds and types of, 21–22, 223; history of, xxiii, 4–7, 41, 120, 240; manufacture of, 16–22, 24, 89, 107–108, 114, 121, 126–60, 168, 179, 217; popular culture of, xviii, 24, 224–25, 232–35, 239; *see also* synthetic twines
binders, xi, xvii–xviii, 40, 184, 233, 238–39; harvesting with, 10, 14, 15, 201–202, 205–207, 229; invention of, 4–7, 32; manufacture of, 14, 16, 126; sales of, 7–8, 11–13, 223
bioregionalism, xxii
Bismarck, North Dakota, 105, 110, 111, 120, 125, 131–34, 136, 146–47, 156, 238
bonanza farms, 9–10
Borden, Robert Laird, xx, 91, 110, 238
borders, borderlands, xxi, xxii, 71–72, 73, 84, 118, 129, 148
Boston, 24, 45, 106, 126, 147
Brandon, Manitoba, xiv, 12, 239
Brantford Cordage Co., 21, 26, 148, 208
Brazil, 26, 47, 81, 100, 198, 226, 228, 235
Bristow, Joseph, 112
British Commonwealth, 110, 112, 171, 215, 219
British West Indies, 198, 200
Bryan, William Jennings, 91, 97–104, 107–14, 116–17, 118, 120, 238
Buffalo Soldiers, 118

Calgary, Alberta, 12, 106, 205
California, xi, 11, 27, 29, 31, 58, 131, 183, 201, 208
Calles, Plutarco Elías, 83, 188, 189, 238
Campbell, Thomas, 10
Campeche, 61, 76, 200
Canada, 84, 122, 123, 125, 126, 158; agriculture in, 11–12, 14–15, 21, 40, 112, 115, 121, 128, 161, 164, 181, 183–84, 186–87, 201, 203, 207, 230; cordage production in, xx, 24, 26, 148, 164, 171, 217, 219; imports of fiber to, 47, 78, 87, 90, 95, 106, 120, 166, 200, 213, 219; international relations of, xx–xxiii, 91, 106, 110–13, 119–20, 170–71; tariffs, 12, 23–24, 123, 131; Parliament of, see Parliament, Canadian
Canadian National Railway (CNR), 21
Canadian Northern Railway, 115
Canadian Pacific Railroad (CPR), 129
Canary Islands, 56
Cannabis, see hemp
Canto, Humberto, 195, 215, 221
Capper, Arthur, 100, 105, 141–42, 150–51, 152, 175–76, 179, 238
Cárdenas, Lázaro, xx, 161, 164, 187–96, 215, 216, 221, 222, 226, 238
Carranza, Venustiano, 92–97, 100–102, 104–10, 113–14, 118–19, 238
Carrillo Puerto, Felipe, 50, 63, 174, 178, 188, 193, 238
Case Co., 11, 205
Casson, Herbert, 2, 3, 8, 10, 14, 17, 18, 87
Caste War of Yucatán, 39, 54
Castor Pacheco, Fernando, 63–64
Cawker City, Kansas, 232–35
Central America, 25, 102, 198, 199
Channing, Arnold, 59–61
Cherokee Indians, 73
Chiapas, 200
Chicago, 2, 11, 16–17, 23, 45–47, 115, 125, 169, 175, 221, 238
Chicago World's Fair, 10
Chihuahua, 92, 118, 211, 230
Chile, 101, 213
China, 56, 80, 121, 237
Christianson, Theodore, 127
Civil War, 5, 122
Coahuila, 87, 91, 92, 187, 210, 230
Coal Creek Rebellion, 123
Colorado, 131, 154, 162, 182, 185, 208
Columbian Rope Co., 107, 221
combine harvesters, 11, 87, 131, 158, 196, 197, 201–12, 229–31, 233

Comisión Exportadora, 174, 175, 177, 178, 179, 199
Comisión Reguladora del Mercado del Henequén (CRMH), 92–96, 109, 116, 137, 147, 149, 165–76, 180, 197, 199
commodities, histories of, xviii–xix; transfer of, xxi, 27, 95
Commonwealth, see British Commonwealth
Comte, August, 42
cordage industry, 7, 16–22, 24, 26, 28, 31, 88, 164, 178, 197; competition with prison twine mills, 147–48, 154–55; impact of Mexican Revolution on, 95–97, 99, 107–109, 112, 115–16, 161, 170, 172, 174, 230; in Canada, see Canada, cordage production in; in Mexico, 87, 90, 214–23, 226
Cordemex, 226, 228
Corral, Ramón, 69, 70–71, 75, 76
Cosío Villegas, Daniel, 75, 77
Costa Rica, 198–99
crickets, see insects
Crimean War, 41
Cuba, xiv, 38, 46–47, 56, 94, 103–104, 113, 214, 217; sisal production in, 30, 158, 198, 200, 223
Cubillas, Alberto, 70, 75
Curtis, Charles, 169–70

Dakota Territory, 9–10
Dalrymple, Oliver, 9–10
Daniels, H. L., 164, 214,
Daniels, Josephus, 102, 109–10, 115, 221, 222, 238
Darwin, Minnesota, 233–34
Davin, Nicholas Flood, 23
Davis, Jonathan, 133,
de Fornaro, Carlo, 26, 36
de Landa, Diego, 32–33, 37
de la Madrid, Miguel, 228
de los Santos, Toribio, 92, 93
decorticators, see rasping machines
Deere, John, see John Deere Co.
Deering, William, 5–7, 8, 10–11, 12, 29
Denmark, 214
Department of Agriculture, see U.S. Department of Agriculture
Department of Commerce, see U.S. Department of Commerce
Department of Justice, see U.S. Department of Justice
Department of Labor, see U.S. Department of Labor

Department of State, *see* U.S. State Department
dependency theory, xviii–xix, xxiii, 46, 53, 66, 90, 231, 236, 239, 240; agricultural, xi, xvii, xviii, xx, 106, 120, 184, 235
depression, *see* Great Depression
Dewey, Lyster, 22, 29
Díaz, Porfirio, 26, 30, 42–43, 45, 48, 56–61, 69, 85, 91–92; policy of deportation (*enganche*), 67–68, 70–71, 73–84, 87–90
Dominican Republic, 30, 98, 103, 237
drought of 1930s, xx, 157, 181–87, 196, 197, 202, 207, 214, 217, 240
Duddridge, Hugh, 13, 213
DuPont Chemical Co., 27
Durango, 187
Dust Bowl, 182–84, 186, 187

East Africa, 111, 158, 171, 176, 179, 198–201, 217, 219, 223, 235
ecological change, xviii, xix, xxii, 1, 161, 235, 236; in Great Plains, 162, 181–87; in Yucatán, 31, 32, 47–53, 229, 238
Ecuador, 30
Edmonton, Alberta, 12
Egypt, 121
ejidos (Mexican communal lands), 41–42, 48, 54, 187, 191, 192, 194, 237
El Salvador, 198, 237
enganche, *see* Díaz, Porfirio, deportation policy
England, 21, 121
environmental history, xix, xxi–xxii, 161, 162, 181–87, 240
ERIC Corporation, 175, 175
Europe, 43, 56–57, 116–18, 121, 161–62, 179, 181, 212, 213–14, 235
Exportadora, *see* Comisión Exportadora

Fall, Albert, 172, 238
Fargo, North Dakota, 23, 29, 105, 234
Farm Implement News, 6, 30, 185, 218
farm machinery, *see* balers, binders, combine harvesters, headers, implements, reapers, swathers, tractors
Farm Security Act, 183
Farmers' Grain Dealers Association (South Dakota), 143, 144
Federal Trade Commission (FTC), 161, 170, 177
fiber, xx, 16, 24; production of, 21–22, 27; studies of, 22, 28–30; supplies of, 27, 30, 41, 91, 95, 105, 114–15, 117, 119; *see also* henequen, polypropylene, polyethylene

fiber industry, *see* cordage industry
Figueres, José, 198
Finland, 214
Fitler, Edwin, 6, 108
flax, 22, 28–29, 30, 31, 106, 147
Flores Magón, Ricardo, 58
Florida, 29, 31, 94, 117, 198, 199
Food Administration, *see* U.S. Food Administration
Food Control Act of 1917, 162
Ford, Henry, 26
Foucault, Michel, 122
France, 47, 121, 184, 210, 214, 223
Free Trade Area of the Americas (FTAA), xxii, 240
Frost, Frederick Tabor, 59–61

Galveston, Texas, 94, 109
García Correa, Bartolomé, 180–81, 187, 188
Georgia, 73
Germany, 47, 117, 162, 184, 199, 214, 223
globalization, xvii, xix, 57, 87, 235
Grain Belt, North American, xix, 2, 120, 201
grain production, xvii, xviii, 1, 3, 14–15, 95, 161, 162, 181, 192
Grand Forks, North Dakota, 29, 96, 105
Grange Movement, 152–53
grasshoppers, *see* insects
grasslands, North American, 1, 162
Great Britain, 47, 112, 171, 210, 217; *see also* British Commonwealth, United Kingdom
Great Depression, 123, 161, 180–81, 187–88, 196, 197, 201, 202, 207, 230
Great Falls, Montana, 23, 29, 106
Great Plains, 11, 16, 24, 26, 31, 40, 110, 158, 178, 239–40; farming in, 8, 91, 97, 146, 157, 162, 177, 179–84, 192, 198, 201–202, 205, 208–10, 225, 230, 234, 238; transnational nature of, xxiii, 1, 7, 120, 162, 182, 212, 229
Grey, Edward, 110–11, 238
Gronna, Asle, 112, 114, 168, 169, 170
Gruening, Ernest, 63
Guadalajara, 79
Guaymas, Sonora, 79, 86
Guzmán, Martín Luis, 84

Haiti, 98, 147, 198, 226
Hamilton, Ontario, 16, 219
Hanley, J. Frank, 130
Harding, Warren, 174, 175, 176, 238
harvest machinery, *see* binders, balers, combine harvesters, headers, implements, swathers

Harvester World, 7, 22, 61, 86, 166–67
Haskins, R. C., 140
Hatfield and Palmer Co., 108
Havana, Cuba, 46, 94, 113, 165
Hawaii, 29, 30, 106, 198
Hawes-Cooper Act of 1929, 123, 157
headers, 11, 131, 201
Hearst, William Randolph, 27, 85
hemp, 22, 27–30, 31, 41, 126, 131, 224
henequen, xi, xvii, xix, 7, 22, 119, 158; decline
    of, 179–81, 187, 197–231; early production
    of, 38–39, exports of, 87, 114, 164; impact
    of Mexican Revolution on, 92, 96; industry,
    xviii–xx, xxiii, 31, 32–66, 78, 82, 88, 158,
    161, 165, 197; rapid rise in production of,
    40–43, 47; uses of, 37–38, 212, 215, 216, 226
Henequen Market Regulatory Commission,
    see Comisión Reguladora del Mercado del
    Henequén
Henequeneros Unidos, 180, 181, 188, 189
henequen-wheat complex, 66, 78, 84, 87, 91,
    121, 161, 184, 197, 235, 238–40; definition
    of, xvii–xx, xxiii, 1
Hermosillo, Sonora, 72, 75, 76, 77, 89
Hodges, George, 139–42, 151
Honduras, xxii
Hooven & Allison Co., 20, 106, 221
Hoover, Herbert, 164, 169, 171–72, 173–74,
    176–78, 199, 238
Houston, 116
Houston, David, 102
Hovland, August, 207
Huastec Indians, 58, 62
Huerta, Victoriano, 92, 100, 101, 102
Hughes, Charles Evans, 176, 238
Hull, Cordell, 219, 220, 238

Idaho, 149, 150
Illinois, 3, 5, 20, 13, 154, 208
implements, 1–7, 23, 86–87; industry, 11–20,
    27, 125, 162, 201–202; *see also,* balers, bind-
    ers, combine harvesters, headers, swathers,
    tractors
India, 129, 198, 215, 217
Indiana, 14, 21, 107, 124, 130, 132–33, 138,
    139
Indonesia, 199
Industrial Workers of the World (IWW),
    144–45, 203
International Harvester Co. (IH), 14, 61, 87–
    88, 159, 162, 186, 194, 195, 197; creation of,
    7, 10–11, 126; in Canada, 12, 16, 205, 208,
    210, 219; in competition with state prison

twine mills, 130, 137, 140, 141, 143, 147–48,
    149, 153–55; impact of Mexican Revolu-
    tion on, 92, 94, 95, 97–99, 101, 107–108,
    114, 164–65, 173–75, 202, 207; in Mexico,
    86–87, 211, 221–22; twine manufacturing,
    xix–xx, 22, 25, 30, 45, 46, 164, 179, 198,
    216, 223–25, 234, 239
insects, damage from, 7, 31, 41, 148, 154, 157,
    181, 182, 196, 210
Iowa, 131, 154, 155
istle fiber, 22, 29
Italy, 47, 56, 184
Izábal, Rafael, 69, 71–72, 79

Jamaica, 198
Java, 21, 41, 56, 158, 176, 179, 199, 200,
    235
John Deere Co., 11. 149
Johnson, Magnus, 233
jute, 29, 129, 164, 198, 214, 215, 217

Kansas, 28, 86, 100, 105, 112, 131, 148–49,
    154, 194, 232–35; adoption of combine in,
    202–205, 208–209; drought in, 182; prison
    twine plant, 21, 96–97, 105, 107, 124, 130,
    131, 132–33, 135–42, 148–55, 158–59;
    wheat production in, 95, 141–42, 158, 162,
    168, 169, 175, 185–86, 203, 239
Kearful, Francis, 173
Kentucky, 11, 27, 28, 30, 122, 123, 124, 125,
    128–30, 131, 138–39
Kenya, 199, 200, 226
Kingston Penitentiary, 21, 29, 30, 122, 123,
    124, 125, 128–30, 131, 138–39
knotters (knotting devices), 5–6, 7, 13, 31, 32
Korea, 56
Kosterlitzky, Emilio, 71–72
Ku Klux Klan, 117

labor, xix, xx, xvii, xviii, 10, 17, 235, 236; in
    grain harvesting, 3–4, 7, 8, 162, 202–205,
    211, 229; in henequen fields, 36, 39, 46,
    52–66, 67–90, 190–92, 231, 234; unions,
    122, 123, 138; *see also* prison labor
LaFollette, Robert, 58
Landon, Alf, 31, 238
Lansing, Robert, 84, 112, 116
Latin America, xii, xviii, xix, 42, 85, 102, 103,
    119, 180, 239
Leavenworth Federal Penitentiary, 131
lechuguilla fiber, 29
Leopold, Aldo, 183
Lethbridge, Alberta, 12

Lincoln, Nebraska, 116, 131
Linnaeus, Carolus, 37
López Portillo, José, 228
London, 58, 77,110, 199
Los Angeles, 58, 77, 110, 199

Macdonald, John, 123
Madagascar, 226
Madero, Francisco, 57, 58, 82, 9–92
maguey fiber, 22, 35
Malthus, Thomas, 14
manila fiber, *see* abacá fiber
Manitoba, 11, 29, 95, 106, 115, 129, 131, 162,
    185, 187, 207
Marijuana Tax Act of 1937, 27
Marsh, Charles, 6
Marsh harvesters, 3–4, 5, 6
Maryland, 120
Massachusetts, 20
Massey-Harris Co., 11, 12–13, 202, 212
Mauritius, 198
mauritius fiber, 22, 198
Maya Indians, 37–39, 44, 53–54, 56–59, 62,
    66–68, 80–82, 192, 194, 223
Mayo Indians, 68
McCormick, Cyrus, 1–2, 5–7, 11–12, 14,
    24–26, 39, 46, 86, 201
McCormick, Cyrus Jr., 6, 10–11, 12, 26,
    114
McCormick, Harold, 175
McCormick Harvesting Machine Co., 1–3, 4,
    6–8, 10–11, 98, 125–26, 147, 159
McCumber, Porter, 168
McKinley, William, 98, 103
Menocal, Mario, 113
Mennonites, 12, 24
Mérida, Yucatán, 38–39, 43, 45, 60, 64, 78,
    80, 82, 89, 195, 199; cordage companies in,
    215, 216; during the Mexican Revolution,
    92, 93, 96, 96, 104, 105, 108, 165, 174
Mexican Revolution, 26–27, 29, 81–84, 89,
    91–92, 100, 117, 161, 187, 238
Mexico, xix, xxii, 33, 184; as cordage pro-
    ducer, xx, 214–23, 226; as fiber producer,
    xvii, 31, 37, 41–42, 106, 200, 226–27;
    economic growth in, 41–42, 44–45, 48, 68,
    69, 90, 236–37; military in, 75, 76, 79, 81;
    relations with Canada, xxiii, 92, 110–13,
    171, 213, 219; relations with the United
    States, xxiii, 30, 98, 101, 102, 116–18, 171,
    220–22
Mexico City, 56, 61, 62, 78, 83, 100–102, 188,
    221–22, 237

Michigan, 138, 154, 157, 201; prison twine
    plant, 21, 100, 124, 130, 132, 148, 153, 156,
    169
Milwaukee, 23, 107
Milwaukee Harvester Co., 11
Ministry of Agriculture (Canada), 162, 239
Minnesota, 11, 26, 28, 100, 124, 126–28,
    130–31, 134, 146, 154, 157; farming in, 7, 8,
    107, 162, 186, 209; prison twine plant, *see*
    Stillwater State Prison
Minnesota Farm Machinery Co., 11, 126–27
Minot, North Dakota, 156
Mississipppi, 11
Mississippi River, 23, 136
Missouri, 11, 21, 98, 124, 130, 149, 150–51,
    154, 232
Mobile, Alabama, 47, 103, 198
Molina, Olegario, 45, 46, 51, 60, 62, 75, 78,
    85, 165
Monroe Doctrine, 103
Montana, 10, 29, 106, 131, 154, 162, 182, 185,
    202–03
Monterrey, 112
Montes, Avelino, 45, 92, 95–96, 108, 109, 114,
    115, 126, 165–66, 174
Montreal, 26, 47, 129, 166
Moore, Hiram, 201
Morelos, 91
Morgan, J. P., 11
Moisés, Rosalio, 78, 79
Mother Jones, 58
Motherwell, William R., 29, 115, 148, 238
Mozambique, 198, 226

National Cordage Co., 24
National Public Radio (NPR), 234–35
Nayarit, 76
Nebraska, 14, 97, 98, 106, 116, 153, 154, 162,
    185, 202–203
Nervo, Amado, 69
Netherlands, 21, 214, 217
Netherlands Antilles, 198
New Bedford Cordage Co., 108
New Brunswick, 129
New Deal, 123–24, 182, 207
New Jersey, 128
New Mexico, 117, 182
New Orleans, 16, 22, 47, 109, 136, 171, 187,
    188, 198, 219
New York (state), 107, 108, 114, 122, 123, 221
New York City, 21, 24, 43, 47, 85, 94, 104,
    120, 129, 132, 136, 144, 172, 187–88;
    CRMH office in, 166, 171, 213

New Zealand, 22, 106, 111, 135, 171, 198, 219
Nicaragua, 98
Nonpartisan League, 31
Norbeck, Peter, 144
North America, 41, 137, 161, 171, 181, 184, 197, 217, 239; agricultural production in, xi, xvii, xx, 200, 207, 214; interrelated economy of, xviii–xix, xxi, xxiii, 88
North American Free Trade Agreement (NAFTA), xxii, xxiii, 235–37, 240
North Carolina, 186
North Dakota, xii, 15, 29, 30, 96, 105, 112, 114, 149, 154, 167–68, 239; farming in, 109, 115, 153, 162, 182, 184–86, 209; prison twine plant, 21, 124, 130, 131–35, 146–47, 151–52, 156, 158, 169, 198, 225, 239
Northern Ireland, 126
North West Mounted Police, 123
Norton, Patrick, 112

Oaxaca, 56, 76
Obregón, Álvaro, 81, 82, 92, 101–102, 171, 178, 200–201
Oklahoma, 7, 21, 73, 111, 162, 182, 185, 202–203, 208; prison twine plant, 124, 130, 132–33, 149–50
Ohio, 21, 106, 128
Olson, Floyd, 157
Ontario, 12, 16, 20–21, 26, 29, 47, 122, 127–28, 130, 148, 239
Ontario Central Prison, 21, 124, 127–28, 139
Opata Indians, 76
Order of the Patrons of Industry, 24
Ortiz Argumedo, Abel, 92, 93, 94, 95, 104, 105, 113, 165
Ottawa, 21, 24, 129, 213, 215, 239
Oviedo, Fernández de, 37

Palomo, Florencio, 222
Panama, xix, 103
Pan-American Commission, 166, 169, 171, 174, 175
Paris, 42, 119, 239
Parliament, Canadian, 24, 123, 238
Peabody, Henry W. Co., 24–26, 45, 96, 106–109, 126, 137, 147, 169, 174, 188, 198
penitentiary twine plants, 21, 26, 97, 107, 121, 124–60, 166, 169, 198, 233, 235
Peoria Cordage Co., 20, 107, 108, 109, 112, 221
Pershing, John, 118
Peru, 35, 121
Philadelphia, 6, 108, 122

Philippines, 6, 24, 30, 41, 106–107, 111, 113, 135, 176, 198, 212, 235; U.S. occupation of, 31, 42, 117
phormium fiber, 22, 29, 198
Pima Indians, 76
plains, *see* Great Plains
planatation system (Yucatán), 40–41, 54, 56–59, 78, 80, 81, 88, 92–93, 165, 190
Plano Manufacturing Co., 11
Plymouth Cordage Co., 20–21, 30, 97, 100, 144–48, 154–55, 167, 169, 176, 195, 199, 200, 219–22
polyethylene, 158, 225
polypropylene, 225
porfiriato, see Díaz, Porfirio
positivism, 42–43, 45
Prairie Provinces, 11–14, 29, 91, 105, 115, 129, 201–203, 207–209, 212, 219, 229; drought in, 181, 183, 185; "Last Best West," 162
Prison Activist Research Center, 160
prison labor, xx, xxiii, 11, 121, 123–25, 133, 137–39, 142–46, 160, 240
Progreso, port of (Yucatán), 49, 76, 77, 79, 93, 108–10, 112, 174, 238; blockading of, 94–98, 100, 102, 104–105, 115, 119, 143, 166, 170, 221
Puerto Rico, 29, 30, 31, 198

Quebec, 29, 129
Queen City Twine, 21
Quetzalcóatl, 216
Quintana Roo, 33, 54, 76, 81, 95, 104

railways, Yucatecan, 44–45, 48–49, 54, 76, 108–109, 181
rasping machines (decorticators, *desfibrado-ras*), 49–50, 55, 191, 238
Rausehenberger Co., 107
reapers, 1–3, 5, 12, 13, 14, 19, 39, 201
Redfield, William, 112, 114
Red River Valley, 9, 10, 29
Reed, Clyde, 148, 155
Regina, Saskatchewan, 12, 15, 23, 30, 129, 131, 205
Reguladora, *see* Comisión Reguladora del Mercado del Henequén
Rendón, Victor, 166, 167, 169–71
revolution, *see* Mexican Revolution
Ricardo, David, 42
Richardson Construction Co., 85–86
Rockefeller, John D., 175
Rodríguez, Abelardo, 189

Roosevelt, Franklin, 27, 123, 124, 182, 217, 219, 221, 238
Roosevelt, Theodore, 102, 103, 119
Russia, 41, 47, 161, 195, 210

Saint Paul, Minnesota, 16, 17, 23, 28, 29, 30, 238
Salinas de Gortari, Carlos, 237
San Francisco, 135, 239
Santa Ana, Antonio López de, 39
Saskatchewan, 24, 29–30, 106, 131, 182, 183–85, 187, 207–208, 212, 224–25, 239; wheat production in, 12, 13, 15, 23, 115, 161
Saskatchewan Farmers Union, 225
Saskatoon, Saskatchewan, 12, 29, 106, 120
Savala, Refugio, 67, 71, 74
Sayre, L. E., 4
Scotland, 29
Senate, see U.S. Senate
Sherman Anti-Trust Act, 26, 168, 170, 175
Silliman, John, 100, 101, 104, 108, 109
Sinaloa, 75, 86, 93, 200
Sioux Falls, South Dakota, 23, 125, 136, 142, 145, 154, 155–56, 238
sisal, 34–35, 105, 107, 109–10, 120; as a commodity, xi, xvii, xix, 90, 114, 126, 131–33, 141, 151, 168–71, 174, 198, 228; as a fiber, 7, 22, 127, 135, 147, 153, 158, 164, 178–79, 225, 231–32; attempts to raise in United States, 29, 31; in East Africa and Asia, 198–201, 214, 217, 219, 223; uses of, 37–38, 212, 215, 216, 226
Sisal Sales Corporation, 175, 177, 178
Sisal Situation, xx, 91–120, 172, 173, 175, 197, 221, 238
socialism, 159, 173, 174
Socialist Party of the Southeast (PSS), 165, 166, 171, 181, 188, 189
Sonora, 53, 66, 67–90, 92, 93, 118, 182, 211, 230, 235; Spanish colonization of, 69; sisal production in, 200
South Dakota, 104, 133, 143–45, 149, 153–54, 156–57, 162, 207, 209–10; drought in, 182, 183, 185, 186, 239; prison twine plant, 21, 121, 124, 130, 134, 142–46, 148, 150, 153–56, 158–59, 160, 169
Soviet Union, 214; see also Russia
Spain, 47, 56, 214
Spanish-American War, 46, 117, 168
Spencer, Herbert, 42
Spring-Rice, Cecil, 110–11, 112–13, 120, 170–71, 181, 188, 189
Standard Rope and Twine Co., 21

Stillwater State Prison, Minnesota, 11, 21, 107, 124–32, 136–38, 148, 150, 153–56, 160–69
Stony Mountain Penitentiary, Manitoba, 131
Sumners-Ashurst Act of 1940, 123–24
swathers, 207
Sweden, 214, 223
synthetic twines, 158, 196, 197, 225–26; see also polyethylene, polypropylene

Tabasco, 80
Taft, William Howard, 61, 98, 102, 103, 119
Tampico, Veracruz, 58, 100–101
tariffs, 12, 23, 38, 123, 127, 131, 217, 219–20, 237
Tanganyika (Tanzania), 111, 199, 200, 214, 226
Tamaulipas, 200
Tennessee, 117, 123
Tetabiate, 70, 71
Texas, 6, 8, 39, 94, 130, 149, 162, 182, 200, 202–203, 212
Thompson, William, 112
Toronto, 12, 21, 105, 111, 127, 129, 213
Torres, Luis, 69, 70
Townley, A. C., 31
tractors, 9, 10, 184, 202, 203
transnational history, xvii, xxi, 235, 240
Tucson, Arizona, 73
Turner, John Kenneth, 43, 58–62, 72, 75–81, 88–89
twine, see binder twine

Uganda, 199, 200
unions, see labor
United Farmers of Manitoba, 148
United Fruit Co. (UFC), 25, 199
United Kingdom, 112, 217; see also Great Britain
United Nations, 226
United States, 122, 164, 181; imports of fiber, 47, 87, 95, 114–15, 159, 200; international relations of, xx, xxii, xxxiii, 89, 91–120, 96, 102–103, 116–19, 173; trade with Mexico, 7, 38, 84, 90, 92, 100, 103, 115, 117, 119–20, 237
U.S. Army, 83–84, 89
U.S. Calvary, 118
U.S. Department of Agriculture (USDA), 22, 29, 102, 115, 120, 161, 175–76
U.S. Department of Commerce, 7, 30–31, 72, 112, 114, 120, 161, 174, 176–77, 198–99, 238

U.S. Food Administration, 164–65, 171–72, 173, 177, 214, 239
U.S. Department of Justice, 161, 177, 239
U.S. Department of Labor, 7
U.S. Marines, 100, 117
U.S. Navy, 101, 109, 114, 115, 120, 239
U.S. Senate, 161, 168, 170, 172
U.S. State Department, 12, 26, 61, 72, 90, 166, 172, 175, 176, 219–20, 238; during Mexican Revolution, 95–97, 100, 105, 107–109, 112–15, 120
U.S.S.R., *see* Soviet Union

Venezuela, 177
Veracruz, 58, 76, 79, 85, 94, 100–102, 117, 118, 221
Vietnam, 238
Villa, Francisco ("Pancho"), 91–92, 101, 102, 118, 119
Virginia, 1
Vulcan, Alberta, 10

Wallace, Henry, 175, 238
Wall Rope Works, 108
Warner, Fred, 130
Washington, D.C., 99, 104, 107, 108, 109, 113, 164, 237, 239
Washington (state), 11, 131, 154, 201
Williams, Robert, 132–33, 134, 149
Western Canadian Cordage Co., Ltd, 106
wheat, harvesting of, 6, 11, 141–42; in Sonora, 86–87; prices for, 162, 183, production of in North America, 1–3, 5, 9, 10, 14–16, 21, 91, 95, 107, 110, 115, 116, 130, 184, 186, 204, 208, 224
Wilson, Woodrow, xx, 141, 176; policies during Mexican Revolution, 91, 97–106, 109, 112, 114, 116–20, 221, 238; policies during World War I, 162, 164
Winnipeg, Manitoba, 12, 21, 129, 208, 238
Wisconsin, 5, 27, 28, 29; prison twine plant, 21, 124, 130, 132, 148, 153–55, 158, 169

Withington, Charles, 4
wire grass fiber, 28, 31
Whitlock Cordage Co., 107
Wichita, Kansas, 120, 239
Wobblies, *see* Industrial Workers of the World
World War I, 10, 14, 95, 110–18, 141–42, 161–65, 171–79, 183–84, 199, 202, 213, 220
World War II, 27, 124, 187, 211–13, 214, 223
Works Progress Administration, 182
World's Largest Ball of Twine, 232–35, 240
Wyoming, 162

Xenia, Ohio, 20, 106

Yankovich, "Weird" Al, 233–34
Yaqui Indians, xix, 56–57, 58–63, 66, 67–90, 236
Yaqui River, 62, 68, 77, 82–83, 85–86
Yaqui Valley, 68, 70, 71, 73, 74, 85–86, 93, 211, 236
Yucatán, 32, 66–67, 72–73, 75–81, 85, 127, 136, 141, 159, 167, 169, 240; agrarian reform in, 187–88, 189, 196, 222; agriculture in, xviii, 40–42, 48, 50, 52, 57, 161; economic collapse of 181, 208, 230–31; fiber production in, xix, xx, xxiii, 7, 22, 24–25, 28, 31, 92, 102, 106, 115, 133, 135, 147, 156–57, 158, 161, 164, 168–69, 173, 177, 179, 185, 199, 210; government of, 27, 30, 38, 45, 48, 92, 95; historiography of, xxiii; Mexican Revolution in, 82, 83, 92–97, 104–10, 113, 120, 161, 165, 167, 170, 172, 197; physical features of, 32–34, 47, 48, 50, 52, 57, 161; Spanish colonization of, 37–38, 52; twine production in, 87, 90, 214–23

Zamudio, Samuel, 193
Zamná (Mayan sage), 37
Zapata, Emiliano, 91, 101, 102
zapupe fiber, 22, 200

CPSIA information can be obtained
at www.ICGtesting.com
Printed in the USA
LVHW111247040123
736430LV00003B/180

9 781623 490478